Advances in Discourse Processes

VOLUME I

DISCOURSE PRODUCTION AND COMPREHENSION

Discourse Production and Comprehension

Volume I in the series
ADVANCES IN DISCOURSE PROCESSES

ROY O. FREEDLE *, Editor*
Educational Testing Service

ABLEX PUBLISHING CORPORATION
Norwood, New Jersey

Ablex Publishing Corporation
355 Chestnut Street
Norwood, New Jersey 07648

ISBN 0-89391-001-5
Printed in the United States of America

Contents

Theoretical Orientations

Empirical Orientations

SOCIOLINGUISTIC AND PSYCHOSOCIAL EMPHASES

Preface to the Series

Roy O. Freedle, *Series Editor*

This series of volumes provides a forum for the cross-fertilization of ideas from a diverse number of disciplines, all of which share a common interest in discourse — be it prose comprehension and recall, dialogue analysis, text grammar construction, computer simulation of natural language, cross-cultural comparisons of communicative competence, or other related topics. The problems posed by multisentence contexts and the methods required to investigate them, while not always unique to discourse, are still sufficiently distinct as to benefit from the organized mode of scientific interaction made possible by this series.

Scholars working in the discourse area from the perspective of sociolinguistics, psycholinguistics, ethnomethodology and the sociology of language, educational psychology (e.g., teacher–student interaction), the philosophy of language, computational linguistics, and related subareas are invited to submit manuscripts of monograph or book length to the series editor. Edited collections of original papers resulting from conferences will also be considered.

Volumes in the Series

Preface to Volume I

The full development and deeper understanding of the structure and function of discourse in social communication and its internal representation in the individual can only come about from a vigorous interaction of what are currently separate disciplines. The present edited collection of multidisciplinary papers is offered as a stimulus to this ultimate goal. Represented here are a wide variety of approaches to the study of discourse: sociolinguistics, psycholinguistics, teacher—student interaction, conversational turn-taking, speech acts in developmental psycholinguistics, mathematical representations of discourse structure, the clinical interview, the interactionist approach to discourse, language production theories, Gricean constraints in discourse, and other related issues.

It seems reasonable to expect that the ready confluence of these disciplines, with their special methods and emphases, will lay the foundation for more rapid growth of the discourse field, and a fuller appreciation of its complexity.

Special thanks are due Laraine Schwartz, Richard Hurtig, and Susan Weiner for their extensive intellectual support in matters great and small as this volume took shape.

The Educational Testing Service's continuing financial support of this editorial effort is gratefully acknowledged.

ROY O. FREEDLE

Introduction to Volume I

Roy O. Freedle
Educational Testing Service

The scientific study of the structure and function of language has witnessed a lawful and cumulative progression: the initial effort involved the study of language's sound systems; later, the units of interest broadened to include morphology (Bloomfield, 1933), then single sentences (Chomsky, 1957), and more recently multisentence discourse contexts (Crothers, 1972; Frederiksen, 1972; Grimes, 1972; Kintsch, 1974). In all these recent efforts, the focus has been on intralinguistic regularities. An additional expansion has occurred at approximately the same time with the study of multisentence contexts – this expansion involves the study of the structures and internal semantic relationships of discourse as well as its extralinguistic relationships with the socio-physical setting. In this category we find emphasis on language's naturalistic uses: communicative competence (Gumperz & Hymes, 1972), dialogue's rules of social sequencing (Schegloff, 1968), and the varieties of linguistic repertoire (Ferguson, 1973).

Corresponding to each evolutionary step in the scope of language study there has been a shift in emphasis regarding the natural *unit* by which language can be most fruitfully studied. A crucial point for those studying discourse today involves the debate between those who maintain the single sentence to be the largest unit necessary for studying any language issue (e.g., see Katz & Fodor, 1963) and the more recent suggestion that texts are the natural unit (Frederiksen, 1973; Kintsch, 1974). A related shift in units has occurred among some computational linguists, especially Winograd (1972), the developer of programs which handle English *dialogue* in restricted pragmatic settings. Such settings require not only a multisentence context representation but also an implicit set of rules for social sequencing, with the computer playing one of the roles of a "social" communicator.

This glimpse of the natural history of research in language and discourse, though brief, suggests the necessity of a multidisciplinary perspective for coming to a fuller understanding of discourse' structure and function. The current set of papers was prepared for this volume by invitation of the editor, in part to foster the growth of this multidisciplinary effort. In addition to representing several of the many disciplines that deal with discourse — sociolinguistics, psycholinguistics, linguistics proper, sociology of language, ethnoscience, educational psychology (e.g., classroom interaction), clinical psychology (e.g., the clinical interview), computational linguistics, and so forth — the particular contributors were also asked, whenever possible, to develop explicit models of the relationship between discourse *production* and comprehension. Several authors were also prompted, whenever appropriate, to deal with special problems associated with the analysis of *dialogue* as opposed to the more traditional analysis of extended monologue. Finally, a third novel perspective on discourse was encouraged among a few of the authors familiar with the relationships between the *sociocultural* realm and its effect on discourse processing in either naturalistic or experimental settings, and its possible effect on the processing of monologue or dialogue.

Discourse and the sociolinguistic perspective. Of the three novel emphases that were encouraged among the authors, perhaps one requires a more detailed rationale: the sociocultural or sociolinguistic realm.

Language communities exist with a variety of discourse genres (Gumperz & Hymes, 1972). Particular genres are designated to be appropriate for particular speakers and listeners and for particular occasions. Other genres serve particular functions in the culture. The structure and function of each special language must be understood in the total context of all the language varieties which a language community finds it needs to carry out its cultural goals and activities. What has this to do with discourse production and comprehension? One possibility, hinted at in several of the chapters, is that the *strategies* which we bring to bear in comprehension (from a constructivist approach) can be regarded as likelihood judgments that come from one's experiences in the naturalistic world. In other words, our social interactions and other naturalistic experiences suggest bases (or schemata) for *which* presuppositions are likely to be correct in comprehending the covert intensions of a speaker. From fragmentary cues (e.g., of the kind considered by Searle, 1969) in the text we are often able to wisely deduce, among other things, the motivations of the author; this ability stems from our real world experience in the language community. There is the interesting possibility that an extensive survey of these naturalistic patterns could be undertaken with their frequency of occurrence noted, along with preconditions for eliciting judgments of social "well-formedness" for a particular genre and genre-sequencing. The knowledge resulting from such a survey would presumably enter into a description of the semantic strategies that discourse processors must use to *efficiently* carry out a structural analysis of discourse, be it dialogue or monologue. Such knowledge may also figure in the pragmatic strategies that discourse *producers* bring to bear in achieving socially valued goals which just happen to be advanced in the form of discourse (see Freedle, 1975).

Such novel use of the sociolinguistic orientation in the cognitive realm of discourse processing can also clarify the reasons for subcultural differences (and individual differences) in the use of discourse. That is to say, not every group of people share identical sociophysical environments. Ethnic and socioeconomic differences introduce a variety of semantic expectations and values from which discourse errors in production and comprehension can accrue.

This brief characterization of how a sociolinguistic perspective can figure in discourse processing theories should suffice to illustrate why several authors were encouraged to explore some of these possibilities. Although I shall not go into any detail, the different ethnographic functions served by dialogue, as opposed to monologue, partly account for the different structural properties of these genres. Thus an ethnographic or sociolinguistic stance could conceivably enlighten us not only with respect to the appropriateness conditions for using *dialogue* as opposed to extended monologue (in either speaking/listening or writing/reading), but also as to when language *production* itself is more appropriate than maintaining silence. Therefore, an ethnographic or sociolinguistic perspective lies in part behind each of the novel emphases of this book, in production as well as comprehension, dialogue as well as monologue, psychosocial linguistics as well as traditional psycholinguistics.

The organization of this volume. While there are many ways in which the resulting contributions to this volume could have been grouped, four categories were settled upon: theoretical; empirical with an emphasis on psychosocial or sociolinguistic aspects; empirical with a psycholinguistic emphasis; and empirical with an applied focus.

The opening group of papers by Clark and Haviland, Chafe, Frederiksen, Hurtig, and Valian primarily reflect new theoretical perspectives. The chapter by Clark and Haviland provides extensive theory and data for an examination of how information foregrounded in the "given" parts of a sentence influences the processing operations of the "new" sentence information: they refer to this as an analysis of the given–new contract. Chafe's chapter introduces a theoretical account of how nonverbal knowledge may be converted into verbal propositions. Frederiksen's paper examines the problem of units of information with respect to discourse structure, discourse productions, discourse comprehension, and the representation of discourse's semantic relationships in human memory. Hurtig's chapter comes to terms with the problem of whether the analysis of multi-sentence contexts must necessarily abandon any or all of the theoretical and empirical work associated with single sentence analysis. Finally, Valian's chapter provides a highly critical review of a variety of theories put forth over the last few years to account for the nearly intractable complexities of language production.

As indicated above, the remaining chapters were classified as representing primarily an empirical orientation.

The first subgroup of the empirical chapters have a sociolinguistic or psychosocial orientation. These include chapters by Rosch; Hall, Cole, Reder, and Dowling; and Freedle, Naus, and Schwartz. The chapter by Rosch represents an interesting methodological advance in empirically separating the encoding and decoding aspects of dialogue that occur in a semiconstrained communication task. In addition, Rosch studies racial and socioeconomic differences in the production and comprehension of messages generated in this communication task. The chapter by Hall *et al.* examines issues in the study of language varieties and their effect on the encoding and retrieval of information in stories presented to both black and white children. The chapter also compares different language patterns which emerge in young children as a function of formal and informal settings. The chapter by Freedle *et al.* examines how self-instructions, rather than experimenter provided instructions, can sometimes differentially prime the psychosocial information in stories, so that the encoding and retrieval of prose information is affected. The age of the intended listener (child versus adult) is the primary social variable that is explored.

The second group of empirical studies deals partly with more traditional psycholinguistic issues. Stenning's chapter focuses in part upon the function of article definiteness as a cohesive device in text structure. Weiner and Goodenough focus upon the cognitive decisions that language users make in their conversational "moves." In pursuing this, Weiner and Goodenough's contribution is very closely allied with the sociology of language. Finally, Dore's paper investigates the development of speech acts in young children by establishing an elaborate coding system for every utterance made by the participants in a dialogue, regardless of their age. Of these three, that of Weiner and Goodenough could equally well have appeared in the psychosocial section; their inclusion in the psycholinguistic section is due primarily to the way in which the material is developed.

The third and final group of empirical studies, while also partly psycholinguistic in their underlying concepts, nevertheless illustrate how discourse issues can be pursued in the applied domain. In particular, the chapter by Rochester and Martin has a clinical orientation in examining problems in discourse cohesiveness through the clinical interview. The chapter by Moore investigates teacher—student interaction using a simulated "classroom" topic with the computer playing the role of "student." This methodology is innovative of the manner in which it partially controls one-half of dialogic interaction. The contribution of Meyer, while touching upon a number of educational implications of prose research, also succeeds in being highly theoretical by introducing procedures for measuring the hierarchical structure of prose — a fact which brings us almost full circle to the beginning chapters of the book.

Concluding Comment. The existence of a multidisciplinary discourse series, of which this is the first volume, permits a gathering together of these many diverse strands of research and theoretical perspectives. Each discipline has much to offer by way of new methods and new topics. While the present volume primarily represents how psychologists have used these other disciplines as a rejuvenating stimulus for extending a psychological theory of language, it seems a reasonable expectation that future volumes which enlist the contributions of other language experts will help lay the foundations for rapid growth in the field of discourse, along with a full appreciation of its complexity.

REFERENCES

Bloomfield, L. *Language.* New York: Holt, Rinehart, & Winston, 1933.

Chomsky, N. *Syntactic structures.* The Hague: Mouton, 1957.

Crothers, E. Memory structure and the recall of discourse. In R. Freedle & J. B. Carroll (Eds.), *Language comprehension and the acquisition of knowledge.* Washington, D.C.: Winston, 1972.

Ferguson, C. A. Language problems of variation and repertoire. *Daedalus,* 1973, **102** (3), 37–46.

Frederiksen, C. Effects of task-induced cognitive operations on comprehension and memory processes. In R. Freedle & J. B. Carroll (Eds.), *Language comprehension and the acquisition of knowledge.* Washington, D.C.: Winston, 1972.

Frederiksen, C. Cognitive aspects of learning in arbitrary and nonarbitrary contexts. Final Report, Feb. 1973. U.S. Office of Education.

Freedle, R. Dialogue and inquiring systems: The development of a social logic. *Human development,* 1975, **18,** 97–118.

Grimes, J. *The thread of discourse.* Ithaca, N.Y.: Cornell University Press, 1972.

Gumperz, J. J., & Hymes, D. *Directions in sociolinguistics.* New York: Holt, Rinehart, & Winston, 1972.

Katz, J., & Fodor, J. A. The structure of a semantic theory. *Language,* 1963, **39,** 170–210.

Kintsch, W. *The representation of meaning in memory.* Hillsdale, N.J.: Lawrence Erlbaum Associates, 1974.

Schegloff, E. Sequencing in conversational openings. *American Anthropologist,* 1968, **70,** No. 6.

Searle, J. R. *Speech acts.* London: Cambridge University Press, 1969.

Winograd, T. Understanding natural language. *Cognitive psychology,* 1972, **3,** 1–191.

*This book is
affectionately dedicated
to my mother and father
Goldie and Edwin*

1
Comprehension and the Given–New Contract

Herbert H. Clark
Stanford University

Susan E. Haviland
University of California, Irvine

Conversations are a cooperative enterprise. A speaker cannot communicate effectively to his audience unless he adheres to certain conventions. At the very least he must speak a language known to his audience, comply with its phonological, syntactic, and semantic rules, and talk in an audible voice. But many of the conventions he follows have more to do with what he says than with how he says it. He must talk about topics he believes his audience can understand, make his part of the conversation coherent with the rest, and say something worthwhile. The important question, then, is, what precisely are the conventions people follow to ensure the smooth give and take of information?

Grice (1967), in an important work called *Logic and conversation,* has brought together under one theoretical umbrella the conventions he thinks are necessary for successful communication. The overriding convention, according to Grice, is what he calls the Cooperative Principle, which consists of the following simple precept to the speaker: "Be cooperative." But the speaker is expected to be cooperative in four general ways, which Grice represents as four maxims:

Quantity: Make your contribution no more and no less informative than is required.
Quality: Say only that which you both believe and have adequate evidence for.
Relation: Be relevant.

Manner: Make your contribution easy to understand; avoid ambiguity, obscurity, and prolixity.

The cooperative principle, together with these four maxims, constitutes a type of social contract. The speaker agrees to follow these maxims, and the listener agrees to assume they have been followed.

These four maxims are more than just guidelines for the well-mannered speaker. They influence the very interpretations the listener attaches to what the speaker has said. In Grice's scheme the maxims are normative rules and do not by themselves constitute the cooperative principle. Under special circumstances the speaker can violate a maxim without violating the cooperative principle. In these instances, however, the speaker must make his violation overt, make it appear intentional, so that the listener will realize he actually meant to violate the maxim. Imagine, for example, that someone has said *It's such a lovely day today* when it was clear to both speaker and listener that there was a terrible storm raging outside. Here the listener would assume the speaker was violating the maxim of quality intentionally, and he would draw what Grice calls a conversational implicature. He would assume the speaker is still being cooperative and therefore must have meant something by the explicit violation. The listener could then figure out just how the utterance was meant — in this case, it was meant to be taken as an ironic comment on the weather, not as a purely informative communication. On the other hand, a speaker can violate a maxim covertly or even unintentionally, and then accurate and effective communication with the listener will normally break down. Imagine, for example, that our speaker had said *It's such a lovely day today* when he knew about the storm raging outside, but the listener did not. Again, the listener would assume that the speaker was being cooperative, but this covert violation of the maxim of quality would lead the listener to believe that the weather was in fact fine, which is incorrect. If this violation was intentionally covert, the speaker would be lying; if it was unintentional, he would be misleading. In summary, intentional overt violations lead to coversational implicatures; intentional covert violations produce lies; and unintentional violations lead to less malevolent breakdowns in communication.

Grice's approach has far-reaching consequences for theories about the process of comprehension. Traditionally, such theories have stressed the syntactic and semantic aspects of utterances. Yet Grice's approach implies that the process must also reflect the cooperative principle, the four maxims, and the way they interact. For instance, a complete theory of the process must explain how *It's such a lovely day today* is taken as merely informative when the listener believes no maxims have been violated, but as ironic when he believes the maxim of quality has been violated. It must also explain, for example, how *I have four sisters* is in most contexts interpreted as "I have *only* four sisters." A speaker with more than four sisters would have been technically correct in uttering this sentence, but he could not use it without violating the maxim of quantity. He would not have been as informative as required. So the listener infers that the speaker meant *I have exactly four sisters.* In general, a theory of comprehension must account for interpretations the listener comes to based on the assumption that the speaker is cooperating with him.

In this chapter we will be concerned with an agreement between the speaker and listener, which we will call the given–new contract, and we shall show how it plays a central role in the process of interpreting sentences in English. As part of the cooperative principle, speakers and listeners have an implicit agreement about how (a) information that is known to the listener, and (b) information that is novel to the listener are to appear in sentences. This is the given–new contract. On the basis of this contract, the listener makes use of a strategy we call the given–new strategy in comprehending the utterances he hears. This strategy, as it happens, leads him to understand some utterances quickly and others slowly, to judge some utterances as appropriate and others inappropriate in certain contexts, and to draw conversational implicatures for some utterances and not for others. We will then show how these and other predictions of the given–new contract are consistent with a variety of linguistic and psychological evidence now available. Finally, we will demonstrate how the given–new contract, like its parent cooperative principle, can be used for good or for ill. By adhering to the contract, the speaker can convey subtle pieces of information either directly or indirectly, and by violating the contract, he can deceive or mislead.

THE GIVEN–NEW CONTRACT

The given–new contract is concerned with a syntactic distinction the speaker is obliged to make between given information and new information. In all languages probably (Chafe, 1970), declarative sentences convey two kinds of information: (1) information the speaker considers given – information he believes the listener already knows and accepts as true; and (2) information the speaker considers new – information he believes the listener does not yet know. In English the distinction is obligatorily marked in what Halliday (1967) has called "information focus," a surface feature closely associated with the intonation contour of the sentence. Consider the sentence *It was Percival who piqued the professor,* which, with normal intonation, has its major stress on *Percival.* Its given information is that someone piqued the professor; its new information, which is conveyed by the constituent containing the strongest stress, is that that someone was Percival. The pattern of given and new in this sentence is inherent in its syntax and associated stress pattern – a topic we will return to later – and does not change with what is in fact known or unknown to the listener. Nevertheless, linguists have traditionally identified this distinction in terms of its obvious function. Halliday (1967) used the terms "given" and "new," Chafe (1970) "old" and "new," and Akmajian (1973), Chomsky (1971), and Jackendoff (1972) "presupposition" and "focus."[1] For convenience we have adopted Halliday's terminology; "old" seems less descriptive than "given" (see Chafe, 1973, p. 112), and "presupposition" has several senses that are easily confused (see Jackendoff, 1972, p. 276).

The given—new distinction, this description suggests, is present in language to serve a specific function. To ensure reasonably efficient communication, the speaker and listener adhere to a convention regarding the use of this distinction in sentences. The speaker tries, to the best of his ability, to make the structure of his utterances congruent with his knowledge of the listener's mental world. He agrees to convey information he thinks the listener already knows as given information and to convey information he thinks the listener doesn't yet know as new information. The listener, for his part, agrees to interpret all utterances in the same light. The result is what we have called the given—new contract, which we view as one aspect of Grice's more general cooperative principle. Like the cooperative principle, the given—new contract consists of a normative maxim (a precept to the speaker as to what he should ideally do) and a set of requirements he may never violate without a breakdown in communication. By relying on the latter requirements the speaker can deliberately and overtly violate the maxim to convey various types of "implicatures" indirectly.

The heart of the given—new contract is the maxim of antecedence, a precept to the speaker that he make sure the listener actually knows the information being conveyed as given information. The precept can be stated this way:

Maxim of Antecedence: Try to construct your utterance such that the listener has one and only direct antecedent for any given information and that it is the intended antecedent.

Consider again *It was Percival who piqued the professor.* For a speaker to utter this sentence, he must be confident that the listener already knows that someone piqued the professor. This knowledge on the listener's part is what we will call the antecedent to the given information of the sentence. Formally, it consists of a node in the listener's memory structure characterized as a nominal that has associated with it one or more propositions in which the nominal serves as an argument. For our example the antecedent is the node in the listener's memory corresponding to "the one who piqued the professor." This particular antecedent is said to be direct since it contains among its associated propositions ones that match the given information precisely. (We will consider indirect

---

[1] "Given" and "new" may also be equivalent to what Fillmore (1971) referred to as the "presuppositional" and "illocutionary" aspects or levels of the "speech communication situation."

antecedents later on.) Since the maxim of antecedence governs the manner in which the utterance is constructed, it can be considered as one specific part of Grice's maxim of manner.

Violations of the maxim of antecedence, like violations of others of Grice's maxims, have two distinct consequences. By violating the maxim deliberately and explicitly, the speaker can convey special types of information. The listener will assume he was meant to recognize such violations and to draw certain inferences. The speaker can exploit this process to convey information not directly contained in the literal meaning of the utterance. On the other hand, by violating the maxim of antecedence covertly or from negligence, the speaker can easily mislead the listener or cease to communicate anything coherent at all. Like other failures to cooperate, such breaches in the given–new contract will typically bring about a breakdown in communication.

From considerations like these, we have proposed elsewhere (Clark & Haviland, 1974; Haviland & Clark, 1974) that the listener makes use of a given–new strategy in understanding sentences. According to this model, the listener represents the content of conversations, as well as other knowledge, in a relatively permanent memory. This knowledge consists of a set of propositions interrelated by indices indicating which propositions are embedded in which, which entities are identical, and so on. This information structure includes not only those propositions underlying the sentences of a conversation – and perhaps not even all of these – but also propositions inferred from these sentences and from the extralinguistic context of the conversation. The given–new strategy is a three-step procedure for relating the current sentence to this knowledge base. At Step 1, the listener isolates the given and the new information in the current sentence. At Step 2, he searches memory for a direct antecedent, a structure containing propositions that match the given information precisely. Finally, at Step 3 the listener integrates the new information into the memory structure by attaching it to the antecedent found in Step 2.

The working of the strategy may become clearer with the concrete example outlined in Table 1. Assume that the listener in a conversation has encountered *It was Percival who piqued the professor.* Assume also that the listener has already stored in memory an interrelated set of propositions, represented here as $p_1, \ldots, p_n$, which includes the proposition E_{37} *piqued the professor* ("a particular individual E_{37} piqued the professor"). E_{37} is meant to represent a constant, a node that refers to a particular "entity" numbered, say, 37; it is to be distinguished from the variable X in the given information. In applying the given–new strategy to the current sentence, the listener first divides its propositional content into that which is given, X *piqued the professor,* and that which is new, $X = Percival$. Then he searches memory for a match with the given information (X *piqued the professor*), finds one (E_{37} *piqued the professor*), and assigns it the role of antecedent. Finally, he "attaches" the new information to

TABLE 1
The Given—New Strategy Applied to the Sentence
It was Percival who piqued the professor

A. Prior memory structure:

$p_1, \ldots, E_{37}$ *piqued the professor*, $\ldots, p_n$

B. Apply strategy to *It was Percival who piqued the professor:*

Step 1: Divide current sentence into given and new.

Given: *X piqued the professor*
New: *X = Percival*

Step 2: Search memory for a unique antecedent that matches the given information.

Antecedent: E_{37} *piqued the professor*

Step 3: Integrate new information into memory by replacing X by the appropriate index in the antecedent.

Add: E_{37} *= Percival*

C. Resulting memory structure:

$p_1, \ldots, E_{37}$ *piqued the professor*, E_{37} *= Percival*, $\ldots, p_n$

---

the antecedent by replacing the X in the new information by the E_{37} of the antecedent. These steps result in a revised memory structure that now contains the proposition E_{37} *= Percival.*

The given—new strategy works perfectly so long as the speaker has successfully followed the maxim of antecedence and the listener can find an exact match for the given information. But suppose the speaker has violated the maxim and the speaker cannot find a direct antecedent. Then, we assume, the listener can turn to one of three procedures: bridging, addition, or restructuring. Bridging and addition are available when the speaker has violated the maxim explicitly and expects the listener to draw certain inferences. Restructuring, on the other hand, is available when the speaker has violated the maxim unintentionally or covertly, and the listener needs the procedure to make sense of the utterance.

1. *Bridging.* When the listener cannot find a direct antecedent, most commonly he will be able to form an *indirect* antecedent by building an inferential bridge from something he already knows. G. Lakoff (1971) provides us with an example where such bridging is required.

(1) John is a Democrat. Bill is honest too.

The second sentence in this sequence, when pronounced with heavy stress on *Bill* and *too,* has as given information that at least someone other than Bill is honest, and it has as new information that Bill is honest. Suppose that the listener's memory structure contains only the proposition *John is a Democrat.*

On applying Step 2 of the given–new strategy to *Bill is honest too,* he isn't able to find a direct antecedent that matches its given information *X is honest* ($X \neq$ *Bill*). To detour around this impasse the listener notes that he could construct a plausible, though indirect, antecedent if he assumed that the speaker, observing the maxim of relation, meant the given information to be provided indirectly by the previous sentence. The listener could then assume that the speaker believes (1) that all Democrats are honest and (2) that since John is a Democrat he too is honest. The inferred proposition *John is honest* can then serve as an antecedent to the given information *X is honest,* since it matches the given information as required. With that the listener can go on to Step 3 of the given–new strategy and integrate the new information successfully into memory.

In this example the listener has assumed that although the speaker has violated the maxim of antecedence, he has not breached the cooperative principle – here that part of the principle we have called the given–new contract. The listener assumes that since the speaker is still being cooperative, he means the listener to be able to find an antecedent but only indirectly. More specifically, the listener assumes that the violation of the maxim of antecedence is to be treated like violations of any other maxim: By violating the maxim the speaker meant him to draw certain inferences, or as Grice called them, implicatures. In this case the listener assumes he was supposed to infer that the speaker believes all Democrats are honest. It should be noted here that the information conveyed by such a sentence as *Bill is honest too* becomes part of the listener's model of the speaker's world and not necessarily part of the beliefs of the listener himself. It is possible for the listener to understand *Bill is honest too* without believing that all, or even any, Democrats are honest.

2. *Addition.* Sometimes it is impossible to find any way of bridging the gap between known information and the appropriate antecedent. Then the listener must add to memory, perhaps hypothetically, a new node (a nominal associated with one or more propositions) to serve as the antecedent to the given information. This often occurs, for example, at the beginning of stories, as with the sentence

(2)   The old woman died.

The given information here is that there is a woman and she is old. But with no prior context, the listener knows of no such woman. He is forced to add a new node to memory corresponding to "the one that is a woman and that is old," use this as the antecedent for the given information in (2), and then proceed with Step 3 of the strategy.

Sentence (2) is a deliberate violation of the maxim of antecedence when it comes at the beginning of a story, yet it is not necessarily a breach of the given–new contract. By violating the maxim, the speaker can be indicating to the listener that there is an old woman whose existence ought to be known at that point. So with this violation of the maxim the listener is again expected to draw an implicature, here that the existence of an old woman is something that shall have to be assumed. As we will discuss later, this implicature is often exploited as an important literary device.

3. *Restructuring.* When the speaker has violated the given—new contract altogether, there are some instances where the listener can still figure out what is being conveyed by restructuring what is given and what is new in the utterance. Consider the sequence in Sentence (3):

(3)   Agnes saw somebody. It was Agnes who saw Maxine.

Assume that the listener knows only what has been conveyed by the first sentence, namely, *Agnes saw* E_{85} , and assume that he is attempting to understand the second sentence. Its given information, *X saw Maxine,* does not match any proposition in memory, hence there is no proper antecedent to which to attach the new information $X = Agnes$. In this instance, however, the listener can restructure the given and new information in the second sentence so that *Agnes saw X* is given and $X = Maxine$ is new. Now there *is* an antecedent in memory for the given information, and the listener can proceed to Step 3 of the given—new strategy and attach the reconstrued new information to the antecedent. Obviously, the listener can turn to the device of restructuring only when the utterance being comprehended has just the right content. It must convey as part of its new information material from which the listener can build the restructured given information. These cases should be relatively rare.

Bridging, addition, and restructuring are all detours around a blockage in the application of Step 2 in the given—new strategy, and as such, they should cause processing difficulty. For each detour the listener must do something extra, and this ought to lead to extra processing time or to a feeling that the sentence was difficult to understand. For example, the second sentence in (1) seems intuitively to require extra time to understand in the context of the first sentence, and Sentence (2) seems to require extra effort as the initial sentence of a story. Unlike bridging and addition, however, restructuring occurs only when the listener perceives that there has been a breach of the given—new contract, not merely a violation of the maxim of antecedence. As with other breaches of the cooperative principle, the listener does not draw any particular implicature, but instead simply fails to see why the speaker said what he said or fails to understand the utterance at all. Thus, the sequence in Sentence (3) seems hard to understand not simply because it requires more processing effort, as do Sentences (1) and (2), but because it is awkward and shouldn't have been put that way. We would accuse the speaker of (3) of having made things unnecessarily hard for us, a judgment we would not apply to the speaker of Sentences (1) and (2).

The given—new contract and its associated given—new strategy, then, have direct empirical consequences, as illustrated in Sentences (1), (2), and (3).

Specifically, they imply (a) some sentences should induce implicatures that others do not, (b) some sentences should be judged as awkward or inappropriate in context where others should not, and (c) some sentences should take longer to comprehend than others. We will take up evidence for these and other consequences of the given–new contract first from a linguistic standpoint and then from a psychological standpoint. Taken together, the facts we will review make an excellent case for the contract and its associated processing strategy.

Before turning to this evidence, however, let us return to the given–new contract and see how it can be formulated more precisely. Earlier we noted that this contract should be viewed as part of the cooperative principle. It therefore consists of a maxim, the maxim of antecedence, plus some notion of what it means for the speaker to be cooperative even when he is not adhering strictly to the maxim. We might formulate this notion of cooperativeness in this way:

> *Given–New Contract:*   Try to construct the given and the new information of each utterance in context (a) so that the listener is able to compute from memory the unique antecedent that was intended for the given information, and (b) so that he will not already have the new information attached to that antecedent.

This contract is fulfilled in the most direct possible way when the speaker has adhered to the maxim of antecedence and the listener has a direct antecedent in memory for the given information. But the speaker does not have to provide given information with a direct antecedent, and then we see the importance of the following three requirements in the given–new contract:

1. *Appropriateness.*   The given part of the sentence ought to convey known, or knowable, information, and the new part unknown information. The given–new distinction ought to be appropriate to the circumstances. Breaches of this part of the given–new contract may sometimes be elementary enough that the listener can rectify them by the process we called restructuring. In many instances, however, the listener will not be able to compute the intended interpretation of the utterance as it was meant to refer to real world objects and events.

2. *Uniqueness.*   The given information provided by the speaker must enable the listener to compute an antecedent that is unique. If the listener finds two or more possible antecedents, he will be unable to decide which of them is the intended antecedent and communication will break down. As with breaches in appropriateness, breaches in uniqueness lead to judgments of unacceptability of the utterance in context.

3. *Computability.*   The most fundamental requirement of all is that the listener must be assumed to have sufficient knowledge and skill to be able to *compute* the intended antecedent. When the maxim of antecedence is fulfilled,

TABLE 2

Violable and Inviolable Requirements in the Given–New Contract and the Consequences of Their Violations by the Speaker

A. Maxim of antecedence
    1. Violation by speaker: Allowed under special circumstances.
    2. Strategy of listener encountering violation:
       a. Bridging
       b. Addition
    3. Consequence of violation: Listener draws an implicature.

B. Appropriateness
    1. Violation by speaker: Not allowed
    2. Strategy of listener encountering violation: Restructuring
    3. Consequence of violation: Listener judges sentence awkward in context.

C. Uniqueness
    1. Violation by speaker: Not allowed
    2. Strategy of listener encountering violation: None
    3. Consequence of violation: Listener judges sentence unacceptable in context.

D. Computability
    1. Violation by speaker: Not allowed
    2. Strategy of listener encountering violation: None
    3. Consequence of violation: Listener judges sentence unacceptable or incomprehensible in context.

the given information will match information in memory directly, and computation will normally be trivial. But when it is violated, and, say, bridging is required, the speaker must be confident that the listener has the information from which he can build a bridge to the intended antecedent and that he has the skill to do so. Whether the intended antecedent is computable or not will depend on all sorts of factors – the listener's beliefs, his sophistication in computing bridges (which children, for example, may lack), and the gap to be bridged – and these must all be judged by the speaker.

For convenience we have summarized our argument in Table 2. This table lists the maxim of antecedence and the three major requirements of the given–new contract, and for each it specifies: (1) whether the speaker is allowed to violate the requirement or not; (2) what strategy the listener turns to when he encounters such a violation; and (3) what consequences the violation has on the way the listener reacts to or perceives the sentence.

LINGUISTIC EVIDENCE

In English assertions, the patterning of information into given and new is closely associated with focal stress (see Akmajian, 1973, Chafe, 1970; Chomsky, 1971; Halliday, 1967; Jackendoff, 1972). Most simple sentences that are spoken with normal intonation have their focal stress — their strongest stress and highest pitch — on the final word in the sentence. So in *Olivia kissed Oscar* the focal stress falls on *Oscar*. There are many other constructions, however, that allow the speaker to place focal stress on something besides the final word, the logical object. The cleft construction *It was Olivia who kissed Oscar* has the function of placing focal stress on *Olivia*; the pseudocleft construction *What Olivia did was kiss Oscar* separates out the whole constituent *kiss Oscar* for focal stress; and the passive construction *Oscar was kissed by Olivia* brings the agent *Olivia*, normally without stress at the beginning of the sentence, into the final position where it receives focal stress. In addition, English allows the speaker to place *contrastive stress* on almost any element in the sentence, as in *OLIVIA kissed Oscar* or *Olivia KISSED Oscar,* and the stressed element automatically becomes the point of focal stress.[2] In short, the speaker, by availing himself of these and other similar devices, can place focal stress on almost any semantic element he wants.

The importance of focal stress is that it always falls on an element in the constituent that conveys new information. We can illustrate this rule with the sentence *It was Olivia who kissed Oscar.* Conceptually, the given information is found by replacing *Olivia,* the constituent containing the focal stress, by a variable X. This gives X *kissed Oscar.* The new information is then provided by the content of the replaced constituent *Olivia,* and that content is used to assign a value to the variable X. This gives $X = $ *Olivia.* In this example the new information consisted of a single noun, but that needn't always be the case. The sentence *What Olivia did was kiss Oscar* has as new information a complete verb phase $X = $ *kiss Oscar*; and the sentence *The BLOND woman kissed Oscar* has as new information only the modifier $X = $ *blond.*

As a practical procedure, one can determine what is given and what is new for a particular assertion by finding the question it is an appropriate answer to.[3] *It was Olivia who kissed Oscar,* for example, is an appropriate answer to *Who kissed Oscar?* What is significant is that *Who kissed Oscar?,* the appropriate question, presupposes that someone kissed Oscar, X *kissed Oscar,* and that is the same as the given information in its proper answer. In effect, the question has as given X *kissed Oscar* and requests the listener to supply a value for that X. The answer has as given X *kissed Oscar* and supplies X with a value in the new information $X = $ *Olivia.* In general, a question and its appropriate answer

[2] Contrastive stress differs from focal stress in its consequences on given and new. For one thing, the given information for contrastive stress carries with it a negative contrast not found in the given information for focal stress. For another, contrastive stress is usually accompanied by a secondary focal stress at the end of the sentence, and this in turn complicates the given–new structure (see Jackendoff, 1972, pp. 258–265). For present purposes we will ignore these complications, since they do not affect our basic argument.

[3] Hiż (1962) applied a similar procedure in his attempt to classify statements about knowledge. He asserted: "Knowledge can be classified according to what questions it answers." This may, however, be true only of the assertions used to convey such knowledge.

share given information, and the answer conveys new information in order to supply a value for the queried information.[4] In brief, to determine the given information for *It was Olivia who kissed Oscar,* replace the Wh- word in the question *Who kissed Oscar* with X; to determine the new information, find the value the answer assigns to that X.

By this procedure it is easy to see that some sentences divide into given and new in several alternative yet legitimate ways. The simple active sentence is perhaps the most flexible of all. *Olivia kissed Oscar,* pronounced with focal stress on *Oscar,* is an appropriate answer to (1) *Who did Olivia kiss?,* (2) *What did Olivia do?,* and (3) *What happened?* These three questions correspond to three different divisions of given and new: (1) *Olivia kissed X* and $X = Oscar$; (2) *Olivia did X* and $X = kiss Oscar$; (3) *X happened* and $X = Olivia kissed Oscar.$ All three solutions, of course, are consistent with the idea that focal stress marks the constituent conveying the new information. The stressed word *Oscar* is simultaneously part of three different constituents: (1) the noun phrase *Oscar; (2) the* verb phrase *kissed Oscar*; and (3) the whole sentence *Olivia kissed Oscar.*

In most sentences definite noun phrases carry given information. In *The judge took a bribe,* it is given that there is an entity that is a judge and that is known to the listener. Such definite noun phrases may be modified by any number of adjectives or restrictive relative clauses, and these become part of the given information too. So in *The old judge that tried my brother George took a bribe,* it is given that the listener knows an entity that fits all the following characteristics: it is a judge, it is old for a judge, and it tried the speaker's brother George. When the listener searches for an antecedent to this noun phrase, he must find an entity that fits all of these characteristics simultaneously.

But this raises an apparent inconsistency in the definition of given and new. In earlier illustrations it appeared that definite noun phrases could occur as part of the new information, contrary to the fact that most definite noun phrases convey given information. Fortunately, this inconsistency is more apparent than real. Consider *It was the judge who took the bribe,* which was said to have the given information *X took the bribe* and the new information $X = the judge.$ Here the new information appears to contain *the judge,* which should be given information. This, however, is not really the case. What is new in this sentence is not the judge himself, but the *identification* of the judge as the one taking the bribe. The new information is the relationship between the judge and the one taking the bribe, the equals sign in $X = the judge.$ To be more precise, the given information should have been written as *X took the bribe and Y is the judge,* and the new information as $X = Y.$ Nevertheless, we will continue to write given

[4] We are speaking here of direct, and not indirect, answers. For example, when asked "Who kissed Oscar?" one could say, "Well I just saw Olivia sneaking out of his room," conveying the answer indirectly (see R. Lakoff, 1973). Indirect answers like these, however, introduce information other than that which is called for in the question and are normally easy to distinguish from direct answers like "It was Olivia."

and new in the less precise form with the understanding that it can always be made precise.

Simple English sentences with normal intonation, as we said, have their focal stress at or near the end of the sentence. In general, therefore, given comes before new. Viewed according to the given–new strategy, this tendency in English makes good sense. Logically, Steps 1, 2, and 3 in the strategy must be carried out in this order. The listener has to identify the given information (Step 1) before he can find an antecedent for the given information (Step 2), and he must do this before he can attach the new information to the antecedent (Step 3). But the listener need not wait until the end of the sentence before identifying the given information (Step 1). As the sentence progresses, he can compute parts of the given information and begin searching for the intended antecedent. When given comes before new, therefore, he may have found the intended antecedent even before he hears the new information. When new comes before given, however, he has a problem. He must hold the new information in abeyance while he waits for the given information and searches for its antecedent. This increases the load on his memory and makes comprehension less than optimal. So the strategy applies most efficiently when given comes before new.

Because given generally comes before new, English sentences also tend to begin with definite noun phrases, delaying indefinite noun phrases until later in the sentence. It is easy to see why. An indefinite noun phrase, because it presupposes the listener does not yet know its referent, has to be part of the new information. So, for example, *It was Ned that a horse kicked and *What a horse did was kick Ned are unacceptable except perhaps as clarifications. Now consider simple active sentences with indefinite noun phrases. Morris kissed a hussy, with normal intonation, allows the new information to have narrow scope (Who did Morris kiss?), medium scope (What did Morris do?), or wide scope (What happened?). But A hussy kissed Morris, with the indefinite subject, allows only the wide scope (What happened?). The questions corresponding to the narrow scope (*Who did a hussy kiss?) and medium scope (*What did a hussy do?) reveal the impossibility of the two narrower interpretations. In passives, similarly, an initial indefinite noun phrase (A hussy was kissed by Morris) restricts the new information to wide scope (What happened?), and in passives, wide scope is particularly difficult to comprehend anyway. Thus sentences with indefinite subjects are particularly restricted in use and should not appear very often.

There is one final point to be raised. The given–new division in sentences appears to be a type of hierarchy, with given itself sometimes consisting of given' + new', given' consisting of given" + new", and so on. The issue is complicated and not well understood, but we can provide a simple illustration of the phenomenon. Compare The young woman who was beautiful left and The beautiful woman who was young left. In both of these assertions it is given that there is a beautiful young woman, and it is new that she left. But when spoken normally, the two sentences appear to induce the listener to search for the antecedent of the given information in two different ways. The first tells the listener that he should know of a set of beautiful women (given') and that he should search this set for the one that is young (new'). The second, on the other hand, tells him that he should know of a set of young women (given') and that he should search this set for the one that is beautiful (new'). It is as if the noun phrase *the young woman who was beautiful* itself has focal stress on the final word *beautiful* so that being beautiful is new' relative to being young and being a woman. In this sense the noun phrase *the young woman who was beautiful* reflects its full sentence counterpart *The young woman was beautiful,* in which it is given that there is a young woman and it is new that she is beautiful, and does not reflect the noncorresponding sentence *The beautiful woman was young.* Such a hierarchy within the given information is most apparent in sentences with contrastive stress, where there are normally two identifiable points of stress in the sentence (see Jackendoff, 1972, p. 258). We conclude that the internal structure of the given information may lead the listener to search for its antecedent in one way and not another. This search strategy has an obvious analogy to the given—new strategy as a whole.[5]

Having outlined some of the principal properties of the linguistic distinction between given and new information, we now turn to three types of "linguistic" evidence for the given—new contract and its associated strategy — awkwardness, unacceptability, and implicature.

Awkwardness

As all good editors know, there are tight constraints on the sentences that can follow one another in good prose. An editor would observe, for example, that the sequence of two sentences in (3)

(3)   Agnes saw somebody. It was Agnes who saw Maxine.

sounds awkward, inappropriate, wrong, and he would advise changing the second sentence to *It was Maxine that Agnes saw* or to something similar. Many judgments of awkwardness or inappropriateness follow directly from the given—new strategy. Such is the case with (3). In two-sentence sequences like this, the first sentence sets up a context, a set of propositions in memory. The second sentence is then interpreted relative to the first. It induces the listener to search for an antecedent to its given information in the propositions stored in memory from the first sentence. If the listener cannot find an appropriate antecedent without restructuring the second sentence, he will consider the speaker to have breached the given—new contract and judge the sequence to be awkward or

---

[5] New information may also consist hierarchically of given' and new' information. When asked *Who did you meet?* one could answer *I met a young woman who was beautiful* or *I met a beautiful woman who was young,* conveying two different patterns of new information to be stored. The difference between them is analogous to the difference between the corresponding sentences with definite noun phrases.

inappropriate. It should be noted that this judgment of (3) could not be made without Grice's maxim of relation. The listener expects each new sentence he hears to be relevant to what has come before. So because he cannot relate the two sentences in (3) without restructuring the second, he judges the sequence to be awkward.

The awkwardness of (3), therefore, is direct evidence for the given–new strategy. Indeed, it is easy to construct an indefinite number of awkward sequences along the same lines as (3). In (4) through (7), we have composed an *a* sequence that conforms to the given–new strategy and is therefore relatively good, and a *b* sequence that does not conform to the given–new strategy and is therefore relatively bad:

(4) a. Olivia kissed Oscar somehow. It was on the ear that Olivia kissed Oscar.
  b. Someone kissed Oscar on the ear. It was on the ear that Olivia kissed Oscar.

(5) a. Olivia did something. What Olivia did was kiss Oscar.
  b. Someone kissed Oscar. What Olivia did was kiss Oscar.

(6) a. Someone kissed Oscar. OLIVIA kissed Oscar.
  b. Olivia kissed someone. OLIVIA kissed Oscar.

(7) a. Something happened. The mouse JUMPED.
  b. Something jumped. The mouse JUMPED.

The *a* sequences are good because the first sentence provides a direct antecedent for the given information in the second. The *b* sequences are bad because the first sentence coincides partly with the given information and partly with the new information of the second.

We assume, more generally, that the listener applies the given–new strategy to every assertion he encounters. It follows that for every assertion with both given and new information — some sentences may convey only new information — we should be able to find a context in which it sounds good and at least one context in which it sounds awkward. Sequences (4) through (7) give evidence for four different constructions, and we claim that we could construct similar good and bad sequences for any other type of assertion.

The appropriateness of questions to their answers provides another sort of evidence for the given–new strategy. Consider the two question–answer sequences in (8):

(8) a. Who kissed Oscar? It was Olivia who kissed Oscar.
  b. Whom did Olivia kiss? It was Olivia who kissed Oscar.

As we noted before, the question *Who kissed Oscar?* has as given information itself that someone kissed Oscar and it requests the identity of that someone. In applying the given–new strategy to its answer, the listener searches for an antecedent to *X kissed Oscar,* finds one in the given information of the question, and attaches the new information $X = Olivia$ to it. This strategy fails in the second sequence, for the question does not contain information that matches the given information of the answer X *kissed Oscar.* The listener is forced to restructure the answer, so he judges the sequence as awkward, as a breach of the given—new contract. Just as there are indefinitely many appropriate and inappropriate context-assertion sequences as in Sequences (4) through (7), there are indefinitely many appropriate and inappropriate question—answer pairs as in (8). For every assertion conveying both given and new information, we claim, there will be at least one appropriate question and at least one inappropriate one. We have found no exceptions. So this too constitutes direct evidence for the given—new strategy.

Linguistic intuitions of acceptability and appropriateness have always been a legitimate source of evidence for theories of linguistic competence. But they are also a potentially important source of evidence for theories of language processing. People come to their judgments of acceptability and appropriateness through a mental process that is part of comprehension. It is quite natural, then, for theories of comprehension to predict which sentences are acceptable and which are not, which sequences are appropriate and which are not. The theory of interest here, the given—new strategy, happens to make such predictions, and so we have appealed, quite legitimately, to judgments of appropriateness. The point is, a judgment of appropriateness is just as much psychological evidence as it is linguistic evidence.

Unacceptability

The given—new contract, it will be recalled, has three main requirements: appropriateness, uniqueness, and computability. So far we have dealt only with appropriateness. Given the first sentence in each sequence, was the given—new structure of the second appropriate to what the listener did and didn't know? When appropriateness was violated, the contract was breached, and the sequences were judged to be awkward or inappropriate.

The speaker can also violate the requirement of uniqueness, and then the listener will judge the utterance to be totally unacceptable. Consider the sequence in (9):

> (9) Two men were watching the dog. The one watching it laughed out loud.

The second sentence here has as given information that some one person was watching the dog. But the first sentence provides two possible antecedents, the man$_1$ that was watching the dog and the man$_2$ that was watching the dog, and there is no clue to determine which man was actually intended. The listener using the given—new strategy has no means to resolve the ambiguity, and so he judges the speaker as having breached the given—new contract and judges the sequence as unacceptable. As this sequence illustrates, violations of uniqueness strike the listener quite differently from violations of appropriateness. When an utterance is inappropriate, the listener can restructure the sentence to get around the blockage at Step 2 in the strategy. But when an utterance violates uniqueness, he has no way to get around the blockage. He is stuck. So while he judges violations of appropriateness as merely awkward, he judged violations of uniqueness as downright unacceptable. For most violations of uniqueness, it takes very little for the speaker to put the sequence right. All he need do in (9), for example, is provide some indication of a difference between the two men, as in (10):

> (10)   Two men were watching the dog. The tall one watching it laughed out loud.

The addition of *tall* is just enough to enable the listener to find a unique antecedent, for of the two men, one must be tall relative to the other.

There are many ways of finding a unique antecedent, even when there appear to be several possible antecedents. Very often the listener can use syntactic information to eliminate unintended Antecedents. Consider (11):

> (11)   John and Bill looked at each other. Suddenly, John hit him.

Him is part of the given information in the second sentence and requires an antecedent. On syntactic grounds alone the antecedent could not be John, for if it were, the pronoun would have to be reflexive. By elimination, the antecedent must be Bill. (The process of elimination, however, requires processing time, as we will discover later.) Or the elimination can be based on semantic considerations. Consider the three sentences in (12):

> (12)   a. The car rolled toward the telephone pole, and it got damaged.
>   b. The car rolled toward the telephone pole, and it hit it.
>   c. The car rolled toward the telephone pole, and it stopped it.

The first uses of *it* in the second clauses of (12) each require an antecedent. In (12a) there are two possible antecedents, and the ambiguity cannot be resolved, leaving the sequence unacceptable.[6] In (12b), however, the first *it* must refer to something that is movable, and so the antecedent is taken to be the car, not the telephone pole. In (12c) the second *it* must refer to something that is movable, and so its antecedent is the car, and the antecedent to the first *it* is the telephone pole. Since the antecedents in (12b) and (12c) can be chosen uniquely, the sequences are acceptable, though they may take time to figure out.

Finally, sequences can be judged unacceptable because they violate the requirement of computability. These violations arise when the listener does not have the information necessary for computing the intended antecedent. For

---

[6] Many will find (12a) to be acceptable for a superficial syntactic reason. When there is no other way to discover the antecedent to a pronoun, listeners are very likely to pick out the superficial subject of the sentence.

instance, we find the sequence in (13) unacceptable because it lacks a unique antecedent for *he:*

(13)   John and Bill entered the room. Suddenly he ran over to the plate on the floor and licked up all the dog food on it.

But if the speaker knew that the listener knew that John was a man and Bill was his dog, then he could be confident that the listener would be able to compute the intended Antecedent for *he,* namely, Bill. Other sequences are unacceptable because the listener cannot find a plausible bridge from the given information to the previous knowledge. Consider (14):

(14)   There was a full moon again on March 15. This time it was Maxine that Max killed.

But if the speaker was certain the listener knew that Max was a werewolf and that werewolves always kill at full moons, then he could be confident that the listener would be able to build the intended bridge between the first and second sentences. At full moon werewolves always kill and it was Maxine that Max killed on this occasion. Note that the speaker can fulfill the given–new contract by relying on information known only to the listener and himself. It matters little whether or not people not part of the conversation can compute the intended antecedents.

Implicature

Perhaps the most significant, yet the most complicated, linguistic evidence for the given–new strategy is to be found in the implicatures the listener is induced to draw in comprehending certain sentences in context. Consider the cleft sentence *It was Olivia who kissed Oscar* in (15) and (16):

(15)   Someone kissed Oscar. It was Olivia who kissed him.
(16)   Oscar had lipstick on his cheek. It was Olivia who kissed him.

In (15) the first sentence (*someone kissed Oscar*) provides the listener with a direct antecedent for the given information of the second sentence (*someone kissed Oscar*). The speaker has adhered to the maxim of antecedence, and the given–new strategy applies without difficulty. In (16), however, the speaker has not adhered to the maxim of antecedence, and the listener is induced to draw an implicature. To apply the given–new strategy successfully, the listener must assume that Oscar had lipstick on his cheek *because someone kissed him* and that the speaker meant him to add this assumption. This assumption constitutes an implicature. The fact that we automatically draw this implicature is evidence that we are applying the given–new strategy in comprehending the second sentences in (15) and (16).

Every assertion with both given and new information, we claim, can be provided with a context in which the listener will be induced to draw an implicature. Since there are indefinitely many assertions, there are indefinitely many instances that support this claim. We will have to be satisfied with a few simple examples:

(17) a. George went to the party last night. It was Samantha who had invited him.
  b. The rat died on the spot. What it had done was nibble on the rat poison.
  c. Jake noticed two people. The woman was sitting.
  d. I consulted my doctor the other day. She said I was fine.
  e. The major of Deadeye is a Republican. Her HUSBAND is honest TOO.
  f. Jake called Jess a Democrat. The insult made her bristle.
  g. Jake called Jess a Democrat. Then SHE insulted HIM.

Most of the implicatures in these examples are obvious. In (17a) the implicature is that George went to the party because someone had invited him. In (17b) it is that the rat had done something that led to its demise. In (17c) it is that only one of the two people was a women — the other could have been a man, a child, or someone else not identifiable as "a woman." In (17d) one implicature is that the speaker's doctor is female. In (17e) the implicature is that the speaker believes all Republicans are honest. In (17f) and (17g) the prominent implicature is that the speaker considers being called a Democrat an insult. Examples (17e) and (17g) have been discussed extensively by G. Lakoff (1971).

As these examples suggest, implicatures are often the very stuff of the message. The reason is clear. In practice speakers do not always adhere to the maxim of antecedence. If they took the effort to spell out all direct antecedents, conversations would become a tedious business, and sentences would begin to sound very repetitious. More commonly, the speaker leaves gaping holes between his sentences that he expects the listener to fill in with the intended implicatures. Indeed, he can count on most listeners to do this swiftly and unerringly, so he can make his contribution brief and efficient. The holes he leaves, however, cannot be too large or he will be violating the computability requirement. It is difficult, for example, to imagine how the ordinary listener would build a bridge between the two sentences in (18):

(18) George Washington was the father of our country. It was Olivia who kissed Oscar.

What does someone's kissing Oscar have to do with George Washington being the father of our country? The unacceptability of this sequence, we argue, follows from the inability to build a bridge, to find an implicature that would connect the second sentence to the first.

The implicatures a listener may draw to connect an assertion with previous knowledge are in no way determinate. Different listeners will build different bridges. Consider the sequence in (19):

(19)   Mavis liked Marvin very much. What he did was give her a diamond brooch.

The given information, that Marvin did something, may induce one of two implicatures – (1) that he did what he did *so that* she would like him or (2) that he did what he did *because* she liked him. Both implicatures make sense, and there may be other alternatives. The skillful speaker, of course, will avoid such ambiguities by anticipating the alternatives and finding some way of narrowing them down to one. Under the strictest interpretation of the computability requirement, the ambiguity in (19) is a breach of the given–new contract. The listener, with two plausible alternative implicatures, has no way of computing which one the speaker intended.

The bridges the listener *could* build to connect a sentence and its previous context are theoretically infinite in number. In (19), for example, one could draw the implicature that Marvin did what he did to please Mavis's mother, to infuriate Mavis's sister, to pay off Mavis's debts, or to effect something else, and it was that that made Mavis like him. There are endless ways of building bridges. Yet most listeners hearing a sequence of sentences will settle on one of a small number of possible bridges. If this were not so the speaker could never count on the listener drawing the implicature he intended, and implicatures would be of no use. What this suggests is that the listener goes about finding the intended bridge in an orderly way. He follows a set strategy he holds in common with other speakers of English. Our guess is that his main goal is to find the most direct bridge to the previous context, assuming no more than he need assume. Other than that, we have no firm suggestions as to how the listener selects one bridge over another. The question remains to be studied with more care.

PSYCHOLOGICAL EVIDENCE

As linguistic evidence for the given–new strategy, we have looked at the awkwardness of some sequences, the unacceptability of others, and the implicatures drawn in still others. The psychological evidence we now turn to comes mainly from measurements of processing time. For the most part we will be concerned with instances where people take longer to comprehend certain sequences than others. Reaction time is a very sensitive measure of processing difficulties, for it can detect mental operations that require only a few hundredths of a second to perform. For this reason we can use decision latencies to test rather subtle predictions of the given–new strategy.

Definite Descriptions

In a recent study (Haviland & Clark, 1974) we examined the time it took people to comprehend sentences containing definite noun phrases. Consider *The beer was warm,* which takes as given that there is a specific quantity of beer and requires the listener to find such a quantity before he can incorporate into memory the new information that that quantity of beer was warm. This sentence appears in the two sequences in (20), each consisting of a "context sentence" followed by a "target sentence":

(20) a. Horace got some beer out of the car. The beer was warm.
      b. Horace got some picnic supplies out of the car. The beer was warm.

In (20a) the context sentence directly establishes the existence of a quantity of beer, so the listener has a direct antecedent for the given information of the target sentence. In Sequence (20b), on the other hand, there is no direct antecedent in the context sentence, and so the listener must build a bridge. He must draw the implicature that the picnic supplies contain a quantity of beer, and it is that quantity that is being referred to by the given information of the target sentence. Since drawing this implicature presumably takes time, the listener should take longer to comprehend the target sentence *The beer was warm* in Sequence (20b) than in Sequence (20a).

To test this prediction we constructed 68 context–target sequences on the pattern of Sequences (20a) and (20b). The sequences came in pairs such that the same target sentence occurred with one context sentence to form a direct antecedent sequence and with another context sentence to form an indirect antecedent sequence. The subjects saw one sequence per pair according to the following procedure. Upon pressing a button, the subject was presented with the context sentence in typed form in a tachistoscope. As soon as he felt he understood it, he pressed the button again, the context sentence disappeared, and the target sentence appeared. As soon as he felt he understood the target sentence, he pressed a second button and the target sentence disappeared. We recorded the time the subject spent looking at the target sentence, the time between the second and third button presses. We assumed that this measure of how long it took the subject to feel subjectively that he understood the target sentence would reflect not only the computation of the propositional content of the sentence, but also Steps 2 and 3 of the given–new strategy, the finding of an antecedent and the integration of the new information in memory. In a carefully counterbalanced design, each subject saw half direct antecedent sequences and half indirect antecedent sequences, but never the same target sentence twice.

The comprehension times, averaged over all 68 sequences and over 16 subjects, were as follows:

Direct antecedent condition: 835 msec
Indirect antecedent condition: 1016 msec

The times were clearly as predicted. The target sentences took around 180 msec longer to comprehend in the indirect antecedent sequences, where bridging was required, than in the direct antecedent sequences, where no bridging was required. This 180 msec difference was highly reliable by the appropriate statistical tests. It is important to note that both (20a) and (20b) are perfectly acceptable sequences, as were all of the direct and indirect antecedent sequences we constructed. The 180 msec difference between them, then, has to be attributed to the difference in normal processing required for the target sentence in these two types of sequences.

But we were not completely happy with this experiment. In the direct antecedent sequences, the word *beer* in the target sentence was preceded by the word *beer* in the context sentence, whereas in the indirect antecedent sequences, it was not. The direct antecedent sequences may have been easier simply because of the repetition of the word *beer,* perhaps making the second instance of *beer* easier to comprehend. To rule out a simple repetition explanation, we therefore constructed new indirect antecedent sequences as illustrated here in Sequence (21b):

(21)   a. Horace got some beer out of the trunk. The beer was warm.
       b. Horace was especially fond of beer. The beer was warm.

Now both the direct antecedent sequence (21a) and the new indirect antecedent sequence (21b) contain the critical word *beer* in the context sentence. But there is a critical difference between the two. In (21a), the context sentence posits the existence of an individual quantity of beer. In (21b), the context sentence does not, and because it does not, there is no immediate antecedent for *the beer* to be found in the context sentence. The reader attempting to comprehend the target sentence (21b) must therefore resort to bridging, and comprehension time for indirect antecedent sequences should still be longer than comprehension time for direct antecedent sequences. Indeed, in a repetition of the previous experiment using these new indirect antecedent sequences we found the following comprehension times for target sentences:

Direct antecedent sequence: 1031 msec
Indirect antecedent sequence: 1168 msec

The indirect antecedent condition took about 140 msec longer, supporting the given—new strategy and ruling out repetition as the sole explanation for the comprehension times observed in the first experiment.

The Adverbs *too, either, again,* and *still*

To demonstrate the generality of these findings, we performed a third experiment in which we constructed similar sequences for target sentences containing the adverbs *too, either, again,* and *still.* Consider the following sentences:

(22) a. Elizabeth is here too.
      b. Elizabeth isn't here either.
      c. Elizabeth is here again.
      d. Elizabeth is still here.

The first, Sentence (22a), presupposes that there is someone else who is here; (22b) presupposes that there is someone else who is not here; Sentence (22c) presupposes that Elizabeth was here before; and Sentence (22d) presupposes that Elizabeth has been here for a while. In given–new terms, these presuppositions constitute the given information, and the assertions, *sans* adverb, contain the new information. For each of the four adverbs, then, we constructed sequences such as (23):

(23) a. Last Christmas Larry became absolutely smashed. This Christmas he got drunk again.
      b. Last Christmas Larry went to a lot of parties. This Christmas he got drunk again.
      c. Last Christmas Larry couldn't stay sober. This Christmas he got drunk again.

The sequence (23a) is a direct antecedent sequence. An antecedent for the given information of the target sentence is provided directly by the context sentence. The sequence in (23b) is an indirect antecedent sequence, for it requires bridging from the context sentence to the intended antecedent. And (23c) is a new type of sequence, which we dubbed *negative antecedent.* These were constructed so that the context sentence contained the negative equivalent of the intended antecedent of the target sentence. The expression *couldn't stay sober* implies *got drunk.* To find an antecedent for the target sentence, therefore, the reader must make this inference, bridging the gap between the context sentence and the intended antecedent. This bridging should take time, making the target sentence take relatively longer to comprehend. In short, the reader should comprehend the target sentence in the direct antecedent sequence relatively quickly and the target sentences in the other two sequences more slowly, since the latter both require bridging.

We constructed a large number of sequences for each adverb, again designed so that each target sentence appeared once in each type of sequence, and we presented them to 27 subjects. The comprehension times were as follows:

Direct antecedent sequence: 1323 msec
Indirect antecedent sequence: 1397 msec
Negative antecedent sequence: 1388 msec

The difference between the first and the second two, though smaller than in the previous experiments, was highly reliable and consistent with our predictions. So again we find support for the given–new strategy.

Cleft and Pseudocleft Sentences

One piece of psychological evidence for the given—new contract is found in the recent work by Hornby (1974) on the verification of cleft and pseudocleft sentences. What he did was read his subjects a sentence and, one second later, present them with a very brief (50 msec) glimpse of a picture and ask them to say whether the sentence was true or false of the picture. The glimpse of the picture was so brief that subjects could not take in all the details of the picture and so they made errors in their verifications. Hornby centered his attention on those sentences that were "false" of the pictures (he had included both true and false sentences) and asked the following question: What is the given and new structure of the sentences that led to the most errors?

The given—new contract leads to straightforward predictions about the errors Hornby's subjects should make. Consider one of Hornby's sentences:

> (24)   It is the boy who is petting the cat.

According to the given—new contract, asking whether (24) is true or false is equivalent to asking whether or not the new information is veridical relative to the intended antecedent of the given information. The reason is this, the listener, believing that the speaker is adhering to the given—new contract, automatically assumes he can compute a unique antecedent to the given information. But there is nothing in the contract to lead him to any comparable assumptions about the veridicality of the new information. The speaker, for example, can provide false new information, violating the maxim of quality and inducing an implicature, still without breaching the cooperative principle. What the listener assumes is to be judged, then, is the new information: Is it veridical for the intended antecedent? In this respect verification is akin to questioning and negation (see Akmajian, 1973; Chomsky, 1971; Jackendoff, 1972). Judging Sentence (24) as true or false is equivalent to answering yes or no to the question *Is it the boy who is petting the cat?* Here the answer is expected to affirm or deny the new information relative to the intended antecedent. And judging Sentence (24) as false is equivalent to asserting the negative of (24). The speaker of the negative sentence *It isn't the boy who is petting the cat,* for example, is denying the new information relative to the intended antecedent of the given information and nothing else. Thus, like questioning and negation, verification leaves the given information of a sentence untouched.

Hornby used two types of "false" sentences, as illustrated in (25) for a picture of a girl petting a cat:

> (25)   a. It is the boy who is petting the cat.
>   b. It is the girl who is petting the dog.

Sentence (25a) is genuinely false in a cooperative context. The new information, that the entity petting the cat is the boy, is not correct. Sentence (25b), on the other hand, violates the terms of the given—new contract. The listener will not be able to find an antecedent that fits the description *X is petting the dog*. We will therefore call (25a) a false sentence and (25b) an uncooperative one. Now subjects had to judge all sentences as true or false. But because they had only a limited time to examine the picture, they had to select which details they would look for and which details they would skip over. Assuming cooperation, they would be expected to check on the new information and ignore details concerning the exact veridicality of the given information. Hence they should be better at detecting the misrepresentation in the false sentences than in the uncooperative ones.

Hornby confirmed this prediction, which he too had made in a parallel line of reasoning. Using a balanced selection of cleft and pseudocleft sentences with both agents and objects in the clefted position, he found the following percentages of failures to detect the misrepresentation:

False sentences: 39%
Uncooperative sentences: 72%

So it was critical whether the misrepresentation in the sentence constituted falsity or uncooperativeness.

Technically speaking, Hornby stacked the cards against any other result by explicitly asking the subjects to judge the sentences as true or false. The false sentences naturally had the edge over the uncooperative sentences. But could Hornby have instructed his subjects to treat the misrepresentations of falsity and uncooperativeness equally? We doubt it. As Horn (1972) and others have argued, English has only very clumsy and indirect devices for qualifying presuppositions, although it has quite simple and direct devices for denying asserted information — new information. More than that, there is no easy way to explain the notion of an uncooperative misrepresentation to subjects, and even if there were, we doubt that they could resist the temptation to assume, as usual, that the speaker was adhering to the given—new contract. We guess that Hornby's findings would have arisen to some degree no matter how carefully the subjects were instructed about the two types of misrepresentations.

In a second experiment Hornby compared the six different types of sentences illustrated in (26):

(26) a. The girl is petting the cat.
     b. The cat is being petted by the girl.
     c. It is the girl who is petting the cat.
     d. It is the girl whom the cat is being petted by.
     e. The one who is petting the cat is the girl.
     f. The one whom the cat is being petted by is the girl.

Hornby presented each sentence followed by a verifying or falsifying picture, just as in the previous experiment, but this time the "false" sentences were all of the uncooperative kind. He found that the six types of sentences varied in how often subjects failed to detect the misrepresentations in them:

Active:	26%
Passive:	68%
Cleft active:	51%
Cleft passive:	80%
Pseudocleft active:	74%
Pseudocleft passive:	92%

Briefly, subjects were most accurate on the simple sentences, less accurate on the cleft constructions, and least accurate on the pseudocleft constructions; in addition, subjects were more accurate on active than passive constructions whether alone, in cleft constructions, or in pseudocleft constructions.

This variation arose, according to Hornby, because some sentences mark given and new information "more strongly or clearly" than others.[7] In particular, new information is more strongly marked when it appears in passive *by*-phrases, when it appears near the end of the sentence, and when it appears to the right of a copula. These three factors place the six types of sentences in just the order Hornby found. But what does it mean to say that given or new information is more strongly or clearly marked in some sentences than in others? For any sentence on any one interpretation, one portion of the content is given and one portion is new, and there is no gradient possible in this dichotomy.

Hornby's findings, we argue, may reflect the following two factors: (1) the alternative given—new patterns permited for a particular sentence; and (2) the hierarchy of given' and new' found within the given information of the sentence. The first factor is straightforward. The simple sentences (26a) and (26b) each have three alternative given—new patterns; (26a), for example, answers the questions *What is the girl petting?, What is the girl doing?,* and *What is happening?* If subjects had formed the broadest of these patterns (the third one), they would have searched both the girl and the dog in the picture and would have been quite accurate in detecting the error. Indeed, the broad pattern is more probable for active than for passive constructions, implying that actives should be more accurate than passives. The cleft and pseudocleft sentences (26c) through (26f), on the other hand, allow only one rather narrow pattern of given

---

[7] Unfortunately, Hornby used all uncooperative and no false sentences in this second experiment, and this procedure clouds the interpretation of his results. It is well known that passive sentences, for example, are often more difficult to verify against pictures than actives (Gough, 1965, 1966; Slobin, 1966). If this is so for Hornby's sentences, (26b) may elicit more detection failures not because passives mark given and new information more strongly than actives, but because passives are generally more difficult than actives. It would have been more appropriate to compare each uncooperative sentence in (26) to a false sentence with the same syntactic structure. Then the strength of the given—new "marking" would be given by the difference between the paired uncooperative and false sentences. With this caution, however, we will assume with Hornby that the sentences are ordered for strength of marking just as he reported.

and new. That pattern would lead subjects in each instance to ignore the parts of the picture corresponding to the given information, hence they would have been less accurate in detecting the error. Hornby's data are in agreement with these predictions.

The second factor that may be involved is the hierarchy of given and new within each sentence. Consider (26c). Its given information is manifested on the surface as *that is petting the cat,* which has an internal intonation pattern with "secondary" focal stress on *cat.* Thus, $X = the\ cat$ is new$'$ information relative to the given$'$ information that someone was petting something. By similar reasoning, the new$'$ information in (26d) is $X = petting.$ Now if the listener were to check the new$'$ information in the picture before the given$'$ information, as he does new before given, he would be more likely to check for the cat given (26c), and more likely to check for the petting given (26d). As a consequence, he would detect the error actually there more often in (26c) than in (26d). The analogous argument can be made for the pseudocleft sentences (26e) and (26f). Hornby's findings are in agreement with these predictions as well.[8]

The two factors just noted provide an account not only for Hornby's data but also for the intuition that some sentences mark given and new information more "strongly" or "clearly" than others. According to our tentative account, this intuition comes about because some sentences have a structure that allows only narrow patterns of given and new and because some sentences have a well-defined secondary pattern of given$'$ and new$'$ within the given information. We stress, however, that this account is tentative. It needs much more investigation.

Personal Pronouns

The personal pronouns *he* and *she* almost always contain given information. On encountering such a pronoun the listener must compute its intended antecedent, and this normally requires a search through memory. In English, however, pronominalization is made even more complicated by the fact that the intended antecedent can sometimes follow the pronoun instead of preceding it. Step 2 in the given–new strategy, therefore, is a rather complicated process, and it is of interest to know exactly how it works. Frederick Springston, in his dissertation research at Stanford University, has examined just this problem, and his findings shed much light on the computation of antecedents in general. We will present one of his findings in detail, and then his general conclusions about the process.

Springston's technique for studying the computation of antecedents was as follows. His subjects were first presented with a sentence containing a pronoun. As soon as they understood it, they pressed a button, and this sentence was

---

[8] This analysis, it should be noted, also predicts that subjects are more likely to detect misrepresentation in the action — say, the girl was lifting, instead of petting, the cat — for (26d) than for (26c) and also more likely for (26f) than for (26e). Hornby did not include misrepresentations of this sort.

immediately replaced by a second sentence, and this second sentence was to be judged true or false as quickly as possible. A sample sequence is shown in (27):

(27) a. Bill said that Sally nominated him.
      b. The person nominated was Sally.

In his experiments, Springston measured the time for the comprehension of the first and second sentences separately, but for purposes of analysis, he used the sum of these two latencies (for true instances only) as a measure of how difficult it was to compute the antecedent of *him*. Then, by comparing various types of pronominal constructions, he was able to make some inferences about the strategies subjects were using to determine antecedents.

Springston first showed that the reader is faster at computing the antecedents for reflexive pronouns (*himself, herself*) than for simple pronouns (*him, her*). Consider the following two sentences:

(28) a. John said that Bill shot himself.
      b. John said that Bill shot him.

The reflexive *himself*, in Sentence (28a), can only have a noun phrase within the same clause as its antecedent, and so the listener can compute it immediately as *Bill*. But for the *him* in Sentence (28b), according to Springston's predictions, the reader will first try a noun in the same clause (*Bill*) as a possible antecedent, find it prohibited for syntactic reasons, and only then try a noun in the next higher sentence (*John*), which in this case can serve as the antecedent. Obviously, this extra processing should take longer, and Springston's data show that it does. According to Springston, the reader generally tries for antecedents in the same clause first and then moves backwards, even when syntactic constraints would seem to make a search of the same clause unnecessary, as in (28b).

To give this notion further support, Springston added gender to these sentences, as illustrated in (29) and (30):

(29) a. John said that Mary shot herself.
      b. Sally said that Mary shot herself.
(30) a. John said that Mary shot him.
      b. John said that Bill shot him.

If the reader searches for the antecedent from the current clause backward, then gender alone ought to help him rule out *Mary* as an antecedent for *him* in Sentence (30a), but it will not help him rule out *Bill* as an antecedent for *him* in Sentence (30b). In contrast, gender should make little or no difference to finding the antecedent for *herself* in (29), since the reader never searches for an antecedent outside of the same clause. Indeed, although Springston's subjects were a little faster on Sentence (29a) than on (29b), they were very much faster on Sentence (30a) than on (30b), where gender was predicted to make a difference. So these results further confirm the notion that the search for antecedents of nonreflexive pronouns begins in the same clause and goes backwards.

Working from a large number of experiments such as these, Springston drew the following general conclusions. First, the reader (and presumably the listener too) searches for antecedents to reflexive pronouns in the same clause and terminates his search on finding the antecedent. To find the antecedent for *himself* in Sentence (28a), the listener need only search the clause *Bill shot himself* and stop on finding *Bill*. Second, the listener searches for possible antecedents for simple pronouns exhaustively, and he determines his choice of an antecedent by the process of elimination. In (28b) he checks both *Bill* and *John* as possible antecedents for *him* and eventually eliminates *Bill* on syntactic grounds. Third, in eliminating candidate antecedents, the listener examines them from the current clause backwards. In Sentence (28b) he checks *Bill* out first and then *John*. Fourth, the listener is able to eliminate candidate antecedents as impossible faster the more syntactic and semantic criteria he has for rejecting them. In (30a) the reader is able to eliminate *Mary* as an antecedent to *him* very quickly because *Mary* is impossible on grounds of *both* syntax *and* gender. Springston demonstrated this phenomenon for a variety of semantic criteria, some of them very subtle. And fifth, the reader has more difficulty finding the intended antecedent when it is in a clause that follows the pronoun or a clause that is dominated by the clause containing the pronoun. Thus it takes longer to find the antecedent to *him* in Sentence (31b) than in (31a):

(31) a. John said that Mary shot him.
      b. Mary shot him is what John said.

And this difference in search time is over and above any difference that might be attributed to the fact that Sentence (31b) is more difficult to understand than (31a) even without pronouns.

Springston's study points to an important direction of investigation: How does the listener go about searching memory for the intended antecedents to given information? If Springston is right, the listener considers some candidate antecedents before others, eliminates them on syntactic and semantic grounds wherever possible, and settles on the candidate antecedent that cannot be eliminated. But this characterization is far from complete. It cannot handle antecedents not directly derivable from prior sentences, and it provides no rule to say when to search further for a direct antecedent or when to draw an implicature for an indirect antecedent. Furthermore, Chafe (1973, 1974) has recently argued that "consciousness" seems crucial to this process, for the speaker must assume that certain antecedents are in the listener's consciousness, not just his memory structure, at the time of utterance. The question of search strategies deserves further investigation.

Wh- Questions

The given—new strategy was designed to account for an important aspect of the comprehension of assertions. Primarily meant to inform, assertions contain given and new information, and the new information is meant to be integrated into memory. But what about other types of speech acts — questions, commands, promises, bets — that are not primarily meant to inform? To handle these, the strategy must be modified, but only slightly. We will examine how it might be changed to handle Wh- questions. How it might be modified to handle other speech acts should become obvious by this examination.

Whereas assertions add information to the listener's memory, questions are meant to elicit information from his memory. But just as assertions indicate the address where the new information is to be added, questions indicate the address from which the wanted information is to be extracted. So questions have given information, but in place of new information they have wanted information. *Who ate my cookies?* has as given that someone ate the speaker's cookies, and it indicates that the speaker wants to know who that someone is. For convenience, we can simply extend the term new information to cover this wanted information, and the resulting analysis is as follows:

(33)   a. Who ate my cookies?
      b. Given: X ate my (the speaker's) cookies.
      c. New: X = Who?

By such an analysis there is in principle a way for Step 1 to divide each question into given and new information, as required. The Wh-word conveys the new information, and the rest of the sentence conveys the given information.

The heart of the revision of the given—new strategy for questions is in Step 3. At Step 1, the listener divides the sentence into given and new, as before. And at Step 2, the listener searches for and finds in memory an antecedent that matches the given information of the question. But at Step 3, the listener must inspect the information attached to the antecedent and use it as the basis for constructing an answer to the question. For *Who ate my cookies?*, the listener would find the antecedent proposition E_{19} *ate the speaker's cookies* in memory, determine that E_{19} was Elmer, and compose the appropriate answer, *The person who ate your cookies was Elmer, It was Elmer,* or, simply, *Elmer.* The point is, the given—new strategy is almost the same for questions as for assertions. It is Step 3 that appears to change with the speech act.

Characterized this way the given—new strategy leads to interesting predictions about the time it takes the listener to answer questions in various contexts. The psychological literature is full of studies in which people were timed as they answered questions. To illustrate how the given—new strategy would apply to them, we will present only one of these studies, Smith and McMahon (1970), and that one only in simplified form. Essentially, what Smith and McMahon did was present their subjects with context–target pairs such as the following:

(33) a. John is preceding Dick. Who is ahead?
     b. Dick is following John. Who is ahead?

The question *Who is ahead?* has as given information *X is ahead of Y* and as new information *X = who?* At Step 2, therefore, the listener has to search for an antecedent to *X is ahead of Y.* The context sentence of (33a) does not convey such information directly, but it does so indirectly. *John is preceding Dick* itself implies the proposition *John is ahead of Dick,* and once drawn, this implication can serve as a direct antecedent for the given information of the question. The context sentence of (33b), however, does not directly imply the right proposition. *Dick is following John* implies *Dick is behind John,* not *John is ahead of Dick.* So to find a matching antecedent for *Who is ahead?,* the listener must draw the further inference that in this context *Dick is behind John* itself implies *John is ahead of Dick.* Such an extra inference should of course take extra time. So questions in sequences like (33b) should take longer to answer than those in sequences like (33a).

Smith and McMahon's answer latencies bear out these predictions. Subjects were able to answer *Who is ahead?* faster than *Who is behind?* for the following context sentences, all of which directly imply *John is ahead of Dick:*

(34) a. John is preceding Dick.
     b. John is leading Dick.
     c. Dick is preceded by John.
     d. Dick is led by John.

Yet they were able to answer *Who is behind?* faster than *Who is ahead?* for the following sentences, all of which directly imply *Dick is behind John:*

(35) a. Dick is following John.
     b. Dick is trailing John.
     c. John is followed by Dick.
     d. John is trailed by Dick.

The difference between the two questions averaged about 300 msec.

In other experiments, psychologists have used questions that contained comparatives, such as *Which is taller/shorter/deeper/shallower?* (Clark, Carpenter, & Just, 1973); superlatives such as *Who is best/worst?* (Clark, 1969); actives and passives, such as *Who did John hit?* and *Who was hit by John?* (Olson, 1972; Wright, 1969); temporals, such as *What happened first/second?* (Smith & McMahon, 1970); and locatives, such as *Where is John?* (Clark, 1972). In each case, the results fit the predictions of the given–new strategy very nicely (see Clark, 1974).

VIOLATIONS OF THE MAXIM AND BREACHES OF THE CONTRACT

As all this evidence demonstrates, the listener relies heavily on the speaker's adherence to the given—new contract. Nevertheless, both the maxim of antecedence and the contract itself are often broken, and, depending on the circumstances, these violations have different consequences. We will distinguish three classes of violation — negligent, covert, and explicit. *Negligent violations* arise from unwitting negligence or misjudgment on the part of the speaker. He constructs sentences without proper regard for what he believes the listener does and does not know, or else he simply misjudges what the listener does and does not know. *Covert violations* are deliberate distortions of given and new for the purpose of deception. Here the speaker realizes he is violating the contract and does not want the listener to realize he is doing so. *Explicit violations* again are deliberate, but they are meant to be noted by the listener as an integral part of his interpretation of the sentence. We noted earlier that explicit violations will always be of the maxim of antecedence, never of the requirements of appropriateness, uniqueness, or computability. On the other hand, negligent and covert violations can be of any aspect of the given—new contract. Explicit violations will be used by the listener in arriving at the intended interpretation of the sentence; negligent and covert violations will normally result in a breakdown in communication. We will examine the consequences of negligent, covert, and explicit violations in turn.

Negligent Violations

As ought to be expected, negligent violations result in comprehension difficulties. Through no fault of his own, the listener has trouble finding the intended antecedent, or even any antecedent, and so he is slowed down in comprehension. Often he finds the wrong antecedent and completely misinterprets the sentence, a fact he discovers only later when his interpretation breaks down. Sometimes he finds more than one antecedent with no way of deciding among them. Or he may have to restructure what is given and what is new before he can find a place for the information in memory. Indeed, these consequences are among those we have examined in the sections on linguistic and psychological evidence.

   The negligence of the speaker can be, simply, in not informing the listener about the topic of conversation. This is illustrated by a paragraph used by Bransford and Johnson (1973) in a study of comprehension and memory. They presented their subjects with the following paragraph:

> The procedure is actually quite simple. First you arrange things into different groups. Of course, one pile may be sufficient depending on how much there is to do. If you have to go somewhere else due to lack of facilities, that is the next step, otherwise you are pretty well set. It is important not to overdo things. That is, it is better to do too few

things at once than too many. In the short run this may not seem important but complications can easily arise. A mistake can be expensive as well. At first the whole procedure will seem complicated. Soon, however, it will become just another facet of life. It is difficult to foresee any end to the necessity for this task in the immediate future, but then one can never tell. After the procedure is completed one arranges the materials into different groups again. Then they can be put into their proper places. Eventually they will be used once more and the whole cycle will then have to be repeated. However, that is a part of life. (p. 400)

As presented here, this paragraph is almost impossible to understand, and Bransford and Johnson's subjects judged it to be hard to understand and had great difficulty in remembering it. The reason is, of course, that there is no clue as to what the paragraph is about. But everything falls neatly into place for the reader told ahead of time that the paragraph is about washing clothes. When Bransford and Johnson's subjects were given this topic beforehand, they rated the paragraph as quite comprehensible, as we would expect, and they could remember significantly more of it.

But why is the topic so important? Apparently, it is the topic that enables the listener to compute the intended antecedents of each sentence in the paragraph. In the first sentence it is given that there is a procedure of some kind. But without knowing that the paragraph is about washing clothes, the reader has no way of computing what kind of procedure was intended. By the process of addition, he merely adds an antecedent reading "there is a procedure," which is not very helpful. Likewise, he needs to know in the second sentence what things are to be arranged, and in the third, what one pile is sufficient for and how much of *what* there is to do. Yet without the topic, he has no means for computing the intended antecedents.

The same point is illustrated in a memory study reported by Bransford and McCarrell (1975). They gave their subjects sentences and, later, gave them the first noun phrase in each sentence as a prompt for them to recall the rest of the sentence. The sentences were of two kinds, as illustrated here:

(36) a. The office was cool because the windows were closed.
       b. The haystack was important because the cloth ripped.

The first was considered easy, since it was easy to understand. The second was considered hard, since it didn't make much sense by itself. To no one's surprise, when given the prompt *the office,* the subjects had little difficulty recalling Sentence (36a), but when given the prompt *the haystack,* they had great difficulty recalling Sentence (36b). But there was an added touch. Some subjects were provided with a different one-word prompt at both the time of presentation and the time of recall, a word that was meant to place the sentence in context. For Sentence (36a) the prompt was *air-conditioning,* and for Sentence (36b) the prompt was *parachutist.* Under these circumstances, the easy and hard sentences were equally easy to recall.

What is going on here? Sentence (36a), it could be argued, is easy because the listener can compute the intended antecedents for the given information in that sentence. *The office* refers to a specific office, and *the windows,* to the windows of that office. Given these antecedents, it is easy to make sense of the two propositions and their relation, especially as we know that offices usually have air-conditioning and that air-conditioning works most efficiently with the windows closed. Sentence (36b) is quite another matter. It is highly unlikely that anyone would figure out from the sentence alone that the appropriate antecedent for *the cloth* was the canopy of a parachute. For this reason it is difficult to make sense of the two propositions and their relation. Once the intended antecedent is made clear by the prompt word *parachutist* then Sentence (36b) becomes as easy to understand as Sentence (36a). The problem with sentences like (36b) only arises because the listener does not have enough information to compute the intended antecedents. Indeed, this seems to be one of the commonest forms of negligent violation. The speaker assumes the listener can bridge certain gaps when in actuality the listener lacks the information that would enable him to do so.

Covert Violations

Covert violations of the given—new contract are meant to deceive. For example, the speaker may construct sentences in which the given information contains something that is not actually true. He knows that the listener must set up in memory an antecedent for this given information and, in so doing, add false information to his set of facts. This way the speaker may communicate false information without asserting it, and the listener may not realize exactly what's happening. Consider the two questions in (37):

(37) a. Did you write this letter?
      b. Do you admit to writing this letter?

The first question merely asks whether the addressee wrote the letter. The second, however, is a leading question. It has as additional given information the notion that writing the letter was bad. If the addressee answers "Yes," meaning "Yes, I wrote the letter," then he has been tricked into acknowledging the truth of the given information as well. If the address says "No," he is only denying the new information, and he is still in agreement with the idea that writing the letter was bad. This may be enough of a deception to serve the speaker's ends. If the addressee happens to have written the letter but wants to correct the given information, he is forced into a complex answer, something like "Sure I wrote it. What's wrong with that?" At the very least, any person listening to this interchange will have accepted for one short moment at least the fact that writing the letter was bad, and this may influence his later acceptance of corrective information. Covert violations like this, therefore, can be used to add new but false information, relabel already known information, plant the germ of an alternative explanation for a fact, or build up prior resistance to a fact. In the hands of a clever pratitioner, such covert violations can be very effective.

A recent study by Loftus and Zanni (1975) demonstrates just how easy it is to use this device for deception.What they did was show subjects a short movie of a car accident and then ask the subjects a variety of questions about the accident. Among these questions were several that violated the given–new contract. For example, half the subjects were asked (38a) and half (38b):

(38) a. Did you see a broken headlight?
      b. Did you see the broken headlight?

In truth, the movie showed no broken headlight, and so (38b) violates the given–new contract (as well as the maxim of quality) since the given information is that there was a broken headlight. The subjects were required to choose one of three answers: "yes," "no," and "I don't know."

What should happen here? The subjects responding to (38a) must implicitly ask themselves two questions: (a) was there a broken headlight? and (b) if there was, did I see it? Only if they can answer "yes" to Question (a) can they ask themselves Question (b), and once asked Question (b), they should be fairly certain of their answer. But the accident happened so fast that these subjects could not even be certain of Question (a), and so they should respond "I don't know" a good proportion of the time. In fact, they responded "I don't know" 38% of the time. In contrast, the subjects responding to (38b) do not have to answer Question (a), since for them the answer is "yes." The given information in (38b) forced them to assume that there was a broken headlight, and they have already set up in memory an antecedent corresponding to this fact. so these subjects are only concerned with question (b), and can be fairly certain about their answer. As expected, these subjects responded "I don't know" only 12% of the time (compared to 38% of the time for the other subjects). Further, if they were committed to its existence, they should be more likely to think they saw the broken headlight, for after all, it was there. And there were in fact more "yes" responses for (38b) than for (38a), 17% as compared with 7%. By a covert violation of the given–new contract, these subjects were essentially tricked into committing themselves to the existence of a broken headlight. This in turn changed their criterion for how much objective evidence they needed to say "yes," "no," and "I don't know."

Explicit Violations

In Grice's scheme, explicit violations of the maxims within the cooperative principle are designed to induce the listener to draw implicatures. Earlier we noted that someone might say *It's such a lovely day today* even though he knew his audience was aware of the fact that there was a violent storm raging outside. In violating the maxim of quality explicitly, he meant to inform his audience not about the weather itself — the literal interpretation of what he said — but rather about how he felt about the known weather. Explicit violations of other maxims induce other implicatures. We have noted in particular that the speaker can violate the maxim of antecedence and, by so doing, convey something in addition to what the sentence says literally.

What is the nature of the implicatures induced by violations of the maxim of antecedence? Consider the sequence in (39):

> (39)   A friend of mine has met both Nixon and Agnew. I have met several crooks in my time too.

The speaker of (39), though he has not said so outright, has conveyed the additional information that he believes both Nixon and Agnew are crooks. In bridging from the first sentence to the second, the listener is led to draw this implicature. But the speaker has done more than that. He has, in effect, used the given–new contract to imply that he believes the listener also assumes that Nixon and Agnew are crooks. The given–new contract requires the speaker to be certain that the listener can compute the bridge from the first sentence to the second, and in this instance, it requires the listener to know that Nixon and Agnew are crooks. By pretending that the listener already knows this, the speaker implies that he and the listener hold this belief in common (though this may not be the case). So this implicature is quite unlike the informing assertion "Nixon and Agnew are crooks," but more akin to the force of "We agree, of course, that Nixon and Agnew are crooks." The implicature, then, can be much more effective than the bald assertion because it is not explicit and because it presupposes common belief. Its effect can also be one of surprise or humor when the implicature required is something unexpected.

A related violation is to introduce new information by means of definite noun phrases or restrictive relative clauses. Consider the following sentence:

> (40)   Bill slipped me a bottle of gin, but the idiot told my wife about it.

The phrase *the idiot* could just as well have been *he,* but by the additional content, it leads the listener to realize that the speaker believes Bill to be an idiot. The mechanism works in the same way as the hidden presupposition example in (39). The effect is again one of implying a common judgment.

There is one particular time when many modern writers explicitly violate the maxim of antecedence, and that is at the beginning of novels or stories. To adhere to the maxim, a writer should always posit the existence of a character, an object, or an event before he talks about it as if it were known to the reader. But modern writers often do not do this. It is instructive to compare, for example, the initial sentences from an old folk tale, *Die zwölf Brüder,* as set down by the Brothers Grimm early in the nineteenth century, with those from

William Faulkner's *The Sound and the Fury*, a twentieth-century novel:

(41) Es war einmal ein König und eine Königin, die lebten in Frieden miteinander und hatten zwölf Kinder, das waren aber lauter Buben. [Once upon a time there was a king and a queen. They lived together peacefully and had twelve children, all of whom were boys.]

(42) Through the fence, between the curling flower spaces, I can see them hitting. They were coming toward where the flag was and I went along the fence.

The purpose of (41) is obviously to introduce the characters that inhabit the story. It marks the beginning of the tale. The purpose of (42), in contrast, is to make the reader think he is stepping into an ongoing story, exactly the effect Faulkner managed to produce. To understand (42) the reader must set up antecedents for each piece of given information and then wait for more complete information. The effect is to make the reader ask, which fence? what spaces? who are "they"? what flag? and so on. The questions produce suspense and an impression of impending action. Stories that begin this way may be difficult to understand at first. Yet the clever writer can introduce just enough information to make the beginning comprehensible, while leaving out just enough to keep up the drama of ongoing tale. The device, nevertheless, is an explicit violation of the maxim of antecedence, since the writer and reader are both aware that the reader cannot really compute the intended antecedents.

The implicature the reader of (42) will draw, therefore, is this. Although he does not know the antecedents he is supposed to know yet, he must accept them as fact; and the reason he does not know them as fact is because he has stepped into the middle of the telling of a story. This type of implicature is not that uncommon. We go through similar reasoning whenever we overhear an utterance addressed to someone else. Since the speaker has not designed his utterance with us in mind, he may have provided given information for which we can compute no antecedents. As surreptitious listeners, we must be content with setting up antecedents by the Step 2 detour we called addition and hope that their true nature will become clear later. Indeed, this is just the class of situations writers exploit when they introduce the reader to the middle of a story. They begin as if the story were being told to someone else and the reader were merely an uninvolved onlooker.

CONCLUSIONS

What we have argued here is that certain processes in comprehension are a consequence of an implicit agreement we all have about conversations. We all assume people are cooperative in their conversations, and in particular we assume they adhere to the given—new contract. By this agreement, speakers attempt to judge what their listeners do and do not know, and they construct their sentences accordingly. They do not deliberately try to deceive their listeners by violating the contract, though they may introduce specific violations of an aspect of it, the maxim of antecedence, in order to convey novel information in a novel way. Listeners rely on the given—new strategy to interpret sentences. When told something, they compute what is given and what is new in the utterance, search memory for an antecedent of the given information, and then add the new information to memory. By relying on this strategy, the listener will draw implicatures for certain sentences, judge others to be awkward or unacceptable in context, and take longer to comprehend those that induce implicatures. All the evidence available so far appears to support these notions.

But the approach taken here may have even broader implications for a theory of comprehension. As Grice (1957) and Searle (1970) have emphasized, a listener trying to understand a sentence does more than determine its propositional or locutionary content. His fundamental goal, rather, is to try to figure out what the speaker intended him to understand by the sentence, and this may require all sorts of inferences. The detailed strategies the listener applies to syntax, semantics, and even phonology may well be geared to these higher-level considerations of interpretation. These strategies should perhaps be thought of as devices in service of these higher goals, rather than as independent devices in their own right. In its essentials, that is the basic idea of the given—new strategy. It is a device that exists because the listener wants to integrate new information into what he already knows, and the device can work only because of an abstract agreement between speaker and listener, the given—new contract. But certainly much more of comprehension is in service of such higher-order goals.

ACKNOWLEDGMENTS

This chapter is based on a paper with the same title presented by HHC at a conference on "The role of grammar in interdisciplinary linguistic research," University of Bielefeld, Bielefeld, Germany, December 1973. We wish to thank Eve V. Clark for her helpful comments on the several versions of the manuscript. This chapter was prepared with support from grant MH-20021 from the National Institute of Mental Health.

REFERENCES

Akmajian, A. The role of focus in the interpretation of anaphoric expressions. In S. R. Anderson & P. Kiparsky (Eds.), *A Festshrift for Morris Halle.* New York: Holt, Rinehart, & Winston, 1973.

Bransford, J. D., & Johnson, M. K. Considerations of some problems of comprehension. In W. G. Chase (Ed.), *Visual information processing.* New York: Academic Press, 1973.

Bransford, J. D., & McCarrell, N. S. A sketch of a cognitive approach to comprehension. In D. Palermo & W. Weimer (Eds.), *Cognition and the symbolic processes.* Washington, D.C.: Winston, 1975.

Chafe, W. L. *Meaning and the structure of language.* Chicago, Illinois: University of Chicago Press, 1970.

Chafe, W. L. Language and memory. *Language,* 1973, **49,** 261–281.

Chafe, W. L. Language and consciousness. *Language,* 1974, **50,** 111–133.

Chomsky, N. Deep structure, surface structure, and semantic interpretation. In L. A. Jakobovits & D. Steinberg (Eds.), *Semantics: An interdisciplinary reading in philosophy, psychology, linguistics, and anthropology.* Cambridge, England: Cambridge University Press, 1971.

Clark, H. H. Linguistic processes in dedutive reasoning. *Psychological Review,* 1969, **76,** 387–404.

Clark, H. H., Difficulties people have in answering the question "Where is it?" *Journal of Verbal Learning and Verbal Behavior,* 1972, **11,** 265–277.

Clark, H. H. Semantics and comprehension. In T. A. Sebeok (Ed.), *Current Trends in Linguistics.* Vol. 12: *Linguistics and Adjacent Arts and Sciences.* The Hague: Mouton, 1974.

Clark, H. H., Carpenter, P. A., & Just, M. A. On the meeting of semantics and perception. In W. G. Chase (Ed.), *Visual information processing.* New York: Academic Press, 1973.

Clark, H. H. & Haviland, S. E. Psychological processes as linguistic explanation. In D. Cohen (Ed.), *Explaining linguistic phenomena.* Washington, D.C.: Winston, 1974.

Fillmore, C. J. Verbs of judging: An exercise in semantic description. In C. J. Fillmore & D. T. Langendoen (Eds.), *Studies in Linguistic Semantics.* New York: Holt, Rinehart, & Winston, 1971.

Gough, P. B. Grammatical transformations and speed of understanding. *Journal of Verbal Learning and Verbal Behavior,* 1965, **5,** 107–111.

Gough, P. B. The verification of sentences: the effects of delay of evidence and sentence length. *Journal of Verbal Learning and Verbal Behavior,* 1966, **5,** 492–496.

Grice, H. P. Meaning. *Philosophical Review,* 1957, **64,** 377–388.

Grice, H. P. Logic and conversation. William James Lectures, Harvard University, 1967, unpublished. Lecture 2 published in P. Cole & J. L. Morgan (Eds.), *Studies in syntax, Vol. III.* New York: Seminar Press, 1975.

Halliday, M. A. K. Notes on transitivity and theme in English: II. *Journal of Linguistics,* 1967, **3,** 199–244.

Haviland, S. E., & Clark, H. H. What's new? Acquiring new information as a process in comprehension. *Journal of Verbal Learning and Verbal Behavior,* 1974, **13.**

Hiž, H. Questions and answers. *Journal of Philosophy,* 1962, **59,** 253–265.

Horn, L. *On the semantic properties of logical operators in English.* Unpublished doctoral dissertation, UCLA, 1972.

Hornby, P. A. Surface structure and presupposition. *Journal of Verbal Learning and Verbal Behavior,* 1974, **13,** 530–538.

Jackendoff, R. S. *Semantic interpretation in generative grammar.* Cambridge, Massachusetts: MIT Press, 1972.

Lakoff, G. The role of deduction in grammar. In C. J. Fillmore & D. T. Langendoen (Eds.), *Studies in linguistic semantics.* New York: Holt, Rinehart, & Winston, 1971.

Lakoff, R. Questionable answers and answerable questions. In B. Kachru, R. B. Lees, Y. Malkiel, & S. Saporta (Eds.), *Papers in Linguistics in Honor of Henry and Renee Kahane.* Urbana, Illinois: University of Illinois Press, 1973.

Loftus, E. F., & Zanni, G. Eyewitness testimony: The influence of the wording of a question. *Bulletin of the Psychonomic Society,* 1975, **5**, 86–88.

Olson, D. R. Language use for communicating, instructing, and thinking. In R. O. Freedle & J. B. Carroll (Eds.), *Language comprehension and the acquisition of knowledge.* Washington, D.C.: Winston, 1972.

Searle, J. R. *Speech acts: An essay in the philosophy of language.* Cambridge, England: Cambridge University Press, 1970.

Slobin, D. I. Grammatical transformations and sentence comprehension in childhood and adulthood. *Journal of Verbal Learning and Verbal Behavior,* 1966, **5**, 219–227.

Smith, K. H., & McMahon, L. E. Understanding order information in sentences: Some recent work at Bell Laboratories. In G. Flores d'Arcais & W. J. M. Levelt (Eds.), *Advances in psycholinguistics.* Amsterdam: North-Holland, 1970.

Wright, P. Transformations and the understanding of sentences. *Language and Speech,* 1969, **12**, 156–166.

2

Creativity in Verbalization and Its Implications for the Nature of Stored Knowledge

Wallace L. Chafe

University of California, Berkeley

Imagine a person who has been involved in, or perhaps has simply witnessed an incident of some kind. Knowledge of the incident has been stored in his long-term memory, and on some later occasion, during a conversation, he recalls it and judges it to be of sufficient interest to talk about. What kinds of processes must this person apply to convert his knowledge, predominantly nonverbal to begin with, into a verbal output? Do these processes give us any insight into the nature of the stored knowledge itself? In what follows I will discuss some partial and tentative answers to these two questions.

The term *verbalization* will be used to cover all those processes by which nonverbal knowledge is turned into language. I want to focus on the respects in which verbalization is creative, in the sense that it requires a speaker to make choices between a multiplicity of available options. The assumption here is that the final verbal output is far from being uniquely determined by the initial nonverbal input from memory. That this is true seems clear enough from the easily observable fact that people rarely use the same words on different occasions to talk about what they nevertheless regard as "the same thing." There is a discontinuity between what one "has in mind" to talk about and what one actually says.

There are two important reasons for this discontinuity. One is that experience is particular, being tied to particular events which involve particular individuals at particular places and particular times. Since it would be impossible for language to communicate every unique event and individual in a unique way, language requires that particulars be interpreted as instances of types. The creative choices a speaker must make in the course of verbalization involve precisely this kind of interpretation. They are decisions as to how to assign particulars to types in such a way that the verbal output will serve its purpose with reasonable effectiveness. In the model and terminology I will be using here these types are of three kinds: *schemata, frames,* and *categories.* I will discuss each in turn, and give examples of variation in the actual choices that have been made, sometimes by different people talking about the same event and sometimes by the same person talking at different times.

A second reason for the discontinuity between what one has to talk about and how one talks about it appears to be the following. Language requires a speaker to "propositionalize" knowledge which is stored not only in nonverbal, but even in nonpropositional form. It seems that the choosing of schemata, frames, and categories requires that one match the internal representations of particular events and individuals with internally represented prototypes. This matching evidently does not take place on an all-or-nothing, yes-or-no basis. The match between a particular and a prototype is rather a matter of degree. Since the matching frequently takes place during verbalization and not before, it cannot be relegated wholly to the stage of perception or storage. We must, in other words, allow for a kind of memory in which both particulars and types retain some analogic content. Thus the existence of creativity in verbalization provides important evidence "that the representation has an internal structure that is itself to some extent analogically related to the structure of its corresponding external object," and another important argument against "the advisability of formulating theories of human behavior solely in terms of discrete processes of verbal mediation or symbol manipulation — as has been characteristic in experimental psychology and in computer simulation, respectively" (Cooper & Shepard, 1973, p. 172).

SCHEMATIZATION

Experience is evidently recalled in "chunks" with varying degrees of content, interrelated in various ways. These chunks appear to be the basic units of memory for particular incidents and events. A person who remembers an incident has it before him in some sense in its totality before he begins to verbalize it, and he may choose to give a summary verbalization to it as a whole:

(1)   Let me tell you about my accident last week.
(2)   Let me tell you about my visit to Washington.
(3)   Let me tell you about what happened on the way to the office this morning.

Even at this stage the speaker has chosen to interpret the incident as an instance of some category: an accident, a visit, something that happened to someone. We will return to the process of categorization below, but for the moment we are interested in the fact that if the speaker is going to say more (as he has invited himself to do), he must get inside this initial chunk and somehow organize the memory of it into smaller chunks.

In doing so he is evidently constrained by the existence in his mind of already established patterns which, following Bartlett (1932), I will call *schemata.* (In works like Minsky, 1974, or Goffman, 1974, the term *frame* is used in a broader way than I use it here, and covers these schemata too. Compare also the *scripts* of Schank & Abelson, 1975.) A schema will be understood as a pattern by which a larger chunk is broken down into smaller chunks. Schemata are available at various levels, in the sense that a chunk within a higher-level schema may itself be broken down into still smaller chunks at a lower level. The following example will show what I have in mind.

I recently asked a group of students to collect personal narratives dealing with some hassle that the narrator had experienced with a bureaucracy. A typical schema to which many of these narratives conformed may be labeled the *runaround.* In a runaround the initial chunk is broken down into (1) a *purpose,* (2) a series of three or more *deflections,* and (3) a *resolution* (often at odds with the purpose). The protagonist begins with a purpose such as registering or transferring credits at the university, exchanging the merchandise at a store, or the like. In trying to accomplish this purpose he passes through a series of deflective episodes in which each attempt is frustrated as a functionary advises him to go elsewhere or come back another time. Finally, in the resolution, either his original purpose is accomplished or the entire exercise ends in frustration.

In the further course of verbalization each of these chunks is itself broken down. The nature of this further schematization can be best illustrated with the schema used in breaking down a deflection. In its most extended form this schema may consist of (1) the protagonist's *arrival* at an office or other place relevant to his purpose, (2) a *wait,* (3) a *request* made of the functionary at this place, (4) a *response* by the functionary whereby the protagonist is told to go elsewhere or come back another time, and sometimes (5) a *remonstration,* followed by (6) a *reiterated response.*

Specific examples of the highest level runaround schema are too lengthy to include here, but a few examples of this deflection schema can be given:

(1) [arrival] The whole line ran to the desk at the other end of the store, and I was at the end once again. [wait] After another ten or fifteen minutes I finally got to the salesman. [response] "Oh no, you didn't get this in my department, you have to go over to the casual section." [remonstration] I told him that Rich had said this is where he bought it, [reiterated response] but he still shook his head and pointed across the corridor.

(2) [arrival] I returned at 9:30. [request] Asking the receptionist if I could turn in my paper to her, [response] I was told that I would

have to speak to the Undergraduate Secretary, who wouldn't be in until after ten.

(3) [arrival] So then I went down to the Institute of Human Development, and I went to the receptionist there. [response] And she was nice, but she didn't real ... she wasn't sure where to direct me, so she sent me off to this other secretary.

It can be seen from these examples that not all the chunks of the deflection schema need be verbally expressed each time the schema is used. The wait, remonstration, and reiterated response are present only in (1), and the request is present only in (2). It is only the arrival and the primary response that are present in all three. An analysis of 70 deflection episodes shows the incidence of mention of these elements to be as follows:

arrival	62
wait	21
request	26
response	70
remonstration	9
reiterated response	9

On this basis it appears that the several chunks defined by a schema differ markedly in status. Some, like the arrival and response, are always or nearly always mentioned when the schema is used. Others, like the wait and request, are sometimes mentioned although in these data they were present less than half the time. The remonstration and reiterated response form a kind of coda to the main schema, each being dependent on the other; but the coda as a whole is present in only a small minority of cases.

In verbalizing his experience according to the deflection schema, then, the speaker evidently must choose which elements of that schema to include and which to leave out. Of course, some elements may be left out simply because they did not happen. Probably the remonstration and reiterated response just did not take place very often within the incidents reported on in these data, and their frequency of actual occurrence. On the other hand, the request must have occurred much more often than is indicated by its frequency of mention. The protagonist is unlikely to have approached the functionary without saying why he was there; the functionary's response must have been a response to a request. But of these two interdependent elements only the response was consistently verbalized.

Perhaps we can attribute this difference to a difference in the salience of these two elements. Although salience is a notion badly in need of study, one might guess that events are salient to the extent that they depart from the bland, routine experience which makes up the greater part of people's lives. The things worth talking about are those which represent significant deviations from this baseline. The response of the functionary is, to the protagonist at least, a greater deviation than the protagonist at least, a greater deviation than the protagonist's own request, which is only a part of his own routine. What is important to us here, in any case, is the fact that verbalizations do show differences in the frequency with which various elements of a schema are mentioned, and that a speaker has to choose which to mention according to some (presumably) continuous scale of salience. Whatever the determinants of salience may be, it does seem that events must be stored in memory with varying degrees of salience attached to them.

Besides choosing which elements of a schema to verbalize, a speaker may actually need to choose the schema itself. It may be true that much of schematization takes place as experience is being acquired. An episode in an administrative office may immediately be perceived by the protagonist as an instance of a deflection. When he later verbalizes his memory of the episode he has no need, then, to decide how to interpret it; he already knows. But this may not always be the case. The following is an example of the use of two different schemata by the same person verbalizing "the same thing" on two different occasions.

During a popular lecture on the history of astronomy, the speaker talked for a while about the Copernican revolution. This portion of his talk was relatively self-contained. It was one major chunk within the larger schema of his entire talk, but we are interested here in the schemata by which he reduced this one chunk to smaller parts. On two different occasions, approximately a month apart, he seems to have employed different schemata for this purpose. In the first talk the speaker began by describing briefly the Copernican model. He then pointed out that it had similarities to the Ptolemaic model. This was what we might call the descriptive phase of his schema, which was then followed by a parallel evaluative phase. He mentioned first the advantages of the Copernican, and then again backtracked to tell about the deficiencies of the Ptolemaic. Finally he jumped ahead to talk about the resistance which followed dissemination of the Copernican idea. The temporal relations of the chunks within this schema are shown in Fig. 1, where C stands for the Copernican model and P for the Ptolemaic.

The second talk made use of a different schema. There were two parallel sections, each following a strict chronology. The first gave a history of the two

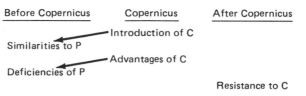

FIGURE 1   Schema followed in first version.

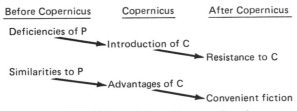

FIGURE 2   Schema followed by second version.

models and their reception. The second focused on the properties of these models. The presentation of the history proceeded from the deficiencies of the Ptolemaic model through the introduction of the Copernican to the resistance to the latter. The presentation of properties retraced this chronology, beginning with similarities to the earlier model, proceeding with the advantages of the Copernican model, and ending with the resulting view that the new model was a convenient fiction. This last chunk, the convenient fiction idea, did not appear in the first talk, perhaps because the schema employed there did not provide a ready slot for it. This second schema is shown in Fig. 2.

The speaker must have had in his long-term memory the overall chunk concerning Copernicus, stored in some way in association with the history of astronomy as a whole. He must also have had in memory the five or six smaller chunks which provided the elements for the two different schemata he chose at different times. Not stored, however, was the specific schema he would use, and in fact he had to choose this schema as he verbalized.

FRAMING

At some point in the course of verbalization the speaker must arrive at chunks that are small enough to be expressed in sentences. That might in fact be regarded as the aim of the schematizing process. The initial, grand chunk was too rich in content to be sententially expressed except by means of a summary. The speaker, therefore, had to break it down through a succession of schemata until he arrived at chunks amenable to verbalization in sentences which would communicate what he judged to be the right amount of detail. This stopping point in schematization is constrained by the existence of what I will call *frames,* in the sense of the so-called case frames described in Fillmore (1968) and elsewhere.

A schema provides a breakdown of a chunk into smaller chunks, but both the larger chunk and the smaller chunk are elements of the same kind. Viewed in terms of space and time, chunks combine a spatial and a temporal particularity. They are holistic ideas of happenings at particular times and places. A frame provides a different kind of breakdown of a chunk. It factors out from the event one or more *individuals,* characterized by particularity in space but not in time. Thus the idea of a particular person or object may take part in a variety of events at different times. It is not tied to a single particular coherent segment of time in the same way as an event. In choosing an appropriate frame, the speaker chooses an appropriate selection of individuals whose involvement in the event he decides to express, and at the same time he assigns appropriate roles to these individuals within the event. Generally, for any one chunk, a variety of options is available to him.

For example, I once showed a group of 80 people a brief film in which there was a transfer of a banana from an older boy to a younger one. In later verbalizing their memory of the event, 76 people used a sentence which contained, in addition to the verb, an agent, a beneficiary, and a patient. That is, they said things like:

The older boy handed/gave/passed the younger boy a banana.

In all of these sentences the same frame was chosen. Three individuals were factored out from the event, later to be verbalized as "the older boy," "the younger boy," and "a banana," or in similar ways, and they were assigned the roles of agent, beneficiary, and patient respectively. But one person said:

Two boys passed a banana.

In so doing he ignored the directionality of the transfer, and treated the event in terms of two agents whose roles were not distinguished. There was no expressed beneficiary. Three other people, furthermore, ignored these individuals altogether and spoke only of the "transference of a banana." Just as we noticed in the case of schematization that some elements of a schema are more salient than others, and therefore more consistently expressed in verbalizations, so too are different elements of a frame. Evidently in this frame the patient or thing transferred is the most essential element.

Here too we may find that the same person makes different choices on different occasions, choosing to frame an event one way at one time, another way at another. The following two verbalizations were produced by the same speaker with respect to one film scene, with an interval of eight weeks between the first and the second:

(1) He picked up some hay and lifted it over the corral fence and into the corral. All of the animals eagerly went after and began eating the hay.
(2) He threw some hay over the top rail of the corral fence to the animals inside.

In (1) the total event was broken down first into two subevents, one involving the transfer of the hay from outside the corral to inside and the other involving the resulting actions on the part of the animals. The first of these was further broken down into three subevents: "picking up," "lifting over," and "lifting into." The second was also broken down further: into "going after" and "beginning eating." Thus, in the first verbalization the initial chunk was analyzed into a total of five smaller chunks before the framing of each of the latter was accomplished. In Sentence (2), in contrast, the speaker immediately chose a "throwing" frame for the whole event, a frame which included an agent ("he"), a patient ("some hay"), a trajectory ("over the top rail of the corral fence"), and a goal ("the animals inside"). Of particular interest are the different roles of the animals in the two verbalizations. In (1) the animals were given an active role, going after the hay and eating it. In (2) they were the passive recipients of the action. As in the case of the two Copernican schemata described above, most of the same elements are present in both versions, but their assignment — this time within frames rather than schemata — is quite different.

CATEGORIZATION

Suppose, now, that the speaker has through schematization arrived at chunks that can be converted into sentences, and that he has taken the first step in the production of a sentence by choosing a frame upon which the sentence can be hung. He must still choose words or phrases that will get across the ideas of particular events and individuals that he has in mind. In the banana transfer example discussed above, 43 people decided to use the verb "hand," 39 chose "give," 10 decided on "pass to," and 3 used "hand over to." One can have in mind a frame, and the ideas of events and objects included in that frame, without having decided on categorizations that will permit effective communication of those ideas. Such categorization is the third kind of choice that is made during verbalization.

Some ideas of particular events and individuals are easier to categorize than others. If we have in mind some object, for example, it may be easy or it may be hard to find a linguistic expression for what we are thinking of. The term that has been used for this variable property of ideas is *codability:* some ideas are highly codable and some are not. Those which are fit smoothly and neatly into the categorial grid on which our language is based. Those which are not cause us a certain amount of difficulty when it comes to verbalizing them.

The richest body of data we have on codability comes from studies of colors and how they are named. In Brown and Lenneberg (1954) it was shown that certain particular colors — those we would call highly codable — tend to be named (1) with short words, (2) with single words rather than groups of words, (3) more quickly, (4) with more agreement between different subjects, and (5) with greater consistency by the same subject. Other particular colors — those we would call less codable — are named either with longer words or with phrases rather than single words, take longer to name, and show less agreement between subjects and less consistency for the same subject.

I have tabulated several of these same measures with respect to various real objects people have seen and later talked or written about. These objects were included within movie scenes or real events where they played some role in some action that was taking place. In verbalizing their knowledge of the action, people found it necessary to express their ideas of these objects in some way. Sometimes they did it easily, sometimes with difficulty. We might consider, for example, the object which was given by the older boy to the younger boy in the transfer example. The amount of agreement found among the eighty subjects with respect to its categorization was as follows:

banana	72
object	5
thing	1
something	1
toy auto	1

Most people, that is, called it a "banana." Five called it an "object," and one person each called it a "thing," "something," or a "toy auto." Probably even these few deviations resulted from failure to recognize the object by people sitting far from the screen, rather than from any real problem in codability. In contrast, the amount of agreement among 73 categorizations of the memory of an object on which children had been seen playing in a playground was as follows:

jungle gym	14	mass	2
object	10	free-form	2
structure	8	slide	2
thing	6	something	1
form	5	shape	1
sculpture	4	mobile	1
toy	4	design	1
apparatus	3	configuration	1
monkey bars	3	device	1
equipment	3	gymnasium	1

No very large proportion of people used any one of these categories. On the basis of agreement among subjects we can say that the idea of the first object was a good deal more codable than the idea of the second. One finds a correlated difference in the consistency with which the same idea is categorized in the same way by the same person at different times. For highly codable items consistency is close to 100%. For items of low codability it is closer to 50%.

Such facts are explainable if we hypothesize that every discrete event and individual in memory has associated with it an "experiential content": the totality of experience which has accumulated in memory with relation to the event or individual. This experiential content must in part at least be stored in analogic form, and not be reducible to any single propositional structure. When a speaker needs to categorize the idea he has of an event or individual, he tries to match the experiential content of that idea with the prototype contents of available categories. The matching process must taken place at least in part in analogic terms, since the match is likely to be a matter of degree and there may, in fact, be no category whose prototype is matched very closely. This matching process cannot simply be a matter of checking one set of propositions against another on a yes-or-no basis.

To say that the idea of some particular object is highly codable is to say that its experiential content matches that of the prototype or focus of some category quite closely (cf. Rosch, 1973). In our first example the idea of the transferred object had an experiential content that matched closely the focus of the category which allowed it to be adequately communicated with the word "banana." The person addressed could then be expected to activate in his own mind an experiential content closely matching the focus of his own experiential content for that category. In the second example, on the other hand, the particular idea being categorized had an experiential content which did not lie close to the focus of any category. Although there was some degree of matching with various categories, including that which enabled the speaker to use the expression, "jungle gym," the match was not especially good with this category or with any other. From the point of view of communicative effectiveness the use of "jungle gym" was not so satisfactory. It would lead the hearer to think that something close to the focus of the jungle gym category was being talked about, whereas that was not the case.

Speakers have a way of coping with low codability; that is what modifiers are for. In a low codability situation the speaker may decide to use an adjective or relative clause to shift the experiential content of a category in a direction that will provide a more adequate match for what he has in mind. For example, the speaker who added the modifier "free-form" to "jungle gym" created thereby an intersection of the content of this property with the content of the jungle gym category. Within this intersection the content of his memory of the object in question fit more comfortably. The prototype jungle gym is presumably imagined as full of bars at right angles. The remembered content in this case was not like that, but contained irregular curved surfaces. By saying "free-form jungle gym" the speaker was able to get across something closer to what he was thinking of. The use of modifiers is what is responsible for another of Brown and Lenneberg's measures of codability: the number of words used. The more modifiers, of course, the greater the number of words. In the two examples before us the average number of modifiers used to verbalize the idea of the banana was .16. For the playground object it was 2.12. This is a large difference, and reflects extremes of high and low codability. Many ideas of particular objects fall somewhere within this range.

It is important to recognize that categorization requires us to recognize not only a continuous scale of codability, but also a form of mental storage in which the uniqueness of particular objects is retained. The perception of an object or event does involve individuation: the registering of a mental unit which is the idea of that object or event. It does not, however, necessarily involve categorization of that idea (contrary to what seems to be implied in Pylyshyn, 1973, for example). Instead, we evidently retain enough knowledge about the peculiarities of a particular object to cause us potential trouble when we try to express that knowledge. People must be so constructed that the unique qualities of particulars are entered and retained to some degree in the mind. Otherwise codability would never be a problem.

HESITATIONS

I have suggested that verbalization requires three major kinds of choices, each involving the interpretation of some piece of particular knowledge in terms of some established type. One kind of evidence that such choices are really being made is provided by the hesitations in speech which are apt to occur whenever a choice presents even a momentary problem. Normal speech is full of hesitations, which for the most part seem attributable to the need to take time to make decisions of the kinds discussed (compare the discussions of Goldman-Eisler, 1968; Maclay & Osgood, 1959; and numerous articles by the latter). As a brief example, representative of many which appear in the verbalization data on which this chapter is based, the second of the lectures on the history of astronomy mentioned earlier included a discussion of the deficiencies of the Ptolemaic model which began as follows:

And . . . well . . . the motivation that Copernicus had was that by this time . . . the Greek model of the universe was . . . uh . . . not working so well.

The initial hesitation, during which there were both pauses and the words "and" and "well," seems to have filled a period of time during which the speaker was making a decision as to *schematization.* It was really at this point that he committed himself to following the second of the two broad schemata outlined above. The pause before "the Greek model of the universe was" allowed the speaker time to choose a *frame* for this clause. Such hesitations typically occur before any part of a clause has been uttered. If, on the other hand, the speaker had been deciding how to categorize the subject of this clause, he would typically have uttered the article "the" first, and then hesitated: "the . . . Greek model of the universe." Finally, the pause before "not working so well" evidently allowed him to decide on a *categorization* for this state in which the Greek model of the universe found itself. Just as categorizing a nominal referent typically leads to a hesitation after the initial articles of the noun phrase, so categorizing an event or state is likely to lead to a hesitation after the first element of a complex verb: here after the word "was." Hesitations, in short, can provide useful clues to the points in a verbalization at which a speaker is engaged in schematizing, framing, or categorizing.

IMPLICATIONS

Figure 3 illustrates the kind of representation of human knowledge that has often been suggested by recent investigators. This particular example is based on one given in Rumelhart, Lindsay, and Norman (1972, p. 206), but I have revised their example somewhat. I believe this diagram is not a straw man, for even though other workers in this area might prefer a representation that differs from this one in some respects, the basic nature of all such representations is the same: they are built up of discrete entities related to each other in a small finite number of discrete ways. This diagram is meant to represent the knowledge which underlies the sentence, "The boy hit the ball with a small bat." The intention is that such a diagram should "describe explicitly how information is represented in the memory" (Rumelhart, Lindsay, & Norman, 1972, p. 201). I want to claim, on the contrary, that no diagram of this kind can possibly represent the basic way in which knowledge is stored, if what I tried to illustrate in the earlier part of this chapter has any validity.

Presumably we are concerned here with the memory of an event. In the diagram this event is labeled E_1. So far so good. We do seem to individuate events in perception and memory, and insofar as this event can be treated as a unit we can represent it with some arbitrarily labeled node. There is no reason to doubt that E_1 has some mental reality. Most likely, however, this event would be remembered as part of some larger incident, or complex of events. To save space I have not tried to show how its integration with other events might be represented in a diagram of this kind, but it is clear that this would be done with labeled arrows showing interevent relations such as "cause," "then," "while," or the like. Rumelhart, Lindsay, and Norman provide an example (209). No such

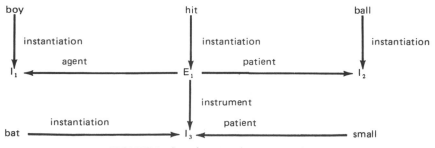

FIGURE 3 Sample network representation.

representations, however, allow for the kind of fact I tried to illustrate with the Copernicus example: that a speaker may choose to schematize the same larger chunk in different ways on different occasions. If knowledge is not necessarily already schematized in memory, if different ways of schematizing it may be chosen at different times, then any representation which suggests an immutable pattern connecting one event with another imposes a structure on memory that is not necessarily there. Furthermore — and this is best illustrated by the examples of hassles with a bureaucracy — different elements in a schema have different degrees of salience. At the very least, then, nodes like E_1 require some kind of indexing to show their relative salience within the larger context. But in the end salience is likely to be a continuous property, so that if these representations were to be wholly faithful to what is in memory it would be necessary to print all the Es in continuously varying sizes, or something of the sort.

But let us turn now to factors which can be seen more directly in Fig. 3. The arrows leading out from E_1 which are labeled agent, patient, and instrument show a case frame for this event. Three individuals are conceived of as participating in the event in these three roles. But again, framing is something that may be decided on in the course of verbalization, and something that may be handled differently in different verbalizations of the same event. Just as one possible variation on the present example, the speark might have verbalized this same E_1 by saying, "The small bat was big enough to get the boy to first base," where the roles of I_1 and I_3 are quite different and I_2 is only implicit.

The point here is like that made with respect to schematization: people often choose how to frame an event in the course of verbalization. A particular frame is not necessarily included as part of their knowledge of the event. And here too the participation of some individuals in an event is more salient than the participation of others, as we saw with the banana in the transfer event. Thus, there may be a continuous range of appropriateness of particular frames to particular events — or of particular elements within a frame.

The remaining arrows in Fig. 3 are all related to categorization. All but one are labeled *instantiation,* which means that E_1 has been interpreted as an instance of the category *hit,* I_1 of the category *boy,* I_2 of the category *ball,* and I_3 of the category *bat.* The point I have been making is perhaps most clearly argued with respect to these cases of categorization. There can be no doubt that some individuals are categorized only during verbalization. For less-codable individuals, categorization is not consistent and typically leads to hesitation. Furthermore, in cases where codability is less than maximum the speaker may resort to modification, as was apparently necessary in this example where "small" was used to modify "bat." The handling of low codability items during verbalization shows clearly that they are not, or need not be, stored in already categorized form. The arrows labeled *instantiation* do not, certainly, in all cases represent how the ideas of events and individuals are stored in memory, but only how the speaker chose to interpret them in the course of a particular verbalization.

What is evidently the case, then, is that all the arrows in Fig. 3, as well as the additional arrows that we can imagine as connecting this event with other events within some larger schema represent, in principle, how knowledge is verbalized but not necessarily how it is remembered. Admittedly some, and perhaps a great many cases of schematization, framing, and categorization are so clearcut, salient, or obvious that they may be part of perception and memory. In such cases the speaker does not need to make choices while verbalizing. But much of what we experience is not this way. Disagreements among speakers, fluctuations by the same speaker, hesitations, and other symptoms show that the kinds of things indicated by the arrows in Fig. 3 are not the basic ingredients of a memory representation.

It is tempting to conclude that the only aspects of Fig. 3 which are necessarily part of memory are the nodes. These nodes fall into two broad classes. Those labeled E_1, I_1, I_2, and I_3 represent particular events and individuals. Those labeled *boy, hit, ball, bat,* and *small* represent categories and properties. Evidently both kinds of units are stored in the mind. In speaking it is necessary to match our memories of particular events and individuals with our stored prototypes of categories and properties in order to find paragraphs, sentences, phrases, and words appropriate to express these particulars. This matching is not done in terms of nodes and arrows as such, but in terms of the experiential content associated with the nodes and arrows. The variability of schematization, framing, and categorization seems to prove that this experiential content exists and that it has analogic properties, for otherwise it seems impossible to explain how the matching of particulars with types takes place.

A bold conclusion to which all of this may lead, and which I think ought not to be rejected out of hand, is that knowledge is not stored propositionally at all, except to the extent that certain schematizations, framings, and categorizations are so salient that they are accomplished during perception or storage rather than during verbalization. In a sense such cases may be a kind of jumping the gun. With some events we already know how to verbalize them the instance we experience them. But the basic form of storage is not to be judged from these cases, and may be of quite a different kind. It may consist of individuated events and objects, each with an associated analogic content, but without established connections in a propositional network — without them, at least, until a need to verbalize them makes propositional decisions necessary.

REFERENCES

Bartlett, F. C. *Remembering. A study in experimental and social psychology.* Cambridge, England: Cambridge University Press, 1932.

Brown, R. W., & Lenneberg, E. H. A study in language and cognition. *Journal of Abnormal and Social Psychology,* 1954, 49, 454–462.

Cooper, L. A., & Shepard, R. N. Chronometric studies of the rotation of mental images. In W. G. Chase (Ed.), *Visual information processing.* New York: Academic Press, 1973.

Fillmore, C. J. The case for case. In E. Bach and R. T. Harms (Eds.), *Universals in linguistic theory.* New York: Holt, Rinehart, and Winston, 1968.

Goffman, E. *Frame analysis. An essay on the organization of experience.* Cambridge, Massachusetts: Harvard University Press, 1974.

Goldman-Eisler, F. G. *Psycholinguistics. Experiments in spontaneous speech.* New York: Academic Press, 1968.

Maclay, H., & Osgood, C. E. Hesitation phemomena in spontaneous English speech. *Word,* 1959, **15,** 19–44.

Minsky, M. *A framework for representing knowledge.* Massachusetts Institute of Technology, Artificial Intelligence Memo No. 306, 1974.

Pylyshyn, Z. W. What the mind's eye tells the mind's brain: a critique of mental imagery. *Psychological Bulletin,* 1973, **80,** 1–24.

Rosch, E. H. On the internal structure of perceptual and semantic categories. In T. E. Moore (Ed.), *Cognitive development and the acquisition of language.* New York: Academic Press, 1973.

Rumelhart, D. E., Lindsay, P. H., & Norman, D. A. A process model for long-term memory. In E. Tulving & W. Donaldson (Eds.), *Organization of memory.* New York: Academic Press, 1972.

Schank, R. C., & Abelson, R. P. Scripts, plans, and knowledge. Paper prepared for presentation at the 4th International Joint Conference on Artificial Intelligence, 1975.

3
Semantic Processing Units in Understanding Text

Carl H. Frederiksen

National Institute of Education
and
The Rockefeller University

Most of the knowledge which humans acquire in a lifetime derives not from unorganized or unstructured stimulus arrays, but from organized informational inputs that possess a high degree of structure. Much of this knowledge is acquired from linguistic messages, or texts, composed of many related sentences. It is apparent that in most situations in which persons are exposed to text, the knowledge which they acquire is itself highly structured, consisting of complex networks of concepts and semantic relations that connect concepts into highly organized propositional structures. A central problem in cognitive theory is to determine the nature and structure of human knowledge including that acquired from linguistic messages.

One strategy for investigating the nature of semantic knowledge is to investigate the semantic structure of texts under the assumption that a text's structure is a reflection of the knowledge structure of the speaker or writer who produced the text. The argument is that if a semantic distinction or structure is manifest in language, it must also represent an aspect of human memory structure. This argument and approach were advanced by Frederiksen (1975a) and underlie other current models of memory structure (e.g., Crothers, 1975; Kintsch, 1975; Norman & Rumelhart, 1975).

One experimental strategy for exploring the nature of semantic knowledge acquired from text is to present subjects with a text which has a known semantic structure and then ask them to recall the content of what they have heard or read. In such situations, subjects typically recall only a part of the semantic content of the text (Crothers, 1972; Frederiksen, 1975b,c; Meyer, 1974). The particular information subjects do recall, however, is not a random selection of individual items of semantic information. Rather, it consists of an organization of highly structured subsets of items of information from the text. Put another way, items of semantic information are not recalled *independently* of one another; they are recalled in clusters of items that are mutually dependent, clusters that correspond to units of semantic information such as concepts, states, events, or other higher-order units. Apparently, understanding a text involves analyzing it into highly structured semantic units that are acquired, stored, retrieved, and in other ways processed as units. These semantic processing units occur at different levels, from units as small as elementary concepts, states, or events, to units that incorporate substantial portions of a text's content. The identification of such processing units is a central question both in the study of processes involved in language production and comprehension, and in the study of the form in which knowledge is represented in semantic memory.

In this chapter I will examine the question of units of information with reference to discourse structure, discourse production, comprehension and information retrieval from semantic memory. First, I will examine the notion of units of information in grammar as developed by Halliday (1961, 1967, 1968) and summarized by Winograd (1972) and Gregory (1972). Then I will apply the notion of units to semantic propositional structures such as those proposed by Leech (1969) and Grimes (1975) as components of linguistic theories; by Simmons (1973), Schank (1973), and Winograd (1972) as computer data structures in language understanding programs; and by Norman and Rumelhart (1975), Kintsch (1975), Crothers (1975), and Frederiksen (1975a) as models of memorial knowledge structures.

I will then consider implications of units of semantic information for our conception of memory structure and discourse processing. Experimental results bearing on these issues will be presented which provide evidence that a discourse is processed as a multilevel structure containing units as "small" as individual concepts and relations connecting concepts, and as "large" as macrostructures consisting of networks of connected propositions. The results also will be seen to shed light on the means by which information occurring early in a text can influence the processing of related information occurring later on in the text.

UNITS IN TEXTUAL AND SEMANTIC STRUCTURES

The notion of *unit* as a general category in the theory of grammar was first introduced by Halliday (1961).[1] A unit is a category set up to account for segments of spoken or written text that consist of recurrently meaningful patterns and/or operate as components of meaningful patterns. Examples of units in English grammar are morpheme, word, word group, clause, and sentence. Morphemes are segments of text (spoken or written) that convey information (i.e., carry meaning) and operate as components of words; words are

---

[1] A category is general if it applies to the description of any language.

informational units that are components of groups, etc. Unit is a general concept that may be manifest differently in different languages.

Attached to units in the theory of grammar is a scale of *rank* or hierarchy. That is, each unit always consists of one or more than one of the units immediately below it in the hierarchy. The rank scale ranges from the largest or more inclusive unit (e.g., the sentence) to the smallest noninclusive unit (e.g., the morpheme). While it is possible to establish a rank scale for any language, a unit occurring higher on the rank scale frequently may be shifted down the scale to operate as a constituent of a unit of equal or lower rank. For example, in English, a relative clause may operate as an element of a noun group. This process is called *rank-shift.*

The definition of the category *unit* makes reference to "recurrently meaningful patterns." A second category, *structure,* is concerned with the nature of the meaningful patterns that comprise a unit. A unit is not a primitive concept; it is defined relative to a theory of the structure of meaningful patterns, i.e., a grammar. In Halliday's conception, a structure describes how a meaningful unit is composed of units below it in rank (and possibly of rank-shifted units of equal or higher rank). The third category, *class,* refers to "a set of items of the same unit (i.e., at the same rank) that show similar possibilities of operation in the structure of the unit immediately above in the rank scale" (Gregory, 1972, Chap. 2, p. 7). For example, different classes of words (e.g., noun, verb) can be defined which operate similarly in the structure of word groups.

The final category, *system,* refers to the limited set of choices available in determining the structure of a unit. Winograd (1972) has presented systems in the form of hierarchical decision trees to account for the structure of classes of groups, clauses, and sentences in English. A sentence thus may be represented as a series of *decisions* governing the structure of the units at different rank levels that comprise the sentence.

While the categories unit, structure, class, and system were intended to apply to the description of natural languages, these categories also may be extended to propositional languages such as those proposed to model semantic memory structure (cf. Leech, 1969). The extension of the categories unit, rank, class, and structure to propositional languages requires that the definitions of these categories be modified to reflect a fundamental difference in the nature of text and propositional structures as abstract *data structures* (cf. Berztiss, 1971).

The simplest type of data structure is a *set,* an unorganized collection of items. The next most complex type of data structure is a *string,* an ordered sequence of items. At one level, a text is a string consisting of an ordered set of lexical concepts and grammatical morphemes. A still more complex type of data structure is a *parenthesized string,* a string in which items may be grouped into substrings that may occur as items in a string. The grammatical structure of a natural language text may be regarded as a parenthesized string. The definition of a unit as a segment of text that consists of a recurrently meaningful pattern refers to a unit as a string consisting of a patterned sequence of substrings or items (in which an item is a unit at the lowest level on the rank scale).

The most complex type of data structure is a *labeled network*. A labeled network consists of a set of labeled nodes that is connected into a graph structure by means of labeled arcs or relations. A string is a special case of a labeled network in which a set of nodes is connected into a linear sequence. A semantic network is a labeled network which consists of a set of concepts, the nodes in the network, and a set of semantic relations that connect pairs of nodes. Semantic networks have been proposed by psychologists as models of the form of representation of information in human memory (e.g., Crothers, 1975; Frederiksen, 1975a; Norman & Rumelhart, 1975; Quillian, 1968), and by computer scientists as computer data structures in language understanding programs (e.g., Schank, 1973; Simmons, 1973; Winograd, 1972).

The category *unit* may be defined for semantic networks as a category of subgraphs of a network that consists of recurrent network structures and/or that operates as a component of a network structure. Just as in the case of text, semantic units have associated with them a rank scale such that each unit always consists of one or more than one unit immediately below it on the rank scale. Furthermore, units may be rank-shifted to occur as constituents of units of equal or lower rank. The categories of structure, class, and system also may be extended naturally to semantic network structures.

To illustrate the application of the concepts unit, rank, class, and structure to semantic networks, I will restrict attention to the network structures proposed by Frederiksen (1975a) as a representation of logical and semantic knowledge acquired from text. I will focus on this model because at present it is the most detailed statement of a semantic data structure for English text and because it was employed in the experiment which I will report in the second half of the chapter. The network structures proposed by Frederiksen (1975a) are similar in many respects to those proposed by other investigators, but are both more general and more detailed than other semantic network structures.

The logical and semantic structures have a number of aspects which distinguish the present network model from other semantic network models. First, the system is well defined in the sense that every relation specified in the system is explicitly defined without reference to linguistic productions. Definitions consist of restrictions on the two slots connected by a relation and a definition of the relation connecting the two slots. Second, the model consists of two network structures: (1) a semantic structure or semantic network consisting of a collection of labeled binary relations which represent events or states and which connect slots containing (in most cases) concepts; and (2) a logical structure or logical network consisting of a collection of labeled binary logical, causal or algebraic relations connecting propositions which are represented as substructures in the semantic network. Third, the model considers in detail the algebraic (and metric) properties of "noncase" (i.e., classificatory, attributive, degree, temporal, locative, and quantifier) relations and defines certain relations having specified algebraic properties (re., transitivity, symmetry, and reflexivity) which may be used to connect propositions containing these noncase relations. What results is a mechanism for representing comparative relations, and relations of relative time and location, tense and aspect. Fourth, the present system contains a stochastic (or probabilistic) element, representing the fact that speakers (or writers) are often uncertain, and hence imprecise, in expressing semantic information involving metric values. They are also often imprecise in specifying case and other nonmetric information. Such uncertainty is often expressed by qualifying propositions with "hedges" such as *may* and *might*. Uncertainty of this latter sort is treated by means of qualifying operators on the truth value of a proposition. Finally, the system distinguishes between "symbolic" and "nonsymbolic" objects and "cognitive" and "noncognitive" actions, both of which involve symbolic content; and develops relations which specify the content of symbolic objects or cognitive (symbolic) actions. (pp. 376–377)

Table 1 identifies six *units* that occur in the semantic and logical networks: concepts, relational triples, event frames, propositions, relative systems, and dependency systems. These semantic units form a *rank scale* in which the concept is the smallest and noninclusive unit and the dependency system is the largest and most inclusive unit. As will be illustrated presently, semantic units may be *rank-shifted* by inserting a unit into a slot in a network structure of equal or lower rank. In addition to identifying units and ranks associated with units, Table 1 lists the *classes* of units that the model specifies at each level of rank. For example, different classes of concepts are defined (viz., objects, actions, attributes of objects, attributes of actions, numbers, degrees, locations, and times) that operate similarly in the structure of relational triples. That is, restrictions on the concept slots in the definitions of relational triples involve these classes of concepts. The category *structure* is concerned with the rules which define each class of semantic unit. These rules are stated explicitly in the paper defining the network structures (Frederiksen, 1975a).

An example of a network structure which contains semantic units at the six rank levels is given in Fig. 1. To facilitate storing and manipulating network structures on a computer, the network is represented as a list of propositions (Fig. 1a) and a list of objects (Fig. 1b). Consider first the proposition list. Each

TABLE 1
Ranked Units in Semantic Structure

Unit rank	Unit	Classes of units
1	concept	objects, actions, attributes of objects, attributes of actions, numbers, degrees, locations, and times
2	relational triple	processive case relations, resultive case relations, stative relations, determiner and quantifier relations, manner relations, degree, locative, and temporal relations
3	event frame	processive event frames, resultive event frames
4	proposition	states, events
5	relative system	nonmetric systems, metric systems, tense and aspect systems
6	dependency system	logical systems, causal systems, conditional systems

```
;--------------------------------------------------------------------
;PROPOSITION LIST: TARGET DESCRIPTION 2
;--------------------------------------------------------------------


    40      (:INDIANA.DUNES)--LOC.1,1-> (:SHORE.L.M)
    41      (:LAKE.MICHIGAN)--HASP-> (:SHORE.L.M)
    42      (:SHORE.L.M)--LOC.0,1-> ('SOUTHEAST)
    43      (:INDIANA.DUNES)--HASP-> (:MOUNDS)
    44      (:MOUNDS)--HASP-> (:SAND)
    45      (:SAND)--I.PAT@ASPCT(HAB)-> ('SHIFT)--MAN.EXT1-> ('SLOWLY)
    46      (:MOUNDS)--EXT1-> ('GREAT)
    47      (:INDIANA.DUNES)--LOC.2,2-> (:INDIANA)
    48      (:INDIANA.DUNES)--LOC.2,2-> (#48)
    49      (:URBAN.CENTERS.D)--CAT-> (:CHICAGO)
    50      (:URBAN.CENTERS.D)--CAT-> (:GARY)
    51      (:URBAN.CENTERS.D)--CAT-> (:INDIANAPOLIS)
    52      (:URBAN.CENTERS.D)--CAT-> (:LANSING)
    53      (:URBAN.CENTERS.D)--CAT-> (:KALAMAZOO)
    54      (:LANSING)--LOC.2,2-> (:MICHIGAN)
    55      (:KALAMAZOO)--LOC.2,2-> (:MICHIGAN)
    551     (:CHICAGO)--LOC.2,2-> (#551)
    552     (:GARY)--LOC.2,2-> (#552)
    553     (:INDIANAPOLIS)--LOC.2,2-> (#553)
    554     (:LANSING)--LOC.2,2-> (#554)
    555     (:KALAMAZOO)--LOC.2,2-> (#555)
    556     ((#48),(#551))--D-> ('NEAR)
    557     ((#48),(#552))--D-> ('NEAR)
    558     ((#48),(#553))--D-> ('NEAR)
    559     ((#48),(#554))--D-> ('NEAR)
    550     ((#48),(#555))--D-> ('NEAR)

    58      (:STEEL.INDUSTRY)--AGT@TEM(PAST)-> ('DEVELOP)+--OBJ1->
+(:AREAS.STEEL)
                                                    /--MAN.EXT1->
+('HEAVILY)
    581     (:AREAS.STEEL)--LOC.2,2-> (#58)
    59      ((#48),(#58))--D-> ('NEAR)--DEG1-> ('VERY)

    60      []--CAU@NEG@TEM(PAST)@ASPCT(CONT)@QUAL(RELATIVELY)->
+('DISTURB)--OBJ1-> (:INDIANA.DUNES)

    61      (:MIDWEST)--HASP-> (:ENVIRONMENT.MDWST)
    611     (:ENVIRONMENT.MDWST)--CAT.ATT-> ('NATURAL)
    612     (:ENVIRONMENT.MDWST)--HASP-> (:INDIANA.DUNES)
    62      (:INDIANA.DUNES)--EXT1-> ('SIGNIFICANT)--DEG1-> ('VERY)
    63      (:CONGRESS)--AGT@TEM(PAST)-> ('AUTHORIZE)+--RESULT->
+(:I.D.NATL.LAKESHORE)
                                                    /--TEM0-> ('1966)

    64      (:CONGRESS)--AGT@TEM(PAST)-> ('ATTEMPT)--GOAL1-> ["65]
    65      (:CONGRESS)--AGT-> ('MAKE)--RESULT-> ["66]
    66      ((:ENVIRONMENTALISTS.2),(:STEEL.INDUSTRY))--PAT-> ('FEEL)
+--THEME2-> ('SATISFIED)

    67      ["65]--CAU@TEM(PAST)-> ["68]
    68      (:GEOGRAPHICAL.PATCHWK)--CAT-> (:I.D.NATL.LAKESHORE)

    69      ()--AGT@TEM(PAST)-> ('PROPOSE)+--THEME1-> ["71]
                                          /--TEM1-> ('RECENTLY)
    71      ()--AGT-> ('MAKE)+--RESULT-> ["72]
    72      (:I.D.NATL.LAKESHORE)--HASP-> (:AREAS.B)
    74      (:AREAS.B)--EXT1-> ('BEAUTIFUL)--DEG1-> ('GREAT)

    75      (:DEPT.OF.INTERIOR)--AGT@TEM(PAST)-> ('REFUSE)--GOAL1-> ["76]
    76      (:DEPT.OF.INTERIOR)--AGT-> ('SUBMIT)--OBJ1-> (:REPORT)
    77      (:REPORT)--THEME1-> ["71]
    78      (:DEPT.OF.INTERIOR)--AGT@TEM(PAST)-> ('BLOCK)--GOAL1-> ["71]
```

FIGURE 1 (a)

```
;----------------------------------------------------------------
;OBJECT LIST:TARGET DESCRIPTION 2
;----------------------------------------------------------------

(:INDIANA.DUNES)              (´INDIANA.DUNES)--DEF->()--NUM0->(´1)
(:LAKE.MICHIGAN)              (´LAKE.MICHIGAN)--DEF->()--NUM0->(´1)
(:SHORE.L.M)                  (´SHORE)--DEF->()--NUM0->(´1)
(:MOUNDS)                     (´MOUNDS)--DEF->()--NUM1->(´PL)
(:SAND)                       (´SAND)--DEF->()
(:INDIANA)                    (´INDIANA)--DEF->()--NUM0->(´1)
(:URBAN.CENTERS.D)            (´URBAN.CENTERS)--DEF->()--NUM1->
 +(´PL)
(:CHICAGO)                    (´CHICAGO)--DEF->()--NUM0->(´1)
(:GARY)                       (´GARY)--DEF->()--NUM0->(´1)
(:INDIANAPOLIS)               (´INDIANAPOLIS)--DEF->()--NUM0->(´1)
(:LANSING)                    (´LANSING)--DEF->()--NUM0->(´1)
(:KALAMAZOO)                  (´KALAMAZOO)--DEF->()--NUM0->(´1)
(:MICHIGAN)                   (´MICHIGAN)--DEF->()--NUM0->(´1)
(:STEEL.INDUSTRY)             (´STEEL.INDUSTRY)--DEF->()--NUM0->(´1)
(:CONGRESS)                   (´CONGRESS)--DEF->()--NUM0->(´1)
(:I.D.NATL.LAKESHORE)         (´I.D..NATL.LAKESHORE)--DEF->()--NUM0->
 +(´1)
(:GEOGRAPHICAL.PATCHWK)       (´GEOGRAPHICAL.PATCHWORK)--UNIV->(´1)
(:AREAS.B)                    (´AREAS)--DEF->()--NUM1->(´PL)
(:REPORT)                     (´REPORT)--DEF->()--NUM0->(´1)
(:AREAS.STEEL)                (´AREAS)--DEF->()--NUM1->(´PL)
(:ENVIRONMENT.MDWST)          (´ENVIRONMENT)--DEF->()--NUM0->(´1)
(:ENVIRONMENTALISTS.2)        (´ENVIRONMENTALISTS)--DEF->()--NUM1->
```

(b)

FIGURE 1   Propositional structure: target description 2.

numbered line of the list is a proposition composed of one or more relational triples and represents a state or event. A proposition consists of slots which are enclosed in parentheses or square brackets and relations which are represented by directed arrows connecting a pair of slots. Slots contain concept labels or proposition numbers; relations are identified by labels inserted in the arrows, for example, --HASP→. Labels for object concepts are preceeded by a colon, for example, (:INDIANA.DUNES), and all other concept labels are preceded by an apostrophe, for example, ('DEVELOP). Parentheses indicate a slot containing a concept; square brackets indicate a slot containing a proposition that is labeled by a number corresponding to a numbered line in the proposition list preceded by a quotation mark, for example, ["72]. Slots may be empty, empty slots being optionally labeled by a number preceded by a # sign, for example, (#48). The label on a relation may be followed by a @ sign plus a label denoting an operator which has been applied to the relation, for example, --HASP@TEM-(PAST)→. Every object appears as a line on an object list (Fig. 1b) that specifies the manner in which each object set has been determined and quantified. Finally, propositions representing events may branch (e.g., Proposition 58 in Fig. 1a). Branched propositions contain an asterisk to indicate where the branching occurs, all branches being listed on lines preceded by a slash and located immediately below the asterisk.

To illustrate, the proposition list in Fig. 1a may be read as follows:

line 40: the object *Indiana Dunes* (definitized and quantified singular on the object list) is located as a region in a one-dimensional object-field *shore* (where *shore* is also definitized and quantified singular);

line 41: the object *Lake Michigan* has as a part the object *shore* (Note that since *shore* also occupies a slot in 40, the propositions are referentially connected. That is, if concept labels are thought of as pointers to entries on a concept list, two propositions are referentially connected if they contain pointers to the same concept.);

line 43: the object *Indiana Dunes* has as a part *mounds*;

line 44: the *mounds* are composed of *sand*;

line 45: the *sand* is the inanimate patient of the processive action *shift*, the action being identified by a manner relation attaching the attribute *slowly* to the action *shift*;

line 58: the *steel industry* is the agent of the resultive action *develop*, the object affected by the action is *areas*, and the action is characterized by the attribute *heavily*; etc.

The units and classes identified in Table 1 may now be illustrated using the network structure in Fig. 1. The units of lowest rank, *concepts*, are represented in the network by labels inserted into the frame ('). Examples of the concept classes in Table 1 are: objects, ('MOUNDS); processive actions, ('SHIFT); resultive actions, ('DEVELOP); attributes of objects, ('GREAT); attributes of actions, ('SLOWLY); numbers, ('1); and locations, the unfilled slot (#48) specifying the location of *Indiana Dunes* in Proposition 48.

Examples of classes of units at the next highest rank, *relational triples*, are: processive case relations, (:SAND)--I.PAT→('SHIFT); resultive case relations, (:STEEL.INDUSTRY)--AGT→('DEVELOP) and ('DEVELOP)*--OBJ1→ (:AREAS.STEEL); stative relations, (:MOUNDS)--EXT1→('GREAT); determiner and quantifier relations, ('INDIANA.DUNES)--DEF→( )--NUMO→ ('1); manner relations, ('SHIFT)--MAN.EXT1→('SLOWLY); degree relations, ('NEAR)--DEG1→('VERY); locative relations, (:INDIANA.DUNES)--LOC 1,1→(:SHORE.L.M); and temporal relations, ('PROPOSE)--TEM1→ ('RECENTLY).

The unit of next highest rank, the *event frame*, is a unit that is composed of a set of relational triples which are connected to an action and identify the various participants in an action, its resulting effects, etc. There are two important classes or event frames: processive and resultive event frames. An event frame consists of an action (which may be processive or resultive) and a network of case relations which specify the immediate structural components of the causal system associated with the action. Event frames reflect the fact that actions, unlike objects, cannot stand alone but involve a system of causes and effects. Yet an event frame does not represent a complete event because it does not specify the time, spatial location, or other characteristics of an event. Thus, an event frame is a component of an event proposition. For example, manner relations may occur as components of an event proposition, identifying an action by classifying it or specifying its attributes. Similarly, stative, locative, and temporal relations may also occur as constituents of event propositions. Examples of event frames are: processive event frames (:SAND)––I.PAT→ ('SHIFT); and resultive event frames, the first line of Proposition 58 and Proposition 76. Note that event Proposition 76 is a unit at both the system and propositional levels and stative Proposition 40 is a unit both at the relational triple and proposition levels.[2] Other examples of units at the fourth level of rank, *proposition,* are: stative propositions, 41–44, 46–55, 551–555, 58A, 61–62, 68, 72–74, and 77; event propositions, 45, 58, 60, 63–66, 69, 71, 75, and 78.

A *relative system* consists of a pair of relative or metric propositions connected by an algebraic relation or function. A relative system contains propositions as constituents and thus represents a fifth level on the rank scale. Examples of relative systems in Fig. 1a are 556–559, 550, and 59, all of which involve relative location. In these examples, an algebraic function – distance – connects two locative propositions.

The unit of highest rank, the *dependency system,* consists of three classes: logical, causal, and conditional systems.[3] Logical, causal, and conditional systems consist of pairs of propositions connected by logical, causal, or conditional relations, respectively. Examples of causal systems in Fig. 1 are: [''65]––CAU→[''68] in 67, and [ ]––CAU→('DISTURB)––OBJ1→ (:INDIANA.DUNES) in 60. Propositions 67 and 60 both contain operators applied to the CAU relation; 60 involves an event having an unstated antecedent cause which is represented by the open slot [ ].

SEMANTIC UNITS IN MEMORY STRUCTURE AND DISCOURSE PROCESSING

Historically, there have been two contrasting approaches to memory structure and organization that differ principally in their conception of units of information in memory – associative models and Gestalt or configural models of memory structure (cf. Foss & Harwood, 1975). In terms of semantic units, associative models allow units of only the first two levels of rank, concepts and relational triples (e.g., Anderson & Bower, 1973; Quillian, 1968). Models of

[2] Units of different rank can consist of the same segment of text in English. For example, the one word utterance *Good,* may be classified as a unit simultaneously at the word, group, clause, and sentence levels.

[3] The term "dependency system" is introduced here to refer to logical, causal, or conditional systems. What these systems have in common is that one proposition is made dependent on another, either logically, conditionally, or causally. The term "conceptual dependency" was used by Schank to refer to any two concepts which are linked by a relation and thus rendered "conceptually dependent."

information retrieval from semantic memory exemplify associative models in which memory structure is conceived of as a network but information is thought to be retrieved in units only at the level of individual concepts and relations (e.g., Collins & Quillian, 1969). In contrast to associative models, configural models suppose that semantic information is represented in memory in units made up of configurations of relational triples. In our present terms, they allow for semantic units of higher rank. However, with certain exceptions (e.g., Foss & Harwood, 1975), configural models have not been explicit in identifying the units of semantic information that occur at higher levels.

Recently, a configural approach to knowledge structure has been developing which is being described as "frame theory" (Minsky, 1975). The notion is that memory is organized into high-level structural units called *frames* which can be adapted to fit new experiences by changing details of the frame. A frame is a network structure for representing situations including visual concepts, experienced events, or the semantic content of linguistic messages. Frames contain slots, some of which may be filled on the basis of input data; others are relatively fixed. Frames may be linked together into frame systems which can represent action sequences, cause—effect relations, changes in conceptual viewpoint, and knowledge structures acquired at the discourse level (Minsky, 1975). Frame theories of knowledge structure clearly involve units at many levels.

The semantic units discussed in the present paper represent units of information which are a property of the networks developed to represent logical and semantic knowledge acquired from discourse. They constitute a set of detailed hypotheses concerning the nature and structure of memory representations and the manner in which semantic knowledge is organized into units at different levels. The theory may be thought of as a sort of low-level frame theory that specifies units out of which frame structures can be built. In addition, certain of the units (e.g., event frames, causal systems) appear to have characteristics usually associated with frame structures (e.g., empty slots, default assignments of concepts to slots, etc.; Minsky, 1975).

If semantic memory is organized into units at varying levels of rank, the processes of retrieving information from semantic memory and linguistically expressing information retrieved from memory ought to reflect in some fundamental way the organization of memory into semantic units. An important problem for psycholinguistic theories of text production is to establish the manner in which semantic units and textual units are made to correspond. For example, a theory of text production would have to account for any correspondence or lack of correspondence between semantic units (such as events) and textual units (such as sentences). Under what circumstances are events linguistically expressed or not expressed in single sentences?

Figure 2 presents a conception of the process of discourse production that distinguishes three decision levels at which the organization of semantic knowl-

Product   **Processes**

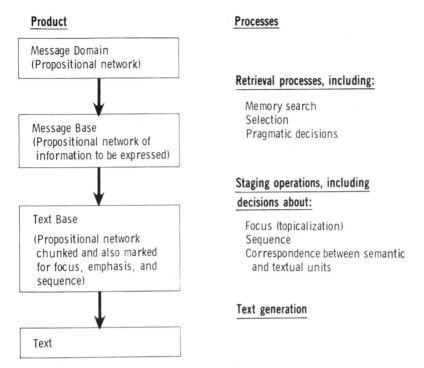

FIGURE 2   Levels of communicative decisions in discourse production.

edge into units ought to be important. In this view, a text results from a series of communicative decisions by which a speaker or writer generates a text from his or her store of message relevant conceptual and propositional knowledge about the world. The store of knowledge from which a textual message is derived is called a *message domain.* These operations involve three levels. First, the speaker or writer retrieves units of semantic information from a message domain which are to be explicitly expressed in a lingusitic message. This retrieval process reflects pragmatic assumptions about what the listener or reader already knows and assumptions about the inferential capabilities of the listener or reader. That propositional knowledge which is selected for explicit incorporation into a message is called the *message base.* Second, the speaker or writer makes *staging decisions* that determine how the retrieved units of semantic information are to be organized into discourse, including decisions about sequence, topicalization, reference, and the correspondence between semantic units and textual units. The message base is thus staged for presentation to a listener or reader (Grimes, (1975). The staged message base is referred to as the *text base.* Finally, the speaker applies his knowledge of sentence structure to generate a sequence of grammatical sentences (text) from the text base. Each of these levels involves decisions that reduce the amount of free variation in text. Presumably, most free variation is eliminated at the level of the text base, text generation involving only the mechanical application of grammatical rules which are appropriate in a speaker's (or writer's) language community. One would expect this process to occur in real time with many interactions among the components of the system.

The process of discourse comprehension also ought to reflect the organization of semantic knowledge into units. Specifically, there are two levels of processing in discourse comprehension that involve propositional data structures. The first processing level, the *interpretive level*, involves those processes by which propositional knowledge is "recovered" from text; the second level, the *inferential level*, involves the generation of new propositional knowledge from a network of propositions which is given — from prior discourse, from context, or from stored knowledge of the world.

An example of the operation of semantic units in the semantic interpretation of text is the "frame-processing" approach to semantic interpretation (e.g., Minsky, 1975; Schank, 1973). In the semantic interpretation of sentences expressing events, a frame processor would retrieve from semantic memory an event frame associated with an action and proceed to fill the slots in the frame using knowledge of English grammar only when necessary to disambiguate the assignment of lexical concepts to slots in the frame. Such "top-down" systems may be contrasted with "bottom-up" systems which use sentence structure and, only when necessary, stored semantic knowledge to generate a semantic interpretation for a sentence (e.g., Winograd, 1972). While higher-order semantic units are important to both types of text processing system, they are absolutely central to frame-processing systems.

Inferential processes operate on units of given propositional knowledge to generate new propositions from given ones. Given propositions may have been derived from a current textual input, from discourse context, from extralinguistic context, or be a part of a person's stored knowledge of the world.[4] While inferences operate on semantic units at a variety of levels (e.g., concepts, frames, events, relative systems, dependency systems, referentially connected propositions, etc.) inferences may also function to *define* higher-order semantic units. Thus, for example, two propositions in a text which are referentially connected may also be related inferentially if one proposition may be derived from the other by inferential operations. Such inferentially related units may be generated as an aspect of understanding a text, even when the inferential connections are not explicitly stated in the text. References to text level structures in papers on discourse analysis frequently involve inferential and referential units (e.g., Crothers, 1975; Kintsch & Van Dijk, 1975).

---

[4] Frederiksen (1976) has worked out a classification of types of text-based inferences.

PROCESSING UNITS IN UNDERSTANDING AND RECALLING
A DESCRIPTIVE TEXT

The preceding discussion has been concerned with exploring the thesis that semantic propositional knowledge is organized into highly structured units at a number of levels and that these units are processed as units in retrieving information from semantic memory, generating linguistic messages, semantically interpreting textual messages, and inferring new propositional knowledge from given propositions. Beginning with Halliday's conception of a unit as a category in the theory of grammar, it was found that by extending the notion of unit to semantic propositional structures, units at six levels of rank could be identified. These classes of units and the propositional structures on which they are based constitute a detailed statement of a theory of processing units in semantic memory. When the processes of discourse production and comprehension were examined, it was found that the organization of knowledge into semantic units should importantly affect both comprehension and text production. Consideration of the inferential component of discourse comprehension led to the expectation that in addition to the processing units implicit in propositional structures there are higher-order semantic units composed of referentially connected propositions that are inferentially related. Such processing units may occur even though the inferential relationships (or operations) which define them are not explicit in a text. Thus, units may exist which represent an aspect of discourse processing rather than an aspect of discourse structure.

Two or more semantic units form a higher-order *semantic processing unit* if the units are components of a semantic unit of higher rank, are connected referentially, and/or are inferentially related, and if the processing of one unit affects or controls the processing of the other unit. The present study was undertaken to investigate semantic processing units in discourse comprehension and recall. Specifically, our goal was to obtain evidence for semantic processing units, both at the levels indicated in Table 1 and at higher levels consisting of referentially and inferentially connected propositions. Furthermore, we wanted to establish that such units are important both during the processing of a text during input as a text is understood, and during recall when previously stored units of semantic information are retrieved and linguistically expressed. Thus, a primary purpose of the study was to establish not only that semantic units are important to discourse processing during recall, but also that semantic processing units including high-level inferential and referential units are important to the processes involved in acquiring knowledge from text.

The study addressed the following specific problems:

(1) to establish that texts contain ranked units of information which are processed as units, both during knowledge acquisition and during recall;

(2) to establish that high-level referential and inferential semantic processing units occur both during knowledge acquisition and during recall;

(3) to establish that such high-level referential and inferential units occur independently of how closely their component propositions are represented in sentence or discourse structure;

(4) to demonstrate that high-level semantic processing units occur during acquisition by establishing that propositions presented early in a text can affect the processing of propositions occurring later in a text to which they are referentially or inferentially connected;

(5) to establish specific inferential processing operations by which propositions presented early in a text affect or control the processing of related propositions occurring later in the text; and

(6) to demonstrate that high-level semantic processing units may be used in retrieving previously stored semantic information by establishing that propositions which connect other related propositions into higher-order referential and inferential units can, when presented last, facilitate retrieval of the related propositions.

The experimental strategy adopted to investigate these issues involved first constructing texts that are derived from known propositional structures (message bases) and that involve manipulating both the semantic propositional information in the message base and the order in which propositions are staged in a text (cf. Fig. 2). Then, a text is presented to an experimental group, after which the subjects are asked to recall in writing the content of the text. Finally, the subjects' recalls are coded against a computer listing of the propositional data structure such as that in Fig. 1 (cf. Frederiksen, 1975a). The available data consist of a large set of dichotomous variables each of which indicates whether or not a subject recalled an item of information from the data structure. In general, three types of measures are obtained: (1) pooled counts of numbers of items recalled from a part of the data structure, (2) estimates of the probability of recall of individual items of semantic information, and (3) statistics that measure the pairwise statistical dependencies among items of semantic information (e.g., joint probabilities, phi-coefficients, tetrachoric correlations).

In the present study, texts were constructed from a propositional structure consisting of two component structures: (1) three descriptive and narrative "target" propositional structures that describe three areas of the Midwest and political events involving these areas (Fig. 1 presents the proposition list for target 2) and (2) a linking structure that connects the three target structures. The link structures are of two types: a *similarity link* which consists mostly of superordinate propositions that describe similarities among the three areas and events involving the areas, and a *causative link* which in addition provides causative connections between the events involving the three areas. A filler structure was also constructed that describes a fourth geographical area and controls for repetition of target information in the two link structures. Texts were written from each message base; each text consists of a link (or filler) text presented either before or after the three target texts.[5] The experimental texts were as follows:

Target Description 1(a)

(1) The St. Croix River forms the border between the states of Minnesota and Wisconsin and is a short drive from the Minneapolis–St. Paul urban center. (2) The river is scenic, winding, and very beautiful; its environment has been disturbed very little. (3) Its upper stretches are a prime stream for canoeing and its lower reaches are pastoral and serene. (4) The development of the lower reaches of the St. Croix is primarily agricultural, consisting mostly of small farms located along the riverbank.

Target Description 1(b)

(5) The governors and congressional delegations of Wisconsin and Minnesota have supported making the St. Croix River a part of the Federal Wild and Scenic Rivers System, as have local communities and citizens' organizations. (6) The National Park Service and Department of the Interior have opposed the plan.

Target Description 2(a)

(1) The Indiana Dunes are located along the southeast shore of Lake Michigan and consist of great mounds of sand that are forever slowly shifting. (2) They are close to Chicago, Gary, Indianapolis, and the Michigan cities of Kalamazoo and Lansing. (3) The Indiana Dunes are a very significant part of the natural environment of the Midwest and have been disturbed very little. (4) The Dunes are very near areas that have been heavily developed by the Steel Industry.

Target Description 2(b)

(5) The Indiana Dunes National Lakeshore was authorized by Congress in 1966. (6) The Lakeshore is a patchwork resulting from attempts by Congress to satisfy both environmentalists and the Steel Industry. (7) It has recently been proposed that additional areas of great natural beauty be added to the Lakeshore. (8) The Department of the Interior has blocked action on the proposal by refusing to submit a report on the project.

---

[5] Complete listings of the propositional data structures for the experimental texts are available from the author.

Target Description 3(a)

(1) The Cuyahoga River between Cleveland and Akron has carved a deep valley into the flat northern Ohio landscape. (2) The Cuyahoga Valley is generally primitive and has innumerable features of scenic, natural, and historical significance. (3) The valley is lightly populated. (4) Many of the valley's residents are descendants of the early pioneers who settled there. (5) The small communities located in the valley have maintained a bucolic and pleasant style of living. (6) The Cuyahoga Valley is near the Cleveland and Akron metropolitan areas.

Target Description 3(b)

(7) Citizens' groups recently have proposed creating a 20,000 acre Cuyahoga Valley National Historical Park and Recreation Area to preserve the natural and historical aspects of the valley, to permit greater numbers of people to visit the area, and to preserve the style of living in the valley. (8) The proposal was supported by all members of the House Subcommittee on Parks and Recreation except the Park Service representatives.

Similarity Link (a)

(1) Three geographical areas of the Midwest will be (have been) described. (2) Each of these three areas is near at least one major urban center. (3) One is near areas of heavy industrial development. (4) Two of the areas are lightly populated, their development consisting for the most part of farms and small communities. (5) All three areas have very irregular boundaries. (6) Each of these areas has significant recreational, historical, or natural features and each has remained relatively undisturbed despite its proximity to urban centers.

Similarity Link (b)

(7) Each of these three areas also has been the subject of a recent proposal to protect the area from future development. (8) The proposals would prevent the future development of an area in one of two ways. (9) First, an area would be made into a park to be administered by the National Park Service, or second, it would be incorporated into an existing unit already administered by the National Park Service or the Department of the Interior. (10) In each of these cases, the proposal has been supported by local communities, citizens' groups, or environmentalists and has been opposed by the National Park Service, the Department of the Interior, or by representatives of the National Park Service.

Causative Link (a)

(1) Three cases will be (have been) described. (2) Each involves a proposal to protect an area from development, either by creating a park to be administered by the National Park Service or by adding the area to a unit already administered by the Park Service or the Department of the Interior. (3) Each area has as yet remained relatively undisturbed. (4) In each case, a proposal strongly supported by local communities, environmentalists, and citizens' groups has been opposed by the Park Service, its representatives, or the Interior Department. (5) The Department now appears to be more concerned with avoiding administrative problems resulting from irregular boundaries, industrial pressures, inholdings, access rights, and heavy rates of visitation, than with preserving our natural and historical environment.

Causative Link (b)

(6) The three areas described are near urban centers and hence would have high rates of visitation; one is near areas of heavy industrial development and thus is subject to industrial pressures. (7) Two are lightly populated, resulting in problems associated with inholdings, access rights, and control of visitation. (8) All have irregular boundaries, making control of visitation difficult. (9) Thus, despite the areas' significant historical, recreational, and natural features, the National Park Service is no longer interested in administering them.

Filler Control (a)

(1) Cape Cod National Seashore is located near Boston and other urban centers of the northeast. (2) Cape Cod has significant recreational, historical, and natural features and has remained relatively undisturbed despite its proximity to urban centers and areas of industrial development. (3) Cape Cod is lightly populated; its development consists primarily of farms, small communities, and resort areas. (4) The boundaries of Cape Cod National Seashore are very irregular; most of the northern Cape is included within the boundaries of the Seashore. (5) Summer residents of Cape Cod include people who come every summer from California and the Midwest.

Filler Control (b)

(6) Recently, it has been proposed that several hundred acres of ocean front property be added to Cape Cod National Seashore to protect these areas from future development by resort, hotel, and motel interests. (7) The proposal would thus create a new enlarged park for the enjoyment of future generations. (8) The

entire area would become a single park which would be administered by the National Park Service. (9) Local communities, citizens' groups, and environmentalists have supported this proposal, while the Park Service, the Department of the Interior, and representatives of the Park Service have opposed the creation of a new enlarged park.

The nature of the inferential connections between the target and linking structures can be determined by comparing each of the propositions underlying the linking paragraphs to those propositions in the target structures to which they are referentially connected. Such a comparison reveals that the linking propositions are of three types:

1. *Redundant propositions* which occur both in the linking structure and in one or more targets; for example, Proposition 69 in target 2 (cf. Fig. 1 and Sentence 7, Target Description 2) occurs in the Similarity Link (Sentence 7) and in the Causative Link (Sentence 2) propositional structures.

2. *Frame propositions* which contain slots into which target propositions may be inserted, for example, Propositions 71, 72, and 73 in target 2 (cf. Fig. 1 and Sentence 7, Target Description 2) may be embedded in the result slot of Proposition 226 in the similarity and causative link structures (Sentence 7 in the Similarity Link text and Sentence 2 in the Causative Link text):

226 ( )--AGT@TEM(PAST)→('PROPOSE)*--GOAL1→["227]
      /--RESULT→["229]

3. *Superordinate propositions* which are derivable from one or more target propositions by replacing one (or more) concept in a target proposition with a superordinate concept class (which includes the target concept as a member), for example, Proposition 59 in target 2 (cf. Fig. 1 and Sentence 7, Target Description 2) is a special case of (i.e., is subordinate to) Proposition 208 in the similarity and causative link structures (Sentence 2 in the Similarity Link text and Sentence 6 in the Causative Link text):

208 ((#206),(#207))--D→('NEAR)

The design thus involves two experimental factors: (1) the *type of linking structure* connecting the three target descriptions (filler, similarity link, and causative link) and (2) the *staging order* of the linking information (link structure first, link structure last). Since sex differences previously have been found in discourse recall (Frederiksen, 1975b,c), sex was also included as a factor in the design. The design provides information relevant to the problem areas raised previously in the following ways:

1. Primary evidence for semantic processing units corresponding to the ranked units identified in Table 1 is given by interitem dependencies in recall.

2. High-level inferential units may be established by looking at higher-order clustering in the dependencies in recall of units established at lower levels.

Both (1) and (2) involve testing clustering hypotheses derived from the propositional data structure, derived in the first case from units implicit in the propositional structures and in the second case from considering inferential relationships between referentially connected propositions in the link and target propositional structures.

3. The primary evidence for the independence of higher-order propositional structures from their proximity in a text is the occurrence of inferential processing units which include propositions from both link and target structures since such propositions are widely separated in the experimental text.

4. The staging order manipulation provides a means of demonstrating that high-level semantic processing units occur both during acquisition and during recall, the primary evidence being a link type by staging order interaction.

5. Three specific inferential processing operations can be explored using the present passage: *selective processing* through elimination of redundant information from a propositional structure; *slot-filling,* a kind of frame processing operation in which target propositions are inserted into slots in the frame provided by previously acquired linking propositions; and *superordinate inference,* using relationships between previously acquired superordinate propositions and subordinate target propositions in the acquisition of subordinate target propositions. The primary evidence for these specific processing operations would be effects of link type on the probability of recall of individual target propositions previously classified as redundant, embedded, or subordinate.

Subjects were 129 University of California undergraduates, about 20 of whom were tested in each of the six cells. Oral presentation of the text was followed by free recall. The number of words in the experimental text and reading time were controlled as was time available for recall. To insure uniformity of expression, the three target texts were recorded only once and then spliced either before or after a linking or filler text. All clicks between texts were erased from the tapes. The average reading time for all passages was about five minutes; pauses between the three targets and linking passages were approximately one half to one second. Sufficient time was allowed for recall to insure that time was not an important factor in limiting recall.

In presenting the results, we will consider first pooled counts of the number of items of target information recalled, then proportions of subjects recalling individual target propositions, and finally measures of the pair-wise statistical dependencies among target propositions. Tables 2 and 3 present a summary of the results indicating the effects of linking structure type and staging order on the pooled number of items recalled from the target propositions. The statistical significance levels reported are based on unweighted means analyses of variance

TABLE 2
Mean Number of Target Items Recalled with Filler, Similarity, and Causative Linking Structures Presented First and Last[a]

	Order			
Linking structure	Target last	Target first	Pooled mean	Difference[b]
Filler[c]	54.43 (23)	74.50 (24)	64.68	
Similarity	50.55 (20)	86.75 (21)	69.09	4.41
Causative	76.62 (21)	79.00 (20)	77.78	13.10[d]
Pooled mean	60.50	79.84	70.25	
Difference		19.34[e]		

[a]Numbers in parentheses indicate the number of subjects in the experimental group.
[b]Difference is from pooled filler score.
[c]Filler is a control for repetition of information from the targets in the linking structure.
[d]$p < .10$.
[e]$p < .005$.

(unequal cell frequencies are reported in Table 2). In general, there is considerable within-cell variability in these data, reflecting the fact that people differ very substantially in the amount and kind of information they are able to recall from text. The results indicate, first, an order main effect, that is, more target information is recalled when the target information is presented first. Since, under the filler condition, no new information was presented that related to the three target passages, this order main effect cannot be attributed to effects of the information presented last on retrieval processes; rather, the order effect appears to represent simply a tendency to acquire more semantic information from the earlier parts of a text. Numerous substantive interpretations of such a primacy effect are possible (e.g., selective effects of staging order on the degree of importance attributed to information presented early, increased time available to process information presented early in a text inferentially, etc.) and need to be addressed in future research.

Second, consider only the causative linking structure and filler conditions. The results indicate first a main effect of the causative linking passage on the

TABLE 3
Mean Difference between Similarity and Filler Groups and between Causative and Filler Groups in Number of Target Items Recalled with Linking Structure Presented First and Last

	Order		
Difference	Target last	Target first	Mean difference
Similarity–filler	−3.88	12.25	−16.13[a]
Causative–filler	22.19[a]	5.00	17.19[a]

[a]$p < .10$.

acquisition of information from the target passages. Thus, presenting causative linking information as a part of the passage resulted in more target information being acquired, whether or not the causative information was presented before or after the target information. The increased levels of recall of target information when the causative information was presented last clearly indicate a retrieval effect — linking information connecting target propositions referentially and inferentially increases the likelihood that the target propositions will be retrieved and recalled. Thus, there is clear evidence that high-level semantic processing units are used in retrieving previously stored semantic information. Evidence for an effect associated with acquisition is given (Table 3) by the fact that the causative linking structure has a greater effect when it is presented before the target information (target last: mean difference = 22.19) than when it is presented after the target information (target first: mean difference = 5.00). Thus, there is evidence that indicates that causative propositions presented early in the text affected the processing of propositions occurring later in the text and thus that high-level inferential processing units occurred during acquisition. Furthermore, these results also indicate that high level inferential processing units occur even when their component propositions do not occur in close proximity in a text. Thus, the occurrence of high-level semantic units is not simply a reflection of how these units are expressed in a text. That is, these units reflect semantic structures, not purely textual structures. In summary, we have found evidence that is consistent with the interpretation that high-level inferential semantic processing units occur in processing discourse both during comprehension and recall of a text.

The effects of the similarity linking passage on the acquisition of target information require further comment. The similarity linking structure was included in the design to permit investigating effects of kind and extent of linking information on high-level processing units in discourse comprehension and recall. Observe in Table 2 that when the similarity information was presented last, it facilitated recall more than did the causative information, but when it was presented first, it had a small negative effect. The former effect on recall is consistent with the results obtained with the causative linking passage. The larger retrieval effects associated with the similarity passage may be due to the fact that the similarity passage does not introduce any *new* information that cannot be derived from the target passages by means of low-level inferences. That is, it summarizes the similarities among the three target descriptions, while the causative passage in addition introduces new events and causative links between the new events and the events and descriptive information in the targets. If similarity information is more useful in retrieving target information than causative information and if more similarity information was acquired from the similarity passage than from the causative passage, then the present result would be expected. Evidence consistent with such an interpretation is presented in Table 4. More similarity information was acquired from the similarity passage than from the passage that included both similarity and causative information.

TABLE 4

Mean Number of Items Recalled from Similarity Structure for Groups Presented with Similarity and Causative Linking Structure First and Last[a]

| Linking structure | Order | | Pooled mean | Difference |
	Target last	Target first		
Similarity	35.35 (20)	39.62 (21)	37.54	
Causative	28.24 (21)	25.10 (20)	26.71	-10.83^{b}
Pooled mean	31.71	32.54	32.13	
Difference		0.83		

[a]Numbers in parentheses indicate the number of subjects in the experimental group.
[b]$p < .005$.

The failure to find similarity effects when similarity information was presented first is subject to several interpretations.[6] However, whatever interpretation is made of this result, the data as a whole indicate that the nature of the linking propositions and the order in which the propositions are staged are both important factors in determining what higher-order processing units occur and when they occur — during comprehension, during recall, or both.

One further observation can be made from Table 4, that is, there are no significant effects of staging order on the level of recall of similarity linking information. This absence of significant order effects is important because it relates to a possible interpretation of the order by link type interaction in level of recall of target information that was found in comparing the causative and filler conditions. The interpretation of this interaction which was proposed earlier is that it provides evidence that the linking information affected the processing of target propositions during acquisition. An alternative is that it was a result of differences in the amount of similarity information acquired under the two order conditions. If more similarity information was acquired when it was presented first (a primacy effect), then the greater amount of target information recalled under this condition could reflect the greater amount of similarity information available for use in retrieving target information. However, since staging order did not affect the amount of similarity information acquired, the only remaining interpretation is that linking information presented early in the text did affect the processing of related propositions as they occurred later in the text.

The specific inferential operations by which propositions presented early in a text are employed in processing other related propositions occurring later in the text can be investigated by examining the probability of recall of individual target propositions that have been classified on the basis of their relationships to

---

[6]Discussion of these interpretations is beyond the scope of the present paper. A number of subsequent experimental conditions were tested to investigate alternative explanations and suggest that the effect reflects multiple causes.

linking propositions. Three categories of target propositions were identified on this basis: *redundant* propositions, *embedded* propositions which may be inserted into slots in frame propositions, and *subordinate* propositions which are derivable from superordinate propositions in the linking structure by replacing one (or more) conceptual classes in the superordinate proposition with subordinate conceptual classes. Associated with each category of target proposition there is a specific type of inferential processing operation.

When a redundant proposition is encountered in semantically interpreting a target passage, it may be recognized as old information and eliminated from the memory structure which is built up for the target passage. Primary evidence for such *selective processing* would be a lower probability of recall of a target proposition when it was preceded by redundant linking information than when it was preceded by unrelated filler information. Data relevant to establishing this type of inferential text processing may be found by examining the proportion of subjects recalling each redundant proposition in the target passages under the target-last conditions. Specifically, we will compare the proportions of subjects in the groups that were presented with the filler and causative passages followed by the target passages. The relevant data are presented in Table 5. There are three instances of redundant propositions in the target passages. As predicted, in each case, the proportion recall is lower under the causative condition. Note that this result is opposite in direction to that obtained from the pooled recall data. Furthermore, there are in target 1 two sets of propositions that are structurally identical, one set which is redundant (Propositions 35 and 36) and the other which is not (Propositions 24–27, 29, and 31). It is interesting to note that for the unrelated propositions there is no difference in the proportion of subjects recalling the propositions while for the redundant propositions the difference is as predicted from the selective processing hypothesis.

The second type of inferential processing, *slot-filling*, involves using previously acquired propositions as frames into which target propositions are inserted. The general prediction is that propositions that were classified as embedded, because

TABLE 5
Estimated Probability of Recall of Redundant Target Propositions

Target	Propositions	Unit	Type	Condition		
				Filler		Causative
1	24–27, 29, 31[a]	Triple	Action + goal	.457	$=^b$	.405
1	35, 36	Triple	Action + goal	.674	$>^b$	.119[c]
2	69	Proposition	Event	.313	$>^b$	.124[d]
3	104	Proposition	Event	.357	$>^b$	.191[d]

[a]Nonredundant information (included for comparison).
[b]Predicted relation.
[c]$p < .0001$.
[d]$p < .10$.

they can be inserted into slots in propositions in the linking structure, will be recalled with higher probability when they were preceded by frame propositions than when they were preceded by the filler. The relevant data are presented in Table 6 (which, along with Table 7, is based on the same two experimental groups as Table 5). For every instance of an embedded target proposition, the outcome is in the predicted direction; however, the effect appears to be weaker than in the previous table. Note, however, that since the propositions in Tables 5 and 6 are for all practical purposes recalled independently, each comparison in Table 6 constitutes an independent test of the same hypothesis. Thus, for this passage there appears to be somewhat weaker evidence for slot-filling than for selective processing as an inferential text processing operation.

The evidence for *superordinate inference,* using given (previously acquired) superordinate linking information in processing new subordinate target propositions, is given in Table 7. Numerous instances of subordinate propositions occurred in the targets, each of which is indicated in Table 7. The prediction is that the probability of recall of a target proposition will increase when it has been preceded by a proposition superordinate to it. As can be seen in Table 7, for every instance of a subordinate proposition, the prediction is in the predicted direction, the differences being significant in all but two instances (by a one-tailed test of differences between proportions). Thus, there is strong evidence for superordinate inference as a third specific mechanism by which given information is used in the top-down control of the processing of new related propositions.

It remains to examine the results that are relevant to establishing that semantic processing units occur during comprehension and retrieval which correspond to the ranked units identified in Table 1. Data relevant to this problem are the pairwise statistical dependencies among items of semantic information in recall. If two or more items of semantic information are found to be mutually dependent in recall, then together they form a semantic processing unit. Any

TABLE 6
Estimated Probability of Recall of Embedded Target Propositions

Target	Propositions	Unit	Type	Condition		
				Filler		Causative
1	20 (Result)	Triple	Locative	.218	$<^a$	$.397^b$
1	32, 33, 34 (Goal)	System	Case frame	.261	$<^a$	.357
2	71, 72, 73 (Theme result)	System	Case frame	.309	$<^a$	.418
3	106 (Theme result)	System	Case frame	.316	$<^a$	.465

[a]Predicted relation.
[b]$p < .10$.

TABLE 7
Estimated Probability of Recall of Subordinate Target Propositions

				Condition		
Target	Propositions	Unit	Type	Filler		Causative
1	9,1,12	Relative system	Distance	.402	$<^a$	.476
2	556–559,550	Relative system	Distance	.370	$<^a$	$.643^b$
2	551–555,54,55	Triples	Locative	.130	$<^a$	$.313^c$
2	59	Relative system	Distance	.145	$<^a$	$.429^b$
3	90	Proposition	Event	.168	$<^a$	$.347^c$
3	981, 101	Relative system	Distance	.130	$<^a$	$.326^c$
3	991,102	Relative system	Distance	.160	$<^a$	.198

[a]Predicted relation.
[b]$p < .05$.
[c]$p < .10$.

text has associated with it a large set of items of semantic information that correspond to items of information in its propositional message base. Given a large set of items, the problem is to determine whether items of semantic information cluster into mutually dependent sets that are recalled together and to determine what correspondence exists between such item clusters and the semantic units predicted by the theory.

In the present paper, results will be presented for the propositional data structure given in Fig. 1 (corresponding to Target Description 2). The results presented are typical of the results obtained with the other target passages. Table 8 contains the mean interitem tetrachoric correlations for the propositions expressed in Target Description 2(a) (p. 62) which consists mostly of stative propositions describing the Indiana Dunes, and Table 9 presents the interitem correlations for the propositions expressed in Target Description 2(b) (p. 62) which consists mostly of events involving the Indiana Dunes. In both of these tables, a proposition was included only if its level of recall was sufficient to permit investigating its dependency on other items. Tetrachoric correlations were chosen since they are the only measure of interitem dependency in recall that does not reflect the level of recall of the items. The pattern of results using phi coefficients is the same except that differences in level of recall complicate the picture. While it is possible to fit mathematical models expressing particular structural hypotheses to these data (e.g., Christoffersson, 1973; Rotondo, 1975), the clustering of items and the relationship of the clustering to the propositional data structure appears to be sufficiently clear that more sophisticated analyses will not be described in the present paper.

Consider first Table 8. The diagonal elements of the matrix contain mean interitem tetrachoric correlations for the items in the indicated propositions; a one indicates that a single item was used as an index of that proposition. Since in

TABLE 8

Interproposition Correlations: Target 2, Descriptive Part[a]

Proposition	Unit	Type	40	41	42	43	44	45	47	48	551	552	553	554	555
40	Triple	Locative	.982												
41	Triple	Stative	.915	.993											
42	Triple	Locative	.809	.928											
43	Triple	Stative	.309	.309	.300	.866									
44	Triple	Stative	.321	.310	.307	.826	.981								
45	Proposition	Event	.342	.317	.129	.610	.769	.982							
47	Triple	Locative	.000	-.149	-.215	.008	.147	.169	1.–						
48[bc]	Triple	Locative	.337	.504	.392	.330	.298	.294	-.271	1.–					
551[b]	Triple	Locative	.093	.219	.191	.359	.344	.267	-.180	.646	1.–				
552[b]	Triple	Locative	.368	.512	.416	.269	.220	.279	-.098	.657	.652	1.–			
553[b]	Triple	Locative	-.127	-.010	-.048	-.020	-.165	.060	-.143	.385	.508	.592	1.–		
554[b]	Triple	Locative	.228	.449	.172	.110	-.184	.226	.103	.468	.361	.653	.594	1.–	
555[b]	Triple	Locative	.259	.363	.213	.188	.067	.125	.067	.431	.158	.666	.393	.696	
49[b]	Triple	Stative	.126	.282	.161	.156	.234	.217	-.052	.475	.930	.529	.456	.470	.252
50[b]	Triple	Stative	.439	.577	.403	.143	.182	.357	.025	.496	.478	.943	.468	.646	.604
51[b]	Triple	Stative	-.077	.035	-.017	-.044	-.133	-.026	-.128	.377	.470	.560	1.000	.543	.304
52[b]	Triple	Stative	.235	.421	.156	.058	-.218	.188	.059	.356	.265	.505	.587	.978	.623
53[b]	Triple	Stative	.178	.362	.299	.244	.083	.177	.044	.322	.077	.479	.394	.623	.954
54[b]	Triple	Locative	.184	.349	.142	.089	-.167	.116	.125	.282	.411	.590	.536	.926	.638
58[c]	Proposition	Event	.265	.077	.282	.139	.051	.050	.159	.226	-.201	-.121	-.302	-.140	.079
58A[c]	Triple	Locative	.429	.308	.312	.058	-.002	.115	.152	.591	-.152	.095	-.046	-.051	.021
59[c]	Rel. Syst.	Distance	.382	.326	.103	-.059	-.094	.183	.062	.552	-.140	.068	.103	.046	.057
60	Proposition	Event	.152	.230	-.016	-.065	.123	.157	-.175	.323	-.169	-.011	.114	.074	.100

Proposition	Unit	Type	49	50	51	52	53	54	58	58A	59	60
49[b]	Triple	Stative	1.—									
50[b]	Triple	Stative	.587	1.—								
51[b]	Triple	Stative	.392	.408	1.—							
52[b]	Triple	Stative	.482	.632	.575	.915						
53[b]	Triple	Stative	.220	.525	.293	.686	.954					
54[b]	Triple	Locative	.553	.615	.564	.869	.582	1.—				
58[c]	Proposition Event		-.116	-.090	-.295	-.072	.043	-.119	1.—			
58A[c]	Triple	Locative	-.102	.133	-.117	-.034	-.029	-.150	1.000	1.		
59[c]	Relative system	Distance	-.069	.127	.017	.061	.029	-.093	.464	.952	1.—	
60	Proposition Event		-.131	.108	.145	.098	.204	-.208	-.062	.182	.278	.971

[a]Mean tetrachoric correlations.
[b,c]Higher-order units composed of indicated propositions.

the scoring procedure employed, the unit scored is for all practical purposes the triple, the diagonal elements are of interest only when a proposition consists of units larger than a triple.[7] In Table 8, Proposition 45 consists of the event indicated in Fig. 1 which includes a processive case frame, an aspect operator, and a manner relation. The fact that the mean correlation for the items from which Proposition 45 is composed is .982 provides strong evidence that a semantic processing unit exists corresponding to this event proposition. Examining the off-diagonal correlations in Table 8, a number of clusters of high correlations may be seen. The semantic units corresponding to these clusters consist of referentially connected propositional units. For example, the cluster consisting of Propositions 40, 41, and 42 is connected referentially by the object (:SHORE.L.M); and in the referential unit consisting of 43, 44, and 45, 43 and 44 are connected by (:MOUNDS), 44 and 45 are connected by (:SAND), and 44 thus connects 43 and 45 referentially. Propositions 48 and 551–555 are connected by distance relations into a relative locative system which specifies the location of (:INDIANA.DUNES) relative to the locations of several midwestern cities. It can be seen that there is strong evidence for a semantic unit in memory corresponding to this relative system. The cluster consisting of Propositions 49–53 are connected referentially through the concept (:URBAN.CENTERS); and 52 is referentially connected to 54 through (:LANSING) ($r = .926$). Each locative proposition in the set 551–555 is referentially connected to a stative proposition in the set 49–53 through the concepts (:CHICAGO), 49 and 551 (.930), (:GARY), 50 and 552 (.943), (:INDIANAPOLIS), 51 and 553, (:LANSING), 52 and 554 (.978), and (:KALAMAZOO), 53 and 555 (.954). A still larger referential cluster involving these semantic units and Proposition 54 is apparent and is composed of the propositions marked by footnote *b* in Table 8. Finally, two other units are apparent in Table 8, a referential unit consisting of Propositions 58, 58A, and 59, and a relative locative system consisting of propositions indicated by footnote *c*. These clusters correspond to all of the structural and referential units which exist in Target Description 2(a) and account for virtually all of the large correlations in Table 8. Thus, there appears to be a very close correspondence between the structure of interitem dependencies in recall and the organization of the propositional structure into units at varying levels.

[7]In the experiment reported here, recall protocols were scored against a graph structure rather than a proposition list display of the message base. Since a graph structure depicts referentially connected propositions as branching from their common concept nodes, such nodes are marked as recalled whenever any proposition containing that node is recalled; thus complicating the analysis of interitem dependencies. In presenting the results, all such items were eliminated and other items within a proposition were used as indices of recall of the proposition. Note also that all experimental dependencies among items were removed by retaining only one item from an experimentally dependent set (i.e., a set consisting of items that were perfectly correlated and thus always scored together).

TABLE 9
Interproposition Correlations: Target 2, Narrative Part[a]

| Proposition | Unit | Type | Proposition | | | | | | | |
			63	65	66	68	69	71	73	78
63	Proposition	Event	1.–							
65[b]	Proposition	Event	.004	1.–						
66[b]	Proposition	Event	.021	.829	.779					
68[b]	Triple	Stative	.203	.322	.361	.844				
69[c]	Proposition	Event	–.050	.177	.148	.183	.870			
71[cd]	Case frame	Event	.241	.226	.200	.204	.235	.968		
73[cd]	Triple	Stative	.247	.181	.165	.163	.221	.800	.615	
78[d]	Proposition	Event	.055	.051	.049	.126	.113	.301	.221	.952

[a]Mean tetrachoric correlations.
[b,c,d]Higher-order units composed of indicated propositions.

The clustering in recall which is apparent in Table 9 reflects clusters corresponding to different kinds of semantic units than those in Table 8. The propositions in Table 9 consist entirely of events and stative propositions which are embedded in event frames. The lowest level clusters which occur correspond to propositions (as indicated by the diagonal elements of the matrix). At the next level, clusters occur which consist of event frames together with propositions which occupy slots in their respective event frames, for example, in the cluster composed of Propositions 65 and 66, 66 occupies the result slot in 65; and in the cluster 71, 73, 73 is embedded in the result slot of 71. At the next level of clustering, Proposition 71 is embedded in 69 (indicated by footnote c in Table 9), and 71 is embedded in the goal slot in 78 (footnote d). The cluster indicated by footnote b is a causal system composed of Propositions 65 and 68 which are connected by the causal proposition 67 (cf. Fig. 1a). The small dependencies remaining in the table appear to be accounted for by a weak referential unit that is composed of propositions containing the concept (:I.D.NATL.LAKESHORE). Thus, there appears to be a very close correspondence between the embedding structure of the propositional structure and the dependency structure of the items in recall.

While one should of course be cautious in drawing too strong conclusions from a single study, especially one based on a single passage, nevertheless these data appear to provide striking support for the hypotheses investigated, both at the general level and at the level of detailed predictions concerning semantic processing units and specific inferential processing operations. The results also illustrate how much information can be obtained about the processes of understanding and recalling text when free response methods are employed. The task remains to throughly explore the issues raised in this paper. In future research, it is important that more careful attention be given to the problem of selecting or constructing texts for study. Research on discourse comprehension should increasingly employ texts that have been systematically related to other texts. To accomplish this will require that models of text structure, perhaps along the lines suggested in Fig. 2, be developed. Such models could be used as a basis for classifying the texts which subjects in a population studied are likely to encounter and for relating the particular texts used in research to this larger domain of naturally-occurring texts. Such a model would also allow us to begin to investigate the complex relationships that exist between semantic and textual structures.

ACKNOWLEDGMENTS

This research was supported by grant number GS-4023 from the National Science Foundation to the author while the author was at the University of California, Berkeley. Any conclusions or other views expressed here are the author's own and do not represent the views of the National Institute of Education, the National Science Foundation, or any other part of the federal government. No official support or endorsement by the National Institute of Education is intended or should be inferred. The author is indebted to George McConkie for developing the notation used in the computer representation of the propositional data structures and for other helpful suggestions related to this paper.

REFERENCES

Anderson, J. R., & Bower, G. H. *Human associative memory.* Washington, D.C.: Winston, 1973.

Berztiss, A. T. *Data structures: theory and practice.* New York: Academic Press, 1971.

Christoffersson, A. Factor analysis of dichotomized variables. Research Report 73–4. Uppsala, Sweden: University of Uppsala, Department of Statistics, 1973.

Collins, A. M., & Quillian, M. R. Retrieval time from semantic memory. *Journal of Verbal Learning and Verbal Behavior,* 1969, 8, 240–247.

Crothers, E. J. Memory structure and the recall of discourse. In R. Freedle & J. B. Carroll (Eds.), *Language comprehension and the acquisition of knowledge.* Washington, D.C.: Winston, 1972.

Crothers, E. J. Paragraph structure description. Report No. 40. Boulder, Colo.: University of Colorado, Institute for the Study of Intellectual Behavior, 1975.

Foss, D. J., & Harwood, D. A. Memory for sentences: implications for human associative memory. *Journal of Verbal Learning and Verbal Behavior,* 1975, 14, 1–16.

Frederiksen, C. H. Representing logical and semantic structure of knowledge acquired from discourse. *Cognitive Psychology,* 1965, 7, 371–458. (a)

Frederiksen, C. H. Acquisition of semantic information from discourse: effects of repeated exposures. *Journal of Verbal Learning and Verbal Behavior,* 1975, 14, 158–169. (b)

Frederiksen, C. H. Effects of context-induced processing operations on semantic information acquired from discourse. *Cognitive Psychology,* 1975, 7, 139–166. (c)

Frederiksen, C. H. Discourse comprehension and early reading. In L. Resnick & P. Weaver (Eds.), *Theory and practice of early reading.* Hillsdale, N.J.: Lawrence Erlbaum Assoc., 1976.

Gregory, M. The patterns of English. Toronto: Glendon College, York University, Department of English, 1972.

Grimes, J. E. *The thread of discourse.* The Hague: Mouton, 1975.

Halliday, M. A. K. Categories of the theory of grammar. *Word,* 1961, **17,** 241–292.

Halliday, M. A. K. Notes on transitivity and theme in English. *Journal of Linguistics,* 1967, **3,** 37–81, 199–224; 1968, **4,** 179–215.

Kintsch, W. *The representation of meaning in memory.* Hillsdale, N.J.: Lawrence Erlbaum Associates, 1974.

Kintsch, W., & Van Dijk, T. A. Recalling and summarizing stories. *Language,* 1975, **40,** 18–116.

Leech, G. *Towards a semantic description in English.* Bloomington, Ind.: Indiana University Press, 1969.

Meyer, B. The organization of prose and its effect on recall. Report No. 1, Reading and Learning Series. Ithaca, N.Y.: Cornell University, Department of Education, 1974.

Minsky, M. A framework for the representation of knowledge. In P. Winston (Ed.), *The psychology of computer vision.* New York: McGraw Hill, 1975.

Norman, D. A., & Rumelhart, D. E. *Explorations in cognition.* San Francisco: Freeman, 1975.

Quillian, M. R. Semantic memory. In M. Minsky (Ed.), *Semantic information processing.* Cambridge, Mass.: M.I.T. Press, 1968.

Rotondo, J. A. Models of chunk structure. Unpublished Ph.D. Thesis, Department of Psychology, University of California, Berkeley, 1975.

Schank, R. Identification of conceptualizations underlying natural language. In R. Schank & K. Colby (Eds.), *Computer models of thought and language.* San Francisco: Freeman, 1973.

Simmons, R. R. Semantic networks: their computation and use. In R. Schank & K. Colby (Eds.), *Computer models of thought and language.* San Francisco: Freeman, 1973.

Winograd, T. Understanding natural language. *Cognitive Psychology,* 1972, **3,** 1–191.

4
Toward a Functional Theory of Discourse

Richard Hurtig

University of Iowa

> My work consists of two parts: the one
> presented here plus all that I have not writ-
> ten. And it is precisely the second part that
> is the important one.
>
> L. Wittgenstein (1969, p. 35)

Recently, in linguistics and its allied fields, the emphasis has shifted from the analysis of sentences to the analysis of discourse. This chapter will consider the question of how this shift of emphasis can be carried out without rejecting some of the theoretical assumptions and empirical work of sentence-based linguistics and psycholinguistics. An attempt will be made to develop an extension of transformational–generative (TG) theory to the level of discourse.

Transformational–generative linguistics (Chomsky, 1965; Katz, 1973) and the psycholinguistics derived from it (Fodor, Bever, & Garrett, 1974) have at times been criticized (Lakoff, 1970; Olson, 1972) for being theories about "non-natural" linguistic units. That is, as theories concerned with the structure of sentences in isolation and isolated-sentence processing, respectively, they have not dealt with the "more natural" language unit: the discourse. It should be noted however that by expanding the domain of linguistic and psycholinguistic theories to include discourse-level phenomena one has not ipso facto ruled out the methodology or metatheory of TG theory: One can in fact only claim that TG theory sentence-based grammars are insufficient theories of language behavior. Whether the mentalist approach to the study of linguistic science is applicable to discourse analysis remains an open question.

This chapter will attempt to deal with that question by examining the extent to which the conceptual categories of TG theory are useful in the construction of a theory of discourse.

Transformational—generative theory (Chomsky, 1965) has held in one form or another that the central core of the grammar is syntactic and as such has concerned itself with such problems as structural compelxity and ambiguity. The existence of ambiguity has been used as an argument in support of the deep structure—surface structure dichotomy. Critics have argued that sentence ambiguity is a pseudophenomenon in that in the natural language setting ambiguity does not exist. The degree to which a linguistic theory is required to account for perceptual complexity and disambiguation has been considerably altered. Various attempts have been made to develop an interactionist theory of language which would account for linguistic behavior through a dynamic interaction of the formal grammar as well as general nonlinguistic perceptual and production systems (Bever, 1970; Bever, Carroll, & Hurtig, 1976; Fodor, Bever, & Garrett, 1974). Any attempt to extend TG theory to the discourse level will, likewise, have to develop within an interactionist framework in order to remain free of the problems faced in dealing with such problems as structural versus psychological complexity.

A discourse theorist must either motivate rejecting the concept of a sentence grammar or develop an interactionist model which would include a level of interaction between the formal syntactic or structural components of sentence and discourse grammars.

Let us begin our discussion of discourse theory with the question of what it is that a discourse theory is about: Is discourse, that is, a string of successive sentences (where sentence is taken to be the structural equivalent of "utterance") a natural unit of language? In natural speech communication discourse appears to be the operative unit of communication. That is, speech communication appears to involve units larger than the single sentence or utterance. Thus it is the set of successive utterances that we shall call discourse and the subject matter of a theory of discourse. Though discourses are variable in length and complexity, they do appear to be bounded, that is, finite in length. Just as in the case of sentences that fact appears to be a phenomenon which is due to perceptual, production, and social context limitations rather than anything in the formal structure of discourse. Discourses can be monologues, dialogues, or multiperson interchanges. Perhaps most importantly, a discourse appears to have topical or logical structure. Successive utterances in a discourse appear to be linked on the basis of such a topical or logical structure. It is precisely these links which a theory of discourse must account for.

Before constructing any general discourse model, one should consider certain theoretical questions which arise as a consequence of developing an extension of a TG model of language; that is, intuitions about discourse. The following set of questions should not be seen as an exhaustive list, but should be interpreted as suggestive of the types of questions which must be held in mind when constructing a theory of discourse.

1. What sorts of criteria should be used in determining what constitutes a discourse?

   1.1 Is there a distinction among comprehensibility, acceptability, and grammatical judgments with regard to discourses?

2. Is the distribution of discourses (constituents) syntactic in nature? If so, is that distribution representable in a syntactic component of a grammar.

   2.1 If discourses are found to have an underlying structural description, characterizable by some form of phrase marker, are there discourse formation rules similar to the phrase-structure rules of the sentence grammars?

   2.2 Do syntactic transformations operate over discourses? (Can the transentential transformation of pronominalization be seen as an instance of a discourse-level transformation?

   2.3 How are discourse boundaries marked: Can discourse structure be seen as simply a surface-structure phenomenon? or, does discourse in fact have a dichotomy of an underlying structure and a surface-structure level?

3. Would a phrase marker associated with a given discourse constantly be restructured as successive utterances are added to the discourse? That is, is there a sequence: discourse initial phrase marker $\rightarrow \cdots \rightarrow$ discourse final phrase marker? Is it possible then that semantic interpretation would be radically alterable between the initial and final phrase marker? Put simply, does the semantic interpretation change as one passes from utterance to utterance within a discourse?

   3.1 How would a discourse theory handle problems concerning the various relationships among discourses, such as synonomy, antimony, etc.? How will such a theory account for various forms of paraphrase relationships which may hold between discourses? How are individual sentence paraphrasing, statement reordering, and propositional paraphrases to be related? How would the theory account for differences in illocutionary and perlocutionary force of paraphrases? Similarly, how would differences in connotative and denotative force of a specific paraphrase be marked?

   3.2 Given the complexity of discourse paraphrase, how will a theory of discourse handle such phenomena as discourse ambiguity and discourse misinterpretation (garden pathing)? In what respect is discourse ambiguity similar to and dissimilar from sentence ambiguity? Clearly such questions are motivated in that natural discourses are often found to be naturally ambiguous and inadvertently misleading. That is, the intent of the speaker is not always correctly conveyed to the listener (see 4.4).

4. If discourse is a product of more than a linguistic grammar, to what extent is the distribution of the constituent utterances determined by contextual features of social, pragmatic, and logical and cognitive components?

4.1 Is discourse perception a product of a discourse semantic projection mechanism or the product of perceptual organization heuristics?

4.2 Would a discourse formation-rule component be a discourse production model or are the phrase markers and the associated discourse formation rules merely a posthoc descriptive device rather than a psychologically explanatory one?

4.3 To what extent would discourse grammar include or be sensitive to conversational postulates, social variables, contextual settings, or speech registers?

4.4 In what way, if any, will discourse grammar be able to mark the distinction between illocutionary and perlocutionary force? How would one be able to relate surface speech act markers and a speech-act interpretation mechanism?

SIMPLE TG THEORY EXTENSIONS

A general theory of discourse consistent with TG theory will be required to deal with the possibility that similar structure can underlie either a sentence or a discourse. If a discourse and a complex sentence can be derived from each other, than it should be the case that the semantic component of a TG grammar could assign a semantic reading to a discourse: Such a proposal speaks to the questions concerning the formal linguistic structure of discourse (1, 2, 2.1, 2.2, 2.3, 3, 3.1 above).

Katz and Fodor (1963) suggested that discourse readings be obtained by the insertion of "*and*" between all sentences within a discourse and the subsequent application of semantic projection rules. They realized that such a proposal cannot work since sentences are not all conjunctively related at the same level. The semantic rules which project sentence readings depend on phrase markers which express the relations between constituents. Bever and Rosenbaum (1964) have suggested that in discourses the structure of the relations between sentences may be expressed in terms of where in the complex phrase marker the conjunctive *and* occurs. Thus, a discourse containing three sentences can have at least the following three structures:

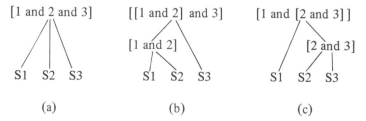

(a)   (b)   (c)

For example, if the following sentences are connected in a discourse, there is a different semantic interpretation corresponding to each of the phrase markers above:

(1) Harry danced.
(2) Susan sang.
(3) I was shocked (by that).

Thus, if discourse constituent phrase markers are available to the projection rules, the semantic component would be able to analyze discourses correctly. Bever and Rosenbaum suggest that such discourse phrase markers which relate to underlying constituent sentences may be generated by a set of discourse formation rules. Such rules generate the discourse phrase marker by combining underlying sentence structures in terms of common elements. Thus, constituents may be combined into a discourse if their readings have common semantic elements. Such rules would be recursively applied until all constituents whose readings contain some common semantic elements are combined.

Thus, the discourse formation rules generate "super phrase markers" in much the same way that cyclical syntactic generation operates in sentence derivations. The discourse formation rules operate on the output of the semantic analysis of constituent sentences, then the generated discourse phrase marker undergoes its own semantic analysis (interpretation).

Discourse formation rules, however, cannot account for all the natural relations between sentences in a discourse.

For instance, consider the discourse:

(1) The professor is in his office.
(2) (a) The air conditioner is working.
     (b) Usually it is broken.
     (c) But the room is cool.
          .
          .
          .
     (n)
(3) He is content.

which can be characterized by the following surface discourse phrase marker

The proper semantic interpretation requires that Sentences (1) and (3) be related in a way closer than Sentences (1) and (2) or Sentences (2) and (3). This is intuitively reflected by the fact that Sentence (2) can dominate an arbitrary number of sentences. There is no way that the projection rules can operate on Sentences (1) and (3) to provide a level of conjunction lower than that between Sentences (1) and (2) or Sentences (2) and (3). The only alternative would be to have Sentences (1) and (3) combined by a discourse formation rule in the underlying discourse structure which would be semantically interpreted and then subsequently separated by a *discourse transformation* to give the derived surface discourse phrase marker.

As in the derivation of single sentences, there are also cases where the same surface discourse has different derivations and exhibits ambiguity due to discourse structural transformation. Thus, cases in which there is ambiguity as to the antecedent reference of a pronoun in a given sentence of a discourse can be accounted for by hypothesizing that the surface discourse structure is derived transformationally from two distinct underlying discourse phrase markers.

Bever and Rosenbaum's suggestion proposes at the discourse level exactly what Katz and Postal (1964) proposed for sentences. There is an underlying discourse structure which is interpreted by the semantic component. Subsequent to the interpretation of the underlying structure using the simple semantic projection rules, that structure is deformed by transformational rules. Since syntactically synonymous discourses and sentences are now generated from the same underlying discourse structure, they will automatically be marked as synonymous.

The Bever and Rosenbaum model can be summarized as a set of serial operations involved in the derivation of a discourse:

1. Underlying sentences (sentoids) are generated by the sentence phrase marker component — the terminal nodes of the phrase marker are filled by the lexicon.
2. The semantic component assigns a reading to each constituent node.
3. The discourse formation rule operates on the semantically analyzed sentences to combine them into underlying discourse structures.
4. The underlying discourse structures are assigned semantic interpretations.
5. The underlying discourse structures are deformed by discourse transformations to produce a string of ordered underlying sentence structures.
6. The underlying sentence structures are deformed by sentence transformations to produce lexically filled-in derived constituent structure.
7. The derived constituent structure is interpreted by the morphophonemics into a sequence of articulatory phonetic segments.

Such a model is not meant to be a psychological process model, but merely a formal linguistic model. It attempted to demonstrate that discourse is amenable to syntactic analyses of the form proposed in TG theory and that the structure of discourse is formally related to the structure of sentences.

WHAT IS THE DISCOURSE "UNIT"?

Our discussion of discourse so far has assumed that the unit of analysis was clearly isolable and that its boundaries were clearly defined. Unlike the sentence whose boundaries appear intuitively clear, the discourse unit is not as clearly definable. The linguistic grammar of discourse operates on the premise that given a discourse it can provide the correct interpretation for that discourse.

Recently, there has developed considerable interest in discourse boundaries; including the examination of speech acts (Searle, 1969) and general rules of conversation (Gordon & Lakoff, 1971; Grice, 1967) as well as the openings and closings in dyadic interactions (Shegeloff & Sacks, 1973). These approaches have attempted to characterize conversational moves (verbal as well as nonverbal behaviors occurring at discourse boundaries). On a parallel with other work in descriptive (structural) linguistics these moves have been categorized on the basis of their distributional characteristics. While such a "movemorphic" analysis meets certain criteria of descriptive adequacy, it fails to meet the more stringent criteria of explanatory adequacy in that without recourse to higher-organizational information (that is, the actual internal structure of a discourse) it is impossible to adequately predict the distribution of the unmarked boundaries (the zero allomovemorphs) of each of the putative distributional categories. Moreover there is nothing inherent in such descriptive analyses to account for the fact that a given sequence without a surface boundary marker can be interpreted by a listener as equivalent to a sequence with a surface boundary marker. Just as the boundaries of the sentence are defined by the structure of sentences rather than by overt boundary markers, so too must discourse boundaries be defined in terms of the structural properties of the discourse itself. Thus, only recourse to the internal structure of the discourse (and perhaps also to nonlinguistic contextual information) will yield an adequate account of discourse boundaries.

Axiom: Discourse boundaries in and of themselves can not constitute an adequate discourse theory.

At the outset we defined the discourse to be topical in structure. Bever and Rosenbaum likewise designed their grammar discourse formation rules to construct discourse phrase markers in terms of the shared semantic readings of constituents (shared topical structure). This notion of topic, however, needs further specification if it is to be of any value in the construction of a theory of discourse. In the absence of a developed theory of topics we must rely on a few general approximations to define a set of operational procedures for dealing with topics.

1. Topics can consist of one or more related propositions (in the sense of formal logic).
2. Topics can be discontinuous as well as contiguous sets of one or more utterances.
3. Topic shifts involve the utilization of propositions not part of the original propositional set (idea).
   3.1 Topic shading is a form of shift which involves the expansion of the domain or scope of the original propositional set.

3.2 Topic fading is a form of shift which involves the establishment of a new propositional set with a link to either a predicate or argument in an antecedent propositional set.

4. Topic transitions or boundaries can be marked or unmarked in the surface configuration of the discourse. Thus, some discourse boundaries may have no syntactic realization.

4.1 Boundaries may be marked either on the basis of propositional content (topical move) or on the basis of propositional form (conversational move).

THE PSYCHOLOGICAL REALITY OF TOPICS

If linguistic theory is to be an investigation into the structure of the mind (Chomsky, 1968), then the descriptive levels proposed in the linguistic theory must be shown to have *psychological validity*. Psycholinguistic research in the 1960s attempted to "prove" the psychological reality of the specific rules posited by the linguists (for example, *coding hypothesis, derivational theory of complexity*) utilizing tasks to supposedly tap perceptual and memory processes. Equivocal empirical findings have led psycholinguists to alter their goals from proving the reality of specific rules to the validation of the structural levels posited by such rules. It is in this context that investigation of the psychological reality of the encoded discourse should be viewed. That is, can the existence of a level of discourse description be motivated by the nature of the perceptual processing of linguistic stimuli?

Recently, Bransford and Franks (1973) reported patterns in the recognition of simple as well as compound predicates in a memory paradigm. Their general finding was that regardless of the nature of the learning sets, compound sentences were (falsely) recognized when they themselves were not in the learning set but their constituent simple predicates were. Likewise, simple predicates were recognized even though they only occurred as constituents of compound sentences in the learning set. Bransford and Franks argue that such results suggest that in the encoding of sentences, predicates and propositions rather than surface forms are stored. In terms of our discussion of discourse, the Bransford and Franks result can be taken as evidence that the encoding of discourse into memory operates in terms of the topical or propositional nature of the discourse rather than the surface linguistic form of the constituent sentences. Bransford and Franks characterize the encoded form of the discourse as an *idea set*. This notion is very similar to the notion of topic which we have been considering.

Hurtig (1974) in a study dealing with the psychological reality of a tense logic demonstrated that the Bransford and Franks *idea set* included temporal information derivable from the constituent predicates. The recognition recall patterns support the hypothesis that the *idea set* can be characterized as an *event space*. That is, subjects' encoded representation of the temporal relations among predicates (events) specified in sentences corresponds to a Reichenbachian tense logic configuration [the relation of events (*E*), the speech act (*S*) and temporal reference points (*R*)]. Furthermore, that representation is built up by a mechanism similar to semantic projection rules and discourse formation rules which incorporates the temporal features of the individual predicates (events) and their respective temporal modifiers (adverbials). These encoded abstract representations were found to be subject to logical laws (Findlay tense laws; a linear time constraint) which altered the *event space* configurations.

The encoded representation (thought) can be seen as derived from inherent (temporal) features of the linguistic structures while the recall of linguistic structure is affected by the logical operations on the abstract representation. Thus, psychologically, the semantic reading of a discourse appears in part to be derived from the semantic feature representation of the constituent sentences.

DISCOURSE BOUNDARIES: TOWARD A FORMAL PROCESS MODEL

The general assumption that discourse boundaries will occur at sentence boundaries has for the most part been universal in discussions of discourse. This conclusion is based on several facts. First, sentences are propositional in nature. Second, since discourses are topical in nature, they will consist of sets of propositions. Therefore by definition one would not expect to find a discourse boundary (propositional boundary) within a single proposition (sentence).

Such an analysis presumes that all sentences have propositional force, that is, topical content. However, utterances can have purely conversational force rather than any propositional or topical force. It should therefore be possible for a topic boundary to occur within an utterance, given that utterance is one with only conversational content. Such a proposal makes certain claims about the processing of utterances in a discourse. Specifically, it hypothesizes that utterances are processed in terms of both their propositional content as well as their conversational content.

Such a formal process model is represented in Fig. 1. Whether such a model represents the psychological process remains an open empirical question. One part of the process (a) analyzes an utterance (sentence) in terms of propositional content and yields semantic representations of event spaces of the form proposed by Hurtig (1974). In the other part (b) utterances are evaluated in terms of their nonpropositional force. That is, in terms of their conversational force (moves). Such conversational moves are further evaluated in terms of their topical reference. That is, certain conversational moves are accomplished by manipulation of the terms of the propositional material, while other moves are

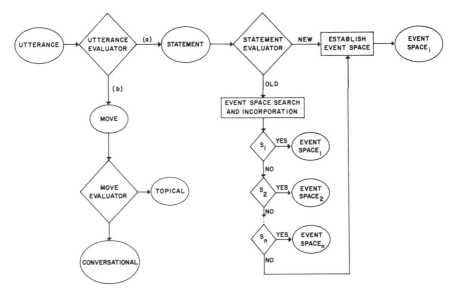

FIGURE 1   A formal process model for discourse.

accomplished by conventionalized conversational forms which do not utilize any of the topics' propositional material.

Thus, the overall semantic reading of an utterance can be seen to be the sum of the *event space* meaning (denotative) and the move or conversational meaning (connotative). Such a proposal attempts to specify the way in which the denotative and connotative meaning can be related within a general process model.

TOWARD AN INTERACTIONIST THEORY OF LINGUISTIC BEHAVIOR

In attempting to characterize the relationship between sentence and discourse grammar within a general theory of language, it will be necessary to make several distinctions at the outset. First, it will be necessary to clarify the goals of the respective grammars. That is, what aspect of linguistic communication does each of the grammars have to account for. In a sense the goals of each of the grammatical theories must be constrained in such a way as to maximize descriptive and explanatory power. In order to accomplish this goal the domain of each grammar must be so characterized as to capture the natural distinction between sentences and discourses.

Optimally, one would not want a discourse grammar to deal with sentence phenomena which would be most adequately treated within the scope of a sentence grammar. Likewise, one would not want to burden the sentence grammar by forcing it to account for discourse level phenomena.

Research in psycholinguistics in the last 10 years has not been totally limited to the investigation of sentence-based phenomena. In fact, numerous studies have been conducted in order to determine the effect of linguistic context on the perception and subsequent recall of sentences. Slamecka (1964) demonstrated the effect of contextual constraints on the acquisition and recall of sentences. Frase (1968, 1969) demonstrated an effect of text organization on acquisition and subsequent recall. Frase concluded that verbal problem-solving behaviors are subject to constraints imposed by the temporal arrangement of syllogistic terms. Furthermore, Freedle and Graae (1965) found that the recall of sentence pairs presented in speeded speech conditions (accelerated 2.5 times normal speed) could be affected by the meaningfulness of successive sentence pairings.

Following Sachs' (1967) demonstration of a nonsurface syntactic memory trace for sentences, various investigators have proposed semantic or propositional models of sentence memory (Anderson & Bower, 1973; Crothers, 1972; Frederiksen, 1972; Kintsch, 1972; Tulving, 1972). These studies generally support the notion that the text or discourse is the unit of organization in memory.

Koen, Becker, and Young (1969) dealing with written texts attempted to demonstrate that subjects' ability to determine paragraph boundaries results from both semantic and structural cues in the linguistic sequence. This study was viewed as a demonstration of the psychological reality of the paragraph. Such a line of investigation, however, remains to be further examined.

Bransford and Franks (1973) and Johnson, Bransford, and Solomon (1973) have demonstrated in a variety of experiments that recognition of novel sentences by subjects is not determined on the basis of surface structure of sentences in acquisition materials, but rather on their propositional form or the implications that can be drawn from those propositions. Jarvella and Collas (1974) found that intentions of utterances are coded into memory. Wertsch (1975), utilizing a Bransford and Franks paradigm, has demonstrated that the false recognition of items is subject to the listener's assessment of the speaker's perceived intentions. Thus, not only logical implications but also the perception of the nature of the speech interaction appears to affect the encoded form of linguistic materials. This can be seen as a demonstration of an interaction between some form of formal linguistic representation and other systems of knowledge, in this case, those relating to sociolinguistic variables.

In contrast, in another line of research several investigators have demonstrated the psychological "primacy" of the sentence (and its underlying structure representation; the clause) (Bever, Garrett, & Hurtig, 1973; Bever & Hurtig, 1975; Jarvella, 1971, 1973). Utilizing sentence memory, sentence completion as well as click detection paradigms, these studies have demonstrated that the clause is the maximal linguistic unit in short-term memory. The findings have been taken as support of the hypothesis that the processing of linguistic material proceeds clause by clause. That is, as successive linguistic material is processed, information concerning the previously processed clause is no longer available in short-term memory.

One might view this work on sentences as well as the work on discourse memory as yielding theoretically contradictory results: The discourse memory studies, in a sense, proving the psychological "reality" of the discourse or text and the sentence memory and click detection studies proving the psychological "reality" of the clause or sentence. Such an interpretation of the results of these two lines of research could lead to the false presumption that one of the two lines of research is dealing with the pseudophenomenon or that some of the empirical findings are simply the result of a specific experimental manipulation. However, it is possible to interpret both the results of the discourse studies as well as the sentence studies within a single coherent theory of language. Such an account is possible if we put into perspective the nature of the empirical questions set by the respective groups of investigators. One can view the findings as speaking to different components of the general speech encoding process. The research on sentences might best be characterized as investigations into the on-line perceptual segmentation process, while the work on discourse has been more concerned with the general representation of linguistic constituents in semantic long-term memory.

Those linguists and psycholinguists who are promoting an interactionist theory of linguistic behavior (Bever, Carroll, & Hurtig, 1976; Fodor, Bever, & Garrett, 1974) have proposed a functional relationship between the formal grammar and the subsystems of speech perception and production. Within this framework the domains of the grammar and of the perceptual system have been so delineated as to maximize the descriptive and explanatory power of the respective components of the linguistic system. The grammar is spared the complexity of having to account for certain linguistic sequences with constraints which can be accounted for on the basis of some general perceptual or production principles, motivated on independent grounds. Thus, the total linguistic behavior can be seen as the result of the operation of a formal linguistic grammar, perceptual and production systems, and the interaction of the grammar and the perceptual and production principles.

By expanding the domain of investigation from the sentence to the discourse one can follow the same sort of functional interactionist approach. The formal linguistic structure can be characterized as the interaction of a formal sentence grammar and a formal discourse grammar, as well as the interaction of both these formal linguistic systems and the perceptual and production principles or devices operative at both sentence and discourse processing levels.

In order to carry out such a program, it is necessary to determine at least some working hypothesis as to the limits or the characteristics of the domain of the respective theories. In order to do this, it might be worthwhile to examine the types of arguments raised in support of the existence of both discourse and sentence grammars. Thus, we are faced with the task of determing what aspect of the total linguistic behavior falls within the domain of constraints on sentence structure, discourse structure or associated cognitive systems such as the general perceptual or production routines utilized in speech.

In addition to the argument based on the intuitive naturalness of discourse units, it has been argued that not all properties of sentences are accountable by sentence grammar. Some of these properties have been attributed to perceptual systems (e.g., incomprehensibility of multiple embedded sentences) while others appear to have formal linguistic properties (e.g., discourse equivalence relations). This form of argument is analogous to that utilized in the criticism of American descriptivist (taxonomic) linguistics. That is, just as it was impossible to utilize only information about the distribution of subordinate structures (morphology and phonology) in the characterization of lexical items, so too it would appear that it would not be possible to account for all of sentence structure without recourse to superordinate phenomena, in this case discourse structure. There are a variety of sentential sequence constraints which have been difficult to account for within the limits of a sentence grammar. Obvious examples are tag questions, the placement of contrastive sentential stress and polysentential ambiguity (pronominal antecedents). Such constraints are more parsimoniously accounted for by either discourse level structure or by constraints due to general perceptual systems (see Bever, Carroll, & Hurtig, 1976).

However, one should not take these arguments for the existence of discourse grammar as arguments against the existence of sentence grammar. On the basis of the same data base, one could argue that the sentence appears to be the maximal syntactic unit. That is, the sentence is the largest linguistic unit whose structure is syntactic.

While discourse might have certain linguistic properties and therefore a formal syntactic or formal semantic component, certain constraints within discourse can be characterized as being extralinguistic. Examples of such extralinguistic constraints are:

1. Gricean conversational postulates.
2. Truth conditions (pragmatic constraints).
3. Logical-scope relationships.
4. Social interaction variables which constrain both types and tokens of linguistic utterances as a function of context of the linguistic communication, participants in the communication, and perhaps even subject matter.

The preceding constraints can be characterized as a consequence of the interaction of language with other formal systems of knowledge. Such constraints can be contrasted with constraints due to processing systems. Specifically, limitations on processing load which might constrain the number of logical arguments to be incorporated in a single proposition in memory or limits on the degree to which propositions may be self-imbedding.

Thus, one can talk about an interaction between the formal structure of sentences and the structure of discourses on the one hand, and the interaction of the structure of discourse with other systems of formal knowledge on the other hand. In addition one can limit the scope of the linguistic grammar (thereby increasing its ability to state linguistic universals) by accounting for certain distributional constraints by recourse to theories of percpetual and production mechanisms. The nature of such general segmentation heuristics which can be applied to nonlinguistic stimuli as well as simple or complex linguistic strings has been discussed by Bever (1970) and further specified in the treatment of problems of grammaticality and acceptibility by Bever, Carroll, and Hurtig (1976).

RESOLUTION: TOWARD A MODEL

It would seem reasonable to conclude with a few statements concerning the nature of the relationship of sentence grammar and discourse grammar and the relevance of psycholinguistic research to a general theory of discourse.

It will be necessary to account for the interaction of the linguistic constituents of the two respective systems of grammatical description. The nature of the definition of the linguistic constituents described by each of the theories will have to be constrained so that statements within one grammar will be compatible with those within the other. Toward this end, a more systematized account of what constitutes a syntactic unit as opposed to what constitutes a semantic (logical) unit must be forthcoming.

From the general description of work in both sentence and discourse grammar, it would appear that sentence grammars have primarily attempted to describe more syntactic constituents while investigations into discourse have been primarily concerned with more semantic (logical) or cognitive constituents.

Furthermore, the fact that complex sentences and discourses are not always clearly distinguishable must be dealt with. In written text, punctuation conventions distinguish the two. In spoken discourse, the distinction is much less apparent. To some extent the account of intersentence relations in discourse and constraints on derivations of complex sentences should be formulated in such a way as to assess the degree to which aspects of propositional sequencing are determined by the syntactic structure of sentences as opposed to the propositional structures in semantic memory.

Just as determinations must be made concerning the assignment of a specific constraint to the domain of the sentence grammar or the discourse grammar, so too it will be necessary to determine to what extent those constraints belong in either grammar as opposed to a general description of a perceptual or production device.

It will be necessary to determine whether complex constraints might be most parsimoniously accounted for by recourse to a description of the perceptual heuristics as opposed to some complex derivational constraints. The effect of such parsimony is to allow the grammar to state relevant generalizations about language. That is, just as Bever (1970) and Bever, Carroll, & Hurtig (1976) have argued that the grammar need not be burdened with complex derivational and transderivational constraints since certain aspects of complex linguistic constructions could be accounted for on the basis of an interaction between the grammar and a general theory of perception and production, so too at the level of the discourse it might be possible to account for certain complexities on the basis of an interaction of the grammar with certain perceptual and production heuristics rather than by some complex constraint on the structure of discourse units. Furthermore, the constraints might be due to nonlinguistic systems of knowledge (e.g., variables of social interaction, and the formal proporties of logical reasoning).

An important empirical question which speaks directly to the issue of such an interaction of various components of language is the degree to which linguistic context (discourse) has an effect on sentence processing heuristics as determined in a variety of studies in psycholinguistics over the past 10 years. We are currently studying in our laboratory the effect of linguistic contexts on the processing of sentence ambiguity. We are attempting to test the hypothesis that there is an effect of deep structure ambiguity at the level of immediate linguistic processing (following the paradigm of Bever, Garrett, & Hurtig, 1973, Exp. 2) even in the presence of an antecedent disambiguating context even though the discourse as a whole was not subject to ambiguous interpretation.

Our general hypothesis concerning the relationship of sentence grammar, discourse grammar and the psychological processes operative in the encoding of sentences and discourses is that the sentence (clause) is the on-line perceptual unit while the discourse (*idea set/logical event space*) is the unit of cognitive

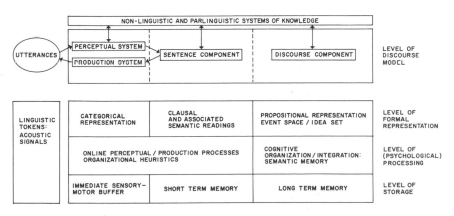

FIGURE 2   A functional model of discourse.

(semantic) memory. Put in other terms, the discourse is the cognitive organizational unit while the sentence (syntactic structure) is the production planning unit.

Such an hypothesis sees the existing research on both sentences and discourse in linguistics as well as psychology not as irreconcilable theories of linguistic behavior but rather as hypotheses concerning the various subcomponents of a *total language system* of the form represented in Fig. 2.

POSTSCRIPT

Traditionally, a discipline determines its own domain of investigation and is evaluated in terms of its success in meeting its theoretical goals. When two or more disciplines share a certain theoretical goal then it is not clear that their domain of investigation can be independently determined. It would seem that in the investigation of discourse, the disciplines of linguistics, psychology, and ethnomethodology share a theoretical goal. That is not to say that they are all interested in identical accounts of language. However, they do share the same object of analysis; the complex behavior of language. In that respect it becomes more difficult to determine what part of the behavioral complex reflects an aspect of the formal linguistic structure or of the behavioral apparatus which must realize that structure. Thus each discipline must proceed in cognizance of the general dimensions of the others. Just as the psychologist must account for the mapping of behaviors to abstract representations so too must the linguist take into account the effect of the behavior mechanisms in determining which apparent constraints or complexities are truly a function of the formal linguistic structure (abstract representation).

It is apparent that the discipline of linguistics or the psychology of language or ethnomethodology cannot be as simple as it used to be.

ACKNOWLEDGMENT

Supported by PHS Postdoctoral Training Grant # MH 08260-11

REFERENCES

Anderson, J., & Bower, G. A. *Human associative memory*. Washington, D.C.: Winston, 1973.

Bever, T. G. The cognitive basis for linguistic structures. In J. R. Hayes (Ed.), *Cognition and the development of language*. New York: Wiley, 1970.

Bever, T. G., Carroll, J., & Hurtig, R. R. Analogy or ungrammatical sequences that are utterable and comprehensible are the origins of new grammars in language acquisition and linguistic evolution. In T. G. Bever, J. J. Katz, & D. T. Langendoen (Eds.), *An integrated theory of linguistic ability.* New York: T. Y. Crowell Press, 1976.

Bever, T. G., Garrett, M. F., & Hurtig, R. R. The interaction of perceptual processes and ambiguous sentences. *Memory and Cognition,* 1973, **1**, 277–286.

Bever, T. G., & Hurtig, R. R. Detection of a nonlinguistic stimulus is poorest at the end of a clause. *Journal of Psycholinguistic Research,* 1975, **4**, 1–7.

Bever, T. G., & Rosenbaum, P. The implications of synonymy for the description of natural language. Lexington, Massachusetts: MITRE working paper, 1964.

Bransford, J. D., & Franks, J. J. The abstraction of linguistic ideas: A review. *Cognition,* 1973, **2**, 211–249.

Chomsky, N. *Aspects of the theory of syntax.* Cambridge, Massachusetts: MIT Press, 1965.

Chomsky, N. *Language and mind.* New York: Harcourt, Brace & World, 1968.

Crothers, E. J. Memory structure and the recall of discourse. In R. O. Freedle and J. B. Carroll (Eds.), *Language comprehension and the acquisition of knowledge.* Washington, D.C.: Winston, 1972.

Fodor, J., Bever, T. G., & Garrett, M. F. *The psychology of language.* New York: McGraw-Hill, 1974.

Frase, L. T. Associative factors in syllogistic reasoning. *Journal of Experimental Psychology,* 1968, **76**, 407–412.

Frase, L. T. Paragraph organization of written materials: The influence of conceptual clustering upon the level and organization of recall. *Journal of Educational Psychology,* 1969, **60**, 394–401.

Fredricksen, C. H. Effect of task induced cognitive operations on comprehension and memory processes. In R. O. Freedle & J. B. Carroll (Eds.), *Language comprehension and the acquisition of knowledge.* Washington, D.C.: Winston, 1972.

Freedle, R. O., & Graae, C. N. Unpublished research. Washington, D.C.: American Institutes for Research, 1965.

Gordon, D., & Lakoff, G. Conversational postulates. In *Papers from the 7th Regional Meeting,* Chicago Linguistic Society, 1971.

Grice, H. P. The logic of conversation. William James Lectures, 1967, Harvard University, Cambridge, Massachusetts.

Hurtig, R. R. Abstract ideas: The relation of linguistics and psychological time. Research Bulletin 74–54. Princeton, New Jersey: Educational Testing Service, 1974.

Jarvella, R. J. Syntactic processing of connected speech. *Journal of Verbal Learning and Verbal Behavior,* 1971, **10**, 409–416.

Jarvella, R. J. Coreference and short-term memory of discourse. *Journal of Experimental Psychology,* 1973, **98**, 426–428.

Jarvella, R. J., & Collas, J. G. Memory for the intentions of sentences. *Memory and Cognition,* 1974, **2**, 185–188.

Johnson, M. K., Bransford, J. D., & Solomon, S. K. Memory for tacit implications of sentences. *Journal of Experimental Psychology,* 1973, **98**, 203–205.

Katz, J. J. *Semantic theory.* New York: Harper & Row, 1973.

Katz, J. J., & Fodor, J. A. The structure of a semantic theory. *Language,* 1963, **39**, 170–210.

Katz, J. J., & Postal, P. *An integrated theory of linguistic description.* Cambridge, Massachusetts: MIT Press, 1964.

Kintsch, W. Notes on the structure of semantic memory. In E. Tulving & W. Donaldson (Eds.), *Organization of memory.* New York: Academic Press, 1972.

Koen, F., Becker, A., & Young, R. The psychological reality of the paragraph. *Journal of Verbal Learning and Verbal Behavior,* 1969, **8**, 49–53.

Lakoff, G. Linguistics and natural logic. *Studies in generative semantics, No. 1.* Ann Arbor, Michigan: University of Michigan, 1970.

Olson, D. R. Language use for communicating, instructing and thinking. In R. O. Freedle & J. B. Carroll (Eds.), *Language comprehension and the acquisition of knowledge*. Washington D.C.: Winston, 1972.

Sachs, J. S. Recognition memory for syntactic and semantic aspects of connected discourse. *Perception and Psychophysics*, 1967, **2**, 437–442.

Searle, J. R. *Speech acts, an essay in the philosophy of language*. Cambridge, England: Cambridge University Press, 1969.

Shegeloff, E., & Sacks, H. Opening up closings. *Semiotica*, 1973, **8**, 289–327.

Slamecka, N. J. Acquisition and retention of connected discourse as a function of contextual constraint. *Journal of Experimental Psychology*, 1964, **68**, 330–333.

Tulving, E. Episodic and semantic memory. In E. Tulving & D. Donaldson (Eds.), *Organization of memory*. New York: Academic Press, 1972.

Wertsch, J. V. The influence of listener perception of the speaker on recognition memory. *Journal of Psycholinguistic Research*, 1975, **4**, 89–98.

Wittgenstein, L. *Briefe an Ludwig von Ficker*, G. H. von Wright (Ed.) in collaboration with Walter Methlagl. Brenner Studien, Vol. I, Salzburg: Otto Müller, 1969.

5

Talk, Talk, Talk: A Selective Critical Review of Theories of Speech Production

Virginia Valian

CUNY Graduate Center

This chapter is selective in that it ignores speech production models that concentrate on syntactic or phonological levels of processing. Notably, it excludes Fromkin (1971), MacNeilage (1970), Whitaker (1971), and Yngve (1960). It includes Loundsbury (1965), McNeill (1975), Osgood (1963, 1971), and Schlesinger (1971a, 1971b, 1976), who have concentrated on higher-order levels of production. In the first part of the chapter five theoretical aims of a speech production theory are elaborated and the positions of Lounsbury, Osgood, Schlesinger, and McNeill with respect to each summarized. In the second part I present a critical analysis of each theorist, and conclude that each theorist fails for a similar underlying reason: an unwillingness to accord sufficient importance to a specifically linguistic component in the speech production process. Each theorist has a different set of reasons for emphasizing nonlinguistic aspects of production, so that different objections are used in criticizing each position.

AIMS OF A SPEECH PRODUCTION THEORY

Five aims are presented, but the first three are so interrelated that they are in fact different facets of the same aim.

1. To trace the course of production from the initiating idea to the speech expressing the idea. Tracing the course of production requires (a) characterizing the planning units, (b) determining the stages of production, and (c) determining the simultaneous and sequential aspects of planning. There are three major sorts of linguistic units: semantic, syntactic, and phonological. Within semantics would be larger units like the paragraph or smaller units like a complete thought (at present ill-defined notions); within syntax, units like the clause and phrase; within phonology, units like the phoneme. Whether the units can be neatly separated into different major types is unclear, as is whether all of the linguistic units are also psychological units, and vice versa.

Every theory must cope with the fact that production begins with an idea, a conceptual entity, and ends with speech, a linguistic entity. (This is on the assumptions that thought and language are not identical, and that thought does usually precede speech to some extent.) Thus, there must be stages in production, during which concepts are "translated" into structured speech. Each stage will then have its own set of units. To make a claim about units is to make an implicit claim about a particular level of processing, and perhaps also about how many levels of processing are presupposed.

All four theorists discussed here have assumed that planning units exist. Lounsbury proposed the stretch of speech between two pauses as the unit of semantic encoding; Osgood has suggested a variety of units, each appropriate to a different level of processing. McNeill discusses a conceptual unit which is the semiotic equivalent of a sensory—motor schema. For Schlesinger the initial unit is an input marker which contains concepts and their interrelations, similar in structure to a phrase marker. All four are thus concerned with units at an early stage of processing.

2. To isolate the determinants of production. The determinants of production are different: cognitive, linguistic, social, attentional, memorial, etc. A speech production theory must determine how many such major factors there are in speech, to what extent each factor is independent of the others, and in what ways interdependent with the others. A major focus has been the relationship between cognitive and linguistic factors. The factors Lounsbury isolates are syntactic, behaviorist, and probabilistic; that is, his approach combines information theory, S—R theory, and immediate-constituent analysis. Osgood substitutes a form of transformational grammar for immediate-constituent analysis, and retains the other two aspects. Recently he has added a suggestion that perceptual/cognitive events will determine the linguistic form of utterances. Schlesinger also has a behaviorist orientation, but one that combines cognitive factors and linguistic factors, with cognition as the primary determinant. McNeill takes a modified Piagetian position in claiming that action schemas are the basis for speech production; the schema organizes the syntagma, which "unites the organization of speech with the organization of meaning" (p. 18).

3. To account for speech phenomena. Most research in speech production involves naturalistic observation (for exceptions see Forster, 1968a, b; Jarvella, 1972; Lindsley, 1975; Valian, 1971) of such phenomena as where pauses and hesitations occur (Boomer, 1965; Blankenship & Kay, 1964; Goldman-Eisler, 1968, 1972; Maclay & Osgood, 1959), what kinds of speech errors occur (Fromkin, 1971; Garrett, 1975; Shattuck, 1974), changes in speech rate (Butterworth, 1975; Henderson, Goldman-Eisler, & Skarbek, 1966; Jaffe, Breskin, & Gerstman, 1972) and so on. Lounsbury predicted that speech hesitations would occur at points of maximal uncertainty in the speech stream, reflecting his information-theory orientation and providing the basis for the claim that the stretch of speech between two pauses is the primary unit of production. Osgood has also suggested that hesitations mark points of relative uncertainty in speech. McNeill predicts that the locus of hesitations will be related to syntagmas, but primarily discusses the correspondence between gestures and syntagmas. Schlesinger also discusses hesitations.

4. To relate production to perception. The relation between speech production and perception has been little explored, because so little is known about production. Lounsbury speculated, however, that the units of production and perception are different; Schlesinger (1976) considers comprehension and production.

5. To explain child acquisition of language. A theory of speech production must also explain the development of the production system. Schlesinger and McNeill have both explored this problem, and their theories of speech production are at the same time theories of child acquisition of language.

LOUNSBURY

Lounsbury (1965) and the early Osgood (1963) hold that linguistic structure plays a role in speech just insofar as it affects the strength of S–R connections and therefore transitional probabilities associated with a given juncture in speech. Lounsbury seeks to describe language by using the intersection of three approaches: S–R theory, information theory, and a linguistic theory that utilizes immediate-constituent analysis to segment sentences. Lounsbury conceives of speech production as governed by a sequence of S–R associations. The strength of the associations is reflected in transitional probabilities in actual sequences.

Linguistic Structure and Semantic Structure

Lounsbury offers five hypotheses, one of which is that pauses in speech will occur at points that correspond to points of maximal uncertainty (i.e., points of low transitional probability). According to Lounsbury, the linguistic structure of language and "the 'semantic structure' of the culture" are the two variables which most affect the fluency with which people produce speech and the ease with which they understand it. Linguistic structure accounts for "juncture pauses," those pauses which occur between constituents. Semantic structure accounts for longer pauses that tend to occur at points other than divisions between constituents.[1] Lounsbury compares extemporaneous speech and well-practiced speech. In the former case, he suggests, the pauses and uncertainties are due to the speaker's need to think out what is being said as it is being said; thus the location of pauses will be determined by the person's thought processes. In the second case, the pauses will simply reflect the linguistic structure of the material being presented, since no on-the-spot thinking is necessary and therefore there will be no interference with a smooth flow of material. In the case of well-practiced material, the production unit is a linguistic unit, since there will be no effect of semantic planning. Lounsbury also hypothesizes that the perception unit corresponds to the production unit for well-practiced speech. That is, the perception unit is linguistically defined.

How do the two influences, that of semantic structure and that of linguistic structure, fit together in the production (encoding) of speech? Lounsbury adopts Osgood's categorization of the encoding and decoding processes. According to this view, there are three "psychological" levels at which linguistic behavior is organized: a "representational level," an "integrational level," and a "projection" level. Higher-level units subsume lower-level units. Within each level, principles of S–R conditioning are assumed to be active. That is, although it is necessary to posit different levels and different types of processing (e.g., semantic, syntactic, phonetic) in order to account for behavior as complex as speech, it is not necessary to assume that any of these processes requires more than S–R mechanisms for successful operation. Events at a higher level will "reshuffle" the probabilities of events at a lower level.

S–R Sequences and Probability

The following picture of the speech production process emerges. A person has an "intention," which is a response to some previously occurring external or internal stimulus that has been perceived as meaningful. The "intention" is then a stimulus for units of semantic encoding. The particular unit evoked will then act as a stimulus at the next lower level of processing. The process continues until the smallest units have been evoked. At each level of the S–R sequences from habit-family hierarchies, the most probable response is evoked. The choice at a higher level will alter the lower-level probabilities. For example, the

---

[1] Lounsbury was under the impression that juncture pauses were 10 msec or less in duration, which is false (Boomer, 1965).

morphemes indicating verb tense will form a habit-family hierarchy with verbs: the collection of verbs is the stimulus, the possible endings the possible responses. The prevailing probability that a given ending will follow a given verb can be altered by higher-level events. If the present tense is the most probable "ending" but the intended speech is coding a past event, the probabilities will be reshuffled so that a past-tense ending will be evoked.

Speech itself, in this view, can be characterized as sequences of convergent habit-family hierarchies (a convergent hierarchy is one in which a variety of stimuli all evoke the same response). That is, the transitional probabilities from one word to the next become successively higher until the end of a semantic encoding unit is reached. At that point the transitional probability of the next word drops. The speaker pauses. Put another way, each successive word in a semantic unit becomes more and more determined and hence more and more probable. The last word of a unit is maximally probable. Lounsbury's empirical prediction is that hesitations will occur at points of low transitional probability.

Evidence against Lounsbury's Hypothesis

Although some empirical work has been interpreted as supporting Lounsbury (Goldman-Eisler, 1968; Maclay & Osgood, 1959), the data on hesitation loci are not uniform (Blankenship & Kay, 1964; Boomer, 1965) and in any event only indirectly test Lounsbury's hypothesis. (See Valian, 1971, for a more detailed review of this literature.) The one experiment which does directly test Lounsbury's hypothesis (Tannenbaum, Williams, & Hillier, 1965) contradicts it.

In that study subjects were presented with deleted versions of two passages (totaling 440 words and including 56 hesitations) which had been spoken orally by two other subjects as answers to questions. The deleted versions had every fifth word deleted, starting with the fifth, sixth, seventh, eighth, and ninth word, for each of five different groups. Thus subjects heard four words, a blank, and another four words. They were instructed to fill in the missing word. In this way the relative predictability of any word given antecedent and subsequent context, could be determined. The original material was separately examined to determine the positions of unfilled and filled pauses, false starts and repetitions. Each of the three words before and after each hesitation was scored for how difficult it was to guess.

If Lounsbury's hypothesis had been correct the words in the antecedent positions should have been increasingly predictable from furthest to closest to the pause, and the final antecedent word should have been much more predictable than the first subsequent word. In fact, however, the closest antecedent word to the pause was the least predictable of the three-word antecedent sequence, and there was no difference between the other two antecedent words. More importantly, there was no difference in predictability between the immediately antecedent word and the immediately subsequent word. There may be an effect of hesitation type, with filled pauses tending to confirm Lounsbury's hypothesis, but there were too few cases in Tannenbaum et al.'s sample to confirm the effect.

Arguments against Habit-Family Hierarchies

There are other, theoretical difficulties with Lounsbury's approach, such as his assumptions that language is a sequence of S–R associations which are part of habit-family hierarchies and that transitional probabilities are the correct way to capture language regularities. Many criticisms of the general assumptions have appeared (Bever, 1968; Chomsky, 1959; Fodor, Bever, & Garrett, 1974); the following discussion offers additional considerations and concludes that the notion of habit-family hierarchies is inappropriately applied to language use, and that the notion of probability cannot be meaningfully applied to language use.

As mentioned before, Lounsbury accounts for speech in terms of S–R mechanisms operating at different levels. Speech is viewed as a series of S–R associations and each association either is part of a divergent or convergent habit-family hierarchy. If a stimulus unit (word, morphome, whatever) evokes the same response unit (word, morpheme, etc.) as do other stimuli, then the association is a member of a convergent habit-family hierarchy. If, on the other hand, a stimulus unit evokes a variety of response units, then the association is a member of a divergent habit-family hierarchy.

The key assumption behind Lounsbury's approach is that language is appropriately described as a sequence of habit-family hierarchies, that there is "a constant and limited number of alternative events. . . ." That assumption will now be examined, both in the case where "events" means "types" and where it means "tokens," and shown to be false. A "type" refers to the class to which a given object, example, occurrence, etc., belongs. A "token," on the other hand, is an individual member of such a class. Tokens are datable and locatable, whereas types are not.

As Chomsky (1957) and others have pointed out, there is no longest sentence in any natural language and there is no limit to the number of unique sentences that can be produced in any language. If sentences are taken as a unit, there is not "a constant and limited number of alternative events." There are infinitely many "stimulus" sentences that have never been uttered before. Therefore, there are infinitely many S–R units that never occurred before and never will again. If membership in a habit-family hierarchy depends, as Lounsbury says, on either the stimulus or the response being a common member in a cluster of associations (i.e., every habit-family hierarchy must be either convergent or divergent) then language is inappropriately described as a sequence of hierarchies. Most utterances are novel, are neither part of a convergent nor a divergent hierarchy.

This is true even though the number of vocabulary items is finite at any given time. By recursive devices even a two-word vocabulary can be used to generate an infinite set of strings. If the two-word vocabulary were composed of "*a*" and "*b*," there could be a grammar which specified that

$$A \rightarrow ab$$
$$A \rightarrow aAb$$

where $\rightarrow$ means "is rewritten as," and only uncapitalized letters are words. By adding more rules, we would be able to generate strings that would not be solely of the "mirror-language" type. In other words, the sophistication of the rules, not the number of elements which the rules manipulate, is what allows us to generate sequences of unlimited length and an unlimited number of new sequences. Natural language has many recursive devices. In Mohawk, for example (Postal, 1964), even nouns are recursive. This means that indefinitely many new nouns can be formed by combining other nouns. Since language is recursive at the level of a word, a phrase, a sentence, etc., it is not true that, at any given level, there is a constant and limited number of alternatives.

Lounsbury's use of habit-family hierarchies can be attacked independently of the connection between hierarchies and probability. Not only are all utterance tokens novel, neither part of a convergent or divergent hierarchy, but there are no utterance types which are convergent hierarchies. As an example of a convergent hierarchy, Lounsbury offers one in which "a wide variety of stem morphemes converge upon a limited number of suffixes." In the case of stem morphemes and suffixes there are many "responses": "-ing," "-ed," "-s," "-en," no "response" at all, creating the question of what to do with a "no response" (which is the plural present tense of the verb in most cases), since this can "follow" any word at all. If a more abstract entity is placed in the "response" position and called a tense marker (since the regularity that needs to be captured is that all finite verbs have a tense) there are still problems.

1. How does one know what words to place in the stimulus position; that is, how are verbs recognized?

2. How can one account for words which do not exist at present but might in the future and will then take the same endings as present words? (New verbs are constantly being created: Xerox, trash, Vietnamize.)

The solution is to use the same level of abstraction on both sides of the hierarchy. If all verb suffixes are condensed to "tense marker," then condense all verbs to the category "verb." However, once the step of abstraction is taken the hierarchy disappears and the fact that all verbs can be tensed is represented in a simple statement. Thus, the example of Lounsbury's, which is the only one he offers, cannot be handled in terms of an S–R hierarchy.

Argument against Probability

It is important to distinguish the true probability of an occurrence and the estimate of the probability. The estimate of the probability is based on a finite number of cases and is thus subject to error, depending on how biased the sample is. In the case of language, the true probability of the occurrence of any sentence is effectively zero (Chomsky, 1964). There is an infinite number of possibilities from which the one sentence we are interested in will be drawn. Since almost all sentences which have ever been spoken or written are novel, single occurrences, there are very few occurrences on which to base a probability estimate. The only candidate phrases or sentences that have occurred often enough to base any sort of prediction on are clichés and idioms.

The point that the true probability of an utterance is effectively zero (excepting clichés and idioms) holds for conditional as well as absolute probability values. It might be thought that some contexts determine the occurrence of an utterance. For example, if someone is reading the Gettysburg address all the way through, the occurrence of the final sentence has a conditional probability approaching 1. Reading the Gettysburg address, however, is the equivalent of uttering an extended cliché and thus the case does not qualify as a counter-example. Utterances which are not extended clichés have a probability approaching 0, regardless of context, because almost all utterances are unique.

The objection to the use of probability estimates shifts somewhat if sentence or constituent types or content is used instead of individual utterances. The objection here is that probability estimates are functioning as placeholders for an explanation. To the extent that the estimates are valid predictors, it is because they are reflecting underlying regularities about language and language use. (See Bever, 1968, for a related discussion.) For example, assume that there is a limited number of grammatical phrases, such as noun phrase, verb phrase, and so on. The probability that a noun phrase will initiate a sentence could be computed, and would doubtless be quite high, say, .8. The calculation leaves at least two questions unanswered: (1) is there a rule-governed regularity that accounts for the estimate? (2) why is the probability .8 and not higher?

An examination of the structure of language offers an answer to both questions. The underlying structure of an English sentence is noun phrase followed by verb phrase, with recursion possible under noun phrase. This structure is the underlying regularity which the probability estimate attempts to capture. The estimate is not 1.0, even though all sentences (except conjoined sentences) have the structure noun phrase—verb phrase at the underlying level, because transformations can distort underlying structure (through deletion, insertion and permutation) and because underlying constituents can terminate in dummy symbols rather than lexical items. Thus, the objection to the probability estimate is that it offers too little information and thereby gives a misleading picture of language and language use.

The preceding discussion demonstrates that an attempt to capture intuitions about one's native language or to account for regularities of which all speakers are aware, must necessarily fail if based only on the surface structure of sentences. The regularities, such as what is the order of units in a sentence, cannot be stated at the level of surface structure because there are too many apparent counterexamples to the regularity. Transitional probabilities, which are based on surface structure, cannot capture deep structure regularities.

Summary

To summarize, the following three of Lounsbury's hypotheses can be criticized. Hypothesis 1 ("hesitation pauses correspond to the points of highest statistical uncertainty in the sequencing of units of any given order") must be rejected. When the unit is a word, where Lounsbury was "relatively hopeful for the substantiation of the hypothesis," there is no such relationship.

Hypothesis 2 ("hesitation pauses and points of high-statistical uncertainty correspond to the beginning of units of encoding") is perhaps accidentally true, since the first two tend to fall at grammatical junctures. On the other hand, it is definitely not the case that "the stretch of speech from one hesitation pause to the next is a convergent one, that is, one characterized by decreasing statistical uncertainty (increasing transitional probabilities)" which Lounsbury considered would be "strong support for claiming this [stretch] as a unit of encoding."

Hypothesis 3 ("hesitation pauses and points of high statistical uncertainty frequently do not fall at the points where immediate-constituent analysis would establish boundaries between higher-order linguistic units or where syntactic junctures or 'facultative pauses' would occur") must also be rejected, since points of high conditional grammatical entropy do tend to occur at grammatical junctures more than in between, although many pauses occur within phrases.

Finally, neither probability (as used by Lounsbury) nor habit-family hierarchies are useful concepts for language use.

OSGOOD

The early Osgood (1963) position is isomorphic to Lounsbury's. Osgood substitutes a transformational grammar for Lounsbury's immediate-constituent analysis; he substitutes a three-stage mediation theory for a simple Skinnerian one-stage model; like Lounsbury, he emphasizes the probabilistic character of language use. He claims that "an adequate theory of language behavior must be a learning theory, but . . . we neither wish nor require any special theory for language." The later Osgood (1971; Osgood & Bock, in press) emphasizes the role of perceptual and cognitive determinants of what people will say and how they will say it. In both his early and more recent writings Osgood emphasizes that a transformational grammar cannot provide a model of language use. Although true, the statement is largely irrelevant, since no one has ever suggested that a grammar alone provides a model of use; the competence—performance distinction rules the possibility out from the beginning.

The early and later Osgood are criticized separately. The early Osgood is criticized for his treatment of probability, the later Osgood for his treatment of perceptual and cognitive determinants.

Argument against Probability

For Osgood (1963), probability is a useful concept in describing all aspects of the speech production process:

> ... it is a probabilistic business going on at all levels in decoding, associating, and encoding. . . . "control" over behavior is simply the way in which combination and patterning within convergent hierarchies modifies the momentary probabilities of dependent alternatives. (p. 741)

And, "Transitional decisions at supraordinate levels modify the probabilities of units at subordinate levels, but only partially. . . ." (Osgood, 1963, p. 743).
Lounsbury (1965) states:

> The way in which events at superordinate levels reshuffle transitional probabilities at subordinate levels . . . can also be understood in terms of the effects of contextual stimuli upon modulating the 'average' structure of hierarchies. (p. 97)

The precise meaning of these statements is unclear. They seem to say that, depending on the situation, one alternative will become more likely than another, and the choice of this alternative will in turn make some other alternative more likely. This has a prima facie plausibility, but there is a "which-came-first-the-chicken-or-the-egg" regress that takes place if one tries to determine why, at any point, some alternative was the most probable. The only answer is that "combination and patterning within convergent hierarchies modifies (sic) the momentary probabilities of dependent alternatives." It is no use to ask what factors determine the "momentary probabilities." Somehow the probabilities of events are there, and are then reordered by subsequent events. These subsequent events, of course, must have their own probabilities of occurrence which can also be modified by other events.

So, for example, imagine that a friend and I go to a fun house, that having been the "momentarily most probable alternative" available. Since I am at the fun house and not in my office, a different set of speech alternatives will become more probable. But how can one calculate what the probability of any of the items in this set would have been if I had not gone to the fun house? One cannot compare the probability of saying "Well, here we are at the fun house" at the fun house versus at the office, because being at the office would make saying "Well, here we are at the fun house" even less likely than if I had been nowhere at all. That is, every situation "reshuffles" probabilities; but in order to reshuffle them, they had to have some value to begin with, some value before that value was altered by a particular situation. That neutral condition, however, is impossible to obtain. Perhaps it was in recognition of this problem that Lounsbury suggested that "contextual stimuli" modulate "the 'average' structure of hierarchies." That would suggest calculating the probability of saying "Well, here we are at the fun house" in a great many situations and then comparing that "average" probability with the probability that I will say it upon arriving at the fun house (should I ever go there). None of these suggestions is even remotely practicable.

More severe criticisms could be leveled against extensions of Osgood's (1971) use of probability. He writes:

> The still dominant view among generative linguists seems to be that surface forms of sentences are transforms of deeper forms which are themselves sentential in nature. Originally these deeper structures were thought to be "kernel" sentences of active, declarative form; during the past decade they have gradually become more abstract, but still forms of sentences. The implication of the very recent work on presuppositions, as well as of my little demonstrations, would seem to be that what is "transformed" into a surface sentence is not another "sentence" . . . but rather a momentary cognitive state which is not linguistic at all yet has its own complex semantic structure. (p. 519)

It makes no sense to talk about the probability of particular deep structures being reshuffled from occasion to occasion, which in turn reshuffles the probability of various transformations and surface structures. This is for two main reasons:

1. As was mentioned earlier, for probabilities to be reshuffled they must have some prior value, which is now being changed. We must know both values. If the prior value is itself a result of a reshuffling, it is biased. To determine the extent of its bias, we must know how much it was reshuffled, by examining its prior value. And so on. These frequencies of occurrence can never be calculated from some null state, because no null state exists. This criticism, of course, assumes that one can calculate the probability of a given deep structure under any conditions.

2. No deep structures, whether they are linguistic or perceptual, are ever spoken, so we would be in the unusual position of trying to calculate the probability of an abstract entity.

Perception as Determinant of Speech

Let us turn now to the evidence Osgood (1971) offers in support of the hypothesis that our percepts "drive" our speech. He conducted an experiment with a group of 26 adults, all of whom were native English speakers. He asked them to describe a series of 32 actions and events, involving his manipulation of items like cups, balls, tubes, poker chips and a plate. He instructed them to

> ... describe in a single sentence just what you see while your eyes are open; imagine that you are describing things for a hypothetical six-year-old child standing behind a hypothetical screen – that is, use simple ordinary language, not fancy scientific or philosophical jargon; refer to me as *the man* and other objects and events as you see fit. (p. 503)

Only two of his results will be discussed here. The others are more or less similar although intended to illustrate different aspects of the same point.

When an object is used in a sequence of events the number of adjectives used to describe that object diminishes from exposure to exposure, unless there is a large time gap between exposures, in which case the number of adjectives stays the same or increases. Osgood (1971) says,

> Quite evidently, as the speaker presupposes more familiarity with the referent [on the part of the listener], the less the frequency, diversity and complexity of his adumbrations on the head noun. (p. 513)

The presumption of listener familiarity is claimed to be derived from the actual experience of multiple exposure of an object; therefore, it is "perceptually based."

There is no quarrel with the explanation that the speaker gives as much information as (s)he thinks the listener requires and as much as (s)he thinks is relevant and that the amount needed decreases from exposure to exposure. Grice (1967) has developed a set of discourse rules for "conversational implicature" which explicate some of the principles governing conventional discourse. So, for example, although the question "would you like coffee or milk" can be answered with "yes," the answer demanded by the conversational maxim mentioned above (give as much information as is relevant) is "I'd prefer coffee" or "coffee, please" or some equivalent.

Linguistic Conventions Supersede Perception

What can be quarreled with is (first) the determination to anchor the origin of these implicatures in the perceptual experience rather than in people's knowledge of rules of grammar and usage, which Osgood thinks is a great advantage. It is clear from this experiment that the instructions and the subjects' adherence to rules of discourse played as important a role in their subsequent descriptions as did the events themselves. Events like those that occurred in Osgood's experiment happen all the time without comment on the speaker's part. Although these significant factors are not part of the grammar (though this is a matter of debate), they are also not perceptual, nor are they necessarily the result of perceptual events. The same results could have been obtained if Osgood had asked his subjects to close their eyes, had given them an elaborate description of each action and then asked them to describe in one sentence for his hypothetical six-year-old child the scene he had just described. Alternatively, if his instructions had been to describe each scene as if there had been no preceding ones, or to misdescribe each scene, the results would have been different. Thus, the perceptual events alone are neither a necessary nor a sufficient condition for particular speech forms, though there must obviously be enough input of some sort so that the subject will have something to talk about.

Osgood begins "Where do sentences come from?" by saying he is illustrating an obvious but not trivial point. It *is* obvious that if I want to talk about a black ball and a blue ball I will not find myself mistakenly discussing a plate and a tube. Nor will I report that the blue ball hit the black ball if it was the other way around. Nor will I say there were two black balls if I only saw one. It can hardly be a surprise that certain aspects of our language behavior are systematic and rule governed. One of the functions of language is communication and to communicate successfully there must be rules of usage as well as rules of grammar. It is also not surprising that an experiment would show that, just as in real life, when people want to use a count noun to refer to more than one object, they manage to pluralize the noun. Having a convention means that people think they ought to follow it; that is what makes it a convention.

Another of Osgood's results is that when people describe an action, they correctly identify the person initiating the action and the thing acted upon. For example, when a man rolls a ball along a table, people do not get confused and describe a table rolling a ball along a man. Osgood says, "The obvious effect of perceptual 'case' [actor, object of action, etc.] upon sentential case seems to be confirmed" (Osgood, 1971, p. 508). This seems to be a misstatement of the phenomenon, a way of making the phenomenon seem almost surprising. What has been demonstrated is that language offers us the means to describe our experiences and perceptions, to express ourselves. This would seem to be a rudimentary requirement for a language. It is not because the events happened a certain way that the subjects described them as they did; the perceptual situation itself was neither a necessary nor sufficient condition. It is because the subjects were asked to describe what they saw, in a particular way, and because language allows people to express themselves. The perceptual conditions were a backdrop; in this case they were utilized. If perception alone controlled description, people would continually be describing their environment.

There is again an interaction with probability, in that the phenomenon of choosing one syntactic realization over another operates probabilistically. Osgood (1963, p. 743) says, "what follows what within the noun phrase or within the verb phrase is in part optional and therefore probabilistically determined." And again " . . . performance theories must deal with real speaker—hearers who are both fallible and variable, i.e., perform probabilistically . . . " (Osgood, 1971,

p. 521). The conclusion that behavior is probabilistic because it is variable or because it represents one choice out of many does not follow. Variability can be orderly and rule governed. Indeed, Osgood's own results, even his own discussions of some of these results, make it explicit that the subjects' behavior was rule governed.

In a more recent paper Osgood and Bock (in press) develop a model of cognition and speech production, in which the results discussed above are reinterpreted. In particular, the model is more specific about the nature of the perceptuo-cognitive principles which determine word order than was Osgood's (1971). The principles are a refinement of Wundt's suggestion that the most emphasized concept in a sentence appears first. Implications of the three principles are briefly discussed here. Only one of the principles, the naturalness principle, can be called perceptual. It consists of two parts, one of which states that the figure/ground relation finds its reflection in speech in the ordering of figure elements first and ground elements second. The suggestion is intriguing, although a separate theory will be needed to show how the principle can be extended to cover abstract figure/ground relations.

The second part requires that people automatically perceive events in terms of an actor, action, and object and in that order; the speech order reflects the perceptuo-cognitive order. The principle is ad hoc. It is appealed to solely to explain the common word order of actor—action—object; no independent motivation is offered. The only evidence supporting the principle is the result it was created to explain. Even if it is true that perception proceeds as outlined by Osgood and Bock, it remains to be shown that the perception is not parasitic on the linguistic concepts of actor, action and agent. (McNeill makes a similar proposal; the criticisms applied to it below are also applicable here.)

The second of Osgood and Bock's principles, vividness, is more promising than the second part of the naturalness principle, because it can be independently defined. For example, an item is vivid if it is highly meaningful, infrequent, highly imageable, and extremely positive or negative in affect. (It is not clear if "item" refers to the actual object or to the word designating the object.) Although the vividness principle is less important than the naturalness principle, Osgood and Bock show that more vivid items tend to be placed earlier in a sentence. Vividness, then, offers a more precise way of defining Wundt's emphasized concepts, but it is not perceptually anchored in the way the figure/ground relation is. The third principle, speaker motivation, at present amounts to little more than a paraphrase of Wundt. It states that speakers will place first in a sentence that which they wish to emphasize.

Osgood and Bock's principles may be seen as attempts at an initial specification of the rule systems governing language use. The principles reduce the question of whether percepts and concepts "drive" speech to a terminological issue. Certainly the content and form of speech are rule determined; this was never in doubt (except for theorists for whom probability is a central notion).

Some of the rules are linguistic and psycholinguistic; some are cognitive, social, and so on. In the final section of the present paper the proper role of such extralinguistic factors in a theory of speech production is discussed.

SCHLESINGER

Schlesinger (1971a; 1971b; 1976) has presented a theory of speech production which, he claims, makes it unnecessary to posit any syntactic structures underlying language use and therefore makes unnecessary any recourse to innate rules which are peculiar to language. The theory has changed somewhat since 1971; in the 1971 papers, Schlesinger postulates two concepts, the I-marker and realization rules. The I-marker represents the speaker's intentions in the form of "conceptual" entries and the relations that hold among them; realization rules convert these I-markers into utterances. I-markers are part of our innate cognitive, as opposed to linguistic, equipment. They are roughly equivalent to underlying structures, or P-markers, in that for each P-marker there is a corresponding I-marker. The difference between them is that I-markers contain semantic information that P-markers lack and I-markers lack purely syntactic information that P-markers possess. Realization rules are roughly equivalent to transformations. They map I-markers on to utterances. They differ from transformations, however, both in terms of what objects they will accept as input and in terms of the operations they perform on those objects.

The goal of Schlesinger's theory is to show that empiricist learning theories can account for language acquisition and language use. Since the relations contained in I-markers are innate cognitive universals (and thereby also linguistic universals) there is nothing in the I-marker that a child must learn in acquiring language. All that must be learned is a correspondence between I-markers and utterances. Although this is not a trivial task, Schlesinger says, it is one which an empiricist learning theory can explain. In this way, as a learning theorist he need not prove the impossible, that abstract structures can be acquired through experience, nor need he accept the innateness of a language ability which is distinct from general cognitive abilities.

In his more recent work, Schlesinger (1976) suggests that I-markers do, after all, contain linguistic material and that I-markers representing the same cognitive message will differ from one language community to the next. Thus, in addition to I-markers there are cognitive structures, which are universal and innate. Schlesinger continues to reject the innateness of any language-specific knowledge, offering as partial evidence an experiment intended to test Chomsky's (1968) hypothesis that structure-independent rules cannot be learned. He also maintains the claim that syntactic relations like "subject of" can be derived from semantic roles like "agent."

The main arguments against Schlesinger's formulation will take two forms here; first, to show that one of his premises is incorrect, that is, to show that there are syntactic relations which play a role in speech and cannot be derived from semantic relations; second, to show that his theory so duplicates transformational grammar as to incorporate the very information he claims is superfluous,[2] to show that his theory would fail to account for language use if this information were removed.

I-Markers, Intentions, and Situations

What is an I-marker? "Let us use the term *input marker,* or *I-marker,* for the formalized representation of those of the speaker's intentions which are expressed in the linguistic output" (Schlesinger, 1971a, p. 65). It contains nonverbal elements and semantic relations between them. The input is thus some form of the speaker's intentions, the output is what the speaker says, and realization rules operate on the former to produce the latter. An immediate objection concerns the notion of intention; Schlesinger tries to make "intentions" do too much work. When someone talks they (a) have some content to express, as well as (b) having motives for saying it in a particular way, intentions about the effect it will have, etc. The two aspects of speech can and should be distinguished. Without the distinction, Schlesinger (1971a) has problems, as in the following example:

> The I marker is inferred from situational cues. When the mother points to a ball and says: "Give me the ball," the task of the child consists in learning to associate the I marker representing the situation, with the utterance he hears. (p. 69)

In the example the information presented the child is too impoverished for the child to infer the speaker's intention. The mother could, equally plausibly, be intending to give her child a lesson in obedience, grammar, vocabulary, etc.

One can infer, or rather, understand, what the sentence "Give me the ball" means, but that is different from determining what I-marker represents the situation, since the sentence meaning and the situation are not the same. The sentence the mother speaks and her pointing to the ball are only small parts of the situation, and the only parts the child needs to attend to and understand in order to respond appropriately to the sentence. How can Schlesinger explain that the one or two relevant aspects of the situation, among so many nonrelevant ones, are singled out? Any representation which truly covered the entire situation in this example would be far too rich a stimulus for the child to associate with the utterance. There are indefinitely many features of the situation which are true for this situation and no other, although the utterance will continue to have the same meaning. Indeed, the utterance will always have the same literal meaning no matter what situation it occurs in. Schlesinger's trouble

---

[2] Independently, Rosenberg (1972) has made the same criticism.

here is his reliance on cognitive universals. If they are to be brought into the picture there must be some way of eliminating all the irrelevant ones for any given situation and this Schlesinger fails to give.

To put the objection another way, how does the child know which features of the situation are relevant unless it has understood the sentence already? If someone is put into a foreign language community and a speaker says, pointing to a ball, "Give me the ball," in that foreign language, the listener has everything the child in Schlesinger's example has but can only guess what to do. Maybe the speaker is saying that the pointed-to object is a ball, or that the listener should be sure not to touch it because it belongs to someone else. Unless the listener already knows the language the appropriate association between the stimulus situation (or the I-marker representing it) and the speaker's utterance cannot be effected. Schlesinger (1976) is careful to state that an I-marker representing a situation should not be interpreted to mean that an I-marker represents the entire situation, but only those aspects of it which are verbalized in the utterance. The cognitive structures represent the remaining situational elements. Such a qualification is useless because it is circular. There is no independent way to determine the content of an I-marker.

Even though the qualification is unsatisfactory, the above objections concern the impossibility of learning language by association, and do not directly affect Schlesinger's claim that syntax is superfluous in a production mechanism. An examination of that claim follows.

Semantic Roles and Syntactic Relations

Schlesinger (1971a) handles the problem of how thought is mapped into speech in two ways: first by stating that the I-marker represents only cognitions but does so in such a form that purely linguistic rules can operate on them to produce speech; second by assuming that realization rules (rules which operate on I-markers) are not abstract and can be directly inferred from experience in a language community.

Schlesinger's (1971a) goal is to begin with solely cognitive material represented in the form of I-markers. Realization rules will operate on these I-markers to order each of the conceptual elements contained within them and to assign each element a grammatical category. Thus, these rules have the job of turning cognitive input into linguistic output. For this to work Schlesinger must assume (1) that it is meaningful to speak of deriving categories from relations; and (2) that case relations can be mapped in a uniform way onto grammatical relations.

As Schlesinger states, in generative transformational theory, grammatical relations are defined in terms of grammatical categories. The P-marker represents the categories and their dominance relations. Within this framework it is not meaningful to ask if the derivation could go the other way around, if grammatical categories could be defined in terms of grammatical relations. By definition, it is impossible. The relations exist by virtue of some categories being rewritten as other categories.

After the first step of noting the grammatical relations are defined in terms of categories, Schlesinger goes on to say that I-markers contain relations from which categories can be derived. Notice that the relations contained in I-markers are not grammatical relations, but thematic or case relations, because, according to Schlesinger, people perceive the world in terms of relations between actors and actions and not in terms of nouns and verbs. Thus, Schlesinger implies that grammatical categories can be derived from case relations. This in turn seems to imply that there is a sufficiently close correspondence between grammatical relations and case relations, such that case relations will map onto grammatical relations and grammatical categories will be derived from grammatical relations. In Schlesinger's forthcoming monograph, the relations in I-markers are not cognitive, and are partly linguistic but still do not contain syntactic relations like "subject of."

The same basic criticisms can thus be made of both the old and new versions of Schlesinger's theory: (1) semantic roles, no matter how collapsed, will not correlate uniformly with syntactic relations; (2) neither syntactic categories nor syntactic relations are, in Schlesinger's schema, genuinely derived categories and relations; rather, they are stated as primitives and correspondences are drawn. Thus, Schlesinger has not eliminated the separate status of grammatical categories and relations. Since the first of the two criticisms is more important, it will be elaborated at length.

Schlesinger (1971a) assumes that the role of agent will be converted into a subject noun phrase and object into object noun phrase. In response to Bowerman's (1974) examples of sentences where the subject is not an agent, Schlesinger (1976) tries to "assimilate" all nonagent relations to agenthood. Aside from the fact that Schlesinger offers no independent motivation for such "assimilation," and that the assimilation is achieved by pointing to the existence of cases where it is difficult to assign a semantic role (rather like saying that there is no conceptual difference between a teapot and a coffeepot because some pots are hard to assign to either category uniquely), neither Bowerman's examples nor Schlesinger's reply are exactly to the point. Appropriate counterexamples are cases where the semantic roles in two sentences are identical but (1) other semantic aspects can only be defined given a level of syntactic deep structure or (2) where the same semantic role is sometimes expressed as syntactic subject and sometimes as syntactic object. Both counterexamples exist.

Semantic Interpretation Is Dependent on Syntactic Deep Structure

The first is given in Anderson (1971) and Mellema (1974), who present arguments against Fillmore's (1968) case grammar. Anderson points out that the following two sentences have the same case relations:

Bees are swarming in the garden.
The garden is swarming with bees.

In both the bees are the agent and the garden is the locus. The two sentences do not, however, have the same meaning: the first leaves open how large a part of the garden the bees are swarming in; in the second the whole garden is swarming with bees. Anderson calls this property the holistic—partitive feature. He demonstrates that this property depends on the grammatical relations *subject of* and *object of.* Anderson's hypothesis is that if the verb is intrasitive (as in "swarm"), its noun is holistic in subject position (as with "garden") and unspecified with respect to holistic—partitive in object position. He gives several other examples which make the same point. Thus, there are two syntactic pieces of information which are needed to correctly represent sentences of this type: type of verb, a category which does not enter Schlesinger's scheme until realization rules assign an element to a part of speech; subjecthood, a relation which is determined before transformations are applied. These can only be determined at a syntactic level. The example shows that the semantic component must be given certain syntactic information in order to compute a full and correct semantic interpretation. Neither a case grammar, nor, by implication, I-markers, present the information.

The example thus illustrates some of the difficulties with case grammars in general and Schlesinger's modification in particular. The formal apparatus for representing the case relations between these two sentences is the same, which is already something of a failure: it represents two nonsynonymous sentences as having the same semantic relations, and provides no other place for representing their difference in meaning. The theory cannot be patched up by an effort to incorporate the holistic—partitive distinction at the level of the I-marker for two reasons. First, the distinction requires information about subject or object of the verb; that is, it requires syntactic information not present in I-markers. Second, there is no principled way of separating the holistic—partitive distinction from other grammatical distinctions which one would *not* want to include at the I-marker level because they would not have semantic import.

Converse Relations and Syntactic Relations

The second counterexample concerns sentences that exhibit converse relations, like (1), and (2). The following two sentences are fully synonymous (as Schlesinger, forthcoming, also notes):

(1) Jane sold the book to Mary.
(2) Mary bought the book from Jane.

The characters also play the same semantic roles in both sentences. Jane is the seller, or agent, in (1) and (2); Mary is the buyer, or recipient in both (1) and

(2). (The designations "agent" and "recipient" are not crucial; the important point is that the roles remain identical.) Yet, though "Jane" is the agent in (1) and (2), it is the syntactic subject (deep structure as well as surface structure) in (1) and the direct object (deep and surface) in (2). Thus, (1) and (2) are sentences where the semantic role of agent is not mapped into the syntactic relation of subject. Katz (1972) argues that the sentences cannot derive from the same deep structure because, among other reasons, there is no motivation for taking either of the two forms to be syntactically basic (that is, to be the form from which the other is derived), nor for postulating a syntactically "neutral" form from which (1) and (2) would derive.

Schlesinger has two options in dealing with the counterexample. He can postulate one cognitive structure (necessary because the sentences are synonymous) and two different I-markers, from which the two different sentences would automatically result. It is not clear, however, by what principle the two different I-markers will be produced. What distinguishes the two sentences is what the subject—object relations are, in conjunction with what the verb is. But neither the cognitive structure nor the I-marker contains syntactic information like "subject of."

The other option is to postulate one cognitive structure and one I-marker, with different realization rules producing the two different sentences. Since I-markers do not contain syntactic information, however, the option requires that realization rules inject syntactic structure, which is what the model was designed to avoid. The realization rules cannot appeal to lexical differences between "buy" and "sell" because I-markers contain only protoverbal elements not actual lexical items; the only difference between "buy" and "sell" is the subject—object difference and that cannot be placed in the I-marker. Thus, the counterexample seems compelling.

Duplication of Transformational Grammar

The two counterexamples demonstrate that Schlesinger's system fails in part because it omits information present at the level of syntactic deep structure. If the information were inserted the model would work, but the difference between the model and transformational grammar would be the difference between a performance model and the competence model it incorporates. There would not be a difference in the independent status accorded to syntax.

An Experiment on "Language" Learnability

The objections presented thus far indicate that Schlesinger's model is inadequate because it gives insufficient importance to syntactic variables. The attempt to demonstrate the superfluity of syntax fails not only at the theoretical level but also at the experimental level. Schlesinger (1976) presents the results of an experiment designed to bear on Chomsky's (1965, 1968) claims that there are innate linguistic constraints on the language acquisition device, in particular, that transformations are structure-dependent. The claim was tested by having two groups of third-graders learn two types of artificial language of a few "sentences." In one set of sentences agenthood was marked by the presence of a suffix; in the other it was marked by the repetition of the agent term. The first was intended to mimic a standard linguistic device, the second a nonlinguistic device. Both sentence sets were learned equally easily.

There are two objections. The first is that Schlesinger must demonstrate that the children were approaching the sentence sets in the same way as they would approach learning a language, rather than playing a game. The second is that morpheme duplication is a linguistic device, so that the experiment is irrelevant. Postal (1964) uses the example of Mohawk to demonstrate that context-free phrase structure grammars are inadequate. In Mohawk reduplication occurs if the object of a sentence is preceded by a modifier. Under this condition the stem of the object noun is incorporated in the verb, and is also present in its usual position. Considerably more complex duplication also occurs. Mohawk differs from Schlesinger's artifical language in that the duplication is not marking a case of syntactic relation but it is marking a rather intricate syntactic state of affairs.

Summary

To summarize, similar objections to those leveled against case grammar can be leveled against I-markers. Schlesinger has not shown that syntactic information can be derived from I-markers and sometimes has no choice but to include syntactic information within I-markers. The experimental data also fail to demonstrate that syntactic devices are a subset of general learning principles.

McNEILL

McNeill's most recent (1975) theorizing marks a departure from his earlier (1966; 1970; 1971) models of child acquisition of language. His early work stresses the innate, language-specific base of speech behavior. Language is not a derived skill which represents a specialized form of cognitive activity, it is biologically determined. In his presentation of strong and weak linguistic universals, however, McNeill (1971, p. 38) introduced the possibility that some linguistic universals ("weak" ones) were derived from cognition and perception, while others ("strong" ones) were derived not just from cognition and perception, but also from a "strictly linguistic" ability.

McNeill's new model represents linguistic ability as a development of the child's sensory—motor action schemas, which development has empirical consequences in adult speech production. In brief, McNeill claims that the interiorization of action schemas is the prerequisite for speech onset; that the dependence on action schemas is visible in the internal sequencing of children's first utterances; that adult gesture patterns reveal this continued dependence; that action rather than perception is the basis of the child's first multiword utterances; and that speech confers abilities that transcend the limitations of the original action schemas. The evidence McNeill presents for his argument draws on both child and adult speech.

The following critique analyzes the internal coherence of McNeill's argument and the quality of the evidence used to support it. The primary facts that McNeill's theory is intended to explain are the child's early sequencing of words once the child moves beyond the one-word stage, and the adult's positioning of gestures. In terms of the aims of a theory of speech production discussed above, McNeill is concerned to explain the link between child and adult speech, the role of cognition in language, and the determination of speech units.

The Necessity of Interiorization

With respect to children, McNeill wants to explain why some relations are consistently ordered in time, such as the actor—action relation, and others are not, such as action—object. For McNeill, patterned speech becomes possible as a result of the child's interiorization of sensory-motor action schemas. As each schema becomes interiorized the child synchronizes it with a speech action schema describing it. Until an action schema is interiorized, patterned speech describing that action is impossible. (Although McNeill's use of action schemas is inspired by the work of Piaget, 1962, 1963, it is not consonant with Sinclair-de Zwart's, 1973, interpretation of the implications of the Piagetian position on child language acquisition. Sinclair is discussed briefly below.) McNeill (1975) puts it as follows:

> ... the action schemas that guide speech have to be mentally representable. The speech action replaces, as it were, the original action in the process of forming the syntagma. Like any overt action, the action of speech cannot be differentiated from the underlying action schema that guides it; therefore, the original action based on the action schema must be differentiated in order for patterned speech to occur. (p. 367)

This is the central aspect of McNeill's theory. Since speech describing an action can occur simultaneously with the action, however, he finds it necessary to supplement the theory by specifying that what allows for the emergence of patterned speech is the reorganization of the action pattern guiding speech which is effected when interiorization takes place. Interiorization, in McNeill's view, is analogous to taking a photograph, such that actor, action, and object are integrated, while the parts and their relation to each other are maintained. Thus, interiorization is necessary, but the absence of actual action patterns is not necessary in order for an action schema to guide the speech schema.

McNeill offers no arguments for the necessity of interiorization. He also does not offer a mechanism whereby interiorization effects integration of an action schema. He accepts without argument the Piagetian account of the development of action patterns. These considerations to one side, one can examine the predictions McNeill makes about children's word order, how the predictions are derived from his model, and whether the predictions are confirmed by data. McNeill compared different types of action patterns in terms of the temporal ordering of actor, action, object, location, etc., and makes predictions about the ordering of relations like agent and action in children's early sentences.

Word Order Predictions

For example, McNeill analyzes the action of placing an object in a location, stating that the location must be the endpoint of the action and is separable from the action itself, while the action of moving the object cannot be temporally separated from the object being moved. Thus, one would expect that utterances expressing the location of an object would always specify the location last, and either the action or the object first. When there is no movement of the object, nor the logical possibility of any movement, there will be no inherent ordering of object and location, and thus no uniform word order in children's speech. As empirical evidence for this claim, McNeill cites various data of children's speech.

There are several criticisms of McNeill's argument. First, it is not clear in what sense objects and actions are the same sorts of things, such that it makes sense to speak of them as being or not being ordered. Second, in the case of movement locatives, not only is there a final location, but an initial location. Why, on McNeill's theory, should the child fail to mention the initial location, which it does in fact usually ignore? Third, McNeill's claim about the nonorderability of objects and actions would seem to imply that object + location and action + location constructions would appear equally frequently in early child speech. Yet Bowerman (1973) speculates that object + location constructions precede action + location constructions: this was the case for one of her subjects; Bloom's subjects, who were studied at an early stage of development, uttered no action + location constructions, but only object + location constructions.

Fourth, McNeill's distinction between movement and nonmovement locatives on the basis of the logical possibility of movement, seems impossible to draw. It is logically possible for almost anything to be moved. McNeill distinguishes between "pillow here," where the object could be moved, and "mess here," "here mess," "there cow," "ear outside," all of which could not be moved. Cows and ears, however can be moved. Messes are a more delicate matter, since it depends in part on what kind of mess is being talked about. If the mess is the kind that a room can be, then it is true that it does not make much sense to speak of its being able to be moved, but it also seems not to make much sense to speak of the mess being "in" the room; rather, "mess" is a way of describing the condition of the room. To the extent that it does make sense to talk of the mess being in the room, it also makes sense to talk of having moved the mess from the living room to the bedroom when doing some emergency house cleaning.

Word Order Data

Fifth, the data are more refractory than McNeill suggests. There are occasional reversals to the pattern of putting the locative word last. For Bowerman's Kendall (1973), there are:

Doggie slipper (M has recently been talking about putting the slipper on the doggie)
in Daddy (K is preparing to close door on D, who is in the room)
door . . find (K exiting to find D, who she thinks is hiding. Perhaps she thinks he is hiding behind a door.)
back doggie (K putting toy dog behind her on sofa)
inna Mommy (K wants to come in past screen door; K is outside and M is sitting just inside)

There are two cases in which the initial location is mentioned:

Kendall foot (K wants to take her shoe off)
tummy off (K wants shirt off her tummy)
(pp. 238, 239)

When the locative word is "here" or "there," the situation is even more complicated, since it is not clear whether these words are being used locatively or as existential markers. For English speaking children these words occur so often in initial position that investigators initially interpreted them as evidence for pivot grammars (see Bowerman, 1973; Braine, 1963; Brown & Fraser, 1963, for presentation of these data). They also occur in final position. This is problematic for McNeill, because if they are taken as examples of movement locatives they should occur only at the end of the utterance.

For the two Finnish children Bowerman studies, the data do not unequivocally support McNeill's thesis that object will precede location. Bowerman (1973) catalogues the frequency of various word orders in their speech (pp. 163–164). For Seppo at MLU 1.42, there were four cases of object + location and two of location + object; two of object + prolocative, three of prolocative + object; none of action + location, and one of location + action. For Rina at MLUs 1.83 and 1.82, there are three cases of object + location, none of location + object; sixteen of object + prolocative, 97 of prolocative + object; two of action + prolocative, seven of prolocative + action; six of agent + action + location, two of agent + location + action, four of location + agent + verb, two of location + action + agent and one of action + agent + location. Thus, the orders McNeill predicts exist, but so do the orders he does not predict.

Unmotivated Word Order Predictions

More serious logical criticisms can be leveled against McNeill, as an analysis of his predictions regarding the order of agent—action and object—action will make clear. McNeill (1975) says:

> There is a necessary sequence in the performance of any action where the actor is ego, since the intention to act must precede the action itself. Furthermore, insofar as the actions of other people or the actions of objects are assimilated to the same action schemas as organize ego's own actions, this order preference would extend to all actor and action sequences, as has been reported. (p. 364)

This is contrasted with the predicted nonordering for object and action:

> Now, there is no basis in the actual performance of an action for an ordering of the action and its object. (Object in this case does not mean a physical object, but the conceptualization of the object of an action.) The object upon which the action operates is not separable from the action; it does not become the object of the action until the action (or the intention to act) occurs. Thus, the action schema relating action and objects is indeterminate for word order. (p. 364)

The attempt to separate the two types of utterances on the basis of the underlying action schemas is unsuccessful: It is no more possible to separate the agent from its action (intended or actual) than to separate the object from the action. Just as the object does not become the object until the action takes place, so the agent does not become the agent until the action (or intention to act) takes place.

Even if we accept, counterfactually, that an intention to act must precede an action, the intention does not guarantee that the agent "precedes" the action. (It is incorrect to suppose that an intention to act always precedes action, since in the situation described by the sentence "Jane walked in her sleep," Jane is the agent of the action of sleepwalking even though she did not intend to sleepwalk.) The agent is inseparable from the action even in its nonactual, intended form. That is, if a child intends to act in a certain way, say it intends to run, the intention will include both the child as agent and the action of running; one will not be able to assign an order to the two concepts within the intention. This is not to say that the child could not think just about itself, as some sort of generalized agent, or could not think just about running, as some sort of generalized action, but that in this case the child would not be having an intention to act. It would be thinking about the concept of being an agent, and the concept of running.

In the case of the ordering of action and agent, there is also the problem mentioned earlier that agenthood and actionhood are not clearly things which it makes sense to talk about being ordered. Words can be ordered, actions can be ordered (and simultaneous), but agents and actions seem like apples and oranges.

McNeill (1975) attempts a similar argument about possession. He claims that the order possessor—possessed object is predicted on the grounds that it corresponds " . . . to the necessary action sequence involved when the possessor manually takes the (alienable) possessed into possession." (p. 365). Again, the possessor does not become a possessor until in the act of possessing, so that there is no basis for McNeill's prediction. A retreat to intention to possess is also inadequate, because in the intention itself the child is not a possessor unless in the act of possessing.

In summary, McNeill's use of the action schema as a basis for predicting child word orders seems logically unmotivated and not sufficiently supported by the data.

Criticism of Interiorization

Next is the question of why McNeill takes interiorization of action schemas to be a prerequisite for patterned speech. According to his argument, the child must line up the schema for speech, that is, the syntagma, with the action schema guiding it. He does not explain why it should be easier to line up the syntagma with the interiorized schema than with the external action schema itself. It cannot be because it is hard to perform two action schemas simultaneously, since one can talk about one thing while doing another. McNeill (1975) suggests that "there is a kind of snap-shot of the entire integrated action when this is interiorized as a pattern, which includes the significant parts of the action, how they are interrelated, and their sequences" (p. 368). It is not clear what advantage this serves for the child with respect to patterned speech, unless the suggestion is that the child does not know what the significant parts of the action, their interrelations and sequence are until interiorization takes place.

The suggestion has an initial plausibility, but unfortunate implications. It means that whenever the child repeats an action schema it is doing so by accident, since unless the child has the ability mentally to represent actions and states of affairs it will only be able to act either instinctively or unintentionally. Intentions are possible only if mental representation exists. Therefore, to claim that the 18-month-old child is not capable of mentally representing actions and states of affairs is also to claim that the child's behavior is profoundly not what it seems, that its repetitive behaviors are not intentional. The claim may be correct, but it remains to be demonstrated.

Gesture Location

Moving on to adults, McNeill suggests that his model provides an explanation for the locus of gestures and for the difficulty adults have in describing noninteriorized, unfamiliar actions. McNeill (1975) asked subjects to perform familiar and unfamiliar actions, such as tying a knot and assembling an aquarium heater and to describe their actions simultaneously. He gives examples of speech with the accompanying gestures to show that in unfamiliar actions subjects alternate acting and speaking, while in familiar actions the action and description coincide. When asked to describe mental paper folding, subjects' gestures "are initiated with the onset of the speech associated with action schemas" (p. 376). When subjects are discussing more abstract matters, the gestures persist at the beginnings of words which correspond to action schemas.

An analysis of this argument requires a more detailed look at McNeill's use of the terms "syntagma," "action schema," and "semantic relationship." In Table I, as taken from McNeill (1975), the speech of a subject is presented broken down into syntagmas, and correlated with the accompanying gestures. Each action schema is labeled.

McNeill's use of schema is broad. An object, action, location, or state are all action schemas. An action schema, then, is apparently not a patterned action of some sort, but is an agent of an action, a consequence of an action, what have you. It is here that the distinction between McNeill and Sinclair-de Zwart is particularly salient. With respect to linguistic expressions of the young child, Sinclair-de Zwart (1973) says:

> At first the child expresses a (possible) action pattern related to himself, in which agent, action and eventual patient are inextricably entwined. Second, he either expresses the result of an action done by somebody else (but not the action—object link in that case), or an action he performs or is going to perform himself. (p. 23)

> In general one can say that . . . holophrases accompany in the present an action done by the child or interesting to the child; or they express a desire for an action the child wants to perform or to have performed immediately by someone else. (pp. 22, 23)

TABLE 1

Utterance Samples Divided into Syntagmas and Correlated with Gestures and Action Schemas[a]

	Utterance	Gesture[b]	Schema
Syntagma A	One thing	H to R	Object
	I found	H up and down	Action
	about	H in arc	Location
	this um	None	Object
Syntagma B	I − it is correct	H to R, down, up	State
	that	None	None
Syntagma C	That	None	Object
	should be	None	None
	a very difficult task	H to L and hold	State

[a]From McNeill (1975).
[b]H, hand; L, left; R, right.

Thus, for Sinclair-de Zwart an action pattern refers primarily to the action itself, and she predicts the opposite of what McNeill predicts, namely, little consistency in the ordering of a child's early speech.

In McNeill's use it is no longer clear what an action schema is, since almost anything seems to qualify as an example. The pairing of schemas and utterances is also not clearly motivated, as Table I illustrates. Why, for example, is "I found" labeled as "action," rather than agent + action? Why is "should be" classified as "a syntactic process . . . which does not relate to an action schema . . . " (p. 378)? If the process of semiotic extension allows for "about" to be classified as a location schema, could not "should be" be classified as an existence schema? McNeill offers no principles of classification.

The assignment of syntagmas is equally vague. Syntagmas are defined as meaning units pronounced as a whole. McNeill does not specify how to handle the two difficult cases that can arise: (1) when a pause interrupts a meaning unit; (2) when two meaning units are contained within a single pronounced whole. In these cases either meaning alone or pronunciation alone must determine syntagma assignment. McNeill labels "I — it is correct that" as a single syntagma, even though there was a false start involved, and therefore presumably something of a meaning change, indicating that being pronounced as a whole is the principal criterion. If this is so, the inclusion of "meaning unit" must be justified, but is not.

Another difficulty is that there seems to be no direct correspondence between syntagmas and the action schemas which are guiding them. McNeill attempts to account for adult speech on the basis of semiotic extension, which is the use of action schemas for more abstract purposes. It is especially difficult to label action schemas at this abstract level, and McNeill does not suggest any principles by which this could be done. With Syntagma B, "I — it is correct that," McNeill has labeled the first four words as corresponding to the schema "state," but does not justify this label over none at all. If none were assigned, however, there would be a syntagma without a schema, and the hypothesis rules this out.

Summary

McNeill, like Schlesinger, tries to derive linguistic expression from cognition: Schlesinger relies on behaviorist principles; McNeill adapts Piagetian principles. They both address the problem of the interface between thought and language: Schlesinger proposes an input marker which represents conceptual information but is also such that linguistic rules can operate on it to produce speech; McNeill proposes the syntagma as the unit of speech and tries to show its dependence on action schemas. McNeill incorrectly interprets action schemas as logically determining the order of children's early utterances, and does not motivate the interiorization of action schemas as a prerequisite for patterned speech.

PERORATION

A common thread runs through the four apparently diverse positions reviewed here: each accords a derivative, rather than independent, status to syntactic processing. In the case of Lounsbury, who presented his hypotheses before transformational grammar was developed, the emphasis is on probability and habit-family hierarchies. With Osgood, there was first an attempt to incorporate a transformational grammar within his overall view of language as probabilistic and determined by mediational learning principles, and most recently an attempt to derive syntax from perception. With Schlesinger, linguistics is appropriate for describing language, but should not be included in a model of language use. McNeill, formerly the strongest supporter of the innateness of syntactic (and, more generally, linguistic) universals, now shifts to an emphasis on sensory-motor action schemas as the source for patterned speech.[3]

A review of the aims of a speech production theory in the opening pages may suggest why speech production theories have developed as they have: the aims are considered proper, even though they are in fact too comprehensive and would require accounting for facts and phenomena which are heterogeneous and do not all lie in the same domain. Since the aims are wrong, the theories which try to meet them are also wrong. Instead of setting boundaries on the subject matter of a speech production theory, investigators have assumed that anything that affects speech processing and acquisition is something that would ideally be accounted for in a theory of speech production. The acquisition of syntax as a problem to be explained has been eliminated, but at the cost of requiring a theory which will explain everything else.

A similar phenomenon has occurred within linguistic theory. A very abbreviated discussion of the phenomenon follows. G. Lakoff (1971) has argued that a linguistic theory should account for whatever determines the distribution of morphemes in speech, including speakers' beliefs, habits, extralinguistic knowledge, and the like. Fillmore (1972), continuing in this vein, advanced the "new taxonomy," which states that a formal linguistic theory is impossible. Chomsky (1973) pointed out that this conclusion followed automatically from the requirement that all facts affecting usage be included in a linguistic theory. Katz and Bever (1976) argue that such an approach obliterates the competence—performance distinction by confusing a wide range of nongrammatical phenomena with questions of grammar. The alternative they suggest is the one originally offered by transformational grammar (Chomsky, 1965), namely, that a grammar

---

[3]It should be noted that there is no reason, in advance of the facts, to prefer a model without a syntactic component over a model with a syntactic component. Nor is there a reason to prefer a model with few innate constraints over one with many innate constraints. These are empirical questions, and in the absence of evidence, it is theoretical prejudice to hold a position on them. The arguments presented above are intended to demonstrate that the evidence does not support the claims of Lounsbury, Osgood, Schlesinger, and McNeill.

is a theory of linguistic knowledge, not use. Linguistic performance should be accounted for, but not within a theory of competence.

The confusion about theoretical boundaries in grammar is similar to the confusion about the aims of a speech production theory. The similarity between these confusions suggests that they will have similar solutions. In grammar the solution is to distinguish between grammatical and nongrammatical phenomena. In speech production the solution would accordingly be to distinguish linguistic processing (the proper domain of a speech processing theory) from external factors which affect processing. An analogy with the operation of a machine may clarify the distinction. A bread-making machine executes, through its components, a certain class of operations: it mixes ingredients, it kneads, it places the dough in a rising chamber, it kneads the dough again, it shapes it into loaves, and so on. Among the things it does not do is determine what the initial ingredients will be; thus, it does not determine whether the bread will be raisin pumpernickel or whole wheat. Further, outside agents can interfere with the process at any stage, for example, by not allowing the dough to rise by putting it into the second kneading operation directly after it exits from the first one. Finally, factors such as the temperature of the plant in which the machine is housed and the amount of ambient wild yeast, will also affect the running of the machine and the quality of bread that is made. These external factors affecting the machine's operation can be collectively called the *inputs* and distinguished from the *machine* itself.

In the case of a bread-making machine, the distinction between the machine itself and the inputs is clear-cut; on the other hand, the distinction between the *language machine* and its inputs, though equally clear conceptually, is difficult to draw in practice. One way out of this difficulty is to start with a case that seems clearly outside the language machine and then explore the relation between that case and others where the determination is less clear. For example, a speech production theory is not expected to include a theory of personality, even though personality variables might affect, say, the choice of lexical items. Personality variables are not part of the language machine, but are an input to it.

In contrast to the clear case of personality is the unclear case of cognition. The theorists discussed above have suggested not only that cognitive or perceptual variables are part of the language machine, but, in effect, that there may be no such independent system in speech production as a language machine. The latter, more radical, proposal has already been argued to be untenable. To answer the question of whether cognitive variables are part of the language machine or input to the machine it will be helpful to compare cognition and personality. If personality is accepted as being an input, and if cognition does not differ from personality in a way relevant to decisions about its inclusion in the language machine, then cognition should also be accepted as another input. Although the question as to whether cognition differs in principle from personality cannot be definitively answered, it can be said that no evidence yet presented suggests that they are different. Thus, a tentative conclusion is that cognition is outside the language machine.

Two implications of this conclusion are of interest. One is that attempts to establish the primacy of one or another aspect of speech are pointless. If there is a language machine, a cognition machine, a personality machine, and interactions among these and other machines, then it is ill formed to speak of any machine as primary. Each serves its own function. The second implication is that the task of a speech production theory can be simplified, not by eliminating syntax, but by restricting the range of facts to be explained to a homogeneous domain. The approach advocated here is similar to that taken by Fodor, Bever, and Garrett (1974) and Garrett (1975). They view speech production as a translation process, in which a message in a mental computational "language" is translated into speech, thus presupposing a mechanism which converts messages into speech. The notion of a language machine presented above makes explicit the nature of this presupposition.

The approach just outlined for clarifying the aims of a speech production theory is the same as the approach already followed in work on speech perception. There, research has focused on the linguistic principles which determine the course of speech comprehension and interpretation; in so doing it has presupposed a language machine for speech perception. The history of psycholinguistics has established the fruitfulness of this presupposition.

ACKNOWLEDGMENTS

The material on Lounsbury and Osgood is based on the introduction of a doctoral dissertation submitted to Northeastern University. I would like to thank T. G. Bever for his comments on these sections, and J. J. Katz for his comments on the final section. C. E. Osgood and I. M. Schlesinger kindly criticized my criticisms; I hope they will not have considered it a thankless task.

REFERENCES

Anderson, S. On the role of deep structure in semantic interpretation. *Foundations of Language,* 1971, 7, 387–396.

Bever, T. G. Associations to stimulus–response theories of language. In T. R. Dixon and D. L. Horton (Eds.), *Verbal behavior and general behavior theory.* Englewood Cliffs, New Jersey: Prentice-Hall, 1968.

Blankenship, J., & Kay, C. Hesitation phenomena in English speech: A study in distribution. *Word,* 1964, 20, 360–372.

Boomer, D. S. Hesitation and grammatical encoding. *Language and Speech,* 1965, 8, 148–158.

Bowerman, M. *Early syntactic development.* Cambridge, England: Cambridge University Press, 1973.

Bowerman, M. Discussion summary – development of concepts underlying language. In R. L. Schiefelbusch & L. L. Lloyd (Eds.), *Language perspectives – acquisition, retardation, and intervention.* Baltimore, Maryland: University Park Press, 1974.

Braine, M. D. S. The ontogeny of English phrase structure: The first phase. *Language,* 1963, **39**, 1–14.

Brown, R., & Fraser, C. The acquisition of syntax. In C. N. Cofer & B. Musgrave (Eds.), *Verbal behavior and learning: Problems and processes.* New York: McGraw-Hill, 1963.

Butterworth, B. Hesitation and semantic planning in speech. *Journal of Psycholinguistic Research,* 1975, **4**, 75–88.

Chomsky, N. *Syntactic structures.* The Hague: Mouton, 1957.

Chomsky, N. Review of Skinner's *Verbal Behavior. Language,* 1959, **35**, 26–58.

Chomsky, N. Formal discussion. In U. Bellugi & R. Brown (Eds.), *The acquisition of language.* Monographs of the Society for Research in Child Development, 1964, Vol. 29, No. 1.

Chomsky, N. *Aspects of the theory of syntax.* Cambridge, Massachusetts: MIT Press, 1965.

Chomsky, N. *Language and mind.* New York: Harcourt, Brace, Jovanovich, 1968.

Chomsky, N. Lecture. MIT: February 15, 1973.

Fillmore, C. J. The case for case. In E. Bach & R. Harms (Eds.), *Universals in linguistic theory.* New York: Holt, Rinehart, & Winston, 1968.

Fillmore, C. On generativity. In S. Peters (Ed.), *Goals of linguistic theory.* Englewood Cliffs, New Jersey: Prentice-Hall, 1972.

Fodor, J., Bever, T., & Garrett, M. *The psychology of language.* New York: McGraw-Hill, 1974.

Forster, K. I. Sentence completion in left- and right-branching languages. *Journal of Verbal Learning and Verbal Behavior,* 1968, **7**, 296–299. (a)

Forster, K. I. The effect of removal of length constraint on sentence completion times. *Journal of Verbal Learning and Verbal Behavior,* 1968, **7**, 253–254. (b)

Fromkin, V. A. The nonanomalous nature of anomalous utterances. *Language,* 1971, **47**, 27–52.

Garrett, M. The analysis of sentence production. In G. Bower (Ed.), *Advances in learning theory and motivation.* Vol. 9. New York: Academic Press, 1975.

Grice, H. P. Logic and conversation. William James Lectures, Harvard University, 1967.

Goldman-Eisler, F. *Psycholinguistics: Experiments in spontaneous speech.* New York: Academic Press, 1968.

Goldman-Eisler, F. Pauses, clauses, sentences. *Language and Speech,* 1972, **15**, 103–113.

Henderson, A., Goldman-Eisler, F., and Skarbek, A. Sequential temporal patterning in spontaneous speech. *Language and Speech,* 1966, **9**, 207–216.

Jaffe, J., Breskin, S., & Gerstman, L. J. Random generation of apparent speech rhythms. *Language and Speech,* 1972, **15**, 68–71.

Jarvella, R. Starting with psychological verbs. Paper presented at the Midwestern Psychological Association, Cleveland, May, 1972.

Katz, J. J. *Semantic theory.* New York: Harper & Row, 1972.

Katz, J. J., & Bever, T. G. The fall and rise of empiricism. In T. G. Bever, J. J. Katz, & D. T. Langendoen (Eds.), *An integrated theory of linguistic ability.* New York: Crowell, 1976.

Lakoff, G. Presupposition and relative well-formedness. In D. Steinberg & L. Jakobovits (Eds.), *Semantics.* Cambridge, England: Cambridge University Press, 1971.

Lindsley, J. R. Producing simple utterances: How far ahead do we plan? *Cognitive Psychology,* 1975, **7**, 1–19.

Lounsbury, F. G. Transitional probability, linguistic structure and systems of habit-family hierarchies. In C. E. Osgood & T. A. Sebeok (Eds.), *Psycholinguistics: A survey of theory and research problems.* Bloomington, Indiana: Indiana University Press, 1965.

Maclay, J., & Osgood, C. E. Hesitation phenomena in spontaneous English speech. *Word,* 1959, **15**, 19–44.

MacNeilage, P. F. Motor control of serial ordering of speech. *Psychological Review,* 1970, **77**, 182–196.

McNeill, D. Developmental psycholinguistics. In F. Smith & G. A. Miller (Eds.), *The genesis of language.* Cambridge, Massachusetts: MIT Press, 1966.

McNeill, D. *The acquisition of language.* New York: Harper & Row, 1970.

McNeill, D. The capacity for the ontogenesis of grammar. In D. I. Slobin (Ed.), *The ontogenesis of grammar.* New York: Academic Press, 1971.

McNeill, D. Semiotic extension. In R. L. Solso (Ed.), *Information processing and cognition: The Loyola symposium.* Hillsdale, New Jersey: Lawrence Erlbaum Assoc., 1975.

Mellema, P. A brief against case grammar. *Foundations of Language,* 1974, **11**, 39–76.

Osgood, C. E. On understanding and creating sentences. *American Psychologist,* 1963, **18**, 735–751.

Osgood, C. E. Where do sentences come from? In D. Steinberg & L. A. Jakobovits (Eds.), *Semantics.* Cambridge, England: Cambridge University Press, 1971.

Osgood, C. E., & Bock, J. K. Salience and sentences: Some production principles. In S. Rosenberg (Ed.), *Sentence production: development in research and theory.* Hillsdale, New Jersey: Lawrence Erlbaum Assoc., in press.

Piaget, J. *Play, dreams and imitation in children.* New York: Norton, 1962.

Piaget, J. *The origins of intelligence in children.* New York: Norton, 1963.

Postal, P. Limitations of phrase structure grammars. In J. A. Fodor & J. J. Katz (Eds.), *The structure of language.* Englewood Cliffs, New Jersey: Prentice-Hall, 1964.

Rosenberg, S. Semantic constraints on sentence production. Paper presented at the Midwestern Psychological Association, Cleveland, May, 1972.

Schlesinger, I. M. Production of utterances and language acquisition. In D. I. Slobin (Ed.), *The ontogenesis of grammar.* New York: Academic Press, 1971.   (a)

Schlesinger, I. M. Learning grammar: From pivot to realization rule. In R. Huxley & E. Ingram (Eds.), *Language acquisitions: Models and methods.* New York: Academic Press, 1971.   (b)

Schlesinger, I. M. Production and comprehension of utterances. Unpublished manuscript, 1976.

Shattuck, S. R. Speech errors: An analysis. Unpublished doctoral dissertation, MIT, 1974.

Sinclair-de Zwart, H. Language acquisition and cognitive development. In T. E. Moore (Ed.), *Cognitive development and the acquisition of language.* New York: Academic Press, 1973.

Tannenbaum, P. H., Williams, F., & Hillier, C. S. Word predictability in the environment of hesitations. *Journal of Verbal Learning and Verbal Behavior,* 1965, **4**, 134–140.

Valian, V. V. Talking, listening, and linguistic structure. Unpublished doctoral dissertation, Northeastern University, 1971.

Whitaker, H. A. Neurolinguistics. In W. O. Dingwall (Ed.), *A survey of linguistic science.* College Park, Maryland: University of Maryland, 1971.

Yngve, V. H. A. A model and an hypothesis for language structure. *Proceedings of the American Philosophical Society,* 1960, **104**, 444–466.

6

Style Variables in Referential Language: A Study of Social Class Difference and Its Effect on Dyadic Communication

Eleanor Rosch

University of California at Berkeley

Are there social class differences in language that actually render lower-class or middle-class speech a better tool for interpersonal communication? The rationale for such a question lies in the convergence of three traditions of research. First, linguistic variations associated with social status do exist; in fact, class differences in phonological, lexical, and grammatical rules are one of the signs by which status is identified by members of the community (Cazden, 1966; Labov, 1970; Williams, 1970). However, no evidence has been found that present English dialectical variation on this level of analysis is large enough to constitute any but the most minimal blocks to communication (Weener, 1969). Other descriptive studies have counted the frequencies with which particular language forms occur in the speech of different classes, finding some consistent differences: middle-class speakers tend to talk more, use more varied vocabulary, and employ more varied and complex grammatical constructions than do lower-class speakers; however, in this case also, there have not been empirical studies that demonstrate the effect of variables such as these on any measurable aspect of communication (Fries, 1940; Hess & Shipman, 1965; Loban, 1963).

Studies in the second research tradition provide an opposite perspective—broad theoretical accounts of social class differences in what is talked about in a communication situation. For example, Bernstein (1962) distinguishes between the restricted communication code of the lower class, which is used among a closely knit group with shared assumptions, and the elaborated code of the middle class, which can be used to communicate information to strangers. And

Schatzman and Strauss (1955) describe the relative egocentrism with which lower- versus middle-class speakers related to interviewers their common experience of a tornado. Such claims involve many aspects of life besides language and have proved very difficult to test in a manner which is both a reasonable operationalization of the theory and also contains necessary controls (Higgins, 1971).

In the third research tradition, class differences in overall accuracy of communication are measured. Communication accuracy has been precisely defined operationally by methods of measurement such as Cloze procedure (Cherry-Peisach, 1965), teaching—learning (Hess & Shipman, 1965), or encoding—decoding (Krauss & Rotter, 1968; Ruth, 1966); however, in these studies, there was no attempt to isolate specific language variables affecting accuracy.

The purpose of the present study was to combine these three traditions of research — that is, to locate and explore specific language variables which (a) differed across social class, (b) were sufficiently general that they might reasonably affect communication, and (c) were sufficiently specific that their effects on communication accuracy could be measured under controlled conditions. A major problem in design was the level of linguistic analysis to be used. Given that class differences in phonological and grammatical rules did not seem to affect communication, what units of language might reasonably be expected to do so? A pilot study was performed using a coding task and arrays of abstract figures and Frois-Wittmann faces as stimuli to determine what class differences in language of the desired type might actually occur. Class differences appeared to be present in the following variables: whether the whole stimulus or part of it was referred to in the description, whether the description used "metaphorical" or "descriptive" language, and how many different things were said about the stimulus. A second problem in design was the communication task to be used. The method of coding (Brown, 1966) designates any two-person communication task in which a speaker encodes one referent in an array to a listener, separated by a visual screen or a lapse of time, who must try to decode the message and select the identical referent. This method makes possible an operational definition of communication accuracy, the separation of communication accuracy from many other factors, and the control of the linguistic variables provided the decoder. Coding is not a situation identical to any encountered in everyday life and may be the type of formal situation which favors middle-class performance (Labov, 1970). However, the aim of the present research was *not* to determine whether there were social class differences in communication skill per se; it was to determine whether class differences in linguistic variables could be isolated which, as such, affected communication accuracy.

The general plan of the present research was: (a) to have middle-class (MC) and lower-class (LC) speakers encode stimuli in a standardized communication situation — that is, to have them describe one stimulus out of an array with the purpose of enabling a future listener to pick out that stimulus; (b) to analyze these encodings to discover if significant class differences could be found in language variables (specifically those identified by the pilot study) which might reasonably be expected to influence communication; and (c) to use the dependent variables of the first experiment as independent variables for a second — that is, to present, in isolation, examples of each significant variable found in (b) obtained from speakers of each class to decoders (listeners) of each class. The decoding accuracy scores so obtained would indicate not only the general accuracy with which each class understood the messages of its own and the other class but also how well particular types of message which had shown class differences in initial production were understood within and across class. An examination of race, sex, and individual differences was included within the same basic design. A general discussion of the significance of the results is reserved until the end of presentation of the data. At the outset, however, it should be stated that the study, as well as establishing several empirical findings of interest, provides a demonstration of the fact that use of social class as an independent variable in research on communication or cognition is probably not as fruitful a strategy to pursue as has been assumed in the lines of research from which this study was initially derived.

EXPERIMENT I: ENCODING

The basic hypothesis of the first experiment was that there are social class differences in the variables of encoding "style" isolated by the pilot study; that is, that MC subjects refer more to parts of the stimulus, use less "metaphorical" language, and say more different things about the stimulus than do LC subjects. Of concern also were the effects of stimulus type (abstracts and faces); the interrelations of style variables (such as length of encoding and use of metaphors) with each other; the relation of these style variables to the units of language analysis (such as grammatical complexity) previously found to show social class differences; and class or other group effects in the content of the imagery of the encodings.

Methods

Subjects. Subjects were 143 10-year-old children divided into class and sex as follows: MC — boys 23, girls 21; LC White (LCW) — boys 25, girls 27; LC Black (LCB) — boys 24, girls 23. The criterion for defining MC was that the child's caretaker have a professional occupation, for LC that the child live in a government housing project. An MC Black group was not available. Middle-class subjects were tested at the university; LC subjects were tested in poverty program offices in their area of residence. All subjects heard of the project by advertisement through the place of testing and were paid volunteers. Because of the methods of recruitment, both MC and LC subjects tended to be children who used recreational facilities at the place of testing and were already familiar with and at ease in that setting.

Stimuli and procedures.   Stimuli were five arrays of abstract figures (shown in Heider, 1971) and five arrays of Frois-Wittman faces (Schlosberg, 1952). The abstracts were figures which had been previously found to elicit low agreement in what they were named (Krauss & Glucksberg, 1969). The stimuli were mounted on cardboard, the target figure or face below the others of the array. A practice array of abstracts and one of faces consisting of entirely different stimuli preceded encoding of the five experimental arrays of each type. Abstract arrays were always presented first. The subject was told to describe the target so that any other boy or girl his age could pick out that one if it was mixed up with all the others just from what he said about it. The subject was prompted once to say more if he stopped after uttering only one "unit" of encoding. Test sessions were tape recorded.

Coding and analysis of the data.   Each encoding of each child was first divided into "units" each of which was then classified as to "type." Interjudge reliability measures obtained through use of those rules were high (.84—.98). A "unit" was roughly a single "statement" or piece of information about the cue figure or face (e.g., "It looks like a spaceship." "His mouth's open."). The identifiable unity possessed by a "unit" was not literally a "bit" of information nor did it necessarily correspond to grammatical boundaries, but rather was the identify of a single "image" about the cue stimulus.

Each unit was classified on two dimensions:

1. *Whole—part.*   A whole unit was a "statement" which referred to the whole face or line drawing; a Part unit was a statement referring to part of the face (e.g., eyes, nose) or part of the figure (e.g., "The top looks like a . . . ").

2. *Inferential—descriptive.*   An Inferential unit was a statement that went beyond the "givens" of the stimulus to describe metaphorically — for a face, attributions such as emotion, state, character, occupation, or events in which the man might be involved; for an abstract, naming or description of an object which the lines on the paper "looked like."

Units were Descriptive if they described the physical properties of the stimulus face or figure (e.g., "His eyes are closed." "It's got a line sticking out on the bottom."). Logically either Wholes or Parts could be either Inferential or Descriptive. As the end product of classification, each subject was credited with a number of scores which represented: the total number of units he had given, the percentage of those units that were Whole and Inferential (WI), the percentage that were Whole and Descriptive (WD), the percentage Part and Inferential (PI), and the percentage Part and Descriptive (PD). Scores for these variables were analyzed separately for the abstract and fact stimuli. These language variables, on the level of the whole unit, will be referred to as "style" variables.

A number of more traditional language variables, "internal to the unit," were also coded: adjectives, dependent phrases and clauses, negatives, and comparative words. The subject received scores for the percentage of images which contained each of these variables; because of the low frequency of some, the scores were combined for abstracts and faces.

Class and sex effects for each variable were tested by analysis of variance; abstracts and faces were analyzed separately where meaningful. Tables of complete data for all ANOVAs and all t tests are available in Heider (1969).

Results

Class effects. Striking social class differences in encoding style were revealed by two modes of analysis. In the first place, the number of units and percentage of units of each type contained in the total encoding record for each class were very different. Table 1 shows class means for the style variables. All Fs were significant. As can be seen, there were large and highly significant class differences both for abstracts and faces in the number of units given (MC said many more different things about the stimuli than LC), in WI% (a far greater percentage of the units given by LC were Whole—Inferential), and in PD% (a far greater percent of MC units were Part—Descriptive — WI% and PD%, of course, are not independent). The percentage of PI units given by any class was small; almost nonexistent for the faces stimuli. Whole—Descriptive units were so rare that they could not be analyzed.

There were no sex differences. Within the lower class, there were no significant race differences. None of the interactions with sex or race reached significance.

The second mode of analysis considered the composition of individual encodings. The majority of MC encodings (84%) were composed of a combination of WI and PD units, while only 21% of LC encodings contained both types of unit. Thus, not only were MC encodings longer (composed of more units) than LC, but they were also likely to contain two styles of description; whereas, the unit(s) of an LC encoding were more likely to be of only one type.

Stimulus effects. The basic finding about type of stimulus was that it failed to affect class differences or individual consistency. It was thought that abstract figures would be less familiar to LC than to MC subjects; whereas, facial expression would be equally familiar to both classes. If familiarity with the type of stimulus materials were a factor in the production of class differences, there should be significant interactions between class and stimulus; none were found. Although faces tended to elicit more units and a higher PD% from all subjects, the relative distances between LC and MC scores were not significantly different for the abstract and face stimuli.

TABLE 1
Means of Encoding Style Variables

Stimulus	Social class		
	Middle class	Lower-class White	Lower-class Black
	Number of units		
Abstracts	21.0	8.7	8.9
Faces	27.3	9.6	10.8
	WI% of total units		
Abstracts	27.7	74.5	83.5
Faces	38.0	83.3	79.6
	PD% of total units		
Abstracts	54.9	12.4	7.5
Faces	51.8	13.4	18.2
	PI% of total units		
Abstracts	17.4	12.3	7.0
Faces	10.1	2.9	2.3

Note: Middle class differed from both the lower-class Whites and lower-class Blacks on all t tests.

Type of stimulus failed also to disrupt individual style consistencies. If encoding style variables were measures of general traits within subjects, they should be correlated between abstracts and faces; they were: number of units $r = .88, p < .01$; WI% $r = .89, p < .01$; PI% $r = .17, p < .05$; PD% $r = .66, p < .01$. The percentage of encodings containing units of more than one type was also highly correlated between abstracts and faces: $r = .73, p < .01$. These correlations were the more informative since the meaning of a "part" of the stimulus or a "metaphor" about the stimulus were, at face value, quite different for the abstracts and faces.

A possible ambiguity in the meaning of this consistency arises from the fact that abstracts were presented first and that a PD style might have been suggested to MC subjects by the abstracts and carried over to the faces. To test this possibility, 13 additional MC and 7 LC subjects were tested with the faces stimuli preceeding the abstracts. The same distribution and consistency of encoding style variables as reported for the main study were obtained.

Interrelations between the style variables. Several questions were raised by the interrelations of the style variables with each other. In the first place, total number of units was highly correlated with PD% and showed a high-negative correlation with WI%, not only across, but also within, social classes. For example, correlation coefficients of number of units and WI% (abstracts and faces combined) were: classes pooled $-.70$, $p < .01$; within MC $-.51$, $p < .01$; within LCW $-.67$, $p < .01$; within LCB $-.72$, $p < .01$. The question thus arose as to whether one of the variables, number of units or style of units, could be an artifact of the other — particularly whether a preference for Parts could be an artificial result of verbal fluency (for example, a talkative subject who is motivated to produce many images runs out of metaphors for the Whole stimulus and must turn to PD descriptions)? Several findings argued against such an interpretation:

1. Class differences in WI% and PD% remained significant even when number of images was controlled by analysis of only the first unit of each encoding (WI abstracts $F = 25.78$, $p < .001$; WI faces $F = 11.77$, $p < .001$; PD abstracts $F = 2.185$, $P < .001$; PD faces $F = 8.30$, $p < .01$).

2. Split half correlations between the percentage of each style in the first and last halves of each encoding that had more than one unit were high (.92 for WI, .95 for PD). This indicated that the first and last parts of encodings were not taken from different populations of response.

3. Proportion of PD first units correlated highly with total number of units ($r = .47$, $p < .01$) showing that a subject who would later give many units was more likely to begin with a PD unit than a subject who would later give few units. There was, of course, the opposite possibility, that number of units was an artifact of the subject's preference for describing Parts of the stimulus (e.g., one unit can designate a whole object; however, if a subject wants to describe parts he must give a separate unit for each part). The major argument against such an interpretation was the finding that subjects who gave many Part units gave, in addition, more Whole units than subjects who gave few Part units.

In effect, how much a subject said and whether he talked about Parts appeared to be, not aspects of the same variable, but separate variables whose correlation could not be predicted from the definition of each variable alone.

A second relation between style variables was that between the Part–Whole dimension and the Inferential–Descriptive dimension. In the data of the present study, approximately 90% of all units were either Whole and Inferential or Part and Descriptive (see Table 1); PI units were rare, and WD units almost nonexistent. The small percentage of PI responses was probably due to the stimuli used. On Rorschach cards, where the figures are more complex and segmented than the encoding figures and where the instructions are to give Inferential responses (tell what it looks like), PI responses (D) of over 50% are common. On the other hand, the virtual absence of WD responses seems due to the nature of Descriptive language. Other than designation of size or overall shape, there is little Descriptive that can be said about a whole face or a whole line figure.

In short, it can be asserted that the close association between the dimensions of encoding length (number of units), Whole–Part, and Inferential–Descriptive was an empirical relationship not a relationship that could be derived analytically from the definition of any one of the variables alone.

Relation of encoding style to other linguistic variables. Several language variables "internal to the unit" were analyzed. Those which showed significant class differences were: number of words per unit, percent of adjectives, percent of negatives, number of dependent phrases, and number of dependent clauses. Sex, race (within LC), and interaction effects were not significant. These language variables were highly correlated with the style variables — for example, a high percentage of adjectives correlated with a high number of units, high PD% and low WI% — and the correlations were significant within social class, as well as for all classes combined (see Heider, 1969, for supporting data). These correlations implied that the encoding style which contained a large number of units and a high percent of PD units was also one, even within social class, in which the individual units were likely (a) to be long, (b) to contain elaborations of the information contained in the basic "image" of the unit (e.g., "It's a house *with a pointy* roof"), and (c) to be phrased in relatively complex grammatical form. Thus encoding style, as defined in the present research, does correlate with the variety and complexity variables previously studied in analysis of differential production frequencies in class language.

Unit content. A final variable which might reasonably be expected to influence communication was the communality of the content of units, that is, the extent to which the content of units (the basic "images" of units) from different encoders was the same. For example, if MC subjects tended to call one figure a *key* and LC subjects to call it a *spaceship* one would predict better within than between class communication of that figure. Using the encodings of a randomly selected third of the subjects, two communality measures were computed: (1) the distribution of the two most common WI and PD unit contents for each encoding, and (2) the percentage of rare unit contents (images of only one occurrence). There were *no* class differences in occurrence of the most common WI units. PD units, of course, were largely confined to the MC, but those PD units given in LC encodings were the more common ones. The percentage of single occurrence units was higher in the MC than either LCW or LCB for both WI and PD units. There were no sex or LCW–LCB differences.

Discussion

The basic hypothesis of the experiment was confirmed; there were significant class differences in encoding style. LC subjects produced fewer units, referred more to the whole stimulus and used more Inferential language than did MC encoders. Encoding style was consistent across type of stimulus for all classes. The style variables correlated with those grammatical variables previously found to differ between classes. The content of the common descriptions did not differ between classes. Although the existence of marked social class differences in style was clear, what style meant and why styles should be associated with social class was not.

Differences in amount said is a consistently reported finding in class language research (see introduction). Middle-class subjects also have been found to give a greater number of responses on the Rorschach than LC (e.g., Ames & August, 1966). Various theories (such as Bernstein, 1962) suggest that such differences in fluency come about because MC parents, more than LC, value and reinforce speech in general in their children. On the other hand, linguists such as Labov (1970) argue that supposed class differences in fluency are actually responses to the formal nature of the experimental situation; Labov points to the importance of verbal interaction and play in the natural setting of ghetto life. In actual fact, accounts of MC and LC verbal interactions outside of formal settings are largely imaginary extrapolations from limited data; there have been few ecological studies of actual speech occurrence and reinforcement contingencies in LC and MC homes.

Individual differences in attention to parts versus wholes (cognitive style) has long received attention as a dimension of personality (e.g., Kagan, Moss, & Sigel, 1965; Witkin, Dyk, Faterson, Goodenough, & Karp, 1962). That there are class differences on this dimension was suggested indirectly by the work of Kagan et al. (1965) on impulsivity and directly by Rorschach studies (Ames & August, 1966). However, all studies using the same names for variables are not necessarily dealing with the same, or even closely related, variables (a fact overlooked by Cohen, 1969). In the present research, subjects who used the WI encoding style exclusively in the communication task were quite capable of perceiving embedded parts when specifically directed to do so; subjects with high PD% were not more likely to sort pictures on the basis of similarities in parts of the picture than were subjects with high WI%; nor was the coding of Wholes in the present research attributable to impulsivity (Heider, 1969, 1971a, b). Thus the origin and meaning of Part—Whole preferences in coding style in the present study remains an open question.

Another relevant factor is that style differences in the present research occurred in a communication task — subjects were not simply asked to describe abstracts and faces but asked to talk to a future listener. The social class differences in style in the present study were like differences Ervin-Tripp (1969) found between formal and informal modes of speech of MC speakers; MC communications intended for a friend were shorter and more metaphorical than those intended for a stranger. Other studies indicated that, in length and use of rare words, encodings which people intended for their own use resembled the LC style of the present study; those intended for another's use resembled the MC style (for example, Krauss, Vivekananthan, & Weinheimer, 1968). Do LC speakers (as Bernstein, 1962, might argue) not have a formal mode of communication? Does the experience of LC children give them reason to believe that any unknown listener will be more *like themselves* than MC children believe? (Bott, 1957, found that the roles of friend, neighbor, and relative all tended to be occupied by the same individuals for British working-class families, by different individuals for MC families). Or were the LC encoding more "egocentric" than MC?

The Inferential—Descriptive dimension, although it could be rated with high reliability by judges, was not an easily characterized dimension. (It should be noted, at the outset, that the words used in both types of description were part of nontechnical English vocabulary — unlike the technical geometric terms used by Brent & Klamer's, 1967, MC but not LC subjects). In defining the dimension, it was implied that descriptive language was somehow closer to what was actually "given" in the stimulus than Inferential language; however, such an interpretation cannot be accepted literally. The same language which would be categorized as Descriptive if used to refer to the faces (mouth open, slanted eyebrows) would be clearly Inferential if used for the abstracts; while the kinds of terms which appeared in Descriptive accounts of the abstracts (line, opening) were not used at all to talk about the faces. Is something different given in line drawings than is given in photographs of faces? (Of course, some subjects may have used Descriptive language because they believed it closer to what was "given" and thus more "exact.") Nor can Inferential—Descriptive be unequivocally characterized on a "concrete—abstract" dimension; both metaphors and descriptions in terms such as "openings" and "points" can be argued the more abstract mode of thought. The meaning of Inferential—Descriptive language also remains an open question. The present research was actually not designed to answer questions raised in the preceeding discussion of style; it was, however, designed to pursue the actual effects of style differences on decoding accuracy of the listener.

EXPERIMENT II: DECODING

The second experiment was designed to determine the effects of coder group (particularly class) and the effect of encoding style on decoding accuracy. It was also designed to assess individual consistencies in communication skills. In regard to the overall accuracy of MC and LC coders, several contradictory hypotheses were possible. Equally tenable were predictions of no class difference (complexity and style are only aesthetic variations of no consequence for effectiveness of communication), of MC superiority (MC language is a better tool for task performance), and of LC superiority (the simpler language and less idiosyncratic imagery of the LC can be more generally understood). An interaction between class of encoder and class of decoder (greater accuracy of within than between class communication) is predicted by the claim that the languages of different social classes, especially LCB, are radically different but equally efficient "dialects."

A number of aspects of encoding style were of interest. One major difference between MC and LC encodings was length. MC encodings were quite redundant;

the same information distinguishing the cue stimulus from other stimuli in the array was repeated in many units of an encoding. Did sheer length improve communication? The majority of MC encodings contained not only repetition but repetition in different styles (WI and PD); did the presence of both styles improve communication? Another major class difference was in use of the Whole–Part and Inferential–Descriptive dimensions; both classes used WI units, but only MC encodings contained a large proportion of PD units. One characteristic of Descriptive language appears to make it particularly suited to the information requirements of an unknown listener; it is "impersonal." "It looks like a hat" could communicate effectively only if "hat" conjured up similar images for encoder and decoder; "It's got a point sticking out on each side on the bottom" seems less dependent for its referential import on idiosyncratic connotation, associations, and imagery. Since most subjects in the present study were strangers to each other, it can be predicted that Descriptive language is generally better understood than Inferential and is a more effective lingua franca for communication across social class lines. The second experiment was, of course, also designed to analyze and deal with the many possible questions concerning interactions between style and coder group.

A final set of questions which Experiments I and II together were designed to explore concerned individual consistencies in communication skill. To make possible such an analysis, the same subjects were used in both experiments. Specific hypotheses tested were that skill as an encoder (the production of encodings which were correctly identified by other subjects) is correlated with skill as a decoder and that preference for one style over another in encoding is correlated with relatively greater skill in decoding that style.

Methods

Subjects. The same subjects used in the encoding study were recalled after a two-week interval. Only two subjects failed to return for the second experiment.

Materials and procedure. Visual stimuli for the decoding task consisted of the same abstract and face arrays as were used in encoding. Stimuli for each array were mounted, in a row, in scrambled order, on strips of cardboard.

The verbal descriptions used as decodings were derived from the encodings. Encodings were classified on three dimensions for the purpose of dividing them into decoding arrays: Whole–Part, Inferential–Descriptive, and Complete–Partial (included to test some effects of redundancy). Encodings were divided into six types on the basis of these dimensions:

1. Composite: The encoding consisted of at least one WI unit and at least one PD unit. The entire description uttered by the encoder was read to the decoder.

2. Complete WI: The entire description of the encoder consisted of only WI unit(s). The entire description was read to the decoder. (Number of units was variable depending on the number given by the encoder).

3. Partial WI: The description read to the decoder consisted only of WI units, but this description originated as part of a Composite, an encoding which had other kinds of units included. The other kinds of units were removed; therefore, what the decoder heard was no longer the entire description as the encoder uttered it.

4. Complete PD: The description of the encoder consisted of only PD units, and was read in its entirety to the decoder.

5. Partial PD: The equivalent of Partial WI. In Partial PD, all units of the encoding which were not PD were removed.

6. Partial PI: Only units which were PI were read to the decoder. Entire encodings of PI units were so infrequent that it was impossible to make a complete category of these.

Each decoder was given one of each of these six types of encoding from each class and sex of encoder. Each decoder received a different set of actual endocings but the same types were included for each subject. The subject's own encodings were excluded from the verbal materials he decoded. To control effects of array difficulty, decodings were balanced so that each type of encoding from each class and sex were distributed evenly over each array for each class and sex. Some types of encoding for some social classes were more numerous than others; it was thus unavoidable that samples of some types were more widely representative of the subjects tested than others.

In administration of the decodings, the experimenter reads the subject each encoding and the subject pointed to the abstract or face in the array that he thought the encoder had been describing. The encoding was repeated upon request. A decoding was correct if the subject indicated the stimulus that the encoder had, in fact, been describing.

Analysis of data. The constraints of forming the decoding arrays out of encodings containing large class differences in style made the data unsuitable for a five-way ANOVA. Therefore, main effects of class and sex of encoder, style of encoding, and whether the encoding was Complete or Partial were tested by *t* tests. Decoding accuracy could be subjected to ANOVA (class X sex) because each decoder received a decoding array of the same overall composition as each other decoder.

Results

Main effects of coder group on accuracy. Percent of decodings correct and significance test results for each class of encoder and decoder are provided in Heider (1971b). The primary results were that MC encodings were better understood than LC encodings by all classes of decoder, and MC decodings were, likewise, superior to LC for all classes of encoder; that is, MC were both better encoders and decoders than LC. Such general MC superiority is subject to all of the ambiguity of interpretation which gave rise to the present attempt to isolate effect of style variables rather than to measure general accuracy of communication (Heider, 1969; Higgins, 1971; Williams, 1970), and it will not be discussed further.

Main effects of style factors on accuracy.   The most obvious aspect of coding style was sheer length. Effects of length were tested in two ways:

1. Complete and Partial encodings of the same type were compared with each other. There were no significant differences at any level of analysis. This showed that a set of units which subjects had "intended" as complete encodings were not superior in communication accuracy to sets of units of that style which subject had "intended" as part of a larger encoding.

2. A short additional experiment was conducted. Thirteen MC and 15 LC subjects who had not served in the original experiment decoded sets of MC and LC WI and PD encodings which had been matched for length (number of units) across class of encoder. Even under these conditions, MC encodings, both WI and PD, were more accurately decoded than LC.

It seemed clear that length of encodings alone did not account for MC encoding superiority.

A second hypothesis about style effects was that encodings which contained units in both the WI and PD styles would be better understood than encodings containing only one style. The percentage of decodings correct for each type are available in Heider (1971b). In general, across stimulus and class of encoder and decoder, Composite encodings, those which contained examples of both styles, were the best understood kind of encoding.

A third hypothesis was that Descriptive language would be more accurately interpreted than Inferential, particularly across social class lines. This hypothesis was not supported. With class of encoder and decoder combined, WI encodings were better understood than PD.

Interactions.   Figure 1 shows the interaction of class of encoder × class of decoder × style of encoding in graphical form. The results are combined for sex for which no interaction effects were significant. Analysis of the significance of interaction effects was performed in the manner described in Heider (1969).

There were two interaction results of interest. In the first place, there was absolutely no general tendency for within-class codings to be superior to between-class. If anything, there was a slight tendency for the LCB subjects to understand the encodings of other LCB subjects, particularly PD encodings, less well than would be predicted on the basis of their ability as encoders and decoders alone. Only one cell showed a within-class superiority effect, and even that was part of a three-way interaction with style — communication was at its most accurate when MC subjects were decoding the PD encodings of MC encoders. In the second place, for each class of encoder, the style of encoding which was most successfully decoded (that is, the style presumably most skillfully encoded) was the style which each class used most frequently; LC encodings composed only of WI units were better understood than LC encodings composed only of PD units, while for the MC encodings the opposite was true.

Individual consistencies. The most general hypothesis about encoding–decoding relationships on the individual level was that encoding and decoding skill are correlated. Since class differences in both encoding and decoding predetermined the result that cross-class correlations would be significant, only within-class correlations were considered. Not all encodings of all subjects were used as decodings; however, it was possible to find an equal number of subjects in each class group (19 MC, 19 LCW, 19 LCB) all of whose encodings had been presented as decodings in their complete form at least twice. Encoding skill scores for each subject consisted of the number of correct decodings his encodings received. An individual's decoding skill score was simply the number of decodings he identified correctly. The results were that none of the within-class correlations were significant.

The second hypothesis concerning individual consistencies was that encoding style preference would be related to relative skill in decoding each style. There was some confirmation for this hypothesis. Results showed that encoding PD% was significantly correlated with general decoding accuracy within LCW ($r = .34$, $p < .05$). Encoding PD% was significantly correlated with decoding MC PD encodings both within MC ($r = .41$, $p < .01$) and within LCW ($r = .35, p < .05$).

A final hypothesis was that encoding skill in one or another style was related to decoding skill. For purposes of this analysis, success of each individual's WI and PD encodings were correlated separately with his decoding scores. Success of WI encodings was unrelated to decoding skill. However, success of PD encodings were correlated with decoding success within all three classes (MC, $r = .49, p < .01$; LCW, $r = .40, p < .01$; LCB, $r = .44, p < .01$). These correlations were somewhat higher for decoding PD than WI and for decoding MC PD encodings than for other PD encodings. In summary, there was limited support for the hypothesis that encoding style preference was related to decoding skill and more general support for skill in encoding in the PD style as a predictor of decoding skill.

Discussion

The decoding data made it possible to analyze some of the factors involved in encoding skill, decoding skill, and the effect of encoding style on understanding. In the first place, sheer length (number of units of encoding) was not a decisive factor in accuracy. Indeed, MC encodings were much less efficient than LC in the sense that they were approximately three times longer, but only a small percentage better understood, than LC encodings. The repetition of information

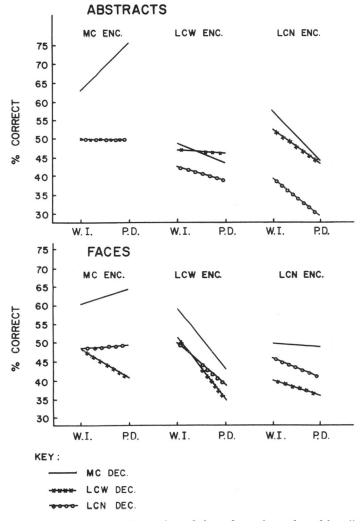

FIGURE 1 Decoding accuracy: Interaction of class of encoder × class of decoding × style of encoding.

in both the WI and PD styles within an encoding did improve accuracy. As shown by the first experiment, the majority of MC but not LC encodings were Composites; had the decodings reflected that actual proportion, MC encoding superiority would have been far greater than the 10% margin obtained. Since style was not an artifact of length, sheer fluency can be eliminated as the effective factor in encoding success.

A second possible basis for communication success which was not confirmed by the present study was the often argued position that MC and LC (particularly

LCB) have different "languages" used to communicate within different "cultures," both "languages" equally effective but not entirely mutually intelligible (as in Stewart, 1965). Such a position predicts two results for the present study:

1. The impersonality of Descriptive language, its freedom of reference from idiosyncratic associations and imagery, should render PD images more effective than WI images as a lingua franca for communication between social classes. This prediction was not confirmed, a finding which implies that impersonality of reference is not a necessary aspect of images that communicate across U.S. social class lines.

2. More specifically, the "different languages" theory implies that within-class decoding scores should be higher than between-class, or that WI units, at least, should have higher communality scores and be decoded more accurately within than between classes. That neither occurred argues strongly that MC and LC have much mutually shared culture in which the way objects look and the meaning and context of facial expressions are mutually intelligible.

An aspect of communication success which was confirmed by the data was the relation between encoding style and decoding skill. Each class was best (was decoded most successfully) when encoding in its preferred style. Within class, although there was no general correlation between encoding and decoding skill as a whole (a result also found by Krauss et al., 1968), preferences for encoding in the PD style and, more definitively, skill in encoding in the PD style were correlated with decoding skill.

Some clues as to the possible dynamics of decoding skill (which may also be related to encoding style preference) were provided by decoding response times. A reasonable strategy for decoding WI is simply to pick the stimulus figure which fits the WI image(s) in a striking way. Successful decoding of PD, on the other hand, requires more complex, serial processing; several of the stimulus figures will probably possess each of the positive, and several be free of each of the negative, attributes mentioned in the encoding. Therefore, adequate decoding of PD ought to take longer than decoding WI. Response latencies of MC subjects in general and skilled PD encoders within LCW and LCB were, indeed, longer for PD than WI, whereas, LC (excluding the few skilled PD encoders) tended to have the same response latencies regardless of the nature of the decoding (Heider, 1969). Thus, both encoding style and decoding skill may be related to habitual strategies of information processing, a possibility which cannot be analyzed further within the context of data from the present experiment (Heider, 1969, 1971a).

GENERAL DISCUSSION

The initial question of this study was whether there were social class differences in language which actually affected interpersonal communication. Both social class and individual differences were found in encoding style in a referential communication task which were related to performance in decoding. Sex and race differences were not obtained. While social class differences served as the heuristic for the discovery of stylistic variation, it is doubtful that an understanding of style can best be pursued through investigation of social class.

Social class is a variable particularly unsuited to the investigation of basic questions in human information processing. Uncontrolled factors such as experience, motivation, and the inherent biases of a formal test situation render any finding of class differences equivocal (Heider, 1969; Higgins, 1971; Labov, 1970; Rosch, in press). More importantly, the level of analysis at which social class is a variable assures that any specific aspect of class life claimed to be related to a specific factor in communication or information processing is probably hypothetical, untrue of members of the "class" as a whole, or at a different level of analysis from a possible viable account of the microstructure of the process under investigation.

Two strategies of investigation of style would appear to be of greater promise than social class for improving our understanding of the way in which stimuli are described in referential communication:

1. Investigations should be performed on the effect of the stimulus — the specific stimulus items and the nature of the array — on perception, encoding, communication, and memory for the stimuli. The stimuli and arrays used in the present study lacked a clearly analyzable informational content and were of a nature such that either the WI or PD mode of description appeared appropriate for them. Class differences in style did not occur when arrays contained an obvious correct encoding of one particular type (Garvey, 1972). The role of the stimulus in information processing may be a far more general and powerful one than individual or group style preferences; it is through an understanding of the role of the stimulus that clues to individual stylistic preferences may occur.

2. A processing model of how stimuli are perceived, analyzed, encoded, and decoded is needed. Without such a general understanding, further theorizing about individual or group differences can only continue on an ad hoc basis. In short, cultural, subcultural, or individual differences in performance on a cognitive or communication task, can only be illuminating if they form one step in the testing of a general theory (Rosch, in press); an endless proliferation of empirical typologies (such as that put forth in the present chapter) either in communication or personality research is, of itself, of neither theoretical nor practical use.

ACKNOWLEDGMENTS

Research reported in this chapter was supported in part by a predoctoral training fellowship to the author (under her former name Eleanor Rosch Heider) #1-F1-MH-049-01. Writing of the chapter was supported by a grant from the National Institutes of Mental Health #1 R01 MH24316-01.

REFERENCES

Ames, L. B., & August, J. Rorschach responses of Negro and White five- to ten-year olds. *Journal of Genetic Psychology,* 1966, **109,** 297–309.

Bernstein, B. Social class, linguistic codes and grammatical elements. *Language and Speech,* 1962, **5,** 221–240.

Bott, E. *Family and social network.* London: Tavistock Publications, 1957.

Brent, S. B., & Klamer, P. The naming and conceptualization of simple geometric forms: a crosscultural study. Paper presented at the meeting of the Society for Research on Child Development, March, 1967.

Brown, R. From codability to coding ability. In J. Bruner (Ed.), *Learning about learning: A conference report.* Washington, D.C.: U.S. Dept. of Health, Education, and Welfare, 1966.

Cazden, C. Subcultural differences in child language: An interdisciplinary review. *Merrill-Palmer Quarterly,* 1966, **12,** 185–219.

Cherry-Peisach, E. Childrens' comprehension of teacher and peer speech. *Child Development,* 1965, **36,** 467–480.

Cohen, R. Conceptual styles, culture conflict, and nonverbal test of intelligence. *American Anthropologist,* 1969, **71,** 828–856.

Ervin-Tripp, S. Sociolinguistics. In L. Berkowitz (Ed.), *Advances in experimental social psychology.* Vol. 4. New York: Academic Press, 1969.

Fries, C. C. *American English grammar.* New York: Appleton-Century, 1940.

Garvey, C. Investigation of child-adult differences in problem-solving communication. Final Report to Office of Education, Project No. 1-C-053, February 1972.

Heider, E. R. Style and effectiveness of childrens' verbal communications within and between social classes. Unpublished doctoral dissertation, Harvard University, 1969.

Heider, E. R. Information processing and the modification of an "impulsive conceptual tempo." *Child Development,* 1971, **42,** 1276–1281. (a)

Heider, E. R. Style and accuracy of verbal communications within and between social classes. *Journal of Personality and Social Psychology,* 1971, **18,** 33–47. (b)

Hess, R. D., & Shipman, V. C. Early experience and the socialization of cognitive modes in children. *Child Development,* 1965, **36,** 869–886.

Higgins, E. T. A social and developmental comparison of oral and written communication skills. Unpublished doctoral dissertation, Columbia University, 1971.

Kagan, J., Moss, H., & Sigel, I. Psychological significance of styles of conceptualization. In J. C. Wright and J. Kagan (Eds.), Basic cognitive processes in children. *Monographs of the Society for Research in Child Development,* 1965, **28,** 73–124.

Krauss, R., & Glucksberg, S. The development of communication competence as a function of age. *Child Development,* 1969, **40,** 255–265.

Krauss, R., & Rotter, G. Communication abilities of children as a function of status and age. *Merrill-Palmer Quarterly,* 1968, **14,** 161–173.

Krauss, R., Vivekananthan, P., & Weinheimer, S. "Inner speech" and "external speech": characteristics and communication effectiveness of socially and non-socially encoded messages. *Journal of Personality and Social Psychology,* 1968, **9,** 295–300.

Labov, W. The logic of unstandard English. In F. Williams (Ed.) *Language and poverty.* Chicago, Illinois: Markham Publishing Co., 1970.

Loban, W. D. *The language of elementary school children.* Champaign, Illinois: National Council of Teachers of English, 1963.

Rosch, E. Human categorization. In N. Warren (Ed.) *Advances in cross-cultural psychology.* Vol. 1. London: Academic Press, in press.

Ruth, D. Language, intelligence and social class: a study of communicative effectiveness within same-class and cross-class pairs. Unpublished undergraduate honors thesis, Harvard College, 1966.

Schatzman, L., & Strauss, A. Social class and modes of communication. *American Journal of Sociology,* 1955, **60,** 329–338.

Schlosberg, H. The description of facial expressions in terms of two dimensions. *Journal of Experimental Psychology,* 1952, **44,** 229–237.

Stewart, W. A. Urban Negro speech: sociolinguistic factors affecting English teaching. In R. W. Shuy (Ed.), *Social dialects and language learning.* Champaign, Illinois: National Council of Teachers of English, 1965.

Weener, P. D. Social dialect differences and the recall of verbal messages. *Journal of Educational Psychology,* 1969, **60,** 194–199.

Williams, F. (Ed.) *Language and poverty.* Chicago: Markham Publ., 1970.

Witkin, H. A., Dyk, R. B., Faterson, H. F., Goodenough, E. R., & Karp, S. A. *Psychological differentiation.* New York: Wiley, 1962.

7
Variations in Young Children's Use of Language: Some Effects of Setting and Dialect

William S. Hall
Michael Cole
Stephen Reder

The Rockefeller University

Gillian Dowley

The University of Chicago

INTRODUCTION

Considerable research has focused on ethnic group and social class differences in language structure and language use. Of special concern has been the implications of such differences for the educational performance of school children. Our own research in this area has been guided by two questions:

1. Are there identifiable cognitive effects of differences between Black English and Standard English that have educational implications?
2. How does the language used in the preschool classroom differ from that used in nonformal settings?

It is fairly well recognized in the scholarly community that Black English Vernacular (BEV) is a separate system, historically connected to Standard English, but possessing distinct phonological and grammatical forms (cf. Baratz, 1969; Hall & Freedle, 1973; Labov, 1970; Simons, 1973). While both comprehension and production differences have been reported for some populations and some tasks (e.g. Baratz, 1969; Labov, 1972; Osser, Wang, & Zaid, 1969), there has been very little direct evidence to support Baratz's contention that standard test performance of Black English Vernacular speakers is systematically depressed by the administration of standardized intelligence tests in Standard English.

A series of studies conducted by Quay (1971, 1972, 1974) provides negative evidence with respect to the influence of dialect on test performance. Working with lower and lower-middle-class Black children in Philadelphia, Quay administered the Stanford—Binet test in its standard form or in a Black English Vernacular form.

In none of her studies did Quay find that standardized test instructions depress the performance of her Black subjects, although a rather extensive range of ages (4—12 years) and subject backgrounds were explored. Item analyses were also carried out to see if the more language-dependent items would show a greater dialect effect, but no consistent effects were discernable.

Williams and Rivers (1972) reached exactly the opposite conclusion from a study of dialect variations in the administration of the Boehm Test of Basic Concepts; nonstandard versions of the test produced higher scores than the standard version, enough better so that when presented the test in a non-standard form (that included vocabulary as well as phonological variations). Williams and Rivers' children scored at levels appropriate to the published norms for children of comparable age and higher socioeconomic levels. Since the Stanford—Binet and Boehm tests are presumably tapping the same cogitive abilities, the results of the Williams and Rivers study was clearly at odds with those produced by Quay, but the source of the discrepancy is not obvious.

In none of this work has there been an attempt to evaluate the influence of dialect usage for larger units of material of the kind that young children often encounter either in school or in various nonschool settings.

In this chapter we will discuss two research studies. The first was an experiment designed to test the hypothesis that dialect differences are likely to be influential when the child must retain and then reproduce a substantial body of material that is both meaningful and interesting to him. For this purpose we used a set of four stories accompanied by illustrative materials. The second study represents our first attempt to extend the seminal observations of William Labov on situational variability in children's language usage.

Labov (1972), pp. 241—254) reports vast changes occurring in a black child's linguistic output when he is moved from a school interview to his living room, the topic is changed, and a friend is present (to name a few of the variables involved). We hoped to be able to produce some of the same changes under somewhat more controlled circumstances as an initial step in developing a theory of the variables controlling children's language usage in the classroom.

STUDY I:
STORY RECALL AND DIALECT

The children who participated in Study 1 were selected from two distinct geographical locations within New York City. All children were approximately 4½-years-old; boys and girls were equally represented.

One group of children, all of whom were Black, were residents of a large urban renewal complex in Central Harlem attending a federally sponsored Head Start Program for 2½ hr per day. Admission to the program required that the children's parents have incomes of $4,000 of less per year for a family of four. Approximately 60% of the children were members of families receiving welfare payments.

The 16 remaining children, all of whom were White, lived in downtown Manhattan and were attending a fee-paying, nonprofit coop nursery housed in the Educational Alliance. Admission to the nursery required that parents of these children worked at a variety of professional and semiprofessional jobs (artists, school teachers, civil servants, etc.). The income of these parents was estimated to be $7,000 per year or above by the program administrator.

Each child was presented four stories for recall during the course of the experiment. Each story contained six picture sequences with an accompanying segment of description and dialogue. The main objective of the experiment was to determine if the language dialect in which the story was told would influence the children's recall of the stories. With this purpose in mind, the accompanying text for each story was written either in Standard English or in Black English Vernacular following the principles described in a number of sources on Black English (Baratz, 1969; Hall & Freedle, 1973). As an illustration of Standard English—Black English contrast, we have reproduced the verbatim protocol for one of the subjects as Table 1.

We were also interested in determining if the race of the experimenter influenced the impact of language dialect. For example, it could well be that black children would perform better to stories told in Black English Vernacular only if the speaker was someone they expected to speak in this dialect.

To test this possibility each child heard and recalled four stories: one in Black English read by a black experimenter, one in Black English read by a white experimenter, one in Standard English read by a black experimenter and one in Standard English read by a White experimenter. The order in which the combinations of dialect-experimenter conditions were experienced was carefully balanced within each of the two basic population groups.

Each child participated in two separate sessions, one with a black and one with a white experimenter. At each session he was told two of the four stories, one in each of the two dialects. The experimenter escorted the child to a table in an area set off from the classroom, with the explanation that they were going to play some story-telling games. The subject was shown the picture books and told

TABLE 1

The Flower Pot Story: Standard English Version

This is Michele. She is watering the flowers. Crash! Now Michele thinks that Mother will be mad. She wants to run away. "I'm not mad," says Mother. "I know you didn't mean to do it. Let's clean up the mess." Michele picks up the flowers. She gives them to Mother. "Don't worry," says Mother, "we'll put them in a nice pot." Now the flowers are okay and the mess is all cleaned up. "Come on," says Mother. "Let's go and make some cookies."

Subject's recall of the story:

Michelle ah waterin' the flower. Michelle broke ah the flowers. Her mother gonna git mad. The mother said, "She isn't mad." The mother said she'll didn't mean it. Michelle ah gived her mother a brand new pot. Her mother say come on like her mother say the flower, the flower is clean up. The End.

Subject's responses to questions about the story:

Experimenter:	John, what is the girl's name in the story?
John:	Michelle.
Experimenter:	Good. Now, John what happened to the flower pot?
John:	It fell. It broke down.
Experimenter:	Who knocked it down?
John:	Michelle.
Experimenter:	Who picked the flowers up from the floor?
John:	Um, the liddle girl gave it to her muddah.
Experimenter:	In the story, tell me, what was Michelle afraid of?
John:	Michelle said her mother'll git mad.
Experimenter:	How did she feel at the end of the story?
John:	Um, she she she she fell uh better.
Experimenter:	Okay, why did she feel better?
John:	Because, uh, uh, because
Experimenter:	What is that?
John:	A rocking chair. So you rock.
Experimenter:	Why does Michelle feel better?
John:	Because Michelle because ah the flowers.
Experimenter:	What is Michelle going to do at the end of the story?
John:	
Experimenter:	Is there anything you can remember?
John:	Macause the girl break the flowers down and she runnin' away. But the Lady of the rockin' chair rock and rock and rock. And she, her muddah get mad. Like her mudder say she didn't mean it. She pick little pieces. Her muddah say come on come on like her muddah say and the end.

The Bicycle Story: Black English Vernacular Version

Here come Peter. He got a new bike. Peter, he don' know how to ride de bike. Dem othah boy — de be laughin at him. Look at Peter. What a jerk! He ain't gon neber learn ta ride no bike. I show ya — Peter say nex time I ain't go fall

(continued)

TABLE 1 *(Continued)*

off. I'ma go ride my new bike all the way up de street. An' dat what he do! He be ridin' – an ridin' – til he git to da park – an he don' fall off eben once.

Subject's recall of the story:

Peter got a new bike. He's lafin at him. Look at Peter. Peter fell off the bike. He don't know how to ride. They was lafin at him cause Peter wuz, wuz a got a new bike wuz he don't know how to ride. Look at that Peter! Peter say he gon fell off. Peter was ridin' ridin' an ridin' just like he's gon' do.

Subject's responses to questions about the story:

Experimenter:	What be de boy name?
John:	Peter.
Experimenter:	That's right. What do Peter have?
John:	A new bike.
Experimenter:	Um hum. What happened to Peter?
John:	Peter is gon' fall off.
Experimenter:	What do de oder boy do?
John:	They wuz lafin at him.
Experimenter:	Then what do Peter do?
John:	Peter is fell down to de street. Peter is fell down to de bike. They wuz lafin.
Experimenter:	Where do Peter go at de end?
John:	The end of de bike.
Experimenter:	Where do Peter go at the end?
John:	That new bike with tires on.
Experimenter:	There be anythin' else you cin remember?
John:	Um huh! Peter was ridin on that bike. He's too big to ride that bike. He was lafin at him. Look at Peter! He rode by. Peter is ridin' *all* the way up to the street. That's just what you gonna do.
Experimenter:	Okay.
John:	An that's the name of that bike.
Experimenter:	Very good, John.
John:	Thank you!

that he was supposed to listen carefully while the story was being told and then would have to tell the story back. The instructions were given in the dialect appropriate to the particular experimental condition.

After the child had completed retelling the story, several questions designed to probe recall were presented in the appropriate dialect, regardless of whether or not the information demanded by the question was present in the child's spontaneous recall of the story. All sessions were tape-recorded and transcribed.

Data Analysis

The data from this experiment were subjected to an analysis of variance employing the following three independent variables: (1) raical group member-ship (Black versus White); (2) experimenter (Black versus White); and (3) dialect of stimulus material (Standard English versus Black English Vernacular). Performance was not analyzed as a function of stories because the design deliberately confounded story with the three variables of primary interest. Three aspects of the group's performance were examined: (1) spontaneity of the child's recall; (2) recall accuracy; and (3) dialect of output.

Findings

Race of experimenter did not significantly affect any of the three performance measures to be discussed below.

Spontaneity of recall. Some of the children were quite hesitant in responding to the experimenter's request for recall. To determine if this hesitancy was related to any of the variables under study, each child's responses to the request for retelling the story were analyzed. A "yes" was assigned to the response if the child had to be prompted, a "no" if the child spontaneously began to retell the story.

On the average, 52% of the stories were retold spontaneously, with no reliable variations in spontaneity as a function of any of the independent variables.

Recall accuracy. The spontaneous recall of each of the stories was scored for recall accuracy. Each of the phrases used in telling a story was considered an item for recall. Hall scored each of the 64 response protocols, item by item, to determine a "percent spontaneous recall" score for each subject on each story. An item was scored correct if the information contained in the item was also contained in the subject's recall, even if the recall was not verbatim. This scoring scheme was then applied independently by two research assistants who did not know the nature of the study or the hypotheses under consideration. There was 94% overlap between the scores assigned; Hall's scores (following an arcsin transformation) were then used as the basic data. The major result was exactly what we would expect if dialect influenced spontaneous recall but ethnic/socioeconomic group did not: the black and white groups performed equally well when tested in their *own* dialects, but the black children did better than the white children in BEV, while the white children did better in Standard English. The disruptive effect of BEV on the white children was particularly pronounced. (Any result reported as significant yielded an F ratio with a probability of less than .05.)

When probed with questions contained in Table 1, there was an overall increase from 25 to 63% in the proportion of correct information for both racial groups.

Dialect of output. Each child's language at the time of unstructured recall was classified in one of four categories: Standard English, Black English Vernacular, Mixed Dialect, and Unclassifiable. Only 2 of the white children used any Black English Vernacular forms whereas all of the Black children did so. Pure use of Black English Vernacular was also rare in this sample; all but 6 of the Black children mixed Black English Vernacular and standard forms in the spontaneous recall; these 6 used BEV exclusively.

Discussion of Study 1

It seems reasonable to say that we have shown in this experiment that one's "parent" dialect is the overriding factor in language performance in our story-recall task. Children produce utterances primarily in their "parent" dialect.[1]

The research also demonstrates that when the dialect in which the to-be-remembered story is read does not match the dialect which the child uses to retell the story, mnemonic interference is produced. The pattern of this interference clearly supports the idea that the black children suffer no generalized language deficit. Rather, differences in language codes are critical when evaluating the children's performance. It can also be noted that the code-related mnemonic interference for recall is not a completely general feature of these children's recall. The probed recall data show clearly that some information which has been stored is not produced at the time of the initial, spontaneous recall. When considered together, the pattern of results in the spontaneous and probed recall provides some information as to how the dialect of presentation influences task performance.[2]

The fact that Blacks recall more information when the task format used is BEV and that whites recall more information when the task format used is Standard English suggests clear dialect effects. Differences between the dialect of presentation and children's native dialect produce a mnemonic "production

---

[1] A caution must be inserted here concerning black children. These children are bidialectical − their production is a mixture of Black English Vernacular and Standard English dialects. We do not know the extent to which the same may be said of their parents, but it is certainly true of their community where Black English Vernacular is not standardized. Consequently, we cannot specify the mix of dialects used by the parents of the black children studied here. This raises the possibility that our "Black Dialect" stories do not represent as close a match to the black lower-class children's parents' dialect as is the case for the white middle-class children, putting them at a relative disadvantage in the story recall situation.

[2] Our findings, particularly those concerning the bidialecticalism of black children, are similar to those recently reported by Ciborowski and Choy (1974) for Hawaiian children. In their research, two groups of school children were presented stories which contained embedded items that were later tested for recall. One group of children was judged to possess competent verbal skills in Standard English and extremely marginal (if any) verbal skills in Hawaiian Islands dialect. A second group of children was judged to possess competent verbal skills in Hawaiian Islands dialect but with only marginal verbal skills in Standard English. An unusual feature of the study was that the dialect speakers were not economically disadvantaged. The pattern of performance showed that the dialect speakers, despite schoolroom ratings, were in fact bidialectical, demonstrating verbal skills both in Standard English and in Hawaiian Islands dialect.

deficiency," analogous to the production deficiency for unrelated materials described in the work of Flavell (1970) and Scribner and Cole (1972).

If this argument is correct, it suggests an explanation of the differences between our results and those of Quay (1971, 1972, 1974). IQ tests may be a poor arena in which to assess the cognitive consequences of dialect usage because of the nature of the task required by them, which is generally much closer to our probe questions than the spontaneous recall.

Other differences between Quay (1971, 1972, 1974) and the present work may also be important. One limitation of the IQ test as an experimental tool is that control over the dialect in which the material is encoded can be manipulated only via the instructions and labeling of the individual items: How the child encodes and mentally manipulates these materials is open neither to control nor observation.

STUDY 2:
LANGUAGE USE IN FORMAL AND INFORMAL SETTINGS

In a very influential paper, William Labov (1970) vividly demonstrates the vast differences in the linguistic resources that black inner-city youngsters bring to a formal testing situation and an engaging conversation with the same adult when a friend is present.

Unhappily, Labov's demonstration has not been systematically followed up by research on the kind of sociolinguistic and situational variables that control young black children's use of their linguistic resources. As a start in this direction, we conducted a study contrasting black preschoolers' language use in a specific "quiz-like" classroom setting with language used by the same children on a trip to their local supermarket.

The children who participated in Study 2 were residents of the same large urban renewal complex in Central Harlem used in Study 1. Altogether, 24 children were included, 12 three-year-olds, and 12 four-year-olds.

The research in which these children participated consisted of two phases. During the first phase, children were taken to the supermarket two at a time for 1 hr. The trip began with the children and a tape recorder being placed in a shopping cart. While riding through the supermarket in the shopping cart, the children were engaged in conversation with special care taken to include discussion of five areas of foodstuff: fresh fruits and vegetables, cereals, meats, dairy products, and canned goods. The children were allowed to handle all the goods. Upon their return to the classroom, the children were asked to tell their teachers about the trip. Recordings of the 24 children obtained in the supermarket and the classroom while the child told the teacher about the supermarket were transcribed and analyzed to answer the following questions:

1. What general differences can be observed between speech in the classroom and in the supermarket?

2. Are developmental differences in the speech used by children the same in the two settings?

3. What are the best predictors of recall and language use in the two settings?

4. Can we obtain some hints about the critical factors at work in what we consider to be examples of formal (classroom) and informal (supermarket) conversation?

Findings

Children differed in the speech produced in the supermarket and classroom situations as can be clearly seen from Table 2. In the informal, supermarket setting the average number of words was greater, the percentage of questions attended to was greater, and the average number of words in response to a question was higher. Despite quantitative differences, language used in the two situations was qualitatively similar in several respects: neither the form of utterances (questions, commands, statement/assertions) nor the content they expressed (want/need, family-related, love-like) differed drastically across the two situations.

The second question of concern in this study was whether our measures of linguistic behavior (MLU — mean length of utterance, etc.) would be similarly related to age in the two settings. In order to answer this question we calculated the correlation between age and each of the dependent variables separately for each setting. The results are briefly summarized in Table 3.

With the possible exception of the number of words in responses to a question, it appears that correlations between age and measures of linguistic development are substantial only in the classroom setting. This finding suggests a clear limitation on conclusions we can reach from the vast literature on language acquisition. Considering that the range of ages sampled (3–4 years) was rather restricted, and that data in the classroom setting are consistent with previous

TABLE 2

Summary Data Showing Differences between Speech in the Classroom and the Supermarket

	Classroom	Supermarket	t ratio for difference
Average number of spontaneous utterances per minute	2.4	5.8	3.69[a]
Average length of an utterance	2.9	3.4	2.05[b]
Average percentage of teacher's questions attended to	65.7	92.2	4.67[a]
Average number of words in response to a teacher's question	2.6	3.3	3.03[a]
Number of different grammatical structures produced	3.8	6.9	3.87[a]

[a] $p < .01$.
[b] $.05 < p < .10$.

TABLE 3
Correlations of Age and Speech in Two Settings

	Spontaneous utterances per minute	MLU	Questions attended to (%)	Number of words in response to a question
Classroom	.41[a]	.25	.33	.31
Supermarket	.03	.04	.05	.22

[a] $p < .05$.

results, these findings support Labov's (1972) speculations that our assessments of linguistic development are closely tied to particular interactional settings.

But we would like to be able to do more than speculate about the role of interactional setting. Are the differences in behavior observed in the supermarket and classroom a function of interrogatory style, or some other aspect of the interaction which is controlling the children's speech?

Our first step in disentangling the many factors that might operate to constrain children's verbal behavior in classrooms was to construct a "classroom supermarket." Located within the school, this play shopping environment, when properly used, permitted us to observe the children as they engaged in both formal and informal interchanges with adults.

The "informal" segment of the classroom supermarket began as the child left the home classroom. The experimenter, playing the role of assistant storekeeper, entered the classroom to seek a volunteer to "go to the market." As a rule the main difficulty at this point was to ward off a host of would-be storekeepers. The child who was chosen then got a ride in the marketbasket along with a dozen, common grocery items, and a tape recorder that was left on during the entire sequence.

Once they arrived at the "market," the adult said something along the following lines:

> Wow, look at all the things we have for our store. Let's take 'em out and put them on the shelves, OK? Go ahead, you can take them out and put them any place you want. OK. What's that you're taking out now . . .

These instructions were continued as the child stood up in the cart and placed items on the shelves. Each object was named both to insure the child's attention and to discover what the child labeled each item, since the names often differed from common Standard English usage.

The "formal" segment of the supermarket situation was, in effect, a disguised recall task. A second experimenter, "the lady shopper," entered the store looking for food for a party. She asked the child, who was now out of view of the goods in the store, what she could purchase there. We believed that this segment of the school supermarket scene would provide an analog to the situation the children found themselves in when they returned from the real supermarket and were confronted by the teacher's enquiries as to what they had seen there.

The data for the eight children who participated in all parts of the study (real supermarket, classroom, class supermarket) are presented in Table 4. For purposes of comparison, these eight children's data from the real classroom and supermarket settings are included in the table.

While the number of children is too small to make statistical analysis worthwhile, the pattern of results is certainly striking. When the children are in a setting like they had experienced in the regular supermarket (e.g., exposure time), the two measures that reflect spontaneity and attentiveness (1 and 3) look very much like their supermarket behavior, while the *length* of utterance measures (2 and 4) are as low as they exhibited in the regular classroom. However, when they are asked to recall items from their play supermarket, all measures of performance look like out previous "classroom" linguistic behavior.

These data take us slightly beyond our initial observations. They suggest that not all aspects of a child's speech production are equally controlled by either the environmental–institutional setting or the two interactional "sequence types" that we have tried to sample. But it should be clear that only a few of the possible interactions that can occur in the two settings we sampled have been studied. In all the cases examined, the children are talking with adults, usually in a conversation that is constrained by the fact that the adult is doing a lot of question asking.

When one looks at a randomly chosen few minutes of children's speech in the classroom and the supermarket (thus allowing for segments in which children are talking to each other), one finds that measures of speech production increase in both settings, relative to the structured segments selected for analysis heretofore. Thus, the issue is not just "classroom versus supermarket" but rather the nature of the verbal exchanges that take place in those settings. Both the supermarket

TABLE 4
Language Output for Eight Children

	Classroom (formal)	Recall (formal, school supermarket)	Exposure (informal, school supermarket)	Actual supermarket (informal)
1. Average number of spontaneous utterances per minute	1.6	1.4	4.5	6.04
2. Average mean length of an utterance	2.8	1.4	1.8	3.31
3. Average % of adult's questions attended to	68%	77%	92%	92%
4. Average number of words in response to adult's question	2.3	1.3	1.5	3.01

and the classroom allow for the kinds of exchanges that we have glossed as "formal and informal." However, it appears to us that the classroom is more likely to produce the former and the supermarket the latter.

CONCLUSION

The two lines of research summarized in this chapter have produced results which are in no way contradictory to the results of previous research in this area. Yet the conclusions to which we are led are quite different than those that one is likely to encounter in the literature.

The reason for this apparent contradiction is to be found in a difference in initial assumptions about the conditions necessary for understanding children's linguistic abilities. With a few exceptions, such as Labov's pioneering research (see also Shatz & Gelman, 1973), investigators of children's language have restricted themselves to a narrow range of interactional settings, usually located in a classroom and usually involving exchanges between adults and children with the adult playing the role of interrogator. Under these conditions, young, Black children do, indeed, use a rather limited array of their total linguistic resources.

The task of our current research is to follow the logic of these results and to design more comprehensive and rigorous means for sampling language behavior across a wide spectrum of commonly encountered interactional situations and subject populations. This seems to us the most promising path to reaching beyond vague assertions about situational variability and the increasingly sterile debate about language differences and language deficits.

ACKNOWLEDGMENTS

A more detailed version of Study 1 appeared under the title: "Story Recall in Young Black and White Children: Effects of Racial Group Membership, Race of Experimenter, and Dialect." *Developmental Psychology,* 1975.

The research reported in this chapter was supported by grants from the Carnegie Corporation of New York to The Rockefeller University for Michael Cole and William S. Hall and PHS GM 21796 to the laboratories of Professors George A. Miller and Michael Cole at The Rockefeller University.

REFERENCES

Baratz, J. C. A bidialectal task for determing language proficiency in economically disadvantaged Negro children. *Child Development,* 1969, 40(3), 889–901.

Ciborowski, T., & Choy, S. Nonstandard English and free recall: An exploratory study. *Journal of Cross-Cultural Psychology,* 1974, 5, 271–281.

Flavell, J. H. Developmental studies of mediated memory. In L. Lipsitt & H. Reese (Eds.), *Advances in child development and behavior.* Vol. 5. New York: Academic Press, 1970.

Hall, W. S., & Freedle, R. O. A developmental investigation of standard and nonstandard English among black and white children. *Human Development,* 1973, 16(6), 440–464.

Labov, W. The logic of nonstandard English. In F. Williams (Ed.), *Language and poverty.* Chicago, Illinois: Markham, 1970.

Labov, W. *Language in the inner city: Studies in the Black English Vernacular.* Philadelphia, Pennsylvania: University of Philadelphia Press, 1972.

Osser, S., Wang, M., & Zaid, F. The young child's ability to imitate and comprehend speech: A comparison of two subcultural groups. *Child Development,* 1969, 40, 1063–1076.

Quay, L. C. Language dialect, reinforcement, and the intelligence test performance of Negro children. *Child Development,* 1971, 42, 5–15.

Quay, L. C. Negro dialect and Binet performance in severely disadvantaged black four-year-olds. *Child Development,* 1972, 43, 245–250.

Quay, L. C. Language dialect, age, and intelligence-test performance in disadvantaged black children. *Child Development,* 1974, 45, 463–468.

Scribner, S., & Cole, M. Effects of constrained recall training on children's performance in a verbal memory task. *Child Development,* 1972, 43, 845–857.

Shatz, M., & Gelman, R. The development of communication skills: Modifications in the speech of young children as a function of listener. *Monographs of the Society for Research In Child Development,* 1973, 38, No. 5.

Simons, H. D. Black dialect and reading interference: A review and analysis of the research evidence. Department of Education, The University of California at Berkeley, Berkeley, California. Mimeo, 1973.

Williams, R., & Rivers, W. Mismatches in testing from Black English. Paper read at the Annual Meeting of the American Psychological Association, Honolulu, Hawaii, 1972.

8

Prose Processing from a Psychosocial Perspective

Roy Freedle

Educational Testing Service

Mary Naus

Haverford College

Laraine Schwartz

Educational Testing Service

In this paper we explore a novel approach for analyzing a selective but highly important aspect of the structure of prose: its social structure. By this we mean that there is implicit and explicit information in the structure and content of a given prose passage that designates among other things characteristics of the author of the passage and characteristics of the intended listener of the passage. We hypothesize that this social information about author and intended listener affects how a subject in a laboratory setting will process, store, and retrieve the prose information when it comes time to recall the passage. In other words, the social information contained in prose can significantly affect the information-processing steps engaged in by an experimental subject. For these reasons our model is designated as a psychosocial processing model. An important consequence of our psychosocial model is that it affects the conditions under which lexical simplification (called deconfabulation) will occur; it also predicts a special set of circumstances under which the lexical entries of the original passage is either left intact (called same-order confabulation) or is made more complex (this being one type of higher-order lexical confabulation). Data are presented which evaluate various aspects of the psychosocial model. Additional distinctions are introduced concerning processing steps engaged in while the prose text is being processed (called "on-line" processing) in contrast to steps engaged in when reconstructing the prose information — this later phase is called "off-line" processing. Some exploratory methods for examining these two processes are presented.

A PSYCHOSOCIAL COMMUNICATION APPROACH TO PROSE

While a number of different methodologies for researching the structure and comprehension of prose have emerged in recent years (e.g., Crothers, 1972; Frase, 1972; Frederiksen, 1972; Freedle, 1972; Kintsch, 1974; Meyer, 1975; Rothkopf, 1972), they primarily consider the information processor in a psychosocial or cognitive-social vacuum with prose structure being represented by concepts lacking in the structural aspects for which prose is primarily intended — namely, social communication and social persuasion. While a full scale exploration of how sociocultural patterns influence cognitive assessment of multisentence contexts will take many years to clarify, some modest psycholinguistic inroads into this line of thinking have recently been made (see Freedle, 1975, 1976; Freedle & Hall, 1976; Hall & Freedle, 1975). We extend this work by attempting to analyze the transaction of social knowledge that occurs under the influence of a single factor: *the age of the intended listener.*

We can best illustrate the assumptions of the psychosocial model by referring to Fig. 1.

The part of Fig. 1 labeled "normative paradigm" for prose research makes explicit reference to neither the psychosocial characteristics of the author of the text passage, the intended listener of the passage, the experimental listener (the experimental subject is the experimental listener), the projected or actual listener to whom the experimental subject is to construct his or her retelling, nor the characteristics of the experimenter. These factors have not been listed presumably because early researchers either overlooked them or did not regard them as relevant to their immediate interests.

We shall argue that the psychosocial factors listed in the part of Fig. 1 called "A new communicative psychosocial paradigm" can critically affect how the text information is processed and/or can critically affect how the information is transformed at the time of recall. In listing these factors we intend to make overt that which is usually presupposed; this will eventually lend itself to a more explicit information-processing model that includes decisional steps which assess the pragmatic intent of the author (A_i) and the pragmatic appropriateness of each sentence of the text for the intended listener (L_j).

A clear way to demonstrate that we do make implicit psychosocial judgments when listening to prose is to give some examples. Suppose you heard the following: "Myths are experiencing a rebirth of interest in modern society. The science-minded Victorians believed that myths were trivial superstitions . . . . " It

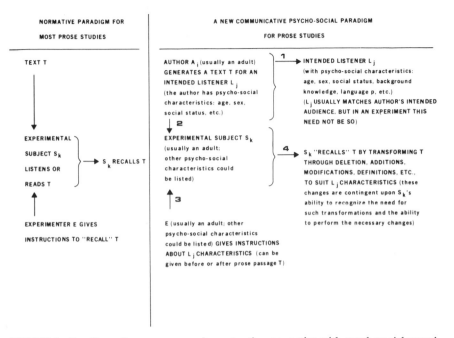

NORMATIVE PARADIGM FOR

MOST PROSE STUDIES

A NEW COMMUNICATIVE PSYCHO-SOCIAL PARADIGM

FOR PROSE STUDIES

TEXT T

AUTHOR A $_i$ (usually an adult)
GENERATES A TEXT T FOR AN
INTENDED LISTENER L $_j$
(the author has psycho-social
characteristics: age, sex,
social status, etc.)

1 → INTENDED LISTENER L $_j$
(with psycho-social characteristics:
age, sex, social status, background
knowledge, language p, etc.)
(L $_j$ USUALLY MATCHES AUTHOR'S INTENDED
AUDIENCE, BUT IN AN EXPERIMENT THIS
NEED NOT BE SO)

2

EXPERIMENTAL

SUBJECT S $_k$

LISTENS OR

READS T

→ S $_k$ RECALLS T

EXPERIMENTAL SUBJECT S $_k$
(usually an adult;
other psycho-social
characteristics could
be listed)

4 → S $_k$ "RECALLS" T BY TRANSFORMING T
THROUGH DELETION, ADDITIONS,
MODIFICATIONS, DEFINITIONS, ETC.,
TO SUIT L $_j$ CHARACTERISTICS (these
changes are contingent upon S $_k$'s
ability to recognize the need for
such transformations and the ability
to perform the necessary changes)

3

EXPERIMENTER E GIVES

INSTRUCTIONS TO "RECALL" T

E (usually an adult; other
psycho-social characteristics
could be listed) GIVES INSTRUCTIONS
ABOUT L $_j$ CHARACTERISTICS (can be
given before or after prose passage T)

FIGURE 1   Paradigms for prose research contrasting normative with psychosocial experimental designs.

is possible to make some inferences about psychosocial characteristics of author and intended listener from the very first word of the first sentence, namely, "myths." Additional words and the complexity of the concepts suggest that the passage comes from an educated adult of Western society; it seems likely that the author is addressing someone of similar educational background and age. Social status of both is less clear-cut but our prejudices and knowledge of the culture would probably suggest the upper-middle class.

You probably agree that such information *is* implicit in or inferrable from the short passage just presented, but you may still maintain that it in no way alters how we process the information and that it certainly has little to do with how we would recall the information if asked to do so. But imagine that you were told before you heard the excerpt that you must retell this passage to a young child who is interested in what you have to say. The way you will respond to the various lexical items and phrasing of the text now will have quite another significance. The "raw" text has taken on new import and recall no longer seems to be the simple "memory" task that it once seemed to be.

You may still protest that the way in which you will selectively listen to the passage may have been altered by this very special and unusual instruction, but nevertheless the "raw" semantic text information and the way it generally is encoded and processed is still in no way affected. To demonstrate that you are mistaken will require a more persuasive example. Suppose the text represented a dialogue from some novel; let the passage read as follows:

Oedipus, the King: Let's make love.
    The Queen: Okay.

Most readers should now see that the social information in this exchange of speaker and listener in the dialogue is critical to discovering the real meaning of the passage. The real meaning is conveyed by our knowledge that a cultural taboo has been violated. *The "raw" information fails to convey the actual meaning.* The way the text is processed and comprehended is affected by our success in projecting our knowledge of permissible social roles for various kinship relations. That is, the real meaning hinges upon discovering that the relationship husband–wife is not sanctioned for the kinship relationship mother–son. This is merely one way in which covert social knowledge can alter the creative comprehension process.

The normative model in Fig. 1 seems to work only because researchers have unconsciously selected materials that were "appropriate" to the psychosocial expectations of their experimental subjects; as a consequence, at least one of the underlying information-processing steps that must take place in assessing the significance and meaning of prose as a genre has been overlooked. We intend to focus upon just these missing steps.

A STUDY DEMONSTRATING THE INFLUENCE OF PSYCHOSOCIAL CHARACTERISTICS IN COMPREHENSION AND RECALL

We shall present the outline of a study and some data which illustrate some of the decisions that experimental subjects make with regard to just one social characteristic: the age of the intended listener. Later we shall attempt to uncover methods which reveal at what point in the comprehension process these age-related decisions are made.

Two texts were selected. One was written by an adult for a child. The other was written by an adult for an adult. In both cases these two texts were evaluated to determine whether the passage as it stood was perceived to be intended for either a child or an adult. The adult passage (referred to as the Myth passage below) was correctly identified as intended for an adult by almost all judges (35 out of 36). For the passage originally intended for a child (referred to as the TV passage below) our judges identified it correctly 30 out of 36 times. Thus both passages contained a sufficiently dense network of cues to allow one to make a clear-cut judgment as to the age of the intended listener.

Eight experimental conditions were studied using adult college students as subjects. Half of the conditions presented the child TV passage first. The subjects were told in advance that they would have to retell the story twice –

once to an adult and once to a child of about four years of age, the order to be determined after they heard the passage. These same subjects were then presented the adult Myth passage. Again they expected to retell it twice – once to an adult and once to a child, with the order determined after they heard the passage. Counterbalancing for order of retelling to an adult or child yields four conditions here. The remaining four conditions involved presenting the adult Myth passage first followed by the child TV passage. Every subject in the experiment therefore generated four stories: (1) a child story retold to an adult, (2) a child story retold to a child, (3) an adult story retold to an adult, and (4) an adult story retold to a child. In all cases, the child and adult to whom they were to retell the passage were imaginary listeners.

The following hypotheses were generated from the psychosocial paradigm. When the actual listener of the subject's retelling *matches* the author's intended audience, minimal changes in the structural complexity of lexicon and syntax can be expected. Thus when a child story is retold by our subjects back to a child, and when an adult story is retold by our subject back to an adult, a match between the actual listener and the author's intended audience occurs. Both of these retellings should be *closer* to the original text structure than those conditions in which our subjects told an adult story to a child, and retold a child story to an adult. The reason this hypothesis makes sense is that if one emphasizes the communicative nature of prose as a genre, a well-formed passage (the reconstructed one produced by our subjects) is one that matches its structure and exposition to the abilities of the intended listener. A socially responsible speaker is one who is aware of his obligation to create a discourse that honors the social contract which underlies an acceptable communicative act (see Clark & Haviland, this volume; also see Grice, 1967).

Since the original child text is assumed to have already matched its structure, content, and exposition to its intended audience (a child) there should be little need for our experimental subject to alter this in retelling the passage back to a child. Ditto for the adult passage which is retold back to an adult. However, when the original passage is retold back to a person who differs radically in age from the originally intended audience, then something will have to be changed if the passage is to be socially well-formed. We shall now suggest just a few of the changes that can be expected.

The Myth passage opens as follows: "Myths are experiencing a rebirth of interest in modern society. The science-minded Victorians . . . . " If this is to be retold to a child who for some reason is interested in what we have to say, several reasonable things may happen. If we want to retain some idea about the concept "myths" then we might (a) use the word "myth" and then define it; we can label this as definitional deconfabulation with the confabulated word "myth" still present in the retelling; or (b) we can substitute some definition of the concept "myth" but choose to delete the word "myth" in the retelling; we shall label this as definitional deconfabulation without the confabulated word present; or (c) we may totally delete this concept as outside the range of the child; (d) if deleted, we additionally might try to substitute some remotely related concept to fill the "gap," or we may feel the need to *tell* a myth rather than to speak abstractly about myths.

In contrast to these possibilities, consider what we might do with the other type of social mismatch that occurs when a child story is to be retold to an adult. Let the child passage begin as follows: "TV cartoons and special shows for you are getting better and better today. Your parents used to think that . . . ." and so on. One might take the expression "TV cartoons and special shows . . . ." and substitute "Public entertainment media for children . . . ." In this case something new has been added; one has inserted a higher semantic node which includes the concepts of cartoons and special shows. When this occurs without mention of TV cartoons we shall call this transformation a higher-order confabulation with respect to the original text. If the person supplies the higher-order semantic nodes and also retains the lower concepts (e.g., TV cartoons and special shows) we will call this higher-order confabulation plus retention of the original level. Notice that for both these kinds of transformations, the use of higher-order confabulation can be rationalized or explained as being responsive to the social demands of communication — one does not want to insult an adult listener by presenting information that is "beneath" his or her current level of knowledge; and, if one is forced to do so by the conditions of the experimental setting, then one can try to honor the social contract of discourse by formalizing the child text so that at least its vocabulary sounds appropriate to the adult listener. Another example in which a more "formal" vocabulary can be used is for the expression "getting better and better" which may invite such substitutions as "becoming increasingly excellent." This latter example does not add any higher-order semantic nodes and so would be classified as a more complex vocabulary selection but at the same level of "confabulation" as the original child text.

The important point to keep in mind is that in contrast with the normative paradigm our psychosocial paradigm rationalizes particular kinds of semantic transformations introduced into a subject's retelling which involve deconfabulation, same-order confabulation, and higher-order confabulation with respect to the original text. The rationalization suggested by a psychosocial orientation emphasizes the necessity of appropriately matching the psychosocial characteristics and abilities of the actual listener. This matching occurs in order to honor the social contract implicit in communicative exchanges at the discourse level.

THE RESULTS OF TWO STUDIES USING A PSYCHOSOCIAL PROSE PARADIGM

The first question that concerned us was whether the actual (projected) listener, to whom our experimental subjects had to retell the TV and Myth stories, would significantly alter the structure and content of the retellings so as to provide clues about the age characteristics of the actual (projected) listener. This question is of interest because our psychosocial model indicates that the structure and content of the original passage (regardless of for whom the original author intended it) would be transformed to match the characteristics of the actual (projected) listener.

A judge was used to sort the stories (four stories from each subject). The stories were presented in random order so that the four stories from any one subject were dispersed randomly throughout the whole collection; this provided a more stringent test than would have been the case had the judge been provided information concerning which subject produced which four stories. The results of this sorting task were very clear-cut. When the experimental instructions requested that the subjects supply an adult version for the Myth passage, our judge identified the end product as an adult story in 23 out of 24 cases; when instructions requested a child version for the same Myth passage, our judge identified the end product as a child story in 21 out of 24 cases. Similarly, when the TV passage whose structure was originally intended for a child was presented by our subjects to a child, the judge identified 22 out of 24 stories as products addressed to a child audience; but when the same TV story was addressed to adults, our judge identified 24 out of 24 cases as appropriate to an adult.

Thus our experimental subjects significantly transformed the information in the original passages to conform to the characteristics of the actual (projected) listener. To make our point even more forcefully, this can be stated as follows. When it comes to a choice of whether the style and content of the original stimulus passage will exert the most powerful effect on what an experimental subject will produce or whether the creative transformations which match the psychosocial characteristics of the actual listener will dominate the retellings of our subjects, it is clear that the psychosocial effects dominate, not the structure of the "raw" stimulus passage. The normative paradigm model is unable to account for such findings, let alone predict the existence of such transformations.

In addition to the above results, two additional groups of experimental subjects were run using the TV and Myth passages. In this case the subjects were not given any special instructions as to whom their listeners would be. In fact these conditions were run in much the same way that the normative paradigm is run: a passage was presented to them, the experimenter asked the subject to recall it in his own words, and the subject recalled it. We were especially interested in whether the subjects would spontaneously give themselves "self-instructions" to alter the structure and content of the TV story or whether they would "parrot" back the structure and content of the original. If they did the latter, it would provide some support for the normative paradigm. Needless to say, the psychosocial model leads us to expect that only the TV story would be radically altered in structure and content to conform to the special experimental conditions of the retelling — the adult experimenter is present, and the adult subject may feel "foolish" retelling material clearly intended for a child in the presence of another adult (unless given good reason to do so by special instructions) and so will alter its structure (style) and content so as to conform to the structure and content that the culture leads us to expect from adults speaking to other adults. The results again are clear-cut. The judge who evaluated who the "actual" listener was for the earlier set of protocols also sorted the retellings produced by the two additional conditions. When the TV passage was presented, all 13 subjects produced adult type retellings. When the Myth passage was presented, the same 13 subjects (counterbalanced for order of presentation across the two types of passages) produced the expected adult type versions. Thus this provides additional evidence in favor of the psychosocial model. In the absence of who their "actual" audience is to be the subjects spontaneously provide "self-instructions" to alter the child TV story so as to make it appropriate for an adult listener. Again, the normative paradigm does not account for this spontaneous transformation of the "raw" stimulus structure.

Our next set of results which are rather clear-cut come from semistructured interviews of our experimental subjects after they finished retelling both versions of the remaining passage. In particular we were interested in the degree to which they were *consciously aware of applying transformational "rules" of a psychosocial type* to the various story reconstructions.

The results are compactly summarized in Table 1. We scanned a transcription of their interview for evidence regarding changes in vocabulary (either simplify it or make it more complex) as a function of whether they were to reconstruct the information for a child or adult. Also we scanned the protocols for statements regarding whether they would add or delete information as a function of the age of the listener. Finally, we were interested in whether these transformations seemed to occur to them while they were listening (on-line) to the original story or only after (off-line) they had listened.

The psychosocial model suggests the following hypotheses:

1. When the original passage was written for an adult, but is to be retold to a child, we expect the vocabulary to be simplified and we expect some information to be deleted only if it is judged beyond the capacity of the actual listener.[1]

2. When the original is intended for a child but is to be retold to an adult, we expect the vocabulary to be made more complex and for information to be

---

[1] A further consequence of our psychosocial paradigm is that it raises an important issue concerning the sampling of stimulus passages for presentation to subjects in prose research. The unconscious sampling of texts which are appropriate to the ability level and interests of the college population which is usually tested using the normative paradigm has masked an interesting question concerning the conditions under which lexical deconfabulation, or same-level confabulation, will occur and under what other conditions higher-order confabulation will occur. Work reported by Kintsch (1974) stemming from the normative paradigm has prematurely settled this question by indicating that same-level confabulation occurs. Our results indicate that additional theoretical empirical work is necessary on this issue.

TABLE 1

Interview Results: Subjects' Awareness of Psychosocial Transformations[a]

Passage stimulus conditions		Response condition	Type of transformation				When transformation would be applied		
Originally written for whom	Name of passage	Actual listener	Simplify vocabulary	Use more complex vocabulary	Add information	Drop information	While listening (on-line)	After listening (off-line)	Both during and after
Adult	Myth	Adult	5	0	9	2	6	11	2
Adult	Myth	Child	19	0	18	10	6	12	2
Child	TV	Adult	1	13	7	3	11	8	2
Child	TV	Child	12	0	13	3	11	8	1
Adult	Myth	Unstated	2	0	4	1	7	4	0
Child	TV	Unstated	0	0	7	1	5	5	0

[a]The first four rows indicate the results of the interview for the psychosocial instructions which involved a total of eight experimental conditions. The last two rows indicate the results of the interview for those conditions approximating the normative paradigm wherein subjects were told nothing about listener characteristics; in fact, the concept of intended listener and actual listener never was raised. The last three columns have a somewhat different import for the last two rows; the interviewer simply asked how the subject tried to remember the information for later recall – was it during exposure to the story or after? Subjects from the psychosocial conditions were asked explicitly about when they were aware of trying to apply the age-related transformations: during or after listening.

added so as to make the content more appropriate and "interesting" to the adult listener.

The psychosocial model makes no predictions about *when* these transformations would take place, so the data will have to speak for themselves in this regard.

Table 1 indicates that when the original story was intended for a child (TV cartoon passage) but is presented to an adult, the conscious awareness of applying a more complex vocabulary in the retelling is spontaneously suggested by 13 out of 24 subjects, and only one person out of 24 suggested using a simpler vocabulary. In general this agrees with our expectations stemming from the psychosocial model.

Twelve out of 24 indicated a simplification of the vocabulary versus none out of 24 for making it more complex for children when the original story is for a child. This result was a surprise since it at first seems to contradict the psychosocial model which indicates that little if any change need be introduced into the original version when the intended listener matches the actual listener. We can account for this discrepancy as follows: subjects indicated that the TV passage was intended for children of about 10–15 years of age, but our instructions asked people to imagine their "actual" listener to be four years of age. Because a younger child has less capacity to handle material than does an older child, this accounts for the high reportage of *further* simplifications of the vocabulary among our subjects. Had we known that the TV passage was perceived as more appropriate for older children we would have altered our instructions for the age of the "actual" listener to equal 10–15 years rather than four years. Given this discrepancy in age, however, we offer this as a post hoc explanation of the seeming divergence from the predictions of the psychosocial model.

Also in Table 1, when the adult Myth passage was used, subjects said they would simplify the vocabulary (19 out of 24 times) when retelling it to a child, and none suggested making the vocabulary more complex. When an adult is the actual listener, thereby producing a match in age with the author-intended listener, no further alterations in the vocabulary should be reported. However, five out of 24 subjects said they would further simplify it (and no one suggested that they would make it even more complex). While five discrepant reports is not large, it actually is not well explained by the psychosocial model.

The spontaneous reports concerning adding and deleting information is a little more difficult to tally because it depends upon qualifying this suggested transformation with respect to competency of the "actual" listener and separating comments which, for example, concern adding or deleting information to improve "style" of the original passage. With these caveats in mind, our initial results also given in Table 1 indicate the following. Subjects believe that they would add clarifying or motivating material to the original "raw" stimulus content when the actual listener is a four-year-old child, regardless of whether the original was the TV or Myth passage (13 out of 24, and 18 out of 24, respectively). Ten out of 24 said they would also delete certain information so as to simplify content when the original was intended for an adult but was to be retold to a child. We shall not dwell on the details provided by our subjects since this will be presented elsewhere. We do wish to state that these results concerning the retention, deletion, or addition of new information across the several experimental conditions has a rationale from the psychosocial perspective but is again not predicted and not well accounted for by the normative paradigm which assumes the preeminent importance of the "raw" information in the stimulus passage.

Finally, Table 1 provides some tentative information concerning subjects' judgments as to *when* they apply these transformations. There is some evidence that the transformations interact with the type of original material. That is, there are more on-line processing decisions when the original story is intended for a child (the TV passage), and fewer on-line decisions when the story was originally intended for an adult (the Myth passage). This interaction suggests the following interpretation. If the original material is difficult to apprehend, then most of the age-related transformations are best handled after the "raw" information is processed. To try to carry out these additional semantic judgments along with material that is difficult enough to handle in its own right may too greatly overload the capacities of our adult subjects. On the other hand, when the original material is easy to understand (as is the TV passage), then more of the age-related transformations seem to occur on-line while the subject is exposed to the materials.

If this is so (and new methods are needed to settle the question) then we can modify our previous claims about just how psychosocial factors affect discourse comprehension and encoding processes in the following way. Early in exposure to the material the subject assesses the relative familiarity and difficulty of the material. Such a decision is an information-processing step in a flow diagram of a full discourse comprehension model. If the material seems to be unfamiliar and hard to assimilate into one's current knowledge structure (encoding), then the subject may decide to pay close attention to the details by rehearsing segments of the passage as he listens. This latter is another step in the information-processing model which involves selection of a cognitive strategy. Such a decision to use a special rehearsal strategy need not block the awareness that some phrases and words encountered indicate the psychosocial characteristics of the author and intended listener. Also such a strategy decision need not block the assessment that such and such a word or phrase must be transformed if the social contract with the actual listener is to be honored. The *depth* to which such a psychosocial transformation will be carried out while the person is listening to the passage may be modified by the difficulty of the material and the difficulty of the required transformation. Thus, it is possible that the greater the difficulty of the passage, the lower the depth of the psychosocial transformation that occurs on-line. If the full transformation has not been carried out during on-line processing, then the remainder of the psychosocial transformation may be accomplished off-line, during reconstruction of the passage.

By "depth" of psychosocial transformation we offer the following possibility. At least two steps (a depth of "two") must underlie such transfomations; first one must classify the word or phrase as inappropriate for the actual listener, and second, one must perform the needed alterations, such as a higher-order confabulation, deconfabulation, or the like. Only the first of these steps may be performed if the material is very difficult for the experimental subject. If the material is easy, both steps may be carried out on-line.

The recall protocols. The results from the subject interview are suggestive, but one should look to the recall protocols themselves to gain further insight, not into when the psychosocial transformations are performed, but into the degree and kind of changes that are employed.

The first set of examples comes from some pilot data which used as the stimulus materials the adult Myth passage referred to above and a child passage which dealt with the structure of the moon and the planetary system — we shall refer to this child story as the Moon passage. Segments from the recall of subjects for a child and adult audience are presented in Tables 2 and 3. We present data from two subjects who responded to the Myth story (Table 2) and two subjects who responded to the child story (Table 3). With respect to the lexicon, the pattern of psychosocial transformations is closely tied to the interview results which we presented earlier. In particular we see that when there is a mismatch between the author's intended audience and the experimental subject's "actual" listener, the subject will formalize the vocabulary and/or introduce higher-order confabulation when a child story is presented to an adult listener; and, when an adult story is presented to a child, the subject will introduce definitional deconfabulations without the head concept (e.g., for the concept "Victorians" which is deconfabulated as "some people a long time ago"), or will introduce definitional deconfabulations with the head concept present (e.g., for the concept "myths" this is rendered as "A myth is a story, a very old story . . . "). Some concepts are deleted, presumably intentionally, as beyond the range of the actual listener (e.g., the concept of "science" was deleted). When the intended listener and actual listener match, a more or less correct paraphrase of the "raw" information is attained in the retelling. This general consistency or recall protocols with the interview suggests that the psychosocial transformations which our subjects believed they used were actually used in the retellings.

Another result which is apparent in Tables 2 and 3 is the selection of a discourse style (formal descriptive versus narrative) as a function of who the "actual" listener was to be. Regardless of the stimulus material, our pilot

TABLE 2
Prose Data Illustrating Psychosocial Transformations of a Story Originally Intended for an Adult

Author's passage (excerpt)	Adult subject to adult listener	Adult subject to child listener
"The science-minded *Victorians* believed that myths were trivial superstitions. . . ." (intended for adult)	"The *Victorians* did not appreciate myths because they were scientifically minded and myths did not reflect scientific knowledge." Comment: More or less correct paraphrase of the author's original passage. (Subject L.A.)	"A myth is a story, a very old story. *Some people a long time ago didn't think that myths were very important . . . and didn't help us with our daily lives.* (No reference to "science") Comment: Defined "myth." Decomposed "Victorians" into more 'elementary' concepts. Deleted reference to "science." (Subject L.A.)
"The science-minded *Victorians* believed that myths were trivial superstitions. . . ." (intended for adult)	"*Victorian society* expected the notion of myths to be irrelevant to their scientific discoveries." Comment: More or less correct paraphrase of original passage. (Subject L.R.)	"*People who lived about 100 years ago* knew a lot of stories that they thought weren't good stories so they didn't believe them." Comment: Decomposed "Victorians." Overgeneralized the lexical item "myths" into "stories." Deleted reference to "science." (Subject L.R.)

subjects tended to select a formal mode for adult listeners and a narrative mode for child listeners. Explicit mention of style shifts did not occur very often in the interviews. Another result not spontaneously mentioned in interviews concerns the use of dramatic intonation when the "actual" listener was a child. Our subjects almost invariably employed a "sing-song" intonation which is sometimes referred to as "baby-talk" intonation when a child was to hear the passage (see Freedle, 1976).

We now direct our attention to the protocols from the main study described earlier and compare a small portion of the materials which have already been scored with the interview results. Our focus here will be on the occurrences of deconfabulation, higher-order confabulation, and same-level confabulation. Other distinctions will be introduced to complete the categorization process. In particular from the Myth passage we shall present data on how subjects transformed the lexical entry "myths" for adult and child listeners. From the TV passage originally intended for a child listener we will also present how the same

TABLE 3

Prose Data Illustrating Psychosocial Transformations of a Passage Originally Intended for a Child

Author's passage (excerpt)	Adult subject to adult listener	Adult subject to child listener
"The moon looks bigger than the stars. The moon is much smaller than the stars, but the moon is much closer to us than any star. That is why it looks so big. . . . " (intended for child)	"There . . . are optical illusions that play tricks on you in your perception of the bodies in the universe. What looks to you as if the stars are smaller than the moon is actually a deception because the moon is much smaller than the stars. . . ." Comment: Introduces higher-order confabulation by categorizing the phenomena as "optical illusions" and as "perceptual"; also includes higher-order semantic node of "universe" along with lower-order retention of concepts of "stars" and "moon." Style shifts to a more formal descriptive one rather than a narrative one. (Subject L.K.)	"To you . . . the stars look much smaller than the moon . . . but actually that's not true. . . . The stars are much larger than the moon, they are simply farther away. . . . " Comment: Makes more explicit statement about "truth" conditions than original. Otherwise it is rather close paraphrase of original?; retains original narrative style. (Subject L.K.)
"The moon looks bigger than the stars. The moon is much smaller than the stars, but the moon is much closer to us than any star. That is why it looks so big. . . ." (intended for child)	"The passage points out the effect of *distance* on the *size* of the stars. The moon looks larger than the stars but in actuality is much smaller. Comment: Inserts "higher" semantic nodes abstracting the facts of the passage into "distance" and "size" relations; still retains lower concepts. Style shifts to formal descriptive rather than narrative style. (Subject M.S.)	"Even though the moon looks bigger than the stars, this is only because it is very close to you." Comment: More or less correct paraphrase of original passage which was intended for a child. Retains narrative discourse style. (Subject M.S.)

subjects transformed the string "TV cartoons and special shows" as a function of the age of listeners. The results are presented in Tables 4 and 5.

Table 4 shows that the subject retains the original lexical concept "Myths" when addressing an adult (17 out of 24 times) but retains this concept only two out of 24 times when addressing a child. This is expected by our psychosocial model. The other striking difference appears in the frequencies for the category

TABLE 4

Some Psychosocial Transformations Observed in the Orally Recalled Prose Passage Originally Intended for an Adult

Response category	Example(s)	Frequency of use to adult listener	Frequency of use to child listener
Identity transformation	Says "Myths" as in the original text	17	2
Deletion transformation	No reference to "Myths"	0	0
Higher-order confabulation			
a. without Head Item "Myths" present	"Verbal art expressing a form of religion"	0	0
b. with Head Item "Myths" present	"Myths are an aspect of religion"		
	Comment: in form of a definition but uses a higher-order semantic category "religion" where "myths" is intended as a strict subset.	} 0	} 0
		0	0
Definitional deconfabulation			
a. without Head Item "Myths" present (implicit deconfabulation)	"Some old stories" "Same legends"	0	6
b. with Head Item "Myths" present	"Myths *are* old stories" "Myths, *or* stories, . . ."		
	Comment: the definition does not use a higher-order semantic category, but instead one of about the same level and perhaps of greater familiarity.	} 3	} 22
		3·	16
Conjoining of same-level categories with Head Item	"Myths *and* stories" "Myths *and* legends"		
	Comment: it is possible that the subject intended a definitional deconfabulation, but the syntactic conjoining leaves this in doubt.	4	0
		$N = 24$	$N = 24$

called Definitional Deconfabulation in which on 22 out of 24 occasions the experimental subject introduces some simplification of the original lexical concept "Myths" purportedly to match the capabilities of his young listener. The same transformation occurs very infrequently when addressing adults. This effect is also expected on the basis of our psychosocial model.

Using a within-subject comparison, and classifying every difference across age of listener as to whether it was or was not predicted by the psychosocial model gives the following result. Only one subject out of twenty (four subjects were

TABLE 5
Transformations for the String "TV cartoons and special shows . . . . " When Orally Recalled for an
Adult or Child: Passage Originally Intended for a Child

Response category	Example(s)	Frequency of use to adult listener	Frequency of use to child listener
Identity transformation			
a. full identity	Says "TV cartoons and special shows"	0 } 15	0 } 15
b. close paraphrase	"Cartoons, TV shows . . . ."	15 }	15 }
Deletion transformation			
a. total deletion	No mention of TV cartoons and/or special TV shows	0 } 2	0 } 8
b. deletion of one concept	Either says "TV cartoons" or "Special TV shows"	2 }	8 }
Higher-order confabulation			
a. without Head Items present	"The mass media for children. . . ."	0 } 7	0 } 1
b. with one or both Head Items present	"The mass media for kids such as TV cartoons. . . ."	6 }	1 }
c. conjoining	"Cartoons and educational programs"	1 }	0 }
Definitional deconfabulation			
a. without Head Items present	"Spider Man"	0 } 0	0 } 0
b. with one or both Head Items present	"TV shows like Spider Man. . . ."	0 }	0 }
Conjoining of same-level categories with Head Item concepts	"Morning shows for kids, Special Shows, and TV cartoons. . . ."	0	0
		$N = 24$	$N = 24$

undecidable) violated the psychosocial model. By a sign test (one-tailed) this was significant at $p < .001$. Since a random difference between the two age groups is "predicted" by the normative model (or, to be more precise, no prediction at all is made by this model regarding age) we must take this result as supportive of the psychosocial model. Similarly we must note that this result for the actual transformations used in their recall generally agrees with what the subjects said they did during the interview.

Table 5 presents a similar but weaker result when the stimulus passage was originally intended for a child. The subjects use a few more deletions when addressing a child as contrasted with an adult; this is not strictly predicted by our psychosocial model, but the result is interpretable when we remember that subjects seemed to believe that the original passage was intended for a slightly older child than we told them to address; hence, they deleted a little more than expected so as to match the lower competence of a four-year-old as opposed to a 10—15-year-old. Also, more higher-order confabulations are used when addressing adults as opposed to children (7 versus 1). This is again expected by the psychosocial model. Finally we note that there is a heavy use of the identity transformation category regardless of the age of the listener. This in itself was not predicted by the psychosocial model.

As before, a within-subject comparison is possible using just their two retellings: to a child and to an adult. The number of differences across these versions which are predicted by the psychosocial model were determined. The results indicate three violations out of a total of 16 scorable subjects (but eight subjects' data did not point to a clear psychosocial distinction). A sign test (one-tailed) showed such a difference is significant at $p < .011$. Hence, we again have some weak support for the psychosocial model as opposed to the normative model.

In summary, we have presented a number of selected results which contrast two approaches to the characterization of a select subset of the types of decisions that subjects make in comprehending and reconstructing prose passages. We have argued that previous models[2] have ignored a very critical but obvious aspect of prose processing, namely, decisions that relate in part to the psychosocial characteristics of the author and intended listener of a passage. Further, we have found that experimental assessment of the two models lends support to the psychosocial model. We therefore conclude that future models of prose processing must include, as a prominent aspect of the comprehension process, explicit decisions which reveal how the subject transforms the "raw" information in a text so as to honor the social norms required in the performance of any well-formed communicative act, including the act of reconstructing a prose passage.

ACKNOWLEDGMENT

The data collection and analyses were made possible by internal funds from Educational Testing Service to author R. F.

REFERENCES

Asch, S. E. *Social psychology*. Englewood Cliffs, New Jersey: Prentice-Hall, 1952.
Crothers, E. Memory structure and the recall of discourse. In R. Freedle & J. B. Carroll (Eds.), *Language comprehension and the acquisition of knowledge*. Washington, D.C.: Winston, 1972.
Frase, L. Maintenance and control in the acquisition of knowledge from written materials. In R. Freedle & J. B. Carroll (Eds.), *Language comprehension and the acquisition of knowledge*. Washington, D.C.: Winston, 1972.

[2] After this work was completed, some earlier work which deals in part with the effects of social information on memory for prose came to the authors' attention. Asch's (1952) review of this literature on sharpening and leveling of selected lexical items in prose should provide further impetus to the models considered in this paper.

Frederiksen, C. Effects of task-induced cognitive operations on comprehension and memory processes. In R. Freedle & J. B. Carroll (Eds.), *Language comprehension and the acquisition of knowledge.* Washington, D.C.: Winston, 1972.

Freedle, R. Language users as fallible information-processors: implications for measuring and modeling comprehension. In R. Freedle & J. B. Carroll (Eds.), *Language comprehension and the acquisition of knowledge.* Washington, D.C.: Winston, 1972.

Freedle, R. Dialogue and inquiring systems: the development of a social logic. *Human Development,* 1975, 18, 97–118.

Freedle, R. Human development, the new logical systems, and general systems theory: preliminaries to developing a psychosocial linguistics. In G. Steiner (Ed.), *Piaget, and beyond.* Vol. VII in the series: Psychology of the 20th Century. Zurich, Switzerland: Kindler Verlag, 1976, in press.

Freedle, R., & Hall, W. S. An information-processing approach to some problems in developmental sociolinguistics. In K. Riegel & J. Meacham (Eds.), *The developing individual in a changing world.* Zurich, Switzerland: Kindler Verlag, 1976, in press.

Grice, P. *Conversational conventions.* William James Lectures, Harvard University. Unpublished mimeo, 1967.

Hall, W. S., & Freedle, R. *Culture and language: the Black American experience.* Washington, D.C.: Hemisphere Press, 1975.

Kintsch, W. *The representation of meaning in memory.* Hillsdale, New Jersey: Lawrence Erlbaum Assoc., 1974.

Meyer, B. *The organization of prose and its effects on memory.* Amsterdam: North-Holland American Elsevier, 1975.

Rothkopf, E. Structural text features and the control of processes in learning from written materials. In R. Freedle & J. B. Carroll (Eds.), *Language comprehension and the acquisition of knowledge.* Washington, D.C.: Winston, 1972.

9

Articles, Quantifiers, and Their Encoding in Textual Comprehension

Keith Stenning

University of Liverpool

SOME FORMAL ANALYSIS

This chapter describes an experiment. The experiment investigates subjects' comprehension of English articles and quantifiers. Oddly enough, the above sentences of this chapter, apart from stating something true and germane, provide an example of one of the linguistic relations that are the central concern of the chapter. In the first section I attempt to arrive at a formal account of this linguistic relation; the second section discusses some experiments from the literature in the light of this account; the third section presents an experiment which was designed to contrast predictions stemming from this formal account with those of some other current analyses.

The very first sentence above contains the phrase "an experiment," headed by the indefinite article, and the second sentence contains the phrase "the experiment" which is identical except that its article is definite. In order to comprehend this text a reader must retrieve a relation between these two phrases which is marked by their articles. That, says our intuition, would seem to be a simple matter: The first sentence says something about an experiment, and the second says something else about the *same* experiment. The articles mark this relation of coreference.

However compelling this intuitive account of the relation between these two phrases may appear, closer examination reveals that it is difficult to generalize to other examples of indefinite—definite phrase relations and that it is full of obscurities even when applied to the present example. The first sentence makes a statement of existential force, true just if there is *at least one* experiment which

193

has the property of being described in this chapter. As such, the statement does not contain a phrase that *refers* to an experiment, and so no phrase in the first statement can be related to the definite phrase "the experiment" in the second statement by the relation of coreference. This point can be illustrated by considering an alternative continuation of the first statement. Suppose the second sentence of this chapter read "In fact several such experiments are described." If this second statement were true, it would then be odd to assign any of these experiments the status of being the experiment referred to by the phrase "an experiment" in the first statement. It would also be odd to continue the text with a sentence containing the singular definite phrase "the experiment" without further specification of the intended referent.

Several points emerge about when the first two sentences make sense, and what sense they make when they do. First, the possibility of the occurrence of the phrase "the experiment" related to the earlier phrase "an experiment" is contingent on the membership of the domain of interpretation of the text. If this chapter contains descriptions of more than one experiment, or less than one experiment, its first two statements jointly convey something false. Second, falsity of the statement containing the indefinite phrase infects the status of statements containing subsequent definite phrases related to that indefinite phrase. If there is no experiment described in this chapter, the second statement is also false. The first existential statement and the indefinite phrase that it contains certainly seem to be involved in the interpretation of the second statement containing the definite phrase but it seems that we must search for some involvement other than a sharing of reference.

Consideration of other types of statement that might contain the indefinite phrase reinforce this latter point. Suppose that the first statement of this chapter reads "Every book on human comprehension describes an experiment" and the second statement remained exactly as it is now. Such an opening would be perfectly intelligible, and would be true just in case every such book contained a description of exactly one experiment (perhaps the same one in each book, and perhaps different ones) that investigated subjects' comprehension of English quantifiers and articles. In this case it would be clear that the phrase "an experiment" would not refer to any one experiment since there might be a large number of such books containing descriptions of different experiments. Each of the books must contain a description of a unique experiment, but this uniqueness condition is not the simple one that there be only *one* such experiment described in the domain of interpretation.

Logicians, faced by difficulties that arise from treating existential phrases as referring expressions employ the apparatus of quantifiers and bound variables, and some recent accounts of definite phrases have attempted to identify these phrases with logical variables (e.g., Harman, 1972). This suggestion avoids some of the problems of the simple "coreferential" theory of indefinite/definite phrase relations. On this account the definite article marks the fact that a phrase is related to a particular logical variable. A simplified form of the last example would then be represented as follows:

"Every book describes an experiment. *The experiment* investigates comprehension."

$(x)\ (\exists y)\ (x$ a book $\rightarrow (y$ an experiment $\& x$ describes $y))$. *? (y an experiment & y investigates comprehension)*.

These two formulas are then amalgamated to form:

$(x)\ (\exists y)\ (x$ a book $\rightarrow (y$ an experiment $\& x$ describes $y \& y$ investigates comprehension$))$

The definite article phrase in the second statement is represented by the italicized part of the formula. The question mark signifies that the definite phrase only marks the variable that it is represented by: Its quantificational structure is inherited from the earlier statement and only becomes explicit when the two statements are amalgamated. The redundant conjunct is then deleted.

This account of the phrase relations does not, as it stands, express the uniqueness condition discussed above, but it does explain how the singular nongeneric noun phrase "the experiment" can be related to a large number of elements of the interpretation. Attractive as this theory of definite phrases may be, it presents problems when an attempt is made to generalize it to other examples. An example in which the phrases are plural will illustrate the type of problems encountered. Consider the two sentence text: "Every book on human comprehension describes experiments. The experiments investigate subjects' understanding of the articles." The quantifier related to the indefinite phrase "experiments" is existential, just as it was in previous examples. The quantifier related to the definite phrase "the experiments" must be universal. The same occurrence of a variable cannot be bound by different quantifiers, and therefore the definite phrase cannot mark the phrase as being related to the same variable as its indefinite precursor.

Two candidates for the relation between indefinite and definite phrases have now been presented, and criticized. The first criticism sought to establish that such phrases cannot be coreferential and the second that definite phrases do not simply mark the repetition of variables introduced by earlier indefinite phrases. These two analyses of indefinite–definite phrase relations provide examples of two contrasting approaches to the representation of texts, and, I believe, can point us toward a better analysis of these relations. The Variable theory is an example of what I shall call a semantic approach to the description of texts: its rules attempt to amalgamate the semantic representations of the separate sentences of a text into some agglomerated formal object on the basis of the structure of the sentences. The meaning of the text is then described through interpretation of this larger formal object. This approach has difficulty in representing texts when certain structural features of related sentences diverge (in our last example the type of quantifier related to phrases differed). In contrast, the naive "Coreference" theory of these relations is a pragmatic analysis: it seeks to relate phrases through their relations to objects in the domain of interpretation. I believe that the naive analysis is correct in that it provides a pragmatic account but that it errs in choosing reference as the relation between indefinite phrases and elements of the domain.

What relation could replace reference to improve the analysis? We know that in the example of the first two sentences of this chapter where a singular indefinite article phrase appears, the subsequent statement containing the singular definite phrase is false unless there is exactly one experiment described here. We also know that the first statement, taken by itself, is true as long as there is *at least* one experiment described. So the indefinite phrase does not necessarily introduce a discourse referent even if it is true. It must be true in virtue of a unique instance to introduce an element for the subsequent definite phrase to refer to. Let us informally define a relation *identifies* that holds between an indefinite phrase, the statements in which the phrase occurs, and an element of the domain of interpretation of the statement. An indefinite phrase identifies an element of the domain just if the statement the phrase appears in is true, and true in virtue of a unique instance. The element it identifies is the unique instance. *Identifies* is a pragmatic relation between phrases, statements, and elements of the context, not a semantic property of sentence types.

How are these sets of identified elements related to subsequent definite article phrases? A particularly simple account of the *semantic* structure of definite phrases which will allow us to state this relation is one that regards the definite article as a simple universal quantifier. This account is perhaps most easily motivated by considering plural phrases like the one that occurs in our earlier example: "The experiments investigate subjects' understanding of the articles." If we replace the plural definite phrase by its indefinite counterpart "experiments" the sentence can be construed either universally or existentially. In some contexts one is more plausible, and in others the other is more plausible, but there is nothing particularly universal about plural phrases as such. Definite plural phrases, on the contrary, are always universal. In different contexts our example sentence will be about different sets of experiments, but whatever sets those are the plural definite phrase will quantify universally over the members of that set. When we consider singular definite phrases, there are a number of factors that complicate our intuitions. If the phrase is related to an indefinite phrase that identifies a unique element, this account of the definite phrase will treat it as a universal quantification over a set with only one member, and this at first may seem a little odd. If we treat the definite article as a universal quantifier we must see the uniqueness and existence entailments that it carries in some contexts as features inherited either from explicit existential identifying phrases in that context, or from assumptions that we make about the domain of interpretation of a text. This seems to me to be all to the good. All too often assumptions that we need to make about the context of an utterance get imported into the semantic form of the utterance, and the present case is one in which we can get a much simplified and general account of the definite article by separating those assumptions and treating them pragmatically.

The view of indefinite/definite phrase relations that I have outlined holds that indefinite phrases, in certain contexts, identify sets of elements of the domain, and that definite phrases quantify universally over those sets.

To establish any generality for an account along these lines it would have to be developed to include plural indefinite phrases, phrases within the scope of other quantifiers, relations between indefinite and definite phrases that differ by more than just their articles, and universally quantified indefinite phrases. For example, in the text "Tigers are members of the species *Felix domesticus.* They have stripes" the definite phrase "they" is morphologically quite different from the indefinite phrase "tigers." In addition, the truth of the second statement is not dependent on the truth of the first, as we saw was the case in earlier examples, and this is because the indefinite phrase in this example is universally quantified. Rather than try to pursue formal generality here, I will refer the interested reader to Stenning (1975) for a more complete development of this direction of argument.

The details of this treatment of the articles are less important here than the contrast between semantic and pragmatic theories of textual representation. I wish to entertain the hypothesis that a comprehender of a text may build up a representation of a domain of objects, their properties and their relations, rather than a representation of statement structures, during the comprehension of a text. For the encoding of some texts these two alternative approaches may lead to the same empirical predictions, but for others they will diverge, and this divergence is the topic of the promised experiment. Consider an example where the two encodings would diverge. The following two texts contain very different statement structures but they describe equivalent domains of objects with equivalent properties.

(1) There once was a cat and a dog. The cat and the dog were black and both lived in a house. The house . . .

(2) There once was a black cat that lived in a house. A black dog lived in the house. The dog . . .

The semantic forms of the texts are as follows:

(1) $(\exists x)\,(\exists y)\,(x$ a cat $\&\,y$ a dog$)$.
   $(x)\,((x$ a dog $\vee\,x$ a cat$) \rightarrow (x$ black $\&\,(\exists y)\,(y$ a house $\&\,x$ lived in $y)\,)$.

(2) $(\exists x)\,(\exists y)\,(x$ a cat $\&\,x$ black $\&\,y$ a house $\&\,x$ lived in $y)$. $(\exists x)\,(x$ a dog $\&\,x$ black $\&\,(y)\,(y$ a house $\rightarrow x$ lived in $y)\,)$.

The pragmatic constraints on the occurrence of singular definite phrases subsequent to singular indefinite phrases (the constraints embodied in the definition of *identification*) determine that at this stage of development of the text the domain contains only one cat, one dog and one house, and so both texts can be represented by an encoding of this fact together with the facts that the animals are both black and live in the house.

A NEW LOOK AT SOME OLD EXPERIMENTS

Much of the recent work on textual memory has been designed to demonstrate that the units of a subject's encoding of a continuous text are not isomorphic with the units that linguists employ to describe the semantic properties of sentence types (see for example, Barclay & Reid, 1974; Bransford, Barclay, & Franks, 1972). Inasmuch as this line of research has attempted to characterize positively the subjects' units of encoding it has tended to produce speculations about spatially arranged visual imagery as a possible mnemonic code. It is true that arguments have been advanced that image encoding at the unit of the word, as suggested by Paivio (1969), is inadequate to the representation of continuous text (see Bransford & McCarrell, 1974) but there has been a concentration on the encoding of spatial relations and pictures have been used to provide context for otherwise difficult passages of prose (Bransford & Johnson, 1972). While it seems intuitively likely that visual imagery plays an important and interesting role in memory of some texts, I believe that there is a potential confusion of issues inherent in this focus on visual–spatial imagery codes. The interaction of verbal and visual-imagery codes in human information processing is a legitimate concern but there is a very basic difficulty with research that conceptualizes spatial imagery as the fundamental mental representation of verbal information. We do not possess any formal theory or description of complex images which can classify them into equivalence classes in the way that we do have for linguistic entities; we have no theory of interpretation or entailment for images, nor even any conception of the possibility of such a theory.

In order to illustrate what I mean I shall take the example of Bransford and Johnson's (1972) well-known passage about a serenade. In the conditions of the experiment that concern us here, this passage was presented to two groups of subjects who saw different pictures of the objects mentioned in the passage. One of the pictures represents the objects in the causal and spatial relations that they have to each other in the passage and the other picture represents them in different causal and spatial relations. These two groups of subjects then heard the passage, registered a judgment of its comprehensibility and recalled the passage. The subjects who saw the picture congruent to the passage rated it as much more comprehensible and remembered far more of it than did the other group. The experimenters concluded that the subjects' encoding of the picture presented as context interacted with the incoming verbal information from the passage to determine these differences in performance. The subjects who saw the "appropriate" picture, although all the objects mentioned in the passage were represented in it, could not integrate the incoming information because they did not have the information about how these objects were related.

If the balloons popped, the sound wouldn't be able to carry since everything would be too far away from the correct floor. A closed window would also prevent the sound from carrying, since most buildings tend to be well insulated. Since the whole operation depends on a steady flow of electricity, a break in the middle of the wire would also cause problems. Of course, the fellow could shout, but the human voice is not loud enough to carry that far. An additional problem is that a string could break on the instrument. Then there could be no accompaniment to the message. It is clear that the best situation would involve less distance. Then there would be fewer potential problems. With face to face contact, the least number of things could go wrong. (Bransford & Johnson, 1972, p. 719)

I would like to suggest that this type of experiment can be performed using linguistic context rather than pictorial context, and that if this were done, it would allow us to employ well-developed formal representations of the informational situation. The three following passages serve as introductions of the text that this experiment used. The first, I suggest, is roughly equivalent informationally to the appropriate picture, the second to the inappropriate picture, and the third to a properly neutral introduction of the objects in the domain of interpretation of the passage.

In the scene I am about to describe, *a man* is serenading *a girl* who is at *an open window of a fifth floor apartment.* The sound of *his guitar* is not loud enough to carry on its own, and so he has *a microphone* near the guitar that is connected by *a wire* to *a speaker.* The speaker is supported at the level of her window by *a bunch of hydrogen balloons . . .*

In the scene I am going to describe, *a man* holding *a bunch of hydrogen balloons* is talking to *a girl.* Beside them *a guitar* leans against *a five story apartment building* and *a microphone,* connected by *a wire* to *a speaker* stands on the man's left . . .

In the scene I am going to describe there is *a man, a girl, a five story apartment building, a bunch of hydrogen balloons, a guitar, a microphone, a speaker* and *a wire . . .*

Each of the objects in the domain of the passage is introduced by an indefinite noun phrase (or by relation to an earlier introduced definite phrase in the case of "his guitar") that occurs in an existential statement. The differences are differences in the relations that are asserted to hold between these objects. A formal theory of the relation between these indefinite phrases and the subsequent definite phrases in the passage provides a precise abstract account of the class of models that yield consistent interpretations of each of the different passages that result: such a theory provides an articulated description of contexts and allows precise control of the relation between context and later information in the investigation of subjects' performance.

My intention is not to detract from the earlier research, or to minimize the importance of visual images or imagery. My hope is that developments of a large existing body of knowledge of logical theory can provide a positive characterization of the formal constraints on subjects' units of encoding, and more clearly define questions of the use of visual imagery. The salient characteristic of pictures as compared to linguistic descriptions, is that they force the representer to be determinate with regard to distinctions that language allows him to remain vague about. The picture that the experimenters here call "the incomplete context" cannot just represent the objects of the domain of interpretation. They must represent them in some relation to each other, and these relations conflict with the relations stated to hold in the passage. Even if the objects were simply lined up in a blank field they would still be related to each other spatially in a way that would be inconsistent with the passage. Of course, such a bleak picture could carry the warning "Construe these objects as just a spatially unrelated list!" but it would then have moved one step toward a linguistic code. This observation suggests an important question about visual images: how like pictures are they? Berkley pointed out the insufficiency of images that are like pictures for the representation of word meaning. If your mental image of a dog is really like a picture of a dog it must be specific with regard to many visual characteristics that language allows us to be vague about. As pictures become more diagrammatic they allow more and more features to remain unresolved, but they also become more and more reliant on conventions for their interpretation. Our formal representation of linguistic texts allow us to state, at least in some cases, exactly what is determined and what is vague about a message and therefore to look for the types of overdetermination in subjects' encoding of those texts that we should expect from certain visually based codes. It may be that the mental visual images that function in textual comprehension tasks are highly "diagrammatic" and are tagged with much interpretative information in a more abstract code. It is particularly difficult to see how our representation of some quantificational information in a visual code could be otherwise.

The arguments and experimental evidence against adopting linguists' units of semantic representation as a basis for psychological theories of text processing have seen, I believe correctly, the shortcomings of these units to stem from the fact that they are sententially based and not easily amenable to theories of either linguistic or nonlinguistic context. Many of these arguments are not only valid psychological criticisms but also point to shortcomings in formal theories of meaning. One direction that has been taken to improve the formal theories has been the writing of text grammars (see for an example of this approach applied to indefinite—definite phrase relations Van Dijk, 1973). These grammars attempt to extend the insights of transformational grammar to the textual domain, generating all and only well-formed texts and their syntactic and semantic descriptions. A systematic development of the Variable Theory of definite phrases sketched here would fall in this line of inquiry. The theory attempts to build a single formal object from the separate sentences of a text, and to do all semantic interpretation on that object. I have sketched one hasty argument against one particular treatment of one particular suprasentential relationship. This will not suffice to establish the correctness of any general approach but it suffices to suggest an alternative. The text grammar approach sees the text as progressively building up statement structure: The sketch of a treatment of indefinite—definite phrase relations that employed the relation of identification sees the existential statements containing indefinite phrases as progressively building up a domain of interpretation of elements and their set relations. The subsequent definite phrases were then interpreted on this domain. This construction of a domain can continue through the course of the text as new objects are introduced. This approach suggests that the article system of English plays a crucial role in expressing various uniqueness properties of sets of elements in the domain of the text. Again, by way of illustration, I shall take a well-known text from an experiment by Frase (1972). I shall omit some filler sentences.

> The Fundalas are outcasts from the other tribes in Central Ugala. It is the custom in this country to get rid of certain types of people. The outcasts of Central Ugala are all hill people. The hill people of Central Ugala are farmers. The farmers of this country are peace loving people (p. 341).

Frase found that subjects made few of the possible inferences based on the conditional form of the statements of this passage. The relevant sentences of the passage might be sketched as follows:

(x) $(x$ a Fundala $\rightarrow x$ an outcast$)$. (x) $(x$ an outcast $\rightarrow$ a hill person$)$.
(x) $(x$ a hill person $\rightarrow x$ a farmer$)$. (x) $(x$ a farmer $\rightarrow x$ is peace loving$)$.

It was pointed out in the discussion in Frase's paper that this passage would be much more natural if noun phrases were pronominalized across sentences, and that if this were done subjects would not have trouble drawing the inferences. This intuition seems wholly reasonable (though so far as I know untested), but if it is correct, that is not because the same information would be expressed in a more cogent style, but rather because the information would be changed. Pronominalized, the passage would read:

> The Fundalas are outcasts from the other tribes of Central Ugala. It is the custom in this country to get rid of certain types of people. They are hill people. They are farmers. They are peace loving people.

Note that beyond the problem of finding the antecedent of the pronoun "they" there is no need to amalgamate information from different premises in order to perform the inferences Frase was concerned with. Now there is an additional oddity about the passage which becomes clear when we consider the problem of finding this antecedent. The second sentence, which Frase does not regard as a premise, contains the indefinite noun phrase "certain types of people" which would most naturally occur as an introducing statement for the first statement of the passage. This observation is related to another: that, as the pronominalized passage stands, the antecedent for "they" would most likely be "outcasts from other . . . Ugala" or "certain types of people" but it might be "the Fundalas," and by this choice hangs some crucial properties of the set relations of the domain. If we pick either of the first two suggestions as antecedent, the resulting interpretation will not determine whether all outcasts are Fundalas, or only some. If we pick "The Fundalas" as the antecedent, the representation determines that all Fundalas are outcasts *and* they are the only outcasts. A still more natural passage would be:

> It is the custom of Central Ugala to get rid of certain types of people. These outcasts are the Fundalas. They are hill people . . .

This passage makes the set of all Fundalas identical to the set of outcasts in the domain of interpretation. The pronominalized sentences then are still of conditional form but the antecedent is the same in each case, and although these conditionals do not fix the set relations of the consequent properties, all these other sets are related to the originally introduced set. Where the logical relation between succeeding sentences is mediated by the transitivity of the conditional (see the transcription of the original) inference demands the combination of information about all the sets mentioned.

What implications do these two contrasting types of textual organization (organization through related definite antecedents, and organization through chains of indefinite consequents which become definite antecedents) have for semantic and pragmatic memory representations? In the example texts about the cohabiting cat and dog which were chosen to contrast the two types of encoding, three unitary sets of elements were identified and relations among them were stated to hold. Although nothing in the semantic form of the sentences indicated that the cat, the dog, and the house were distinct elements, it is reasonable to assume that as English speakers we possess the knowledge that they must be so. In the present example, when the text is organized by repeated definite antecedents, a set of outcasts is identified, and various other sets of elements (farmers, hill people, etc.) are related to that set. These phrases are not followed by related definite phrases and so the question of exactly what sets of elements in the domain they identify, if any, does not arise. Their semantic impact can be represented in terms of properties of the set of outcasts. On the other hand, when the textual organization is through the transitivity of conditional assertions these indefinite phrases in the consequents are followed by definite phrases, and so the representation of the sets of elements they identify becomes crucial to the accurate representation of the text. Furthermore, unlike the cat, the dog and the house, the sets of Fundalas, outcasts, farmers, hill people, and peace lovers are not disjoint and the text does not provide enough information to represent the contents of the domain. The information that is provided is only sufficient to entail that the sets are nested, but not that they are coextensional or proper subsets. The number of different possible relations between the five sets is very large. This information cannot be definitively represented by adding new members to the domain, or by tagging existing members with new properties.

If a subjects' favored strategy for representing texts is to try to build up a characterization of the contents of the domain it can be seen that these two types of textual organization will present very different levels of difficulty for him, and these levels of difficulty are at least consistent with our intuitions about the relative comprehensibility of the texts.

The contrast that I have attempted to draw between what I have called semantic and pragmatic encoding for these example texts parallels the applicability of image codes to these texts. The texts that are easily and accurately represented in terms of the contents of their domains are intuitively ones that could easily be represented by an image. An image of a black dog and cat in a house, or an image of a set of outcasts who are Fundalas, farmers, hill people, and peace lovers would seem to be a plausible representation of our two examples. It is difficult to construct an image that represents Frase's original text without going beyond the information in the passage and making particular unwarranted assumptions about the set relations in the domain. A theory that regards specification of the domain of a text as the unit of encoding can remain conveniently neutral as to whether the information is represented in an image or in some verbal or conceptual form, and is much easier to relate to nonlinguistic context than a theory that picks linguistic propositions as its unit of representation.

THE EXPERIMENT

Up to this point I have attempted to sketch a pragmatic account of the relation between indefinite and definite noun phrases and to reexamine some of the existing experimental literature from its point of view. The experiment I am going to describe was designed to investigate a narrow range of linguistic examples which enable us to contrast the predictions of such a pragmatic account with those of semantic accounts that see statement structures as the subjects' unit of encoding.

Semantically, nongeneric indefinite article phrases are related to existential quantifiers. The semantic representation of definite article phrases is controversial: on the theory suggested here their semantic representation simply contains a universal quantifier. On Russell's theory of descriptions (Russell, 1905) their semantic representation contains both an existential and a universal quantifier. While controversy makes it difficult to specify the exact semantic disparity between the two types of article phrases, it can perhaps be agreed that the semantic contribution of the two articles must differ at least by the difference between an existential and a universal quantifier. This same semantic divergence between the formal quantifiers can be expressed in English by the contrast between "all" and "some," and in this case the English terms do not diverge in their pragmatic relations as the articles do: neither phrase relates to a contextual precursor (either a linguistic or nonlinguistic precursor). The articles and these two English quantifiers share a further linguistic feature that is helpful in the design of an experimental investigation. The two pairs of words both occur in environments in which they condition a contrast in meaning, and both occur in environments in which they do not condition any contrast. This feature makes it possible to estimate subjects' ability to remember features of the wording of a text independently of its meaning. The linguistic design of four different conditions of the experiment was as follows:

1. *The quantifiers in contrast.* A sentence in each experimental text was selected so that it could contain either "all" or "some" and that the choice between these two words determined that the statement made would have universal or existential force respectively.

2. *The quantifiers in paraphrase.* Another sentence was selected so that it could contain either "all" or "some" and that either choice would determine that the statement made would have universal force. An example from a passage that described plans for a tennis tournament read as follows:

$$\begin{Bmatrix} \text{Someone} \\ \text{All those} \end{Bmatrix} \text{who} \begin{Bmatrix} \text{wins} \\ \text{win} \end{Bmatrix} \text{enough of these games} \begin{Bmatrix} \text{goes} \\ \text{go} \end{Bmatrix} \text{through to the tourna-}$$

ment proper.

Although the sentence with "someone" is ambiguous between an existential and a universal reading the passage was selected so that only a universal reading of this sentence would make sense.

3. *The articles in contrast.* In the text examples discussed earlier, changing the article on the critical phrases changes the meaning of the text. Sometimes such changes result in anomaly (a definite phrase is used without sufficient context) and sometimes they result in the introduction of new elements into the interpretation of the text. The examples used in the experiment were all cases in which the phrases were singular. The noun phrase always occurred twice, once in each of two adjacent sentences and both occurrences were identical except for the nature of their article. The phrases were always related to a unique element of the domain of interpretation which was not otherwise mentioned in the text. The anomaly that results from certain article combinations was avoided in the following manner. The two adjacent sentences were chosen so that either could, if it contained the indefinite article, identify the element in question, or could, if it contained the definite article, refer back to the previously identified element.

The articles therefore always occurred in the sequence (indefinite–definite) but the containing sentences could be reversed in order. An example of the two forms of one of the experimental texts was as follows:

(a) *A truck* is being loaded with rubble. A driver is waiting by *the truck* for a bulldozer to finish loading.
(b) A driver is waiting by *a truck* for a bulldozer to finish loading. *The truck* is being loaded with rubble.

4. *The articles in paraphrase.* A sentence in each text was selected so that it contained an article that could be changed without changing the meaning of the text. Most of the examples were sentences containing a generic phrase in which both articles have universal force.

The paradigm used in this experiment was a modified version of that employed by Sachs (1967). Subjects listened to taperecordings of passages and subsequently made recognition judgments of sentences which had occurred in the passages. After 100 syllables of intervening text subjects' memory for the exact wording of a sentence has decayed to a low level but their memory for the gist of the passage is quite good and not subject to further rapid decay. It is therefore possible to use the paradigm to examine subjects encoding of the gist of the passage by testing to see whether alteration of a linguistic feature in a recognition item can be detected by the subject after such delays. If the subject cannot detect the change, his encoding is presumed to be invariant with regard to representation of that feature. If the subject can recognize the change his representation of the text must discriminate between the presented form and the altered form of the sentence. Such ability to discriminate does not mean that the subject's encoding is like the linguistic feature under investigation but only that he can judge that the altered recognition item is not consistent with his representation of the passage.

With this design it is possible to make the following predictions. If the subject encodes and retains the semantic form of the sentences of the text, whether in the separate forms in which they occur or in some agglomerated statement formed by rules of textual amalgamation, the subject should accurately recognize the differences between the presented sentences and their changed counterparts when those changes are of the type described in the "contrast" conditions above. The semantic forms of both the article and quantifier contrast sentences differ by at least the contrast between the existential and universal quantifiers. Since it is possible that the article contrast pairs differ by more than this contrast they should be at least as well distinguished as the quantifier contrast pairs, and perhaps better.

If, on the other hand, subjects do not represent these differences in meaning as differences in statement form but rather in terms of the contents and properties of the domain of interpretation of the texts, prediction is more complicated. In the quantifier contrast condition the predictions of the pragmatic and the semantic encoding hypotheses do not diverge. The set relations holding between the objects that the *some* and *all* statements are about are different, and so whether the subject encodes the statement that occurs in the text, or encodes the properties of the objects of the domain, his encoding should discriminate the different statements. However, in the article contrast condition, the predictions of the semantic and pragmatic theories do diverge. On the pragmatic analysis of the pairs of target sentences in this condition, both members of the pair make statements about the same unique element of the domain of interpretation. These statements are encoded as properties of this unique object, and once encoded in this way, the encoding will not discriminate between the different semantic forms of the statements that can appear in the text. In the encoding of the example given here, the subject encodes the fact that there is a unique truck mentioned in the passage, that it is being loaded with rubble, and that a driver is waiting by it for a bulldozer to finish loading. There is nothing in such a representation to suggest which of these properties was asserted of the truck by a statement containing a universal quantifier and which by an existential statement. On this hypothesis, the subject should be no more accurate in the article contrast condition of the experiment than in the article paraphrase condition. On this hypothesis the comprehender must appreciate the semantic form of the statements of the text at the time of input or he could not extract the correct relation between them, but there is no reason why he should maintain this form in memory. The paraphrase conditions provide controls for the memory of wording which is not correlated with contrast of meaning, and so in both paraphrase conditions low accuracy of recognition is predicted.

Method

The subjects listened to a recording of one practice passage and ten experimental passages. After each passage the subjects made five recognition judgments, indicating which of two typed sentences was the one they had heard and recorded their confidence in this judgment on an eleven-point scale, for each of the five judgments. The pairs of sentences differed by just the linguistic features that were under investigation, and this feature was underlined to help in their location by the subject. The order of passages and the order of tests after each passage was randomized. Each subject was presented each of the target forms of the sentences in each linguistic condition an equal number of times, and all the target sentences occurred in both of their forms.

Results

The subjects' performance was scored by assigning the positive value of the confidence scale to correct responses and the negative value of scale to incorrect responses. The subjects were therefore scored on a scale from −5 to +5 with a zero point. The mean scores for the four main conditions, subdivided by stimulus states, are shown in Table 1.

Two separate analyses of variance were performed, one on the quantifier conditions (quantifier type by context type) and the other on the article conditions (article type by context type). Each subject's mean score in each condition was computed and a two factor analysis with repeated measures on both factors was used. In the analysis of the quantifier conditions, the main effects of type of context and of type of quantifier were both significant at the $p < 0.01$ level, and the interaction between the two factors was significant at the $p < 0.05$ level. In the analysis of the article conditions, the main effects of type of context and type of article were both insignificant ($p < 0.1$) but the interaction between the two factors was significant at the $p < 0.05$ level. These figures also appear in Table 1.

DISCUSSION

The Quantifier Conditions

Viewing the results of the quantifier conditions in terms of the accuracy data, the effects of context type accord well with earlier results in the literature. The distinction between *all* and *some* was more accurately recognized when those

TABLE 1
Mean Recognition Scores

	Contrast contexts $N = 500$ responses		Paraphrase contexts $N = 500$ responses
Quantifiers	"Some"	1.79	0.01
	"All"	2.79	2.07
	Mean	2.29	1.05
	$N = 1000$ responses		$N = 500$ responses
Articles	"A"	0.38	0.49
	"The"	1.12	0.18
	Mean	0.75	0.34

Analysis of variance (quantifiers)		
Factor A: Contrast/Paraphrase	$F = 15.5$	$p < 0.01$
Factor B: "All"/"Some"	$F = 20.7$	$p < 0.01$
Factor A × Factor B	$F = 5.0$	$p < 0.05$

Analysis of variance (articles)		
Factor A: Contrast/Paraphrase	$F = 0.26$	$p > 0.1$
Factor B: "A"/"The"	$F = 2.39$	$p > 0.1$
Factor A × Factor B	$F = 5.5$	$p < 0.05$

elements conditioned a contrast between the existential and universal quantifiers than in contexts where both elements were related to the universal quantifier in logical form. The absolute scores were actually quite close to those obtained by Sachs for her mixed collections of semantic and formal changes when tested at 160 syllables delay. This overall result is consistent with either the 'semantic encoding' hypothesis or the 'pragmatic encoding' hypothesis. It does serve to demonstrate that however the contrast between the quantifiers is encoded, it does survive in memory in this paradigm about as well as the other distinctions of meaning that have been investigated in similar experiments.

The Article Conditions

The main result of the article conditions, that the type of context does not significantly affect accuracy of recognition, supports the pragmatic encoding hypothesis. Subjects were not able to discriminate in the recognition tests the different semantic forms of the statements that contained the article phrases at the time of presentation. In retrospect, this is not a very surprising result: it accords very well with our naive intuitions about what we can remember about passages, and our naive intuitions about what the articles mark. The pairs of sentences which contained the articles were deliberately designed to be interchangeable in order, and the naive referential theory of the relation between indefinite and definite article phrases does not ascribe them very different semantic forms, so it is not too surprising that if we cannot remember the order of the sentences occurrence we will not be able to reconstruct the nature of the articles they contained. There is a temptation in the very obviousness of this result to reject its implications. It is tempting to see the divergent semantic forms that have been proposed for the article phrases as a philosopher's fiction and to propose that they play no part in the real world of sentence processing. This temptation sometimes surfaces in the form of claims that the articles really mark not semantic distinctions but psychological distinctions between speaker's and hearer's ability to recognize referents. If such claims are to be more than relabeling of problems, they must explain how we are so good at talking about things that we cannot recognize. I believe that any serious attempt to do this in a way that can account for the full range of relationships between indefinite and definite phrases would be bound to invoke semantic distinctions between these phrases. It has become a commonplace for psychologists to complain that linguists focus their attention too much on sentences and ignore their context, but there is a danger in the opposite tendency to account for a sentence's meaning in some narrow range of its possible contexts and to ignore the sentence's other possibilities. In the case of definite phrases, these possibilities are infinitely varied. The same definite phrase may appear in an infinite number of different contexts, and in each be related to a different indefinite article phrase, and each of these indefinite phrases can itself be in the scope of an infinite number of different quantifier configurations, and all of these differences between contexts will affect the interpretation of the definite phrase. There is every reason to suppose that speakers of English represent the definite article in a way that allows them to treat this variety with equanimity. I have tried to sketch one analysis for this ability. That analysis ascribes a simple semantic form to definite article phrases, a form that contrasts with the indefinite phrases that have been discussed here, along with certain pragmatic rules which relate that semantic form to a potentially infinite variety of linguistic and nonlinguistic contexts. In the light of such an analysis, the experimental results suggest that subjects comprehending these experimental texts process the semantic form of these phrases in order to extract the right relations between sentences in the texts but do not retain that form as a permanent part of their representation of the texts.

Analogous arguments have been advanced before. Bransford and Franks (1971) argued from subjects' failure to detect the amalgamation of presentation sentences into complex recognition test items that the subjects' unit of encoding cannot be the sentence deep structure. Bransford, Barclay, and Franks (1972) have also shown that subjects tend to recognize their own inferences about spatial relations of objects mentioned in passages, as if these inferences had been explicitly presented. It has been the purpose of this chapter to propose that the analysis of the articles provides a particularly fertile field for the development of an alternative approach to textual representation. If it is correct that the articles cannot be adequately described in terms of rules for *textual amalgamation,* then the articles provide evidence that the extension of methods of description developed for sentences are not appropriate for the description of texts. If it is correct that indefinite—definite phrase relations can be analyzed in terms of a pragmatic relation between phrase, statement, and domain, then the articles also suggest that we already possess a formal method for describing the properties of the domain of interpretation of texts.

In comparing the type of formal representation of article relations proposed here with other recent work on the representation of discourse, the current proposal can be seen to be strikingly conservative. It adopts a standard logic as its language of semantic description and augments that logic with some pragmatic rules that relate sentences to their context of occurrence. Most recent work in this field has rejected this position. Kintsch (1974), in reviewing arguments against the adoption of a standard logic for the description of discourse and appealing for the development of a "natural" logic, states that:

> ... several investigators in psychology and artificial intelligence have at least tried to make fresh starts and to construct semantic memory models with a more or less specific disregard for standard logic. Representative examples of this kind of approach are Anderson and Bower (1973), Collins and Quillian (1969), Rumelhart, Lindsay, and Norman (1972), Quillian (1968, 1969), Schank (1972), Simmons (1973), and Winograd (1972), as well as the current work. (p. 46)

The apparent divergence between terms of the standard predicate calculus and their English relatives have been discussed at great length in the philosophical literature. Some problems involved in extending the predicate calculus to the representation of natural language have been well known since Frege but these problems are not the ones for which psychologists have been proposing alternative treatments. On the contrary, the adoption of *"natural logics"* has been proposed as an explanation for apparent divergences that can often be better explained by supposing that the relation between the calculus and English is more complex than the proponents of *natural logics* have supposed. Grice (1967), for example, has argued that the predicate calculus connectives can represent accurately the semantics of English connectives such as "and," "or," "not," but that the semantics of a term does not exhaust its contribution to the meaning of utterances in which it appears, and this semantic account should be augmented by pragmatic maxims of communication. Something like these rules will be required whether the logic that describes the semantics of English is standard or natural.

It is often difficult to assess how seriously these natural logics diverge from their standard counterpart. Kintsch, for example, proposes that quantifiers such as "all" should be treated as predicators, and a sentence such as "all men die" should be analyzed as (DIE, MAN) & (ALL, MAN). It is difficult to tell whether this is anything more than a suggestion that we adopt a logic with a nonstandard syntax (several different syntax schemes are already used for predicate calculus) since no explicit semantics is stated for these formal representations, and what does emerge from our understanding of the programs that manipulate them does not seem to be nonstandard in any important respect. This raises another criticism that Kintsch brings against standard logic, namely that it draws a sharp distinction between syntax and semantics. Since in English this distinction is not born on the sentences' face, this, Kintsch claims, counts against standard logic as a language for the description of English semantics. This argument rests on a confusion of evidential problems that we encounter in building a theory of English meaning, with properties of a completed theory.

Examination of the treatment of indefinite—definite phrase relations in the various proposals that have emerged for textual representation from this line of investigation reveals that they adopt a treatment which resembles what I have called the naive referential theory. Kintsch (1974), for example, states that:

> It is assumed that a lexical noun entry by itself is always singular, unique, but unspecified. Thus the lexical entry HOUSE appears in the surface structure as *a house,* meaning one nonspecified house. The original meaning of the indefinite article is therefore the numeral *one.* (p. 47)

Whatever it may be for an entry to be singular, unique, but unspecified, the word "one" in the most salient reading of the sentence "One example does not make a theory" cannot be related to any unique object, specified or unspecified. Kintsch states that "Attempts to account for quantification in natural language by taking the existential and universal quantifiers and primitives have not been impressively successful and at best result in quite clumsy expressions" (p. 50). There is an impressive list of unsolved problems of representing quantifiers in natural languages, but there is no list at all of solutions to these problems in terms of natural logic. I have tried to argue that the offensive semantic complexity that emerges from the usual predicate calculus translations of English sentences can be reduced by a theory that ascribes simple semantic structures and some relatively simple pragmatic rules with which those structures interact.

The strategy of selecting simple linguistic structures as the departing point for empirical research is undoubtedly a good one. In the experiment described here, the article contrast sentences were all related to single unique referents in the texts in which they appeared. The researchers that Kintsch lists also choose examples of this type when they represent article relations. Choosing simple examples is one thing, but basing a purportedly general theory of textual representation on a restricted range of examples that that theory happens to fit is quite another. To do so is to lose the benefit of the enormous amount of formal work that has been done in the description of natural languages using predicate calculus. Admittedly this work has been done with a different focus of interest and with some implicit idealizations in mind that are not acceptable to a psychologist interested in actual texts, but the work has produced a formal logic of great generality, an extensive knowledge of the natural language examples that are most problematical, and some understanding of just how much more there is to a theory of meaning than the bare bones of a semantic theory of sentences.

ACKNOWLEDGMENT

This research was supported in part by PHS Grant GM 21796 to The Rockefeller University.

REFERENCES

Anderson, J. R., & Bower, G. H. *Human associative memory.* Washington, D.C.: Winston, 1973.

Barclay, R. J., & Reid, M. Characteristics of memory representations of sentence sets describing linear arrays. *Journal of Verbal Learning and Verbal Behavior,* 1974, **13**(2), 133–137.

Bransford, J. D., Barclay, R. J., & Franks, J. J. Sentence memory: A constructive versus an interpretative approach. *Cognitive Psychology,* 1972, **3**, 193–209.

Bransford, J. D., & Franks, J. J. The abstraction of linguistic ideas. *Cognitive Psychology,* 1971, **2**, 331–350.

Bransford, J. D., & Johnson, M. K. Contextual prerequisites for understanding: Some investigations of comprehension and recall. *Journal of Verbal Learning and Verbal Behavior,* 1972, **11**, 717–726.

Bransford, J. D., & McCarrell, N. S. A sketch of a cognitive approach to comprehension: Some thoughts about understanding what it means to comprehend. In W. B. Weimer & D. S. Palermo (Eds.), *Cognition and the symbolic processes.* Hillsdale, New Jersey: Lawrence Erlbaum Assoc., 1974.

Collins, A. M., & Quillian, M. R. Retrieval times for semantic memory. *Journal of Verbal Learning and Verbal Behavior,* 1969, 8, 240–247.

Frase, L. T. Maintenance and control in the acquisition of knowledge from written materials. In R. O. Freedle & J. B. Carroll (Eds.), *Language comprehension and the acquisition of knowledge.* Washington, D.C.: Winston, 1972.

Harman, G. Noun phrases derived from variable binding operators. Unpublished manuscript, Princeton University, 1972.

Kintsch. W. *The representation of meaning in memory.* Hillsdale, New Jersey: Lawrence Erlbaum Assoc., 1974.

Paivio, A. Mental imagery in associative learning and memory. *Psychological Review,* 1969, 76, 241–263.

Quillian, M. R. Semantic memory. In M. Minsky (Ed.), *Semantic information processing.* Cambridge, Massachusetts: MIT Press, 1968.

Quillian, M. R. The teachable language comprehender. *Communications of the Association for Computing Machinery,* 1969, 12, 459–476.

Rumelhart, D. E., Lindsay, P. H., & Norman, P. A. A process model for long-term memory. In E. Tulving & W. Donaldson (Eds.), *Organization of memory.* New York: Academic Press, 1972.

Russell, B. On denoting. *Mind,* 1905, 59, 479–493.

Sachs, J. S. Recognition memory for syntactic and semantic aspects of connected discourse. *Perception and Psychophysics,* 1967, 2(9), 437–442.

Schank, R. C. Conceptual dependency: A theory of natural language understanding. *Cognitive Psychology,* 1972, 3, 552–631.

Simmons, R. F. Semantic networks: Their computation and use for understanding English sentences. In R. C. Schank & K. M. Colby (Eds.), *Computer models of thought and language.* San Francisco: Freeman, 1973.

Stenning, K. *Understanding English articles and quantifiers.* Unpublished doctoral dissertation, The Rockefeller University, 1975.

Van Dijk, T. A. Text grammar and text logic. In J. S. Petrofi & H. Reiser (Eds.), *Studies in text grammar.* Dordrecht, Holland: Reidel, Publ., 1973.

Winograd, T. Understanding natural language. *Cognitive Psychology,* 1972, 3, 1–191.

10

A Move toward a Psychology of Conversation

Susan L. Weiner

Donald R. Goodenough

Educational Testing Service

INTRODUCTION

The ultimate goal of the psychology of language is presumably to describe and explain the psychological processes responsible for how people can and do talk to each other. One major initial research strategy in forwarding this goal was to develop a body of experimental data on the comprehension of and memory for sentences in isolation. However, it has not been at all clear how current conceptions of sentence processing might be extended to deal with the rapid and continuous production and comprehension processes operating in conversation. Indeed, attempting such an extension raises a number of problems which themselves are suggestive of the shape that a psychology of conversation might take.

One important problem concerns the unit of analysis. It can be argued that the sentence may not be a practical or even a "proper" unit for understanding conversational processes. In the first place, the uttering of any particular set of sentences seems a limited concern, since a wide range of paraphrases of most messages in conversation are possible with minor changes in meaning. Moreover, it has been observed that much of dialogue may not be in sentential form (Chapanis, 1975). Further, while sentence-based models of speech comprehension have received wide attention, models of speech production have been notably lacking. It would appear that focusing on a unit that could be equally useful for speech production and comprehension processes would be warranted.

A second problem concerns the effects of social variables such as the relative power and status of the participants. Such variables have been shown to affect the structure (Hymes, 1974) (and thereby presumably the production and interpretation) of conversation, and therefore must be included in any psychological model of conversational processes. It is difficult to see, however, how social factors might be included in current models of sentence processing. Indeed, the psycholinguistics of sentences has treated such variables as largely theoretically irrelevant.

The present chapter describes our first attempt to create a psychology of conversational process by tackling some of the difficulties described above.

THE CONCEPT OF A CONVERSATIONAL MOVE

As a general theoretical framework, we have chosen to employ a game theory approach. Using games as analogies to language behavior is of course not new. This approach has a variety of roots (e.g., philosophy, Wittgenstein, 1953; mathematical game theory, Rapaport, 1960; social psychology, Harré & Secord, 1972; Robinson, 1972), and has attracted attention because it provides a number of useful concepts and clues as to how a psychology of conversation might be developed. First, and most obviously, it is a rule-governed conception in which it is possible to describe systems of rules functioning at the various levels of conversational processes, for example, social, cognitive, linguistic, affective. Second, the fact that games and conversations require participants to generate sequences of exchanges which are constrained not only by general rule systems but also by what the other participant(s) has(have) done allows their strategies, plans, and tactics to be identified. Third, it provides a potentially very useful unit for psychological analyses, namely, the "conversational move." Our goal in the present chapter is to elaborate the concept of a conversational move in general, and to develop one class of such moves in some detail.

We have adopted a definition of conversational move as a unit of both speech production and comprehension. On the production side, a move is an action taken by a speaker to accomplish something with words (Austin, 1962; Searle, 1969). A move refers to that entity that people frequently talk about as "having something to say," something which may be successfully or unsuccessfully expressed in a variety of linguistic forms. Thus a move is claimed to be a cognitive unit of production: things known or recognized not to be known (as in, "I don't know what to say about that"). It is also a social unit, since, being part of a conversation, it participates in sequences and exchanges that have effects on other participants and their moves.

On the comprehension side, people readily remember essences of conversation, the very same sorts of abstract "things" known to speakers. In remembering conversations, people naturally reduce the stream of speech to X, Y, and Z as "information" which has been transmitted. A number of psycholinguistic experiments have demonstrated that for connected discourse from a single source, people retain the gist of or semantic information from a passage and rapidly lose at least the surface linguistic structure of the input (Bransford & Johnson, 1973; Fillenbaum, 1966; Sachs, 1967). It has also been demonstrated that listeners go beyond the discrete sentential input to integrate, infer and supply "information" not explicitly stated in the original input. While these experiments suggest strongly that there are cognitive units recalled by a listener, recent variations of this paradigm have shown that recall of the very same passage can be markedly affected by varying its attributed source, for example, whether it comes from one or another opposite sides to a debate (Wertsch, 1975). Thus it appears that "things" abstracted from discourse preserve and integrate social information as well as the particular semantic contents of a passage.

A move need not be isomorphic with conventional social or linguistic units. Most obviously, it contrasts with units of the sentence-bound models of speech production proposed by Marslen-Wilson (1973), Yngve (1960), and others, and with speaking turn units studied by ethnomethodologists (Sacks, Schegloff, & Jefferson, 1974). At present, our operationally minimal unit for a move is an "utterance" (a word, phrase, clause or sentence with terminal intonational contour). Successive utterances falling into the same move category are considered a single move.

SUBSTANTIVE AND HOUSEKEEPING MOVES

The game analogy and the psychological unit of the move provide some basic tools for examining certain processes operating in conversations. Our next question was what kinds of moves might be basic to the fabric of conversation. To aid in answering this question, we used transcripts from three different kinds of conversations. One set of conversations (hereafter the "teacher–student study") came from four-day minicourses on the Mayan civilization, given by experienced male and female teachers to classes of four high school students each, two males and two females. These hour-long class sessions represent more or less natural, self-contained teaching encounters and as such may be said to have realistic beginnings and endings, lesson organization, etc. The second set of conversations came from dyads of female college students who discussed two or three forced-choice problems like those of the Kohlberg moral dilemma type (hereafter the "peer interaction study"). The students were preselected to disagree about the solutions to the dilemmas, and were asked to try to resolve their disagreements. The third group of conversations, the "doctor–patient" set, came from a study of pharmacological treatment of obese patients. The doctors were medical residents and were given the task of finding out as much as possible about their patients' weight history in an effort to relate patient variables to treatment outcome. The three kinds of interactions represent strikingly different kinds of conversations in form and content and were therefore useful in the effort to arrive at a first impression of the generality of various types of moves.

It seemed reasonable, on the basis of intuition and the reading of these transcripts, to begin by distinguishing between two kinds of moves. First, there seemed to be "substantive" moves that made up the subject matter of conversations. Some of these moves appeared to be "genre-specific" and others "content-specific." By genre-specific (consistent with Hymes, 1974, use of genre), we mean moves that may be typical of particular social forms of conversation, such as in a debate, teaching, or casual talk. Moves which specifically reinforce another's answer to a question, for example, may apply in teacher–student conversation but not in casual talk. The identification of genre-specific move categories would appear to depend in part on ethnomethodological analyses, that is, on determining what kinds of conversations naturally occur to accomplish what kinds of purposes. By content-specific moves we mean moves which may be "natural" in communicating a particular subject matter. A taxonomy of such moves would appear to depend in part on analyses of the structure of different domains of knowledge. It is our impression that both conversational genre and content influence the form and function that substantive moves take in the course of a conversation. One can debate a wide range of topics, and the moves in a debate would seem to be determined both by the fact of the debate and by the nature of the topic being debated.

The second class of activities are what we call "housekeeping" or "management" moves. Housekeeping moves are distinct from substantive moves because they appear to add nothing new to the subject matter of the conversation. Instead, housekeeping moves seem to serve semantic content connecting functions, often occurring at the opening or closing of the conversation, and at boundaries between substantive topics within the conversation.

The division between substantive and housekeeping moves seems analogous to the distinction in linguistics between "content" and "function" words. While content words and substantive moves are open classes of language activities encoding particular referential concepts, function words and housekeeping moves are relatively closed classes of language activities which function as "syntactic" linkages and have questionable referential value. In addition, housekeeping moves and function words accomplish essentially the same connecting activities across a variety of conversational forms and content areas.

Housekeeping moves have several features which make them more amenable to research analysis than substantive moves. First, the underlying psychological reality of housekeeping moves can be illustrated and inferred in part from their generality across conversational forms. We also believe that such moves have important psychological functions for conversational participants which can easily be subjected to empirical test. Examples of how this is possible are described below. We have chosen, therefore, to begin our study of conversation by focusing on a type of housekeeping move.

PASSING MOVES: A TYPE OF HOUSEKEEPING MOVE

One way to view conversational flow is to treat the substantive material as being organized into successions of topics; that is, the speech of the participants tends to cohere on a particular subject matter and then to progress to a related or totally new subject. A first question to ask of such a view of conversational organization is how do topical changes come about. We would propose a ground rule of polite conversation that a participant who has contributed new substantive material to the topic under discussion preserves for himself the right to contribute again to the same topic on his next move. We have called this the "topical continuation rule" and make use of it below. In order for changes in topic to occur, both participants must either decline the rights to continue, or one participant must manage the topic shift unilaterally. Who may be responsible for the offer or management of a topic change and exactly which devices are used no doubt depends on a complex of social, personality and situational variables, such as relative status, knowledge, age, aggressiveness of the participants etc. However, the underlying set of possibilities ought to be general, rule governed and specifiable. One general method of topic shifting appears to be the "passing move" (extending Schegloff & Sacks', 1973, term). We have defined a passing move as a turn or part of a turn in which the utterer relinquishes his option to make a substantive contribution to the topic talk of the conversation at that moment, that is, suspends the topical continuation rule.

Passing moves may be classified in several ways. First, it seems useful to distinguish between two kinds of passing moves in terms of the utterance form. One form is defined by a limited set of words such as, "yeah," "well," "alright," "okay," and "mmhmm," words which have been recognized by other investigators as recurrent phenomena in conversation (e.g., Duncan, 1972; Kendon, 1967). These forms occur noninterruptively, have falling intonational contour and are followed by juncture pauses. The functions of such words in conversation have been variously described in recent work as "back-channel responses" by which a listener can indicate that he wants the other speaker to continue (Duncan & Niederehe, 1974), as "passes" by which a participant gives up his turn in a conversation (Schegloff & Sacks, 1973), as "framing moves" by which a teacher in a classroom marks a section in the discourse (Forsyth, 1974). We call this type of passing move an "OK pass" and draw on the work of these investigators in the discussion to follow. A second form called "repetition pass" includes repetitions and close paraphrases by one partner of another's just prior speech.

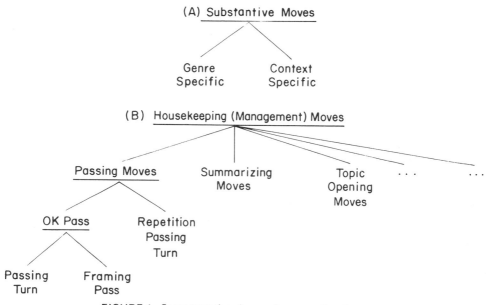

FIGURE 1   Some tentative classes of conversational moves.

A second basis for classifying passing moves has to do with whether the move occupies an entire speaking turn or only part of a turn. Passing moves which occupy an entire turn are called "passing turns," while passing moves that occupy a part of a turn are called "framing moves," following the terminology introduced by Forsyth (1974).

Passing turns may occur in the form of "OK passes" or "repetition passes." However, framing moves occur only in the form of "OK passes" (i.e., repetitions that occupy only part of a turn do not seem to serve a passing function). Thus, we have distinguished three kinds of passing moves, as summarized in Fig. 1.

OK PASSING MOVES

The first type of passing move that we observed was the "OK passing turn." Applying the topical continuation rule to turn taking, conversational partners ought to continue to take turns addressing the topic until one partner declines his right to continue the discussion by emitting a passing turn. The other speaker may choose to exercise his option to continue addressing the topic on his next turn (see Example 1).

Example 1: (Peer Study)

Speaker L: But meanwhile in the time that it would take for them to come up with something that would cool the waters.

Speaker R: Mmhmm
Speaker L: Think of all the — what would happen to the rivers in the few
          years . . .

Alternatively, the other speaker may emit a passing move of his own, thus producing the passing move pair (Schegloff & Sacks, 1973). Each instance of a passing turn by one partner can be interpreted as an offer to change topics, and the other partner(s) may or may not choose to make a matching move. The second member of the passing move pair thus functions as an acceptance of this offer, forming what appears to qualify as an adjacency pair (Schegloff & Sacks, 1973) with special structural significance in conversations that obtain between two (and perhaps more) partners. Typically, no substantive moves occur on the same topic after the passing move pair. However, additional housekeeping moves on the same topic may follow. For example, either speaker may summarize the topic discussion or assess the progress of the conversation at that point before advancing to the next topic. These additional housekeeping moves appear to be optional, however, since one of the speakers often introduces a new topic directly after the passing move pair:

Example 2: (Doctor–patient study)
   Doctor: —and you say, as far as you know, you don't have any other
           illnesses?
   Patient: No, not to my knowledge.
   Doctor: High blood, or diabetes.
   Patient: No.
   Doctor: OK.
   Patient: Mmhmm.
   Doctor: And you desire to lose weight.

In Example 2, the second passing move of the pair is a passing turn, and the speaker, who emitted the first member of the pair was also the speaker who introduced the new topic. However, the second passing move is often a framing move, that is, the speaker who emits the second passing move is the one who introduces the new topic:

Example 3: (Peer Study)
   Speaker L: . . . When you think of a heart machine going, you know, you
             can't imagine that sort of thing.
   Speaker R: Alright, fine.
   Speaker L: Yeah. The next problem has to do with an air raid warden.

In the Examples 2 and 3 above, the passing moves occur in pairs to form a collaborative topic closing. However, passing moves need not occur in pairs in order to mark topic shifts. Indeed, in his discussion of framing moves, Forsyth (1974) has noted that the very same sort of words we are discussing appear singly at topic shifts in teacher's talk in the classroom. Our own teacher transcripts support his observation. Example 4 illustrates a teacher's unilateral use of a framing move.

Example 4: (Teacher–student study)

> LT016: I thought he ["*B–C*" comic strip character] was finished by this time 'cause when I was small he was still going on there. Alright. In a Stone Age society ((uh)) you should possibly have an idea how these people might have lived . . . .

The "alright" in Example 4 qualifies as a passing move in that the speaker chooses not to add further substantive material to the topic just discussed. Furthermore, framing moves of this sort retain the features generally characteristic of passing moves (falling intonation, and juncture pauses), that is, are complete utterances even though they are often single words or phrases that are only part of a much longer speaking turn.

Since the topic shift takes places without explicit collaboration from the other participants, one might expect unilateral framing moves to occur more frequently when one participant in a conversation has relatively greater power, knowledge, status, etc. In effect, the acceptance of a low-status role seems to involve yielding continuation rights before the conversation begins. Hence, a passing move pair is unnecessary for polite topic closing. The expectation that unilateral framing moves characterize the speech of high-status participants is supported by the observations in our data that they do not occur often in the peer interactions, are rarely used by the low-status students and patients, but are often used by the high-status teachers and doctors.

REPETITION PASSES

Repetitions and close paraphrases by one partner of another's just prior speech have been recently observed to have a variety of conversational functions (Cherry, 1974; Keenan, 1974) in child–child or adult–child conversations. Repetitions also occur in the speech of our adult subjects and appear to have identifiable functions. When these repetitions occupy an active turn (repetition passing turns), they appear to have a function similar to that of the OK passing turns, that is, a speaker spends his turn adding nothing new to the conversational content:

Example 5: (Doctor–patient study)

> Doctor: Have you been successful with that [fluid reduction]?
> Patient: Well it didn't seem like I was losing, to me, I mean. Sometime I may lose 5–6 pounds. That's all.
> Doctor: That's about as much as you've lost.

Patient: Mmhmm.
Doctor: What's the highest that you — Is this the most you have ever weighed?

Like OK passes, these repetitions are required to have falling intonation to qualify as passing moves. Such a requirement contrasts with Duncan and Niederehe's (1974) inclusion of a category of "request for clarification," with rising intonation, as a back-channel response. With rising intonation, for instance, the doctor's repetition in Example 5 becomes a substantive move, a challenge of the patient's previous utterance. Thus the doctor's repetition is a question with "Do you mean to say that you started gaining weight when you had . . . " deleted.

Certain similarites and differences emerged between repetition passing turns and OK passing turns that suggest to us that they may have somewhat different conversational functions. First, like OK passing turns, repetition passing turns also occur with passing turn pairs — but only as the *first* member of such a pair. OK passing turns are the second members; three utterances of the same phrase is a conversationally anomalous phemomenon. A second observation is that passing turn pairs beginning with a repetition often have substantive moves following that pair which are on the same topic:

Example 6: (Doctor–patient study)
Patient: I would like to weigh around 135.
Doctor: About 135.
Patient: Mmhmm.
Doctor: And how long has it been since you weighed 135?

By contrast, recall the earlier observation that passing turn pairs with both members as OK passes either have other housekeeping moves or a topic shift directly following the pair.

A third observation also concerns passing turn pairs beginning with a repetition. We described earlier how when OK passes occurred in pairs, the second member might be either a turn pass or a framing move. When the latter occurred, a new topic was introduced within the same turn. Passing move pairs beginning with a repetition, however, do not have framing moves as their second member; only turn passes seem to occur at this point. Put in other words, if a new topic follows a passing move pair beginning with a repetition, it appears more likely to be introduced by the emitter of the repetition than by the emitter of the second member of the passing move pair.

These observations suggest to us that the function of repetition passing turns is a temporizing one, that is, the speaker seems to suspend temporarily the topical continuation rule, preserving for himself both the right to address the same topic again on his next turn or the right to introduce a new topic. OK passes appear to commit the speaker to a definite offer (or acceptance) in changing topics. Repetition passing turns make such an offer ambiguous.

Repetitions occurring in our transcripts which are not passing turns do not clearly have a passing move function. Such repetitions seem to occur most often in teachers' talk in the teacher–student study and appear to have several kinds of housekeeping functions. For example, they acknowledge students' answers to teachers' questions, as noted by Cherry (1974):

Example 7: (Teacher–student study)

Teacher· . . . What did you notice about the shape of the buildings, most of them?

Student: They were perfect.

Teacher: Okay, they were perfect ((haha)). I'm thinking more in terms of geometry now . . . .

They also seem to rebroadcast student speech as a way of the teacher's guaranteeing that the class has heard a student's remark. In addition, they may serve a turn-holding function, buying time for a speaker to finish planning his next move without relinquishing the speaking floor, and to emphasize that the speaker will address the substance of his partner's prior turn. This latter use of repetition seems not to be restricted to teacher's classroom talk.

Some Implications of the Analysis of Passing Moves

We believe that there are several ways in which the above analysis of passing moves and the larger framework in which they were conceived are advantageous. First, it suggests a parsimonious account of conversational endings. In discussing how conversations close, Schegloff and Sacks (1973) propose the following as properties of closing: (a) they occur at the end of the last "mentionable" topic; (b) they are formulated as a section; (c) they are not the place for new information unless new topic introductions are specially marked (e.g., with phrases like "by the way"); (d) they can be introduced with a variety of "preclosing" devices, for example, "free pass," summary statement, aphoristic formulation; and (e) they end with a terminal exchange of adjacent turns like "goodbye – goodbye." We have observed most of these features occurring in the interactions we have studied. It is our view, however, that it is possible to treat closing "sections" as housekeeping topics, having an arrangement of moves within the topic that is much like that within any substantive topic. The terminal exchange then can be regarded simply as a kind of passing move exchange. In addition, as Schegloff and Sacks note, preclosings appear to be ordinary topic closing devices, and as such would appear to retain for the speakers the option of introducing new topic talk whether substantive or housekeeping in nature. Which type of topic talk might ensue thus would seem not to be a function of the way in which the preceding topic is closed as Schegloff and Sacks argue, although it may, of course, be a function of some yet to be defined intertopical organization constraints.

Secondly, and more importantly, our analysis of the characteristics of passing moves can be subjected to empirical test in a variety of ways. Our impressions of the functions of passing moves in conversation are, of course, a series of hypotheses. One set of these hypotheses concerns the effect of passing moves on the internal structure of conversations, that is, the possibility that constraints are posed on the occurrence of different kinds of conversational sequences by the occurrence of passing moves. As one example, we would hypothesize that substantive talk on the same topic will occur less often following an OK passing move pair than pairs of other move types. As another example, if repetitions occupying an entire turn (which also have falling intonation) are indeed temporizing passing moves, then topic shifts should be less likely to follow turn pass pairs whose first member is a repetition than turn pass pairs both of whose members are OK passes. Many additional hypotheses about conversational structure have been suggested by the analysis of passing moves, and in each case it is possible to disconfirm the hypothesis and its underlying theory by simple frequency counts of types of conversational sequences.

The analysis of passing moves also has implications for the effects of social variables on the distribution of conversational moves. For example, we hypothesized earlier that the use of unilateral framing moves as a way of marking topic boundaries ought to occur more often among relatively high-status conversational participants than relatively low-status participants. So too, relatively high-status participants ought to emit "repetition turn passes" more often than low-status participants, since the use of a repetition turn pass preserves for that speaker the right to continue the same topic or change it regardless of whether his partner produces a turn pass of his own.

Further, our analysis has implications for how effectively information is being communicated. If one assumes that when a topic is being discussed the knowledge and experience of the participants relevant to that topic is brought to bear on it ("aroused" or "foregrounded" to use Chafe's, 1972, term), passing moves, if they in fact close topics, should suspend the aroused presuppositions relevant to the topic being closed and thereby contribute to listener comprehension. Thus, subjects may be presented with talk on two separate topics (Topic A and Topic B). The initial statement of Topic B may be understood in one way if heard as part of Topic A, and in another way if heard as part of Topic B. We expect that it will more often be correctly understood as part of the B topic if Topic A is closed by an appropriate move pass (or turn pass pair in collaborative situations).

Finally some hypotheses about recall of conversational material may be suggested. If move passes mark topic boundaries, then their presence should facilitate a chunking of subject matter in a body of conversational material with the consequence of better recall than would occur with the same material given their absence.

As these hypotheses may suggest, the analogy between conversations and games and in particular the use of conversational move as a unit of analysis shows promise of dealing with a variety of relevant variables at different conversational levels within an integrated theoretical framework.

ACKNOWLEDGMENT

This research was supported by Grant MH21989 from the National Institute of Mental Health.

REFERENCES

Austin, J. L. *How to do things with words.* London: Oxford University Press, 1962.

Bransford, J. D., & Johnson, M. K. Considerations of some problems of comprehension. In W. G. Chase (Ed.), *Visual information processing.* New York: Academic Press, 1973.

Chafe, W. Discourse structure and human knowledge. In R. O. Freedle & J. Carroll (Eds.), *Language comprehension and the acquisition of knowledge.* Washington, D.C.: Winston, 1972.

Chapanis, A. Interactive human communication. *Scientific American,* 1975, **232**, 36–42.

Cherry, L. Sex differences in preschool teacher–child interaction. Unpublished doctoral dissertation, Harvard University, 1974.

Duncan, S. D. Some signals and rules for taking speaking turns in conversations. *Journal of Personality and Social Psychology,* 1972, **23**, 283–292.

Duncan, S., & Niederehe, G. On signalling that it's your turn to speak. *Journal of Experimental Social Psychology,* 1974, **10**, 234–247.

Fillenbaum, S. Memory for gist: Some relevant variables. *Language and Speech,* 1966, **9**, 217–227.

Forsyth, I. J. Patterns in the discourse of teachers and pupils. In G. Perren (Ed.), *The space between: English and foreign languages at school.* London, England: Centre for Information on Language Teaching, 1974.

Harré, R., & Secord, P. F. *The explanation of social behavior.* Oxford, England: Blackwell, 1972.

Hymes, D. *Foundations in sociolinguistics.* Philadelphia, Pennsylvania: University of Pennsylvania Press, 1974.

Keenan, E. O. Again and again: The pragmatics of imitation in child language. Paper presented at American Anthropological Association Meetings, Mexico City, November 1974.

Kendon, A. Some functions of gaze-direction in social interaction. *Acta Psychologica,* 1967, **26**, 22–63.

Marslen-Wilson, W. Speech shadowing and speech perception. Unpublished doctoral dissertation, Massachusetts Institute of Technology, 1973.

Rapaport, A. *Games, fights, and debates.* Ann Arbor, Michigan: University of Michigan Press, 1960.

Robinson, P. *Language and social behavior.* London, England: Penguin Books, 1972.

Sachs, J. Recognition memory for syntactic and semantic aspects of connected discourse. *Perception and Psychophysics,* 1967, **2**, 437–442.

Sacks, H., Schegloff, E. A., & Jefferson, G. A simplest systematics for the organization of turn-taking for conversation. *Language,* 1974, **50,** 696–735.

Schegloff, E. A., & Sacks, H. Opening up closings. *Semiotics,* 1973, **8,** 289–327.

Searle, J. *Speech acts.* Cambridge, England: Cambridge University Press, 1969.

Wertsch, J. V. The influence of listener perception of the speaker on recognition memory. *Journal of Psycholinguistic Research,* 1975, **4,** 89–98.

Wittgenstein, L. *Philosophical investigations.* New York: Macmillan, 1953.

Yngve, V. A model and an hypothesis for language structure. In *Proceedings of the American Philosophical Society,* 1960, **104.**

11
Children's Illocutionary Acts

John Dore

Baruch College, City University of New York

Despite the enormous amount of research on child language for the last two decades, the fundamental question of "What must a child learn in order to master his language?" has not been adequately answered. Most investigators have concentrated on the child's acquisition of the phonological, syntactic, and semantic structures of linguistic competence. This notion of competence concerns only the child's grammatical knowledge; the notion was adapted by developmental psycholinguists from Chomsky's (1965, p. 4) distinction between "*competence* (the speaker–hearer's knowledge of his language) and *performance* (the actual use of language in concrete situations)." But it is becoming increasingly clearer that language acquisition involves more than learning grammar. Even if, as Brown (1973) and many other transformationally oriented psycholinguists have claimed, the child is actively inducing the grammatical rules underlying the utterances he hears, it is unarguable that he must also be learning how to use utterances appropriately in actual situations. What is at present controversial (in formal linguistic theory as well as in the study of child language) is how to best describe and explain the many interacting facets of the speaker's overall *communicative competence*. In particular, what is needed is a full characterization of the notion of the appropriate use of language by the child; and, ideally, this specification of appropriateness would complement the recent important discoveries about children's grammatical development. In short, it is time to focus on certain crucial aspects of performance in language acquisition.[1]

---

[1] There has of course been some important research on performance in language development; for example, Bever's (1970) work on the perceptual strategies which affect the acquisition of linguistic structures. But an entirely different aspect of performance, namely the consequences of speech acts on conversations, has until quite recently been neglected.

An adequate model of the appropriate use of language requires a unit of analysis different from the sentence. Sentences are linguists' abstractions from utterances. The phonology and syntax of sentences are evaluated in terms of "well-formedness" conditions; the semantics of sentences is evaluated in terms of the truth conditions of propositions or (depending on which semantic theory one advocates) in terms of the compositional coherence of meanings within sentences. But the appropriate use of sentences in contexts cannot be dealt with on the level of grammar because appropriateness involves such factors as the intentions and beliefs of speakers and the effects of utterances on hearers. Such factors clearly are not properties of sentences themselves, but are characteristics of users of sentences. Moreover, the pragmatics of language use (as distinct from the grammar of linguistic structures) encompasses a larger domain, a domain that includes the relations among utterances in discourse and the rules for constructing conversations. The model of the pragmatics of language use by children which is outlined below assumes that whereas grammar concerns the structures of sentence types, pragmatics concerns the use of sentence tokens in particular contexts in order to convey messages beyond the semantic information of the sentence type. The unit of analysis which we have employed for our investigation of pragmatics is the *speech act.*

The notion of speech act originated in the philosophy of language literature. Austin (1962), for example, was concerned with what we are doing when we are speaking, apart from the truth value of propositions. He viewed utterances as acts, acts such as asserting, questioning, advising and so on. This emphasis on the actual acts of speech (as distinct from the knowledge of sentential rules) has several advantages. First of all, it provides a framework for discussing the intentions, beliefs, and expected effects that are essential components of speakers' uses of utterances to accomplish acts. Second, it provides a basis for explaining the relations between sentences and contexts. Speakers can use the same sentence to perform different speech acts and they can use different sentences to perform the same speech act: for example, the utterance "The door is open" counts as a description in certain contexts when the speaker merely intends to inform the hearer of the state of the door; but the same utterance, in different circumstances, can function as the speech act of requesting the hearer to close the door; moreover, the speaker can achieve the same effect by saying "Close the door" or "Would you mind closing the door?," both of which are different sentence types from "The door is open." And a third advantage of a speech-act framework is that it allows for the possibility of accounting for such phenomena as how speakers actually understand ambiguous and metaphorical sentences, how language is used to negotiate interpersonal relations and to persuade and manipulate others and to be ironic, humorous, aggressive, deceptive and so on.

The purpose of this chapter is to propose a model of certain kinds of speech acts, namely illocutionary acts, that are performed by preschool children. This will be accomplished by revising the notion of speech act in order to apply it to the empirical problem of describing children's uses of utterances as acts in conversations. I will offer (a) some hypotheses concerning the purposes, intentions and effects of illocutionary acts; (b) the results of a study of the illocutionary acts performed by three-year-old children; (c) a typology of their illocutionary acts; (d) a methodology for identifying each type; (e) a description of some of the pragmatic strategies the children deployed; and (f) some examples of the sociolinguistic rules that seem to govern the children's uses of illocutionary acts.

ILLOCUTIONARY ACTS AND COMMUNICATIVE INTENTIONS

Searle (1969) describes the speech act as containing two components: a proposition (defined in terms of a predicating expressing taking one or more referring expressions) and an illocutionary force (which indicates how the utterance is to be taken). Whereas the proposition conveys the conceptual content of the utterance, the illocutionary force indicates whether the utterance counts as an assertion, promise, question or any number of other acts. Illocutionary acts are those speech acts which are performed by speakers *in* producing certain utterances. They were distinguished by Austin (1962, p. 108) from other kinds of acts such as "a luctionary act, which is roughly equivalent to uttering a certain sentence with a certain sense and reference" and "perlocutionary acts: what we bring about or achieve *by* saying something, such as convincing, persuading . . . " and so on. In my discussion of children's language, I will restrict myself to illocutionary acts.

In order to adapt speech act theory to my purpose, I will first make explicit certain fundamental assumptions and hypotheses. To begin with, I want to propose the following:

(1) The basic purpose of illocutionary acts is to affect the beliefs and behavior of other people, especially to change the beliefs and behavior of people with whom one engages in conversation.

If this assumption is correct, we should expect to find the effects (in the form of utterances or actions) of illocutionary acts on hearers. Such effects are described in detail below.

The first major hypothesis I want to propose is:

(2) The primary determinant of the illocutionary force of an illocutionary act is the speaker's *communicative intention.*

A communicative intention (CI) is an intention to induce in a hearer two kinds of effects. These effects are:

(3) a. The expected *illocutionary* effect — that the hearer recognize the illocutionary status of the speaker's utterance.

b. The expected *perlocutionary* effect – that the hearer recognize
what the speaker expects him to do or believe as a consequence
of recognizing the illocutionary act.

For example, if I say to you "What's your name?" I will have achieved my
expected illocutionary effect if you recognize that I have asked you a certain
kind of information question; I will have achieved my expected perlocutionary
effect if you tell me your name.[2] Unlike other kinds of intentions, a CI must be
linguistically marked. That is, it must be conveyed by utterances of certain
grammatical forms; and the illocutionary acts determined by CIs must be
conventionally governed by rules for the use of utterances in contexts such that
hearers automatically recognize speakers' CIs.

At this point I will invoke what I refer to as the *principle of unequivocal
recognizability of communicative intention.* That is, I assume that most often
hearers automatically recognize speakers' CIs in uttering sentences. If this were
not the case, then verbal communication would be difficult, if not impossible.
Some prima facie arguments in favor of this principle are: (a) hearers respond to
most utterance types according to predictable arrays of what can be characterized as "appropriate" responses; (b) occasionally hearers are uncertain of how
to respond because the speaker's CI *is* equivocal to them, in which cases hearers
will typically question speakers about their intentions (I take this to be the
exception that proves the rule); and (c) hearers can undo the expected effect of
the speaker's CI – for example, to the speaker's request of "Can you pass the
salt?," a hearer can reply "Yes, I can" without passing the salt. As this example
indicates, more than grammar is involved in conveying and recognizing CIs. One
specific goal of this chapter is to account for some of the nongrammatical
factors that enable children to recognize unequivocally the CIs of others.

A STUDY OF PRESCHOOL CHILDREN'S ILLOCUTIONARY ACTS

Seven children, four boys and three girls, from white, middle-class backgrounds
attended a nursery two hours a morning, four days a week, over a period of
seven months. The children's interactivity was videotaped regularly.[3] A wide

---

[2] This notion of communicative intention is heavily influenced by Grice (1957) who has
maintained that meaning is largely a matter of intentions to produce effects on hearers and
by Mohan (1974) who distinguished the "intended illocutionary effect" from the
"intended perlocutionary effect." But I have previously described children's utterances in
terms of a somewhat less explicit notion of communicative intention in Dore (1974, 1975).

[3] The laboratory facility and staff, the data collection and some of the data analyses were
supported by a grant from The Grant Foundation to The Rockefeller University. The
research reported here is only part of a much larger study of the same children's language
behavior.

variety of situations (including structured activities like snack time and arts and crafts as well as free play) were systematically sampled. Although the nursery school teacher was almost always present, she was as unobtrusive as possible regarding child-initiated activities. Consequently, the children appeared to engage in relatively unrestrained, spontaneous conversations and more than half of their speech was addressed to other children. The corpus discussed below comes from videotapes of one-hour sessions per month for the last four months of the study. The children ranged in age from 34 to 39 months at the first of these four sessions. The corpus consists of almost 3,000 child utterances, all of which were coded as illocutionary acts.

The decision procedure for coding utterances as illocutionary acts was as follows: determine, in the following order,

a. The literal semantic reading of the primary proposition of the uterance, on the basis of its logical subject, predicate, adverbial phrases and other constituents (according to Katz, 1972);
b. The grammatical and prosodic operators on the proposition;
c. The new, or focused, information; new in relation to both conversation and context (Halliday, 1970);
d. The speaker's related utterances and nonlinguistic behavior;
e. The reciprocal and contingent behavior, both verbal and nonverbal, of his interlocutors (Garvey, 1975); and
f. The contextual features directly relevant to the pragmatic status of the utterance (Lewis, 1972).

Let me exemplify the steps in this procedure. The vast majority of the children's utterances were propositional in structure (though sometimes elliptical), consisting of at least a subject and predicate; for example, the "I" and "am painting" (respectively) in "I am painting." Numerous kinds of grammatical operators applied to propositions: word order converted a proposition to a yes–no question (for example, "Are you painting?"); and a grammatically determined intonation pattern did the same (as in "You're painting?"); and an interrogative pronouns converted it to a Wh-question ("What are you doing?"). The new information in an utterance may be new in relation to the conversation ("Nothing" might be the Wh-answer to the above Wh-question); or information could be new in relation to what was already given in the context, ("He likes to" would be an attribution about the above "painter's" internal state relative to painting).

The single most important indicator of the CI of a given illocutionary act is the speaker's utterances that are contingently related to the target utterance being coded. For example, one boy said to a girl: "Hey, don't sit there!", which was coded as a protest; then he said "I was sitting there" which was contingently related to his first utterance by stating his right to make a protest. The remarks of addressees (the second-most important indicator of CI) most often indicate how the addressee interprets the speaker's CI; children often reply with "Okay" to a speaker's action request in order to verbally encode their compliance. And a third source of evidence for the investigator is the teacher's remarks which were, though often unsolicited, contingently related to a child's utterance to another child. For example, one boy tried to make an action request appear to be a genuine protest by raising his fist and saying, in an abrupt rising falling intonation contour, "Get out of here" to a girl. The teacher immediately asked "Why does she have to?", thereby questioning the boy's right to issue a protest. The girl did not leave.

The context is often crucial in determining the CI of a child's illocutionary act. Contextual features may, in fact, override the literal meaning of a proposition: instead of an event description, "I am painting" would be coded as role-playing if the child were merely waving his arms in the air as he said it; the utterance "We painted the windows" would be coded as a joke if the participants in the conversation respond with laughter because they know that it is obviously untrue, and even unreasonable. In general, the coding of individual illocutionary acts is determined by both "internal" grammatical factors and "external" discourse relation and contextual factors. Most often, the relations among sequences of utterances define the status of individual utterances in the sequence.

Thirty-two types of illocutionary act were performed by the children in the study. Table 1 lists the types and gives the total number of occurrences and percentages for each type. I am not going to discuss Table 1 in any detail. I offer it to give some indication of the types of illocutionary acts we postulated and to give some perspective on the relative proportions among the illocutionary acts our children performed. I do not want to maintain at this stage of the research that the illocutionary act categories have an absolute validity or even that the division of illocutionary act types is the best possible descriptive arrangement. I will say that we achieved a reliability of better than 82% for all sessions for classifying the utterances in the corpus into illocutionary acts; this was measured in terms of the initial agreements of two experienced coders who scored independently. The primary value of our initial coding was to group together all the utterances that we intuitively coded as a single type. The more important task was analysing the conditions common to all occurrences of a type in order to understand how children use each type.

A few additional remarks about the methodology of coding illocutionary acts will indicate the kinds of problems one encounters in the pragmatic analysis of child speech. Not all utterances contained full propositions. Sometimes a child's speech was unintelligible or incomplete, or sometimes clear and complete but nevertheless incomprehensible in the given context, in which cases we coded the utterances as uninterpretable; 7.9% of the corpus was uninterpretable. In other cases, utterances were merely elliptical; a "No," for example, suffices as the complete answer to "Are you painting?" so it is coded as a yes–no answer, implicitly equivalent to "No, I am not painting." Also, the category of illocutionary acts called conversational devices are nonpropositional in structure. These include conversation-position markers like greetings and farewells, filler returns like "Oh" or "What" to rhetorical questions, calls for attention like "Hey" or "John," and utterances like "Here you are" which are completely redundant with respect to the actions they accompany and thus are not propositions containing new conceptual information. Finally, we did not code purely emotional expressions like "Wow!," nor singing or playing with sounds or words because it is not clear what, if any, intentions children expect to convey by such utterances.

Some utterances were double coded, and of these there were two types. The first is definitionally double, given the coding scheme. Responses to Wh- questions, for example, are often also descriptions: a response to "Where's John?" was "He's under the table" which is both a Wh- answer and a location description; 5.5% of the corpus was coded as a Wh- answer plus another illocutionary act. The second type of double coding was problematic insofar as it involved utterances which either lacked sufficient linguistic or contextual information to warrant a specific CI or which fell clearly into two categories. For example, in response to the teacher's request of "Paint your real name on the egg, okay?," a child replied "But I'm Robin Hood" which we coded as both a compliance (because it made explicit his refusal to comply) and a role play (because it simultaneously established a fantasy). Notice that such problematic utterances are not structurally ambiguous in the sense of expressing different underlying propositions. Rather, they are functionally equivocal insofar as the listener may not be sure of how the speaker intends his utterance to be taken. In such cases it is not clear whether the speaker has a single intention (which the listener fails to recognize uniquely) or two equivalent intentions. These exceptions highlight the fact that hearers (and observers) most often automatically and unequivocally recognize the speaker's CI. Merely .3% of our corpus were of this problematic type. Thus totally, 5.8% of the corpus was double coded.

In addition to coding for illocutionary act, we also used six code tags: –R for immediate and exact repetitions of previous utterances; –X for extensions of previous utterances in which the form, but not the CI, changed; –F for utterances whose content was fantasy (these occur in fantasy sequences after Role play initiates the fantasy); –C for utterances which were contingently related to other utterances; –I for indirect forms of illocutionary acts such as "I want some juice" as an indirect action request; and –E for egocentric speech, that is, an utterance not addressed to a listener and concerning which the speaker apparently does not expect any contingent behavior. It is problematic to view egocentric utterances as "intentional," even if we assume that the speaker and

TABLE 1

The Illocutionary Act Types Identified in the Corpus of the Speech of
3-Year-Olds

	Total	%
REQUESTS: solicit information, actions or acknowledgment.		
Yes–No questions: solicit the Hearer H to affirm, negate or confirm the proposition P of the Speaker's S utterance U.	124	4.4
Wh- questions: solicit information about the identity, location or property of an object, event or situation.	208	7.3
Action requests: solicit H to perform an act.	282	10.0
Permission requests: solicit H to grant permission for S to perform an act.	133	4.7
Rhetorical questions: solicit H's acknowledgment for S to continue	18	.6
Total	765	27.0
RESPONSES: directly complement preceding utterances.		
Yes–No answers: complement yes–no questions.	151	5.3
Wh- answers: complement Wh- questions.	154	5.4
Agreements: agree with or deny the P of S's previous U.	91	3.2
Compliances: make explicit compliances with action requests.	88	3.1
Qualifications: qualify, clarify or otherwise change P of S's U.	39	1.4
Total	523	18.5
DESCRIPTIONS: represent observable or verifiable aspects of context.		
Identifications: label an object, event, person or situation.	225	7.9
Possessions: indicate who owns or temporarily possesses an object.	46	1.6
Events: represent the occurrence of an event, action, process, etc.	204	7.2
Properties: represent characteristics of objects, events, etc.	114	4.0
Locations: represent location or direction of objects, events, etc.	43	1.5
Total	632	22.3
STATEMENTS: express analytic and institutional facts, beliefs, attitudes, emotions, reasons, etc.		
Rules: express conventional procedures, facts, definitions, etc.	95	3.4
Evaluations: express impressions, attitudes, judgments, etc.	35	1.2
Internal reports: express S's internal state (emotions, sentiments)	219	7.7
Attributions: express beliefs about another's internal state.	7	.2
Explanations: report reasons, causes or motives for acts, or predict future states of affairs.	34	1.2
Total	390	13.8
CONVERSATIONAL DEVICES: regulate contact and conversations.		
Boundary markers: initiate or end contact or conversation.	5	.2
Calls: make contact by soliciting attention.	57	2.0
Accompaniments: signal contact by accompanying S's action.	30	1.1
Returns: acknowledge, or fill in after, H's preceding U.	48	1.7
Politeness markers: make explicit S's politeness.	12	.4
Total	152	5.8

(continued)

TABLE 1 *(Continued)*

PERFORMATIVES: accomplish acts by being said.

Role plays: establish fantasies.	46	1.6
Protests: object to H's previous behavior.	78	2.8
Jokes: produce humorous effects.	68	2.4
Game markers: initiate, continue or end a game.	5	.2
Claims: establish rights for S by being said.	78	2.8
Warnings: alert H of impending harm.	16	.6
Teases: annoy, taunt or provoke H.	16	.6
Total	307	10.8

UNINTERPRETABLE: are unintelligibe, incomplete or otherwise
incomprehensible utterances.   223   7.9

DOUBLE CODED: are utterances that received two of the above codes.   −163   −5.8

TOTAL: 2,829   100.0

hearer are the same person. These utterances can, however, be dealt with separately for data analyses.

GRAMMATICAL FORMS AND ILLOCUTIONARY ACTS

Utterances tagged −*I* present a special, in fact the crucial, problem for the pragmatic theories thus far proposed in the philosophical (Searle, in press), linguistic (Gordon & Lakoff, 1971), and psychological (Garvey) literatures. The problem is essentially to explain how the same illocutionary act can be accomplished by different grammatical forms – how, for example, an action request can be performed by uttering either "Close the door" *or* "Would you mind closing the door?" This was the most difficult problem encountered in the coding of the children's utterances.

The solution to this problem determines to a large extent the nature and value of one's pragmatic theory. Rather than review and criticize previous solutions, let me propose still another. First of all, I propose that each illocutionary act type is closely associated with a *canonical* grammatical form. (I use the term canonical form in the mathematical sense of "the simplest standard form") Table 2 is a grid that represents the relations between some basic illocutionary act types and the forms that are used to realize them.[4] The X entries along the diagonal indicate the pairings of illocutionary act types with their canonical sentence forms; the vertical ○ entries represent the pairings of noncanonical

[4] I would like to thank George Miller for suggesting the grid form of displaying what I call canonical relations.

TABLE 2

The Relations between Some Basic Illocutionary Act Types and the Canonical and Noncanonical Sentence Forms Used to Realize the Illocutionary Act Types[a]

	Illocutionary Act Types			
	Assertive	Question	Requestive	Emotive
SENTENCE FORMS				
Declarative	X		o	
Interrogative		X	o	
Imperative			X	
Exclamatory			o	X

[a]X = canonical sentence form for corresponding illocutionary act type; o = noncanonical sentence forms for the requestive type.

sentence forms with the requestive illocutionary type. To use examples from our corpus, the children got the teacher to serve them juice by producing the following utterances:

(4) a. Give me some juice!
     b. I want juice.
     c. Can I have some juice?
     d. Oh, there's my juice!

I suggest that while Sentence (4a) is the canonical sentence form for making the action request, Sentences (4b)–(4d) are noncanonical sentence forms which can be equally effective in conveying the speaker's CI. What needs to be explained is how children, by the age of three, can have learned not only the canonical form of illocutionary acts, but also some of the noncanonical forms equivalent in illocutionary value to the canonical. The second major hypothesis I wish to propose addresses itself to this issue, namely,

(5) When a speaker uses the canonical sentence form of an illocutionary act, the expected illocutionary effect and the expected perlocutionary effect are unequivocally recognized by the hearer as a conventional pair, without inferences on the part of the hearer about the beliefs, expectations or motives of the speaker; but when the speaker uses a noncanonical sentence form of the same illocutionary act, the hearer will make inferences of varying degrees concerning the speaker's expected perlocutionary effect.

The inferences that hearers make about a speaker's expected perlocutionary effect are probabilistic in nature and depend upon the shared beliefs of speaker and hearer. Nevertheless, the inferences are conventionally governed by sociolinguistic rules for the use of utterances in contexts. A hypothesis related to (5) is

(6) If a hearer has some belief which makes him question the automatic illocutionary–perlocutionary effect relation of a speaker's illocutionary act of canonical sentence form, he will try to infer a different expected perlocutionary effect on the part of the speaker.

These hypotheses will be exemplified below in the discussion of "pragmatic strategies."

Some experimental evidence from Clark and Lucy (1975) suggests that it takes adults longer to process the "intended sense" of nonliteral forms of requesting than to process the literal form (or what I have called the canonical sentence form of requesting). They hypothesized that the hearer "goes about comprehending the intended meaning of an utterance by (1) constructing a literal interpretation of the utterance, (2) checking its plausibility against the context, and (3), if there is a conflict, bringing to bear certain rules of conversation in order to deduce a conveyed interpretation" (Clark & Lucy, 1975, p. 66). Their evidence is in the form of longer latencies in responding (in terms of matching sentences with visual displays) to utterances like "I would love to see the circle colored blue" as compared to "Please color the circle blue." But their subjects were told that the utterances would be requests, which is not the case in natural conversations. Also, some of their nonliteral request forms are subject to Sadock's (1972) criticism that some indirect speech acts may be processed as idioms. This caveat would also hold for my Hypotheses (5) and (6) above. What is now needed is some forced situation experiments with children to determine how they process noncanonical forms of illocutionary acts. A few utterances in our corpus do indicate that noncanonical forms of illocutionary acts can cause misunderstandings. For present purposes, however, I can only suggest the form of the "rules of conversation" about which Clark and Lucy, among many others, admit "there is little known."

PRAGMATIC STRATEGIES AND SOCIOLINGUISTIC RULES

There is ample evidence from our corpus that children used arrays of different utterances to achieve the same effect on hearers. This section describes the child's choice of one utterance over another in terms of "pragmatic strategies" — strategies for deploying utterances to convey messages beyond the semantic information of the sentence type and beyond the expected illocutionary effect of the illocutionary act type. And I want to argue that these messages are conventionally communicated because they are based on underlying sociolinguistic rules.

The first strategy is called the "direct strategy" because the canonical form of the illocutionary act is used and the conventional illocutionary—perlocutionary effect appears to be unequivocally recognized by the hearer, as in

(7) a. I'm painting.
     b. Get off my blocks.

In (7a), which was coded as an event description, the expected illocutionary effect (EIE) is that the hearer recognize that a description was performed and the expected perlocutionary effect (EPE) is merely that the hearer accept the description as true or accurate. (7b) is a protest, the EIE of which is that the hearer recognize it as a protest and the EPE of which is that the hearer recognize that the speaker wants him off the blocks. (Note that the "appropriate response" can be characterized as the hearer's actualization of the speaker's EPE.)

A second strategy is called the "indirect strategy." We have already seen that (4b) can achieve the same effect as (4a), namely that the hearer recognize that the speaker wants juice. Similarly, the same speaker who uttered (7b) uttered

(8) You're standing on my blocks.

the EIE of which is that the hearer recognize it as an event description; but the EPE is the same as (7b).

A third strategy is called the "metaphorical" because it involves the exploitation of the semantic reading of a proposition (usually its truth value) by producing an utterance in circumstances which prevent it from being taken literally. For example, a child points to a wooden box and says

(9) That's a train.

The EIE is that the hearer recognize the utterance as an identification; but the EPE is that the hearer recognize that the speaker wants him to accept it as a role play. Similarly, utterances like

(10) You can't catch me.

when produced with a sing-song intonation contour in circumstances where the speaker is some distance away from the hearer are not coded as attributions (the EIE) but as gamemarkers (the EPE) since, in this case, the speaker expects the hearer to begin the game of chasing him.

We have identified other strategies such as the use of grammatical tags to convey politeness or to allow the hearer to take the utterance on its illocutionary *or* perlocutionary value; but such phenomena are treated more fully by Ervin-Tripp (1977) and in Dore (1977). The existence of such strategies makes the coding of utterances quite difficult. One must decide, which we were not in a position to at the initial coding, whether one wants to code the EIE or the EPE, or both, of the speaker's illocutionary act. More importantly, one must try to discover the sociolinguistic rules that underly the existence of illocutionary acts and pragmatic strategies.

One final point about strategies: further research on speech acts may reveal that there are really very few "basic" illocutionary act types, perhaps corresponding to grammatical moods or "modalities" like the sentence forms in Fig. 1. If this turns out to be the case, then emphasis should shift to pragmatic strategies, and these would presumably become more sophisticated with age. Consider an example typical of adult conversation: after dinner a guest says to the hostess "May I help you wash the dishes?"; if the guest does not really want to wash dishes, the utterance can not be a genuine permission request; it would, I think, be best described as some kind of politness strategy. Similarly, if the sociolinguistic rule for asserting a proposition involves the speaker's belief that the proposition is true, then lying would be another pragmatic strategy as opposed to being a type of speech act. Now let us consider what such rules might be like.

Following the analysis of speech acts provided by Searle (1969), Garvey investigated requests for action by three- to five-year-olds, using a framework similar to ours, and identified eight "interpersonal meaning factors" which are understood by children to constitute the conditions for requesting: (a) the request and response must be reasonable; (b) the speaker wants the hearer to perform the act; the hearer is (c) willing, (d) able and (e) obligated to do the act; (f) the hearer is the appropriate recipient of the request; (g) he has rights which may conflict with the performance of the act; and (h) before the request, he did not intend to perform the act. For each of these factors, Garvey found sequences of contingent utterances which indicated that the children observe the conditions. For example, one child said "Just start the motor, okay?" and the hearer replied "Okay," in which case the speaker checked the hearer's willingness to comply and the hearer made his compliance explicit. Garvey's data make it clear that the domain of an action request can stretch over large parts of conversations.

We used Garvey's method of examining contingent utterances and behavior in order to discover the conditions for the performative illocutionary types in our corpus. It soon became evident that the performance of illocutionary acts depends crucially on the shared beliefs of speakers and hearers.[5] Accordingly, we formulated the rule for protests as follows:

> (11) a. Utterance U is successful in consummating a protest if both the speaker S and the hearer H believe that U = "I hereby object to

[5] Hutchinson (1971, p. 134), discussing presupposition in adult speech, proposed that "people hold certain beliefs about the world and about their interlocutors as they approach the communicative task. Certain of these beliefs are revealed in the speech act itself, and revealed in a systematic way.

your A-ing," where A is an act that H has performed which
violates some right R of S.

b. Operative belief conditions

1. H has done A.
2. S has the right R.
3. In doing A, H has violated the R of S.
4. S wants H to cease A-ing.
5. H is obligated to cease A-ing.
6. If S had not protested, H would not have ceased A-ing.

Rules for illocutionary acts are sociolinguistic in nature because they require both utterances of certain grammatical forms *and* the operativity of social constructs like rights, obligations, institutionalized roles and procedures and so on. Illocutionary acts are *consummated* only when the relevant beliefs are shared: if, for example, the hearer fails to share an operative belief, the speaker may have protested, but from the hearer's point of view it is not consummated. Obviously, the clearest evidence that a protest is consummated (indeed, is responded to appropriately) is if the hearer actually performs the EPE of the protest. One ironic aspect of protests for children (and one that I think sheds light on the nature of illocutionary acts in general) is that what determines whether or not a protest is consummated is whether the hearer *believes* that the speaker has the right in question. It does not matter if the speaker actually has the right, except in a case where the hearer contests the protest, in which case the speaker can state his right and thereby consummate the protest.

Empirically, we found that when our children manifested their objection by an abrupt rising–falling intonation contour, it never took a requestive tag (like "okay" or "please") and it was never responded to by a simple yes or no compliance. These two findings distinguish protests from action requests. Moreover, Belief Conditions 1, 2, and 3 on protests are not operative in the domain of an action request (cf. Garvey's conditions above). The point is that children have the choice of producing a request or a protest, and their behavior indicates that they distinguish the two quite clearly. Finally, consider the child's utterance of "You're standing on my blocks" mentioned earlier. If we try to explain why such an utterance (which has an illocutionary value of a description) can be equivalent in perlocutionary value to a direct protest, two facts are crucially important: all the belief-conditions for a direct protest appear to be operative in the domain of the indirect utterance; and the utterance actually encodes Belief Condition 1 on protests. I suggest that these two facts alone are a substantial enough information base for the hearer to infer a perlocutionary effect not ordinarily associated with a description.

Another example of a performative rule is:

(12) a. Utterance U is successful in consummating a claim if both the
speaker S and the hearer H believe that U = "I hereby preempt

the right R" where R is some privilege of possession, position, turn, etc. for S.

   b. Operative belief conditions

      1. A procedure is in effect such that rights relative to the procedure can be established for an eligible S by his verbally claiming R.

      2. S has claimed R.

      3. S wants R.

      4. He accepts S's R.

      5. He cannot claim the same R.

      6. There is no other procedure in effect that overrules Condition 1. above.

A sequence which exemplifies some of these conditions for the children is

(13) a. Teacher: Who'd like to wash the table?
      b. Boy I: Me.
      c. Boy II: Me.
      d. Boy I: No, me.
      e. Boy II: Me too.
      f. Teacher: Well, wait a minute. Don't fight. There's three sponges.
      g. Boy II: The big sponge.

In this sequence, Boy I's utterance (13b) was double coded as a Wh- answer to the teacher's Wh- question and as a claim because it effectively secured him first rights at washing the table. Boy II's utterance of (13c) violated Boy I's right since Boy I had already claimed the position of first washer. But when Boy I protested and reasserted his claim (13d), Boy II did not contest Boy I's right, rather he claimed the right to be second washer. Finally, when the teacher said there were three sponges (and therefore three potential "washing" positions), Boy II ultimately got the upper hand anyway by claiming the biggest sponge. Had Boy II persisted in contesting Boy I's claim, he might have left himself open to be thought of as a bully, instead of the leader (with the requisite verbal skills) that he was. So goes life in the nursery!

Apparently, the sets of belief conditions operative in the domain of an illocutionary act change with age, and not merely additively. One condition that children older than those in our and Garvey's study must acquire (since they produced no relevant utterances) in the domain of an action request is that there be a reason for making the request. Otherwise, utterances like "It's cold in here" to convey a request to close the window, or a son's reply of "okay, I'll get up" to his mother's initial utterance of "breakfast is ready," would be difficult to understand. Similarly, the children in our study did not produce single-word utterances like "juice" to accomplish action requests, which utterances seem to work well for adults. However, it seems that although preschool children believe they are obligated to comply with an action request, they may drop this condition as they get older. Some five-year olds in Garvey's study replied with "I don't have to" to some action requests. And many adults report that though it is polite to acknowledge a request, they are not obligated to comply.

CONCLUSION: ILLOCUTIONARY ACTS AND DISCOURSE RELATIONS

The question posed at the beginning of this chapter was "What must a child learn in order to master his language?" It seems indisputable that he acquires grammatical rules, despite conflicting opinions about how rules are represented cognitively. And it has become commonplace to note that he must also learn rules of discourse. The controversial issue is how to treat supragrammatical phenomena. Our empirical investigation of children's illocutionary acts suggests that such acts not only share certain general properties of sentences, but also that the discourse relations among utterances in conversations seem to be in part determined by the structure of illocutionary acts.

The most striking property shared by sentences and illocutionary acts is that, like the sound-meaning relations in grammar, there is no isomorphic relation between the surface forms of utterances and the CIs they convey. Secondly, one relation among illocutionary acts themselves is that different acts seem to share some belief conditions from among a (possibly) universal (but limited) set of relevant belief conditions. Thirdly, illocutionary acts, like sentences, are based upon underlying rules, though the former involve purely social constructs. And finally, contrary to the claims of others, there does not seem to be an infinite set of illocutionary act types, just as the number of sentence types, though large, is not infinite. This last assumption is based upon our observation that children do a limited number of general things when they speak: they give and receive information, get attention and get others to do things for them, express their beliefs and feelings, commit themselves to future acts, establish facts, create fantasies, and communicate humor. Moreover, since acts of different illocutionary values can be used to achieve the same perlocutionary effect, the actual effects of illocutionary acts on hearers are probably more limited than the number of illocutionary act types.

Illocutionary acts affect hearers and the flow of conversation in a number of ways. First of all, when a speaker decides to say something, he chooses one act over another; and this choice communicates not only his specific CI, but often affective information as well. Since the choice of an illocutionary act conveys the speaker's expected effects, hearers are constrained to a relatively circumscribed set of responses. Even when the hearer does not respond with the "most appropriate response" (for example, with the exact information solicited by a question), his response is limited to various kinds of acknowledgments contingent on the speaker's illocutionary act. In examining the request response sequences in our corpus we found that the children produce very few basic kinds of responses to yes–no questions: appropriate (or canonical) yes or no answers, sometimes in sentences or in gesture form; qualifying information, like elaborating on the answer or stating that one can not answer; a question asking for clarification of the initial question; and nonsequiturs (less that 1% of total yes–no replies). There were very few nonsequiturs in our entire corpus, and at least some of them seem to be due simply to failure to hear speakers. In fact, the "rationality" of the children's conversations was quite striking. The evidence, apart from the small number of nonsequiturs, which supports this notion of rationality comes from the patterns of conversational organization that we identified. These patterns can be characterized in terms of Searle's notion of "preparatory conditions" for speech acts and Garvey's notion of "the domain" of a speech act. Consider the following:

(14)   a.   Boy I: What are you making?
     b.   Boy II: A zoo.
     c.   Boy I: Put the animals in the zoo.

It is certainly reasonable for Boy I to find out what is being made before he can reasonably request an action like that in (14c). More than 37% of the Wh-questions our children asked made explicit a preparatory condition operating in the domain of an action request. Another fact that demonstrates that the children organized their conversations in terms of rational plans is that 49% of their Wh-questions were about procedures, possession and taking turns – all institutional facts that are crucial to subsequent interaction.

In view of such findings, we speculate that discourse relations are to a large extent affected by the sociolinguistic rules underlying illocutionary acts. And these rules are not the same type as the "conversational rules" proposed by Gordon and Lakoff: they are not extensions of the grammar because they involve many nonlinguistic shared beliefs about the world; and they are not "formal" rules in the sense claimed by Gordon and Lakoff because, as Katz and Langendoen (1976, p. 16) point out, more "than the form and arrangement of symbols in strings determines the theory's treatment of its subject."

ACKNOWLEDGMENTS

The research reported in this paper was supported in part by a grant from The Grant Foundation to The Rockefeller University's Experimental Psychology Laboratory and in part by a National Institute of Mental Health grant to the author.
For their helpful comments on previous drafts of this paper, I would like to thank George Miller, Catherine Garvey, David McNeill, Susan Ervin-Tripp, Denis Newman, and Maryl Gearhart.

REFERENCES

Austin, J. *How to do things with words.* New York: Oxford University Press, 1962.

Bever, T. The cognitive basis for linguistic structures. In J. Hayes (Ed.), *Cognition and the development of language.* New York: Wiley, 1970.

Brown, R. *A first language.* Cambridge, Massachusetts: Harvard University Press, 1973.

Chomsky, N. *Aspects of the theory of syntax.* Cambridge, Massachusetts: MIT Press, 1965.

Clark, H. & Lucy, P. Understanding what is meant from what is said: A study in conversationally conveyed requests. *Journal of Verbal Learning and Verbal Behavior,* 1975, **14,** 56–72.

Dore, J. A pragmatic description of early language development. *Journal of Psycholinguistic Research,* 1974, **4,** 343–350.

Dore, J. Holophrases, speech acts and language universals. *Journal of Child Language,* 1975, **2,** 21–40.

Dore, J. "Oh them sheriff": A pragmatic analysis of children's responses to questions. In C. Mitchell-Kernan & S. Ervin-Tripp (Eds.), *Child discourse.* New York: Academic Press, 1977.

Ervin-Tripp, S. "Wait for me, Rollerskate!" In C. Mitchell-Kernan & S. Ervin-Tripp (Eds.), *Child discourse.* New York: Academic Press, 1977.

Garvey, C. Requests and responses in children's speech. *Journal of Child Language,* 1975, **2,** 41–60.

Gordon, D., & Lakoff, G. Conversational postulates. *Papers from the Seventh Regional Meeting, Chicago Linguistic Society,* 1971.

Grice, H. P. Meaning. *Philosophical Review,* 1957, **3,** 377–388.

Halliday, M. A. K. Language structure and language function. In J. Lyons (Ed.), *New horizons in linguistics.* Harmondsworth, England: Penguin, 1970.

Hutchinson, L. Presupposition and belief-inferences. *Papers from the Seventh Regional Meeting, Chicago Linguistic Society,* 1971.

Katz, J. *Semantic theory.* New York: Harper & Row, 1972.

Katz, J., & Langendoen, D. T. Pragmatics and presupposition. *Language,* 1976, **52,** 1–17.

Lewis, D. General semantics. In G. Harmon & D. Davidson (Eds.), *Semantics of natural languages.* Dordrecht, Holland: Reidel, 1972.

Mohan, B. Do sequencing rules exist? *Semiotica,* 1974, **12,** 75–96.

Sadock, J. Speech act idioms. *Papers from the Eighth Regional Meeting, Chicago Linguistic Society,* 1972.

Searle, J. *Speech acts.* Cambridge, England: Cambridge University Press, 1969.

Searle, J. Indirect speech acts. In P. Cole & J. Morgan (Eds.), *Syntax and Semantics III.* New York: Academic Press, 1975.

12

The Art of Referring: The Speaker's Use of Noun Phrases to Instruct the Listener

S. R. Rochester
J. R. Martin

University of Toronto

In John Searle's *Speech Acts,* in the paperback version, there is a misprint of a chapter title which reads, "Reference as a Speech Art." In effect, that is the proper title of the present chapter. We are concerned here with a referential "art" — with the speaker's ability to guide listeners to select precise referents of noun phrases. This guidance is not simply the referring of symbols to things which characterizes all language. It is rather a particular referring which marks out some noun phrases as requiring more information in order to be understood, and other noun phrases as requiring no further information.

Guidance which the speaker gives the listener can be helpful or misleading. For example, if the speaker mentions *that old snail,* the listener expects to find more information about *that* snail elsewhere in the utterance context. The information may be in the immediate situation, or in the listener's recent memory of the verbal context. If it is in fact recoverable, the speaker's guidance has been a help; if not, the guidance has been a hindrance to comprehension. Helpful guidance would seem to be an "art" normally available to all native speakers of English.

What we have been calling the "art" of referring, Halliday and Hasan (1976) term "phoricity." Phoricity . . . "embodies an instruction to retrieve from elsewhere the information necessary for interpreting the passage in question" (p. 4). We apply this term to noun phrases in particular. A *phoric* noun phrase contains a clear instruction to the listener which says, in effect, "To interpret me, see elsewhere." Such noun phrases might be as follows: *that old snail, him, the stronger bond.* A *nonphoric* noun phrase, on the other hand, requires no further information in order to be understood. The instruction it seems to carry is, "To interpret me, stay here." Examples of *nonphoric* noun phrases might be: *a snail, a strong bond.*

Phoricity in noun phrases is interesting to psychologists for two reasons. First, since it points to a signaling system which the speaker may use, it probably requires some choice or decision-making on the part of the speaker. Secondly, since it appears to guide the listener, phoricity might have some effect on comprehension. As we suggested, there would seem to be guidance which is artful and guidance which is misleading. To the extent that the speaker accurately and effectively signals what is needed to interpret a noun phrase, the listener should benefit. Such accurate signaling could lead to what Searle (1970) calls "a fully consummated reference . . . in which an object is identified unambiguously for the hearer" (p. 82).

But we already know that phoricity does not tell enough about the art of referring. In a series of provocative studies, Herb Clark and his colleagues (Clark, 1973; Clark & Haviland, 1974; Haviland & Clark, 1974) have shown that the *location* of referents in the utterance context affects listeners' comprehension. For example, consider the following:

(1)   Joan hurriedly left her house.
(2)   *She* hoped never to return to *it.*

Clark finds that utterance combinations like (1) and (2) are readily understood by listeners. There is no apparent difficulty in finding referents for the (italicized) phoric noun phrases in (2). However, listeners are slower to find the referent for *the door* in (3).

(3)   *The door* slammed behind her.

In order to interpret the phoric noun phrase *the door,* the listener must search for a previous identification of *a door* in the verbal context of the utterance. In fact, assuming that (1) is the first utterance in the text, there is no explicit mention of *a door.* Rather, *her house* is given. In our culture, *house* and *door* fall within close semantic range of each other so that a listener could locate the needed referent for *the door* in the noun phrase *her house* by inference, or "bridging." Clark finds that listeners are slower to find referents which require inference from the verbal context than those which are explicitly given.

Clark's work indicates clearly that the art of referring is determined not only by phoricity, but by the actual placement of referents in the utterance context. He has focused on the comprehensibility of text as a function of explicit and implicit referents, and has demonstrated that referent location is important for the listener. In the present study, we focus primarily on the speaker. At a first level, we present a description of the speaker's use of phoricity and, for phoric noun phrases with definite referents, we determine where those referents are located in the context of the utterance. The locations we examine are broader than those distinguished by Clark, for we include Halliday and Hasan's categories of explicit verbal and explicit situational reference, as well as an additional category of implicit reference. In order to provide a useful description, we study the productions of speakers in a variety of situational contexts. One context is an unstructured interview; a second context is a structured task in which ten cartoons were shown to subjects who then described the cartoons and interpreted their content; and in a third context subjects were read a brief narrative and asked to retell it in their own words.

At a second level, we ask whether the speaker's use of phoricity and placement of definite noun phrase referents depends on the skill of the speaker. As we mentioned earlier, the art of referring ought to be available to all native speakers of English. But we know that some speakers are more coherent than others. It is at least possible that coherence is related to facility with a noun phrase signaling system.

How does one find native speakers who clearly differ in coherence? Robin Lakoff's (1973, p. 297) studies of violations of the rules of conversation set us onto an unusual track. She observes that speakers seem to conspire using "a kind of principle of sanity: I assume you're sane, unless proven otherwise, and will therefore assume that everything you do in a conversation is done for a reason. . . . " What if the speaker is *not* sane? Then the use of phoricity might change, and the location of referents for phoric noun phrases might be obscure.

Pursuing this reasoning, we chose to study persons diagnosed as schizophrenic and showing clear signs of thought process disorder. Thought process disorder seems to be a disturbance in language (at least) in which speaker-to-listener signaling systems are breaking down. For young short-term patients, this breakdown does not occur at all levels of language use. Rather, the thought-disordered speaker typically uses a normal lexicon and adequate syntax. What appears to be disrupted is the propositional structure of the discourse. Such speech is described by psychiatrists (e.g. Bleuler, 1950) as being "wooly and vague," containing an "inconsequential following of side issues."

Consider the following sample from a thought-disordered subject:

(4) a. but what's to say there's nothing up in that ice age
     b. the ice age that is yet to come supposedly this summer and this
         winter coming up
     c. you could see quite a recession of them
     d. and then they come on pretty strong

Each segment is rather well formed in itself, but the text of the four segments is not fully coherent. What seems to be problematic here is that Segments (4c) and (4d) contain noun phrases (*them* and *they*) which presuppose for their interpretation something other than themselves. In the terms we've been using, they are phoric noun phrases which require definite referents. But no explicit referents are apparent. This example, and others like it, prompted us to hypothesize that thought-disordered (TD) speakers would differ in their use of phoricity and placement of noun phrase referents from normal speakers.

The important test of this notion is a comparison of TD speakers with subjects who are also diagnosed as schizophrenic but who show no clear signs of thought disorder. These nonthought-disordered schizophrenic (NTD) subjects are identical to TD subjects on several potentially important variables such as drug dosage, length of hospitalization and verbal IQ. However, they are clearly different in the quality of their discourse. In an earlier study (Rochester, Martin, & Thurston, in press), we asked lay judges to evaluate the coherence of interview transcripts for TD, NTD, and normal (N) subjects (the same subjects described in this chapter). On the basis of these ratings of coherence, we correctly identified 75% of TD interview transcripts and falsely identified as thought disordered only 5% of NTD transcripts and 0% of N transcripts. This suggests that TD speakers are more difficult to understand than other speakers, whether the other speakers be schizophrenic or normal volunteers.

To summarize, we have attempted to study one aspect of the art of referring: the speaker's use of noun phrases to instruct the listener. We ask the following questions:

I. How does the normal speaker use noun phrases as referential signals?
   A. What is the balance of phoric and nonphoric noun phrases in normal discourse? That is, how often is the listener asked to recover noun phrase referents and how often are those referents provided?
   B. What strategies are normally demanded of the listener? Given that a definite phoric noun phrase is presented, where does the speaker place the referent for that noun phrase? In the explicit verbal context of the utterance? In the situation? In the implicit verbal context?
   C. Do the answers to (A) and (B) depend on the situational context, that is, on whether the speaker is engaged in an interview, a structured monologue, or a narrative?
II. Is the speaker's use of noun phrases related to the coherence of his/her discourse?
   A. Does the balance of phoric and nonphoric noun phrases in the speech of TD subjects differ from that in NTD and N subjects?
   B. Where do TD speakers place the referents for their definite phoric noun phrases?
   C. Do the answers to (A) and (B) depend on the situational context?

PROCEDURES

Basic Unit of Analysis

As a basic unit of analysis, we used the noun phrase or nominal group. These terms are used interchangeably. Our description of the nominal group derives from early category-scale grammar (Halliday, 1961): a nominal group consists of at least some "head" element and is usually open to premodification by deictics, epithets, or classifiers and postmodification by words, prepositional phrases and relative clauses. Example 5 gives a representative labeling:

(5) *the*   *little*   *stone*   *cottage*   *which John owned*
      Deictic   Epithet   Classifier   Head   Qualifier

Phoricity Categories for Noun Phrases

When speakers use a noun phrase, they provide their listeners with clues for interpreting that noun phrase. This is not to say that speakers *intend* to provide clues, but merely that they do so. We distinguish noun phrases into three categories, according to what we suppose to be similar reference characteristics. At the most basic level, we presume, the speaker indicates whether a noun phrase is complete in itself (a *nonphoric* noun phrase), or requires further information to be understood (a *phoric* noun phrase). If further information is required, the speaker indicates whether that information is generally available to the listener (a *general phoric* noun phrase) or must be retrieved from the particular context of the utterance (a *definite phoric* noun phrase). Examples are given in Table 1 and the categories are explained in detail in Appendix 1.

Retrieval Categories for Definite Noun Phrase Referents

Phoricity of noun phrases is only one part of the art of referring. Phoricity tells the listener to search or not to search for further information, and indicates very generally where the search should be pursued. But instructions embodied in the noun phrase itself do not tell the listener precisely where to locate referents in the utterance context. This search must be performed without instructions from the speaker. An "artful" speaker, we may suppose, would ease the listener's task by placing referents for definite noun phrases in accessible locations.

We distinguish five categories of referent location. Examples are given in Table 2 and the categories are described fully in Appendix 2. The categories are described in terms of strategies which the listener would need to use to recover

TABLE 1
Phoricity Categories for Noun Phrases

Phoricity category	Subcategory	Examples
Nonphoric NP (No referent required)		I saw *a movie* yesterday.
General phoric NP (Referent in context of culture)	1. Common	*One* gets uncomfortable.
	2. Generic	*Psychologists* are conservatives by definition.
	3. Homophoric	*The sun* won't last forever.
	4. Unique	*Fred* works in Ottawa.
Definite phoric NP (Referent in verbal context or context of situation)		Look at *that guy* over there.
		I saw *a more exciting movie.*

referents. The listener may recover referents from the explicit verbal (endophoric retrieval) and situational (exophoric retrieval) context of the utterance. These strategies are suggested by Halliday and Hasan's (1976) analysis of reference as a cohesive device. If no specific referent is provided by the speaker, the listener must somehow supply his/her own. This can be done by inference from a close semantic associate (bridging) or by the creation of a referent (addition). Both of these strategies have been characterized by Clark (1974). Finally, the listener may need to decide which of two or more equally likely alternatives serve as the referent for a definite noun phrase. This strategy we term disambiguation.

TABLE 2
Retrieval Categories for Definite Phoric Noun Phrases[a]

Retrieval category	Location of referent	Example
Explicit referents		
Endophoric	Explicit verbal context	A DONKEY was loaded with salt and *he* went to cross a river.
Exophoric	Explicit situational context	I am reading *this paper* now.
Implicit referents		
Bridging	Implicit verbal context	There's A HOUSE with two people standing in *the door.*
Unclear referents		
Addition	Not clear	A donkey was crossing *the other river.*
Ambiguous	Not clear	A COMMUTER and A SKIER are on a ski lift and *he* looks completely unconcerned.

[a]Italicized item is "definite phoric" noun phrase; small capitals indicate the referent.

HOW SPEAKERS USE PHORICITY AND WHERE THEY PLACE REFERENTS

In this section, we attempt to answer the questions posed on page 248. We study how speakers use phoricity and where they place definite noun phrase referents, for three groups of speakers in three contexts.

Method

Speakers.   Speakers were three groups of 20 subjects each: 40 inpatients who had received a discharge diagnosis in any of the schizophrenias, and 20 volunteers from the community with no reported history of psychiatric disturbance (N). The patients were subdivided into two groups: those who showed clear signs of thought process disorder (TD) according to two senior psychiatrists, and those who showed no such signs (NTD).

All subjects were either native English speakers or had adopted English by the age of 12. They were between the ages of 15 and 52 years, had completed at least seven school grades, and were paid to participate in the study. The groups did not differ in composition according to sex or age, though the patients' educational level and Hartford-Shipley IQ scores are lower than the normals'.

The primary experimental comparison occurs between TD and NTD patients. These groups did not differ in IQ scores and are similar in the mean length of prior hospitalizations (about 2 months), educational level (about 11 years) and other aspects of their socioeconomic status (cf. Rochester, Martin, & Thurston, in press).

Speech contexts.   Each subject participated in three speech situations: (1) an unstructured interview of about a half-hour in duration; (2) a cartoon task taken from Goldman-Eisler (1968) in which the subject described and interpreted ten cartoon pictures; (3) a brief (107 words) narrative, which was read to the subject and retold in the subject's own words.

Discourse was recorded through Uher M822 low-impedance lavelier microphones input to a Uher Royal Delux Stereophonic tape recorder at 7.5 ips. From the interview, 3-min samples of uninterrupted speech were taken and combined. Ideally, samples from TD and other subjects would have been selected at random from the interview. However, this procedure would ignore the fact that only small portions of the TD subjects' discourse showed signs of thought disorder. Thus, for TD subjects, the most thought-disordered sections (as indicated by the judges' comments) were selected. For other subjects, "informal" sections involving slang, laughter and/or increased tempo (see Labov, 1973) were chosen. In the cartoon task and in the narrative, all of each subject's speech was analyzed.

Reliabilities.   One coder (JM) analyzed typescripts of the utterances while listening to them on a taperecorder. A second coder separately analyzed typescripts from 18 subjects, six per group. This was done for each of the three speech contexts for three levels of analysis: (a) selection of noun phrases, (b) assignment of phoricity values, and (c) assignment of retrieval categories. Agreement between coders was high: mean agreement of coders on (a) noun phrase selection was about 95% (range 87–97%); (b) on phoricity values was about 93% (range 88–97%); (c) on retrieval categories was about 88% (range 86–90%). There were no systematic differences in reliability between groups or speech contexts.

Analyses: Phoricity Variables

For each subject, the total number of noun phrases was computed. From this total, the proportion of noun phrases in each of three phoricity categories was determined. Proportions across the three speech contexts (interview, cartoon, and narrative) and across the three subject groups (TD, NTD, and N) were compared using two-way analyses of variance on the arcsin transforms of the proportions. Where F values yielded $p < .01$, Scheffé tests were done to assess the significance of the differences between groups and contexts. Results are presented in Table 3.

Balance. What is the balance of phoric and nonphoric noun phrases in normal discourse? Table 3 shows that for all speakers, normal and schizophrenic, most noun phrases (about 60–80%) are definite phoric noun phrases. A moderate proportion of noun phrases are general phoric (about 20–30%) and relatively few noun phrases (10–15%) are nonphoric. This seems to indicate a gradient of usage of noun phrases according to the dependence of the noun phrase on the utterance context. Independent (nonphoric) noun phrases are rare, and noun phrases which depend fully on utterance context (definite phoric) are most common. This is true virtually without regard to situational context. The single exception seems to occur in narratives, where proportions of general phoric noun phrases match or fall below proportions of nonphoric noun phrases.

Situational context. Does the use of phoricity depend on the situational context of the discourse? Table 3 indicates that context is a significant source of variance in all three phoricity categories. Nonphoric noun phrases are used more in the cartoon contexts than in narratives: about 16% of all noun phrases are nonphoric in cartoon contexts, while only about 11% are nonphoric in narratives (a Scheffé test yields $p < .05$). This result seems straightforward. In the cartoon task, speakers must discuss ten separate cartoons, and this requires extensive identification of things and events. In the narrative, however, there are only a few participants and a few actions to be recounted. In this context, we would expect a high degree of dependence of noun phrases on a few initial identifications.

In interviews, the use of nonphoric noun phrases depends on speakers (groups X contexts yields a significant effect). For normal speakers, about the same

TABLE 3
Proportion of Noun Phrases and ANOVA According to Phoricity Categories

Phoricity category	Interview			Cartoon			Narrative				Groups	Contexts	G × C
	TD	NTD	N	TD	NTD	N	TD	NTD	N			ANOVA	
Nonphoric	.12	.13	.15	.16	.18	.16	.13	.13	.08	df	2,57	2,114	4,114
										F	ns	15.87	2.89
										p		.001	.05
General phoric	.30	.23	.26	.18	.16	.22	.09	.05	.10	F	5.54	70.4	ns
										p	.01	.001	ns
Definite phoric	.56	.63	.58	.63	.64	.78	.82	.82	.81	F	ns	65.9	
										p		.001	
Total noun phrases per subject	55	54	64	146	142	134	24	22	28				

proportion of nonphoric noun phrases are used in interviews as in cartoons: It seems that normal speakers give full identification of several noun phrases in interviews, just as they do in cartoon descriptions. Schizophrenic subjects, on the other hand, seem to use phoricity in interviews just as they do in narratives: that is, they seem to identify only a few noun phrases fully. This could be due to the use of very few topics in interviews (a finding reported by White, 1949) or to the use of several topics in which there is incomplete identification of some referents.

Definite phoric noun phrases are used more in narratives than in cartoons or interviews. This is a highly significant finding, and holds for all speaker groups. Again, number of topics seems an important determinant of phoricity. In the cartoon task, where we established ten separate topics, highly dependent noun phrases are relatively rare; in narratives, where there seems to be no more than a single topic, such dependent noun phrases are more common.

Finally, general phoric noun phrases are most common in the interview and least common in the narrative. (Scheffé tests yield $p < .001$.) This is true for all speakers. What seems important in this finding is the highly structured nature of the narrative, in which speakers are invited only to retell a story, and the relatively unstructured nature of the interview. General phoric noun phrases appeal to the cultural context of the discourse, and seem most appropriate to broad statements. It is easy to justify such appeals in the unstructured interviews, and easy to exclude them in the narratives where the persons and events to be described are already determined.

In cartoon contexts, proportions of general phoric noun phrases are essentially the same as interview contexts. In the cartoon context, speakers were asked not only to describe the events and persons, but to explain why someone might find those events funny. Such an explanation seems to demand broad statements and appeals to the cultural assumptions of the speakers. If this is so, then our findings here are an artifact of the particular task chosen. If, for example, subjects simply described cartoons, appeals to a cultural context would not be necessary and we would not expect strong similarity between cartoon and interview contexts.

Speakers. The only reliable main effect of speakers in their use of phoricity occurs with general phoric noun phrases. Thought-disordered speakers use more of these noun phrases than other subjects, but this effect is significant only in the interview context. In interviews, TD speakers use about 7% more noun phrases in a general phoric category than NTD speakers. This increased appeal to the cultural context occurs because TD speakers used fewer definite phoric noun phrases than NTD speakers.

We can examine this in more detail by analyzing subcategories of general phoric noun phrases (cf. Appendix 1). There is no difference between TD and NTD speakers on three of the four categories, but with generic noun phrases, TD subjects use twice the proportion of noun phrases as NTD subjects (TD: 11% and NTD: 5%). These generic noun phrases mark out a class as a whole, making general identifications. Thus, an increase in TD use of generic noun phrases may correspond to findings that thought-disordered schizophrenic subjects avoid particular personal themes and prefer abstract or universal themes (Maher, McKean, & McLaughlin, 1966; White, 1949).

To summarize, all speakers in all contexts use high proportions of dependent (definite phoric) noun phrases and relatively small proportions of independent (nonphoric) noun phrases. Within a phoricity category, the proportion of noun phrases depends on the situational context of the utterance. Nonphoric noun phrases are used more often in the cartoon context than in the narrative contexts, probably reflecting the number of topics used in each context. Results for definite phoric noun phrases mirror these findings, with most dependent (definite) noun phrases used in narratives and least used in cartoons. Speakers differ little in their use of phoricity. The single main effect was TD subjects' increased use of general phoric noun phrases and reduced use of definite phoric noun phrases, in comparison with NTD subjects.

In order to understand the speaker's referential use of noun phrases more fully, we now examine in detail the 60—80% of all noun phrases which are definite phoric. For each noun phrase, two coders attempted to locate the noun phrase referent (with reliabilities reported on p. 252). When the referent was located or the strategy needed to identify the referent was estimated, each definite noun phrase was assigned to a retrieval category.

Analyses: Retrieval Variables

For each subject, the total number of definite phoric noun phrases was determined. From this total, the proportion of noun phrases in each of five retrieval categories was computed. Proportions across three speech contexts and three subject groups were compared as above. Results are presented in Table 4.

Balance. Given a normal speaker's signal to retrieve a referent from the utterance context, where should the listener search? Most frequently, Table 4 indicates, the listener can find referents in the explicit verbal context of the utterance (in about 70% of the cases). Failing this, and depending on the utterance context, the listener should attend either to the situation or attempt bridging in the verbal context: normal speakers require about 10% bridging and 10% exophoric retrieval from their listeners. Finally, the listener rarely needs to create referents using addition (at most, in 3% of all cases) and never has to disambiguate referents.

Notice that it is much more difficult to generalize about these retrieval categories than it was to describe phoricity categories. We cannot state the case for speakers in general, because there are strong differences between speakers

TABLE 4

Proportion of Noun Phrases According to Retrieval Categories

Retrieval category	Cartoon TD	Cartoon NTD	Cartoon N	Interview TD	Interview NTD	Interview N	Narrative TD	Narrative NTD	Narrative N	ANOVA Groups	ANOVA Contexts	ANOVA G × C
										df 2,57	2,114	4,114
Explicit												
Endophoric retrieval (verbal)	.61	.73	.79	.43	.38	.49	.66	.80	.87	F 7.67 p .005	116.6 .001	3.75 .05
Exophoric retrieval situational)	.33	.20	.14	.44	.55	.39	.03	.01	.00	F 7.51 p .005	73.4 .001	6.78 .005
Implicit												
Bridging	.04	.06	.07	.04	.02	.08	.11	.07	.11	F 11.3 p .001	1.81 ns	2.98 ns
Unclear												
Addition	.01	.00	.00	.07	.04	.03	.19	.12	.02	F 3.46 p .05	30.0 .001	2.46 ns
Disambiguation	.02	.01	.00	.02	.00	.00	.01	.01	.00	F 6.00 p .005	<1	1.19 ns
Total definite phoric noun phrases per S	92	95	87	31	35	40	18	18	22			

and significant interaction effects with context throughout these data. It is even difficult to make broad statements about normal speakers because their retrieval demands on the listener depend on the utterance context.

Explicit reference. Explicit reference includes noun phrases which have their referents in the explicit verbal (endophoric) and situational (exophoric) context of the utterance. Together, these categories include about 80–90% of all noun phrases examined. Since they are so comprehensive, results for endophoric noun phrases tend to be the complement of results for exophoric noun phrases.

Endophoric noun phrases occur most frequently in narrative and cartoon contexts (in 60–80% of the cases) and least often in interviews (in 40–50% of the cases). This is reversed for exophoric noun phrases, which occur most often in interviews (about 40–55% of the cases) and less often in cartoon contexts (in about 15–30% of the cases).

These results seem easy to understand when we recall that exophoric noun phrases include all personal pronouns. Therefore all references to *me, myself, my parents, my plans* and so on are exophoric. Such references should be common in interviews and less frequent in structured tasks, and they are. Certainly, in a context where the speaker is simply to retell a narrative, no personal references or other references to the immediate situation are expected and in fact, they occur only rarely.

These context differences hold for all speakers. However, there are also reliable differences between speakers in their use of explicit referents. Endophoric noun phrases are used significantly less often by TD subjects than by other speakers (Scheffé tests yield $p < .005$ between TD and each other group). This result holds in two of the three contexts, but in the interview, all groups use about the same proportions of endophoric noun phrases.

As we might expect, these findings are mirrored in the results for exophoric noun phrases. Thought-disordered subjects demand more exophoric retrieval than normal speakers. In cartoon contexts, TD subjects are reliably different from all other speakers (Scheffé tests yield at least $p < .05$). In interviews, TD subjects differ from normal speakers (Scheffé $p < .05$) but not from other schizophrenic speakers. And, in narratives, exophoric noun phrases are never used by normal speakers, almost never (1%) by NTD speakers, and occasionally (3%) by TD subjects.

In general, then, TD speakers use proportionately more situational reference and less verbal reference than other subjects. This is seen more clearly in structured contexts than in the unstructured interview. In the interview, TD speakers are not reliably different from NTD subjects.

The contexts where these differences occur seems important to understanding why the group differences between TD and other subjects emerge most clearly in cartoon contexts. Examining these data in detail, we find that differences are not due to the use of personal pronouns but rather to the TD subjects' extensive references to the actual situation. For example, consider the following descriptions of a single cartoon:

(6)   a. here we have a chap in the pillory or in the stocks with both his
         hands and his feet being held by the device
      b. and we have a woman who is seated by his side doing her knitting
      c. and she has raveled the yarn all about his hands and his feet
      d. and is now raveling up the yarn into a ball getting ready for knitting

(7)   a. *she*'s kni/
      b. well *he*'s got yarn in *his* hand and on *his* feet
      c. and *she*'s winding
      d. and imagine winding a ball of wool off of a man who's in the stocks

The examples were chosen at random: Example (6) is from a normal speaker and Example (7) is from a thought-disordered speaker. Exophoric noun phrases are italicized. These examples characterize the data nicely. Normal speakers tend to describe the cartoon in front of them as if the experimenter were unable to see the cartoon. Nonthought-disordered speakers behave in about the same way. But TD subjects describe the cartoon in recognition of the fact that the experimenter is perfectly capable to seeing the events and persons being described.

These findings conform closely to Hawkins' (1973) data with working-class and middle-class English children. Hawkins finds that working-class children use about twice as many referents in the situational context as middle-class children. He concludes that working-class children rely on the listener's awareness of the situation to achieve comprehension while middle-class children rely on differentiations through language.

Our TD and NTD subjects do not differ in social class, so far as we are able to define that variable. These two groups of subjects attended school to about the same grade, have about the same employment history and the same marital status. However, Hawkins' description seems apt for our subjects. This suggests that the differences between use of situational and verbal reference may not be tied to social class or to thoughtdisorder per se, but rather to a style of social interaction. As Millicent Poole (1975) observes in a review of Hawkins' work, working-class children appear to be using an economy of speech while the middle-class response appears unduly remote and "even a little pompous and pedantic." It is the working-class children in Hawkins' study and the TD subjects in our findings who appear to follow the dictum (Grice, 1967): Do not be more informative than required.

Implicit and unclear reference. Implicit reference includes noun phrases which require bridging. About 6% of all noun phrases fall into this category. This proportion does not vary with context, but does depend on the speaker. Normal speakers demand bridging more than other subjects. This result is significant in cartoon and interview contexts (Scheffé $p < .05$).

Unclear reference includes noun phrases which require either addition or disambiguation in order to be understood. On the average, these noun phrases constitute only about 3% of the total noun phrases. However, they seem to be powerful determinants of the listener's response. Evidence for this is discussed in the next section.

Unclear reference is virtually never used by normal speakers. They never use it in cartoons and use it no more than 2% in narratives and 3% in interviews. In contrast, TD speakers use unclear reference rather often: in 3% of cases in cartoons, and in 20% of cases in narratives. Proportions for NTD speakers tend to be small, and differ reliably from those for TD subjects in narratives and interviews (Scheffé p at most $< .05$).

These results suggest subtle differences in the task the three groups of speakers pose for the listener. The normal speaker appears to make the listener's task easy by using many explicit verbal references, and by placing implicit verbal references within immediate semantic range of the listener. Similarly, NTD speakers tend to do this, but provide fewer endophoric references and fewer implicit references. The TD speaker, however, seems to pose a profound problem for the listener: no matter how long the listener searches, he/she will be unable to identify definitely some small number of the TD speaker's noun phrases.

GENERAL DISCUSSION

In the first section of this paper we proposed two aspects to the "art" of referring with noun phrases: phoricity, or the referential characteristics of noun phrases, and retrieval categories, or the location of noun phrase referents in the utterance context. In subsequent sections, we studied the use of these two aspects of noun phrase reference in three situational contexts with three groups of speakers. The data were discussed in detail at that time. In the present section, we engage in a more general discussion, speculating about the psychological relevance of phoricity and retrieval categories for speakers and listeners.

Figure 1 outlines three components of the speaker's use of noun phrases to instruct the listener. In Fig. 1a, the speaker's decisions about the referential form of a noun phrase are portrayed. We assume that the speaker begins with a concept to be realized in speech. The actual form the concept takes depends on what the speaker assumes about the listener's knowledge by determining whether information necessary to identify the concept in question is available in (a) the utterance context, (b) the cultural context, or (c) neither.

Once this assessment is made, the speaker produces a noun phrase with particular referential characteristics (phoricity). This production carries with it

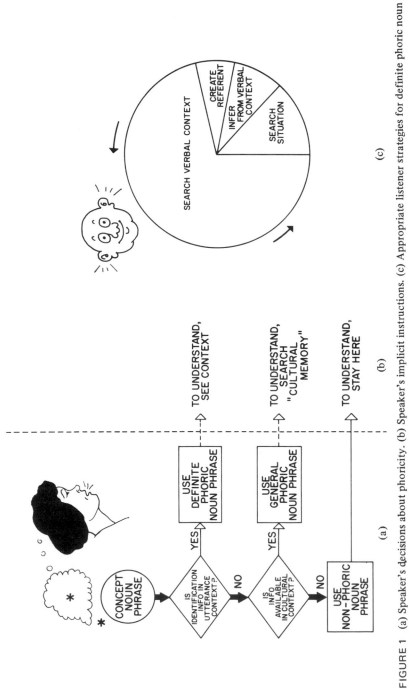

FIGURE 1 (a) Speaker's decisions about phoricity. (b) Speaker's implicit instructions. (c) Appropriate listener strategies for definite phoric noun phrases.

an important fail-safe component: just in case the speaker has evaluated the listener's knowledge incorrectly, he/she instructs the listener where to gain that knowledge. The instructions are contained in the noun phrase itself. As Fig. 1b indicates, the noun phrase contains general instructions about *how* to locate its referent, sending the listener (a) to the utterance context, (b) to a "general cultural" memory store, or (c) to itself.

Given these general instructions, the listener tries to discover exactly *where* the noun phrase referent is located. We do not attempt to describe here the memory search needed to recover referents available in the general culture, nor do we discuss the memory processes needed to understand a noun phrase which contains its own referent. Elements of such accounts are contained in the seminal theories of Norman and Rumelhart (1975) and in the views presented in the Bobrow and Collins collection (1976). However, in Fig. 1c we present a "retrieval wheel" to show the appropriate strategies for recovering referents for the definite phoric noun phrases of normal speakers. Most of the time, the listener should search the explicit verbal context of the utterance, and this would require a search through a short-term verbal memory store; less often, the listener should search the situation, and this would mean searching a short-term (nonverbal) store and also perceiving the immediate situation; occasionally, the listener must infer from the verbal context, and again this would require a search through a short-term verbal store. Finally, and rarely, the listener must create referents when no referents are available through a search of short-term memory and the immediate situation.

We do not know how listeners select a particular strategy for recovering definite phoric noun phrases, or how they decide which strategies to use in particular contexts with particular speakers. We doubt that listeners simply select at random from a pool of strategies having various probabilities of occurrence, although that is the procedure implied by Fig. 1c. Perhaps the probability of using a strategy and the hierarchy of testing those strategies depends on the listener's own placement of referents.

While we are ignorant of the retrieval processes, we can make some educated guesses about the speaker's decisions in realizing a noun phrase in a given form. As shown in Fig. 1a, we hypothesize that the speaker performs a series of tests, first checking if the noun phrase can be identified through the general cultural context. This sequence seems likely because it is efficient. Most noun phrases are definite phoric (from 60 to 80%, depending on the context), so the chance that a noun phrase is definite phoric should be checked immediately. Nonphoric noun phrases are least common, so the chance that a noun phrase is nonphoric should be tested last.

It is possible to test this notion in spontaneous speech by measuring the duration of silences preceding the production of nonphoric, general phoric, and definite phoric noun phrases. According to our formulation, pause time should be longer before nonphoric noun phrases than before Definite Phoric noun phrases, reflecting the increased number of alternatives which need to be tested by the speaker before production of the nonphoric noun phrases can occur. What is the consequence of departing from the procedures shown in Fig. 1? Departures are rare for the operations shown in Fig. 1a and b: all speakers in all contexts tend to use phoricity in similar ways. However, departures are common for the location of noun phrase referents shown in Fig. 1c: TD speakers differ reliably from other speakers in the retrieval demands they place on listeners. To understand the definite phoric noun phrases of a TD speaker, listeners should adjust their search probabilities from those they use with normal speakers. With TD speakers, the ideal strategy is to restrict searches in the verbal context, increase searches in the situational context, restrict attempts to infer from the verbal context, and attempt valiantly to create new referents where none are provided. Finally, the conscientious listener must expect to disambiguate equally-likely referents, a task never demanded by normal speakers.

Noting these differences in speaker usage, we imagine that the differences are significant for the listener. That is, we suppose that the fact that TD speakers demand more addition and more disambiguation than other speakers means that addition and disambiguation are poor strategies to require of the listener. This inference is tenable at least, because addition and disambiguation require recovery of "unclear" referents. But what consequences are there for the listener when speakers demand an increased recovery of situational referents, or require less than normal retrieval from the explicit verbal context? Is comprehension more difficult with these demands?

A direct answer requires a test of listeners' comprehension as a function of differences in referent placements. We provided an indirect answer by asking ten lay judges to read[1] transcripts of the interviews and evaluate the coherence of those interviews without knowing the speakers' identities. A multiple regression analysis was performed to determine whether the location of noun phrase referents contributed to the judges' experience of incoherence. The criterion variable was the proportion of incoherent clauses to total clauses for each subject. Three variables were useful predictors: Addition accounts for 31% of the total variation in the criterion variable ($F = 26.2$, $df = 1$, 58; $p < .001$); disambiguation predicts an additional 3% of the variation, and exophoric retrieval predicts an additional 2% of the total variation.

Thus, we find that some speaker differences are important to judges' comprehension, and some are trivial. Addition makes an important contribution to readers' evaluations, but the use of situational reference is essentially irrelevant. It seems crucial therefore, to discuss speaker differences not merely in terms of significant variations between *speakers* but also in terms of the effects of these

---

[1] We employed readers rather than listeners as judges in order to restrict the judges' decisions to segmental (lexical) features of the discourse, and to eliminate the possible effects of intonation and hesitation phenomena.

variations on *listeners* (and readers). In the present study, small variations in speakers' performance predict large differences in the reported coherence of that performance.

To summarize, the "art" of referring using noun phrases seems to depend most heavily on the location of the noun phrase referents in the utterance context. This aspect of reference varies with the skill of the speaker and affects judges' evaluations of coherence. Phoricity, or the referential characteristics of noun phrases, seems almost constant across speakers and may be less important in its psychological implications.

APPENDIX 1: PHORICITY CATEGORIES FOR NOUN PHRASES

Nonphoric Noun Phrases

A noun phrase is considered *nonphoric* if it does not lead the listener to look elsewhere in the verbal or situational context of the utterance. For example, in

(1) I saw *a beautiful rainbow* this morning.

the listener is not obliged to ask "What rainbow?" in order to interpret the noun phrase. The nonphoric noun phrase, then, is self-sufficient. It presents information as if it were being said for the first time. The main exponents of this class are indefinite noun phrases, that is, any noun phrase preceded by an indefinite article such as *a, some,* or *any*. In addition, noun phrases with a cardinal plus head (e.g. two women) and other cases in which a particular segment of a class is intended (several men, enough men) are considered nonphoric.

Phoric Noun Phrases

Phoric noun phrases require referents in discourse. A noun phrase is considered *phoric* if it prompts the listener to ask "What x?" "Which x?" For example, in

(2) Wow! Look at *that fantastic rainbow!*

the listener is obliged to ask "What rainbow?" It is then necessary to recover the referent, probably in the situational context in this case. The phoric noun phrase is thus dependent on the context of the utterance. It presupposes that its referent is already known by the listener.

Phoric noun phrases can be divided into two classes depending on whether their referents are found in the general cultural context or in the particular context of the utterance. The two classes are general phoric noun phrases and definite phoric noun phrases.

General Phoric Noun Phrases

When the speaker indicates that the referent of a phoric noun phrase is recoverable from the general cultural context of an utterance, four subcategories of noun phrases may be distinguished: (1) generalized, (2) generic, (3) homophoric, and (4) unique.

1. *Generalized noun phrases.* These are characterized by pronouns used in a generalized sense. The referent is treated as if it were given in all possible contexts of the situation (cf. Halliday & Hasan, 1976). Examples are as follows:

> (3) a. *One* never can tell. (any human individual)
>   b. *We* consider it our duty. (the royal or editorial "we")
>   c. *They*'re going to repave Avenue road. (pronouns referring to persons unspecified)
>   d. *It*'s snowing.
>   *It* looks like Snoopy. (pronouns conforming to the structural requirements of the clause)

2. *Generic noun phrases.* These noun phrases mark out a class as a whole. For example, in

> (4) *The tiger* is a vicious animal.

no particular tiger is intended. Noun phrases of this class may lack deictic premodification. For example, *the* is missing in

> (5) Mary is fond of beer.

In addition, the distinction singular—plural and definite—indefinite often is lacking (cf. Quirk, Greenbaum, Leech, & Swartvik, 1972). One could say

> (6) *Tigers* are vicious animals.

and intend nothing different from

> (7) *The tiger* is a vicious animal.

3. *Homophoric noun phrases.* These are noun phrases with referents which are identifiable as part of the cultural situation of the utterance. For examples, we include "the sea," "the moon," and "the stars" which are identifiable in all situational contexts. Certain homophoric noun phrases are inherent in most, though not all contexts. For example, if a daughter asks

> (8) Can I have *the car?*

homophoric reference is entailed if the family has only one car. But to say this in a family with three cars is confusing.

4. *Unique noun phrases.* These have a unique referent available in the general context in which they are employed. The main exponents of this class are proper

names. Typically, article contrast is not permitted with proper names. For example, one can say

(9) I saw *Mary* this morning.

but not "a Mary" or "the Mary." In those few circumstances where proper names do take an article and a postmodifying relative clause, they no longer realize unique reference.

Definite Phoric Noun Phrases

When the speaker indicates that a noun phrase referent lies in the particular context of an utterance, the noun phrase is *definite*. It asks the listener, in effect, to single out some member of a class to which the head noun makes reference. Pronominal, demonstrative, and comparative constructions are the main exponents of this class of noun phrases.

The referent for a definite noun phrase may occur in the situational context of the utterance. For example, if Penny walks into a room and someone says

(10) Here *she* comes now.

then *she* would be a definite phoric noun phrase with *Penny* its situational referent. Alternatively, one might say

(11) *Penny* is always prompt. Here *she* comes now.

In this case, *she* is still a definite phoric noun phrase but now the referent is in the verbal rather than the situational context.

"Complex" Noun Phrases

Thus far, we have discussed only "simple" noun phrases, that is, those which do not include other noun phrases. For example, we have considered *the boy from Ottawa* as two separate noun phrases: *the boy* and *Ottawa*. Now, we examine "complex" noun phrases which we interpret as noun phrases which include another noun phrase. At this point, we consider *the boy from Ottawa* as one complex and not two simple noun phrases.

The distinctions given above provide an outline of the formal and contextual grounds we used to assign "simple" noun phrases to phoricity categories. A more detailed account is presented in Martin (1974). In practice, "simple" noun phrases are frequently contained in other noun phrases, in combinations we designate as "complex." Because the phoric potential of simple noun phrases is mediated by the complex noun phrase containing them, analysis of retrieval strategies examined noun phrases not contained in other noun phrases: For example, "the boy" and "the boy from Ottawa" but not "Ottawa" alone.

When a qualifier element containing another noun phrase is present, the phoricity of the noun phrase as a whole appears to depend on the most deeply embedded noun phrase in the construction. A noun phrase like (a poodle from (that litter)) contains one nonphoric (*a poodle*) and one definite phoric (*that litter*) noun phrase. When the head phrase is itself definite, it points cataphorically to the qualifying group, as in (the boy (I) saw). Since the most deeply embedded noun phrase in these two constructions is definite, we considered the noun phrase as a whole definite as well. For further discussion of these points, see Martin (1975).

APPENDIX 2: RETRIEVAL CATEGORIES

Endophoric Retrieval

Endophoric retrieval is required when a referent must be recovered from the explicit *verbal* context of an utterance. For example,

(1) A DONKEY was loaded with salt and *he* went across a river.

In this case the Definite noun phrase *he* is preceded by its referent DONKEY. A definite noun phrase may also be followed by its referent. When this occurs, the referent is usually given in the immediately succeeding verbal context. For example,

(2) Any *other* person would have been unthinkable; LAWLOR was the only solution.

LAWLOR provides the referent anticipated by *other*.

Exophoric Retrieval

Exophoric Retrieval is required when an explicit referent must be retrieved from the particular *situational* context of the utterance. In ordinary conversations, most exophoric reference occurs with use of personal pronouns. For example, in

(3) *I* patched up *my family*.

both italicized noun phrases are exophoric. For another example,

(4) Are *you* reading *this chapter* closely right now?

both italicized noun phrases are exophoric because they refer to a definite person — you, the reader — and a definite object — this chapter. However, when *you* is used in a generalized sense to refer to any human individual [as in (3a) in a previous section], it is simply a general phoric noun phrase and requires no specific retrieval from the utterance context.

It is critical to consider the meaning of the noun phrase before assigning it to a retrieval (or phoricity) category. Such meaning is not always obvious, however, and the referents can be difficult to guess. This is particularly true when a pronoun has an antecedent in the verbal context. It is difficult to tell whether the pronoun is exophoric or refers to its antecedent. In these cases, we arbitrarily define Exophoric Retrieval as necessary only if no possible unique antecedent for a noun phrase exists in the verbal context.

Bridging

In a noun phrase requiring bridging the information needed for its interpretations is *implicit* rather than explicit in the verbal context of the utterance. The referent is accessible, however, because it falls within the immediate semantic range of the noun phrase to be interpreted. For example, in

(5) I was all packed for *our camping trip* when I discovered *the sleeping bag* was missing.

the sleeping bag falls within immediate semantic range of *our camping trip* and is somehow retrievable from it. In fact to say

(6) I was all packed for our camping trip when I discovered the sleeping bag for our camping trip was missing.

seems redundant and awkward.[2]

Addition

Addition is required when a definite phoric noun phrase has no discernable explicit or implicit referent in the verbal or situational context. In these cases, the listener is forced to create his or her own referent for the noun phrase. For example, to say

(7) A donkey was crossing *the other river.*

---

[2] Bridging is frequent when inalienable possession is involved. For example, one can say "On the road there is a sign with a hand with the fingers crossed." In this example, one could equally well say "its fingers" but instead of this, "the fingers" is bridged from "a hand." Often noun phrases bridge to items that are a part of them. For example, "the chimney" can be bridged from "the house" more easily than "the house" from "the chimney." Note that it is possible to say "the chimney of the house" but not "the house of the chimney." Commonly, a prepositional phrase can be postulated from the bridged noun phrase. This hypothetical prepositional phrase points to the antecedent and confirms that the antecedent does implicitly provide a referent for the bridged noun phrase. One of the keys to recognizing the presence of bridging is to ask if a nonphoric noun phrase would sound strange here or, is a nonphoric noun phrase really necessary? For example, in "Charlie Brown is playing baseball and he even catches the ball," a nonphoric presentation "a ball" does not seem obligatory.

implies that *a river* has already been identified. However, if no referent has been clearly given in the utterance context, the listener must construct such a referent in order to understand the noun phrase in question.

Disambiguation

When a speaker provides more than one referent for a definite noun phrase, the listener must perform an arbitrary disambiguation. For example, the referent is unclear in

(8)   A commuter and a skier are on a ski lift and *he* looks unhappy.

ACKNOWLEDGMENTS

This research was supported by the Benevolent Foundation of Scottish Rite Freemasonry, Northern Jurisdiction, U.S.A., and the Clarke Institute Associates' Research Fund.

We are grateful to Sharon Thurston and Judith Rupp for assisting in the investigation; to Dr. Mary Seeman and Dr. Alexander Bonkalo for their generous help in serving as psychiatric judges of thought disorders; and to Peter Dean, Penny Lawler, Rita Anderson and Judith Gill for their valuable comments on an earlier draft of this paper.

REFERENCES

Bobrow, D. G., & Collins, A. M. (Eds.), *Representation and understanding: Studies in cognitive science.* New York: Academic Press, 1976.

Bleuler, E. *Dementia praecox; or the group of schizophrenias.* New York: International Universities Press, 1950. (Originally published 1911).

Clark, H. H. *Comprehension and the given-new contract.* Paper prepared for conference on The Role of Grammar in Interdisciplinary Linguistic Research, University of Bielefeld, Bielefeld, Germany, December 11–15, 1973.

Clark, H. H. Semantics and comprehension. In T. A. Sebeok (Ed.), *Current trends in linguistics.* Vol. 12: *Linguistics and adjacent arts and sciences.* The Hague: Mouton, 1974.

Clark, H. H., & Haviland, S. E. Psychological processes as linguistic explanation. In D. Cohen (Ed.), *Explaining linguistic phenomena.* Washington, D.C.: Hemisphere Publ., 1974.

Goldman-Eisler, F. *Psycholinguistics: Experiments in spontaneous speech.* New York: Academic Press, 1968.

Grice, H. P. *Logic and conversation.* The William James Lectures, Harvard University, 1967.

Halliday, M. A. K. Categories of the theory of grammar. *Word,* 1961, 17, 241–292.

Halliday, M. A. K., & Hasan, R. *Cohesion in English.* London, England: Longmans, 1976.

Haviland, S. E., & Clark, H. H. Acquiring new information as a process in comprehension. *Journal of Verbal Learning and Verbal Behavior,* 1974, 13, 512–521.

Hawkins, P. R. The influence of sex, social class and pause-location in the hesitation phenomena of seven-year-old children. In B. Bernstein (Ed.), *Primary socialization, language and education: class, codes and control.* Vol. 2. Boston, Massachusetts: Routledge & Kegan Paul, 1973.

Labov, W. *Sociolinguistic patterns.* Philadelphia, Pennsylvania: University of Pennsylvania Press, 1973.

Lakoff, R. The logic of politeness; or minding your P's and Q's. *Papers from the Ninth Regional Meeting.* Chicago Linguistic Society, 1973, 292–305.

Maher, B. A., McKean, K. O., & McLaughlin, B. Studies in psychotic language. In P. J. Stone et al. (Eds), *The General Inquirer: A computer approach to content analysis.* Cambridge, Massachusetts: MIT Press, 1966, 469–503.

Martin, J. R. *Phoricity: A coding manual.* Unpublished manuscript, University of Toronto, 1975.

Norman, D. A., & Rumelhart, D. E. *Explorations in cognition.* San Francisco, California: W. H. Freeman, 1975.

Poole, M. Review of Class, codes and control, Vol. 1 – Theoretical studies towards a sociology of language and Vol. 2 – Applied studies towards a sociology of language by B. Bernstein. *Language in Society,* 1975, **4**, 15.

Quirk, R., Greenbaum, S., Leech, G. N., & Swartvik, J. *A grammar of contemporary English.* London, England: Longmans, 1972.

Rochester, S. R., Martin, J., & Thruston, S. Thought process disorder in schizophrenia: The listener's task. *Brain and Language.* In press.

Searle, J. R. *Speech Acts.* Cambridge: Cambridge University Press, 1970.

White, M. A. A study of schizophrenic language. *Journal of Abnormal and Social Psychology,* 1949, **44**, 61–74.

13

Verbal Teaching Patterns under Simulated Teaching Conditions

Carol Ann Moore

The Ohio State University

Classroom interactions are situations which have considerable impact on nearly everyone's educational and personal development. In spite of the vast research attention such interactions have received, the rules which govern verbal communication and the transmission of information in the classroom setting are still poorly understood. Questions such as how teachers use speech to influence student learning and behavior, what impact teachers' speech has on student learning, and what rules govern teacher—student interaction have remained unanswered.

Until recently, research into classroom verbal interaction has treated teacher utterances as isolated units of speech, both in studies where teaching behavior was observed and in teacher-training studies. However, the lack of consistent relationships between the frequency of particular types of teacher utterances and student achievement (Dunkin & Biddle, 1974; Gage & Berliner, 1975; Rosenshine, 1971b) now demands that teacher speech be examined for its pedagogical significance in context and that patterns of interactive speech be described (Bellack, Kliebard, Hyman, & Smith, 1966; Dunkin & Biddle, 1974; Forsyth, 1974; Mehan, Fisher, & Maroules, 1975; Taba, 1966). This attention to utterance sequences has opened new methodological issues. How, in fact, are the sequential properties of a verbal interaction to be described and rigorously measured without oversimplification or distortion? How can interactive sequences be systematically investigated under experimental conditions?

The purpose of this chapter is to introduce an experimental approach to the investigation of verbal teaching patterns through a simulation technique which standardizes student contributions to the interaction sequence. In order to design a simulation model, several assumptions about teaching were made. These assumptions are:

1. teaching is an interactive process;
2. teachers are decision makers, selecting appropriate teaching actions in view of student feedback and teaching objectives;
3. teachers' utterances make a difference in what and how students learn; and
4. teachers' utterances are influenced by the nature of the content being taught.

TEACHING AS DECISION MAKING

The notion that the teachers are decision makers, selecting among alternative speech acts which can potentially influence student learning, is central to the simulation model. If teacher–student interaction is viewed as a transaction between teacher and student for the purpose of modifying the cognitive framework of students (i.e., for changing students' store of knowledge, conceptual structure, problem-solving strategies, and skills), then it can be hypothesized that teachers use language to motivate, direct, and shape student learning in a step-by-step fashion contingent on student feedback and teaching goals.

Teaching strategy has been defined as a set of verbal actions by the teacher which serve to increase the likelihood of certain educational outcomes and to decrease the likelihood of others (Smith, Meux, Coombs, Nuthall, & Precians, 1967). Such strategies involve actions with engage students in class discussion, clarify course content, and monitor and guide student learning such that incorrect or inappropriate responses are minimized. The teachers' function as a decision maker may therefore be fundamental to teaching and teacher–student interaction. For example, the teacher's ability to estimate adequately the competencies and preferences of the students, to utilize feedback from students, to make hypotheses about student learning at each stage in the teaching sequence and to act accordingly with skill and judgment should influence the nature of the learning taking place (Shavelson, 1973; Snow, 1969).

Smith and associates' definition of strategy is analogous to Bruner, Goodnow, and Austin's (1956) earlier notion of cognitive strategy which was defined as a pattern of decisions in acquiring, storing, and using information to achieve particular objectives. Although Bruner and his associates were not concerned with teaching behavior, their success in studying cognitive strategies under standardized learning conditions suggests that comparable research into the nature of teaching strategies might be useful in building an understanding of complex teaching behavior. The approach employed by the Bruner research group allowed them to identify strategies used by individuals in attaining concepts and to evaluate the effectiveness of particular strategies under different task requirements. Briefly, in their work, subjects learned the defining characteristics of a concept represented by instances in an array of cards which varied on several dimensions, for example, color, geometric form, borders. By selecting cards and receiving immediate feedback on whether or not each card was an instance of the concept, the subject was gradually able to identify the attributes defining a concept. A subject's cognitive strategy was inferred from the pattern of card selections he made while seeking to attain a concept.

As will be seen, an analogous approach to the study of teaching has been taken here in the development of a simulated teaching situation. Students are simulated and the institutional setting, the curriculum content and structure, the teaching objectives, and the mode of communication are standardized. Under these conditions, teacher's sequencing of specific verbal phrases can be documented for any number of teaching sessions and the teaching strategies which emerge can be examined.

TEACHER SPEECH AND STUDENT COGNITIVE PROCESSING

Specification of educationally and psychologically meaningful teaching phrases was an important step in the development of the simulation situation, which specifically isolates teachers' questioning and teachers' presentation of content material for detailed analysis. In the simulation situation, the teacher is given a repertoire of teaching phrases which the teacher must then use as speech units in instructing simulated students. Three functions of teacher's speech relating to student learning were considered in formulating these teaching phrases: encouragement of student thinking, transmission of content structure, and logical operations performed on content in presentation.

Encouragement of Student Thinking

From an educational viewpoint, an important goal of classroom interaction is the transmission of knowledge and of problem-solving techniques. Thus, much of the research investigating teaching has focused on teaching effectiveness and on those aspects of teachers' speech which may be functionally related to student learning. Of concern are the role of teachers' speech in stimulating and maintaining student cognitive processing and the types of mental operations required of or called up in the students during the course of classroom interaction. A guiding hypothesis of this research has been that an increase in teacher–student interaction requiring more complex cognitive processing (e.g., analysis, reasoning) of the students will significantly improve the quality of learning occurring in the classroom (Dunkin & Biddle, 1974).

Schemes[1] for categorizing teacher verbal behavior with respect to implied cognitive processing have been developed primarily on an a priori basis. The intangibility of thought processes leads to many problems in appropriately identifying the cognitive meaning for the student of different teacher utterances. Uncertainty about the nature of cognitive processing actually being required of particular students haunts all research involving cognitive aspects of classroom teaching and learning. If, for example, a student is asked to explain an event (e.g., "Why is the pressure in your car tires greater after driving an hour than it was when you started?"), he may engage in mental operations leading to the generation of a new response arrived at through application of previous learning. However, if the same event were discussed in class yesterday, he would now only have to recall the answer. Therefore, if known, the previous learning history of an individual student may influence how a particular teacher or student utterance would be classified. In addition, the context in which the verbal exchange occurs may also provide clues as to how the student and the teacher are dealing with an utterance.

Teachers' questions. Questioning offers a major avenue for teachers to influence student learning and to gain feedback on the state of student learning. The placement of questions in the teaching sequence and the types of thinking requested of the students could potentially change the subsequent course of instruction. Questions may, therefore, mark important decision points in a teaching sequence. If so, the questions available in the simulation situation needed to be carefully constructed to provide a range of question types which could be used at the teacher's discretion. To ensure such a range, questions falling in most of the general categories defined by the *Taxonomy of Educational Objectives* in the cognitive domain (Bloom, Engelhart, Furst, Hill, & Krathwohl, 1956) were included among the teaching phrases. Widely used in educational research, the taxonomy was first conceived in response to a need felt by college examiners for a theoretical framework which could facilitate communication among examiners and stimulate research on relationships between testing and educational processes. The following classification system was proposed based on cognitive operations considered to be involved in the learner's attainment of educational goals: knowledge, comprehension, application, analysis, synthesis, and evaluation. These categories relate to knowledge, intellectual abilities and intellectual skills and involve processes of remembering, reasoning, problem solving, concept formation, and creative thinking. They are seen as hierarchically arranged from simple to more complex educational goals in

---

[1] See Simon and Boyer (1967, 1970) for a comprehensive compilation of observation schemes, Rosenshine and Furst (1973) for a discussion of types of classroom observation schemes and ways schemes have been used in studying teaching, and Dunkin and Biddle (1974) for a review of classroom research employing major schemes.

relation to the cognitive processing required of the learner. At the bottom of the hierarchy, goals involve the recall and recognition of previously learned information (lower-level goals). Goals in the middle of the hierarchy involve the transfer of learning to new situations, while goals at the top of the hierarchy involve the production of novel, perhaps unique responses and evaluation of these responses by the learner (higher-level goals). Subsequently, Sanders (1966) proposed that the same categories that were applied to questions on tests and to educational objectives could also be applied to questions asked in the classroom during instruction.

In general, the taxonomy categories have been used to distinguish between higher-level and lower-level cognitive requirements of questions. This dichotomy is also maintained in the simulation situation to be described with questions falling in several different higher-level categories included among the teaching phrases. Often, questions falling in the higher-level categories (comprehension, application, analysis, synthesis, and evaluation) are combined for analyses. Studies in which classroom interaction has been observed and coded using taxonomy categories have repeatedly found that teachers use more memory questions than any other category and that teachers' use of higher-level questions is unrelated to pupil achievement (Dunkin & Biddle, 1974; Rosenshine, 1971b). However, this research has focused on the frequency of use of question types without reference to the function of the question within the context of the class discussion. In addition, given the wide variation in classroom and experimental conditions under which questions have been investigated and the persistent issue of methodological limitations, relatively little is known about the possible impact on student learning of teachers' use of questions requiring different levels of thinking from the students (Heath & Neilson, 1974; Rosenshine, 1971b). Indeed, it is highly likely that little progress can be made in understanding the impact of teachers' questions until they are viewed as an integral part of a process of information flow and of personal interaction.

Organization of the presentation.   A second and important avenue through which teachers influence student cognitive processing is the organization of their presentation of material to be learned. How well the teacher organizes subject matter in communication of new information to students can affect how easily students grasp the important points to be learned. Even if the content material itself is well-structured, the teacher must make the underlying content structure clear to the students (Gage & Berliner, 1975). Two characteristics of teachers' explanations which may affect student performance are teachers' sequencing of rules and examples and their use of explaining links (Rosenshine, 1971a). Here, "rule" refers to a "summary statement before or after a series of examples" (Rosenshine, 1971a, p. 205), while "explaining links" refer to prepositional phrases and conjunctive statements indicating relationships among concepts (e.g., cause, means, or purpose). Examples of explaining links would be "if . . . then . . . , " "though" or "in order to." Such explaining links may appear within or between sentences, such that one phase elaborates or expands upon another.

Rosenshine (1971a) compared the minicourse lectures of teachers whose students showed high achievement in the course with those of less effective teachers. With the qualification that rules and examples were defined in the context of particular social studies curriculum content, his results indicated that a pattern of explanation involving an opening statement followed by details and a closing statement — a *rule-example-rule* pattern — was used more frequently by the more effective lecturers. Less effective lecturers tended to provide either an opening or a closing statement, but not both. In addition, more effective lecturers used more explaining links. The implication is that the impact of teachers' presentations on student learning, at least in social studies, may relate both to clear specification of generalizations (rules) and the relationships among concepts and principles and to the sequential characteristics of content presentation (e.g., when a teacher provides a generalization in the course of presentation). In the simulation situation to be described, the specific phrases (i.e., rules, examples, statements of relationships) are specified for natural science content, so that teachers' sequencing of the phrases may be examined.

Content Structure

In addition to aspects of teachers' speech which are oriented toward student thinking and learning, there is a framework provided by inherent content structure to be transmitted to the student in the teaching process. Although learning processes and the content of learning may be distinguished conceptually, they may be integrally related. When a student learns new material, the nature of the cognitive operations he performs on the subject matter presented may be influenced by the structure of the content itself. In an optimal learning situation, content should support and enhance the particular cognitive processing to be fostered in the learner (Taba, 1966, Taba, Levine, & Elzey, 1964). Correspondingly, the types of thinking requested of students should complement content learning.

Shavelson (1974) has defined content structure as "the web of facts (words, concepts) and their interrleations in a body of instructional material [p. 231]." The comparable organization of content in memory for individuals teaching or learning the content is termed cognitive structure. Here a distinction is made between the content structure represented in the instructional materials and the structure of the content as it is stored in the learner's cognitive framework. Thus, instruction involves communication of a particular knowledge structure from one source (e.g., the teacher) to another (e.g., the learner). Shavelson proposes the following model for examining communication of subject-matter structure from teacher to learner in the classroom. The content structure is learned by the teacher and represented in memory as cognitive structure. The teacher then transmits this cognitive structure through an interactive process to students who in turn attempt to learn the web of words and concepts presented. Finally, what the student has learned is represented in his or her memory as cognitive structure.

So far, exploration of the relationship between content structure and cognitive structure has involved comparison of content structure models to measures of teacher or student cognitive structuring of the same content before and after instruction in the content material. Studies investigating the transmission of content structure, as well as the concepts involved, have consistently shown that learners' psychological structure of the content corresponds more closely to a priori content structure models after instruction than before instruction in the content (Johnson, 1967, 1969; Johnson, Cox, & Curran, 1970; Shavelson, 1972; Shavelson & Geeslin, 1973; Stasz, 1974). However, the transmission process has yet to be analyzed systematically to determine the impact of content structure on the teaching process and to identify the manifestations of content structure in classroom discourse. Intuitively at least, there is reason to propose that content structure may influence classroom discussion. Different content structures could affect the degree to which content can be organized for presentation and could call for different modes of problem solving. Extremely different content structure may even call for substantively different teaching techniques. For example, one would hardly expect social studies instruction to be conducted in the same way that physics instruction is conducted. The content material to be transmitted in a physics course usually has a definite underlying structure (e.g., force = mass X acceleration). In comparison, relationships among concepts in social studies are not as clearly defined (e.g., relationships in meaning among the concepts of culture, civilization, and society).

Logical Operations

Finally, teachers' speech should also be influenced by the nature of the logical operations which may be performed on the content. "Logical operations" refer to the language forms which may be employed in communicating content to the students (Smith & Meux, 1962; Smith, Meux, Coombs, Nuthall, & Precians, 1967). For example, logical operations might include defining, designating, classifying, cause–effect explaining, comparing, contrasting, and evaluating.

Addressing the content-logic of instruction, Smith and his associates (1967) analyzed transcripts of classroom discourse for teaching strategies used to reach different instructional objectives. To identify strategies, Smith and associates defined a unit of discourse, a "venture," which encompasses a single topic relevant to a single objective. Eight types of ventures were identified: causal, conceptual, evaluative, particular, interpretative, procedural, reason and rule. A conceptual venture, for example, is concerned with some class or category of events and the label for the class or category. Embedded within ventures are elements of content structure (concepts and interrelations among concepts) upon which different logical operations may be performed. Content structure and logical operations seem to have been considered simultaneously by Smith and associates in defining teaching "moves" as instructional units based on the meaning of what is said by teachers and students. General types of moves identified in conceptual ventures are descriptive moves (attributes), comparative moves (similarities and differences), and instantial moves (examples). The sequence of moves in a venture then defines a teaching strategy. The most common teaching strategies identified in conceptual ventures, for example, consisted of sequences of descriptive moves alone, alternating sequences of descriptive and instantial moves, and alternating sequences of descriptive and comparative moves.

Using programmed texts, Nuthall (1968) has investigated relationships between student achievement and four teaching strategies for conceptual ventures. These four teaching strategies included the three above plus an alternating sequence of comparative and instantial moves. Achievement results indicated that strategies containing comparative moves tended to be less effective for student learning than other strategies, while strategies containing instantial moves (examples) were more effective than other strategies, particularly for students with greater initial knowledge of the material.

With Nuthall's concern for the effectiveness of different strategies for student learning, he is considering both the content-logical aspects of the strategy and the sequence of moves which calls up in the student the type of thinking most conducive to learning the content. The implications are that the most effective teaching strategies may be those where the content logic supports and enhances teaching activities designed to stimulate cognitive processing.

Thus, in developing a simulation situation where teaching patterns can be considered, it was evident that the teachers should have alternative moves that they can make in order to allow aspects of teaching strategies to emerge. In addition, the teaching moves available should represent categories of teaching behavior that teachers are likely to use, that represent aspects of explaining and questioning relevant to student cognitive processing, and that are consistent with the content structure to be transmitted.

SIMULATION SITUATION

As a tool for microscopic analysis of verbal teaching behavior, an experimental method has been developed to simulate a dyadic teacher—student instructional situation where the teacher's sequencing of specific phrases can be documented for any number of teaching sessions with simulated students. Thus, the student half of the teacher—student dialogue is standardized while the teacher's choice

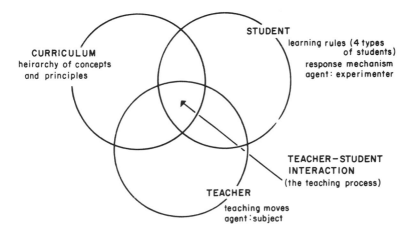

FIGURE 1   Simulation components.

of phrases can be studied in detail. When teachers are allowed to utilize statements and questions in whatever order they find effective for teaching a range of students, teaching patterns should emerge in pedagogically important ways.

The simulation model forms a system with student, teacher, and curriculum components (see Fig. 1).

Curriculum Component

This component consists of a set of interrelated concepts and principles to be learned by the student. In this case, the curriculum involves an hierarchically-arranged set of natural science concepts and principles (Gagné, 1970), the pressure-temperature-volume gas laws (see Fig. 2). Both the verbal statement of these laws (e.g., The pressure of a gas decreases when the volume is increased with the temperature held constant.) and the symbolic representation (e.g., $PV = c$) are included in the curriculum. For the teacher, student learning is evidenced by correct answers to questions indicating the student can state and explain the gas laws in verbal and symbolic forms.

Teacher Component

The second component consists of a repertoire of 86 verbal phrases covering all the concepts and principles in the curriculum. These phrases were carefully constructed to provide a balanced emphasis on laws, relationships represented by laws, examples, symbolic representation of laws, and relationships between laws. Both statements and questions related to rules, relationships, and examples are available for use in teaching each concept and principle. In addition, the

VERBAL FORM

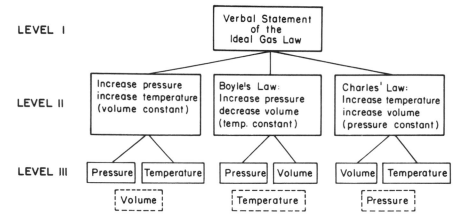

ALGEBRAIC FORM

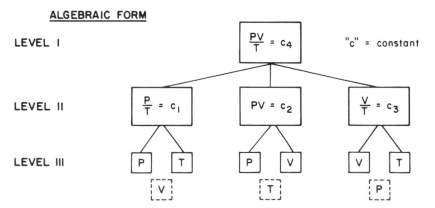

FIGURE 2 Learning hierarchy for the gas laws.

repertoire has been constructed to include under each concept and principle questions which theoretically require the student (1) to simply repeat information already learned — memory or knowledge questions — and (2) to engage in some thinking on his own — higher-order or comprehension questions (Bloom *et al.*, 1956; Sanders, 1966). The types of teaching moves and examples are given in Tables 1 and 2. When a teacher reads one of these phrases in the course of teaching a simulated student, he is considered to have made a "teaching move." The phrases can be ordered in any way the teacher feels is effective for teaching the student, and can be used as many times as the teacher feels is necessary.

Student Component

The third component consists of (1) a set of rules explicitly governing student learning contingent on teacher behavior, and (2) a means for student communication with the teacher. Thus, the "student" is simulated by a set of learning rules and is represented to the teacher by a pair of lights which indicate

TABLE 1
Types of Moves

Level	Verbal statement	Algebraic form
I. Ideal Gas Law	Formal statement	Equation
	Informal statement	
	Relationship	Relationship
	2 Everyday examples	
	Lower-level question	Lower-level question
	Higher-level question	
	Higher-order question[a]	
II. Component Gas Laws (for each law)	Formal statement	Equation
	Informal statement	
	Relationship	Relationship
	3 Everyday examples	
	Lower-level question	Lower-level question
	3 Higher-level questions	
III. Concepts (for each concept)	Formal definition	Symbol
	Informal definition[b]	
	3 Everyday examples	
	Lower-level question	Lower-level question
	3 Higher-level questions	

[a]In addition, there were three higher-level questions which related the component gas laws to the Ideal Gas Law.
[b]There was no informal definition for "volume." An additional statement about volume was included instead.

TABLE 2
Examples of Teaching Moves

Moves relating to the concept of pressure	
Informal definition	The push of a gas against the walls of a container is the "pressure."
Example	If you puff out your cheeks, you can feel the pressure inside your cheeks.
Lower-level question	What does the letter "P" represent?
Moves relating to the pressure-temperature rule	
Formal statement of gas law	The pressure-temperature rule states that change in pressure of a given amount of gas is directly proportional to change in temperature at constant volume.
Relationship	The pressure of a gas decreases when the temperature is decreased, if the volume remains constant.
Higher-level question	Why is the pressure in your car tires greater after driving an hour than it was when you started?
Moves relating to the Ideal Gas Law	
Informal statement of gas law	The Ideal Gas Law says that if the pressure of a gas has increased, the volume may have decreased, the temperature may have increased, or both.
Equation	The Ideal Gas Law is described by the Ideal Gas Equation: $PV/T =$ where c is a constant.
Algebraic relationship	If V decreases or T increases, P increases.
Moves integrating the Ideal Gas Law and the Component Gas Laws	
Higher-level question	In what ways could the pressure of a gas be increased by changing other gas conditions?

whether or not the student can answer a question correctly. The lights are operated by another person (the experimenter in this project) on the basis of the student's knowledge of the subject matter at the beginning of the teaching session, the student's learning algorithms, and the student's increasing knowledge during the teaching session. Four types of students are defined by initial knowledge of the subject matter and learning ability: high knowledge, fast learners (H–F); low knowledge, fast learners (L–F); high knowledge, slow learners (H–S); low knowledge, slow learners L–S).

Knowledge dimension. High- and low-knowledge students differ in the number of concepts, symbols, rules, and equations in the curriculum network that they "know" and "understand" at the beginning of a teaching session. Students can answer all questions about concepts and rules they know upon entering the teaching session. High- and low-knowledge students are defined by the specific knowledge that the students possess (see Table 3). In addition, most students possess some miscellaneous knowledge about everyday phenomena and can answer at least two of the following application questions correctly without understanding the underlying principle: "How are sailboats propelled?"; "Why shouldn't you put an aerosol can in an incinerator?"; and "What happens when you pop a closed paper bag?" High- and low-knowledge characteristics were randomly assigned to two sets (H1–L1; H2–L2), defining eight students when crossed with student learning ability.

Learning ability dimension. Slow and fast learners are defined by learning rules. Although research leading to development of learning and instruction models and corresponding algorithms has begun, there is a general lack of adequate models of subject-matter learning (Atkinson, 1972; Landa, 1968, 1969). Therefore, no one model of learning has been adhered to in development of learning algorithms for fast and slow learners in this project.

Basically, the algorithms represent all-or-none learning of concepts, rules, equations, relationships, and applications, given fulfillment of certain information requirements for learning. In addition, a forgetting function is superimposed on the all-or-none learning paradigm. Rules governing information requirements and sequencing of information for learning are based on several considerations.

TABLE 3
High/Low Knowledge Students

Amount of knowledge	Specific knowledge
High	H1. Pressure, temperature, volume, Boyle's Law.
	H2. Temperature, volume, Charles' Law, T, V, $V/T = c$.
Low	L1. Temperature, volume.
	L2. Temperature, T.

The first is Gagné's (1970) conception of the hierarchical nature of learning, which would predict that concepts need to be learned and understood before principles relating the concepts can be learned and understood. The second consideration has been the experimenter's own ideas about what information ought to be necessary for learning and what differences in informational requirements should exist between fast and slow learners. The third has been pretest and pilot study teachers' reactions to the ways the students learned. A high priority has been given to development of algorithms which have the capacity to *simulate* student learning effectively even in the restricted environment of the experimental situation. For examples of learning algorithms, see Table 4.

Algorithms allow students, particularly the fast learners, to learn both deductively and inductively from examples and statements of relationships. The pilot study algorithms were oriented toward *deductive learning* more than inductive

TABLE 4
Examples of General Rules for Student Learning

Fast learners	Slow learners
Learning rules for concepts	
If the student is given two examples, he learns and understands the concept.	If the student is given the definition and an example, he learns and understands the concept.
Learning rules for component rules describing relationships among gas conditions	
If the student is given a rule when he knows the component concepts, he learns and understands the rule.	If the student is given a rule, plus the relationship underlying the rule when he knows the component concepts, he learns the rule, but he cannot apply it.
If the student is given two examples, plus the relationship exemplified when he knows the component concepts, he learns and understands the rule.	If the student is given an example of the rule when he has learned the rule, he understands the rule and can apply it.
Learning rules for the Ideal Gas Law	
If the student is given the full gas law when he knows the component concepts, he learns and understands the full gas law.	If the student is given the full gas law when he knows the component concepts and at least one component rule, plus he is given the relationship underlying the rule, he learns the full gas law, but he cannot apply it.
Learning rules for integrating component rules and the Ideal Gas Law	
If the student knows Boyle's Law and the pressure-temperature rule, he can compare the two.	If the student knows the full gas law, Boyle's Law and the pressure-temperature rule, he can compare the two component rules.

learning. Since some pilot teachers felt frustrated by the students' inability to draw conclusions from discussions of relationships among gas conditions underlying everyday examples of gas behavior, algorithms allowing more *inductive learning* were added.

Previous knowledge also plays a part in some learning algorithms. Suppose, for example, a student already knows the answer to the question "Why shouldn't you put an aerosol can in an incinerator?" That knowledge can be applied to the learning of the pressure–temperature rule, if the student is asked that question at a relevant point in the teaching session.

Finally, the teacher's *sequencing* of teaching moves is important, particularly for the slow learner. For example, a slow student can learn the rule and the relationship underlying the rule from examples and statements of the relationship involved, but must be given another example after he understands the rule before he can apply the rule himself. None of the students will necessarily know what rule an example is associated with, if the teacher just gives a series of examples.

In general, the student retains the knowledge he has learned in the course of the teaching session. However, if the student does not already possess the necessary prerequisite knowledge and the teacher does not provide sufficient information to fulfill the learning requirements, the student will forget what he has already been told. The slow learner has forgotten by two teaching moves later, while the fast learner has forgotten by three moves later. For example, if a slow learner is given the equation representing a gas law when he does not know what the letters in the equation represent, he will forget the equation. If the teacher asks for the equation two moves later, the student will not be able to answer the question "correctly."

It should be noted here that there is no claim made that individuals do in fact learn scientific concepts and principles according to the algorithms described. These algorithms have been developed for the purpose of simulating a real student in an elementary fashion. They are, however, complex enough to give subjects the impression of teaching a live student and to forbid discovery of the particular learning rules by subjects during their teaching.

Simulation Procedures

Two agents are necessary in the experimental situation: A teacher and a person to follow the student learning rules and provide feedback to the teacher on student learning. In this study, each teacher was presented with a board on which the 86 teaching phrases (see Table 2 above) were placed in random order. After the teacher had rearranged the phrases on the board in a manner which allowed easy access to each, the experimenter moved out of sight behind a screen and the teacher was given the task of teaching the gas laws to each of six students individually. The teacher was responsible for beginning the teaching session by making a teaching move and for maintaining the session by making additional teaching moves, one after another. While technically the teacher only needed to give the number of a teaching move to make the move known to the experimenter, in order to create a more natural situation, the teacher read each phrase aloud. Reading the moves aloud helped to give an impression of continuity across moves and heightened the impression that there was a "student" listening. When the teacher asked a question, the lights provided feedback indicating whether or not the student could answer the question correctly. Since the teacher knew nothing about the student initially, questioning was the avenue through which he could learn about student learning characteristics. Finally, the teacher ended the session when he felt that the educational goals for the session had been met (i.e., when the "student" could state and explain the gas laws, including the equations representing the laws).

The raw data provided are the sequence of teaching moves made by the teacher in teaching each "student" and the student's responses to questions. Teaching moves were audio-recorded as the teacher read the moves and the tape dubbed to indicate "student" responses. Postgame interviews with the teachers were also audio-recorded.

EXAMINATION OF TEACHING PATTERNS

The study presented here addresses two general questions about teaching: "On the average, how do teachers differ in presenting information to students and in questioning students?," and "How are differences in presenting and questioning related to personal characteristics of teachers?" The primary purpose has been to describe verbal teaching patterns in the presentation of information (explaining) and questioning of students under the simulated teaching conditions described. Teachers' sequencing of questions and statements was accepted as the outcome of decisions made in structuring verbal information for the learner and in soliciting and using feedback from the learner. Verbal behavior examined include teachers' use of rules and examples in explaining (Dunkin & Biddle, 1974; Rosenshine, 1971b) and teachers' use of different types of questions (Berliner, 1969; Dunkin & Biddle, 1974; Sanders, 1966). In particular, teachers' placement of questions with respect to topic boundaries and to statements (information giving) are explored to identify the functions questions play in teaching. A second purpose was to explore relationships between teaching behavior and teachers' personal characteristics which could potentially affect teaching behavior. On a priori grounds we may speculate that teaching behavior should be compatible with the general aptitudes and personality of the teacher. Characteristics, selected to provide a wide range of information about the teacher, were amount of teaching experience, sex, intellectual or cognitive abilities (verbal, reasoning, and spatial), and cognitive style (field dependence—independence). Since this was an exploratory study employing a new experimental method, no specific hypotheses were offered predicting the nature of different teaching patterns or the relationship of different teacher characteristics to teaching behavior.

The experiment was designed to test the effects of teaching experience, the sex of the teacher, and student characteristics on teaching behavior in the simulated teaching situation. A four-factor experimental design (teaching experience X sex X student learning ability X student knowledge) with repeated measures on the student factors was employed. Thus each subject taught four students, one of each type: HF, LF, HS, LS. Students were taught in random order with all 24 possible sequences represented across subjects. In addition, since the students were simulated, all teachers taught the same four students.

The 32 subjects included 20 teachers (10 men and 10 women) with classroom teaching experience and 12 individuals with no teaching experience (six men and six women). They were paid volunteers recruited by leaflets distributed around a university and the neighboring communities. The subjects ranged in teaching experience from none to 10 years and in age from 17 to 36 years. Before the experimental session, each subject filled out a general information questionnaire, took four cognitive tests, and passed an achievement test covering the gas laws. The questionnaire asked for general information about the subjects, including teaching experience, age, educational background, and profession. The four cognitive tests were selected to provide a range of information about the teachers which might relate to their teaching in general or to their behavior in meeting the specific teaching requirements of the simulation setting. These tests (French, Ekstrom, & Price, 1963) measure verbal ability (Extended Range Vocabulary Test, Parts I and II), reasoning ability (Necessary Arithmetic Operations, Parts I and II), spatial ability (Form Board Test, Parts I and II), and the field dependence—independence cognitive style (Hidden Figures Test, Parts I and II). Finally, the achievement test measured knowledge of the curriculum content, the pressure-temperature-volume gas laws, at the level of simple problem solving using the appropriate equations. Criterion performance on the test (80% correct) was required for participation.

In the experimental session, each subject taught two practice "students" before teaching four experimental "students." Practice and experimental students differed only in the specific knowledge that high- and low-knowledge students possessed at the beginning of a teaching session. Of the practice students, the high-knowledge, fast learner was always taught first, and the low-knowledge, slow learner was taught second. The four experimental students were then taught in random order. After teaching, each subject was interviewed by the experimenter.

Teaching Variables and Scoring Procedures

From the audio-records of teaching move sequences, variables have been generated to answer questions about the teaching sequences (e.g., "How frequently does the teacher use memory questions? comprehension questions?" "How does the teacher respond to a student response?" "Does the teacher tend to give rules first or does he give rules after some discussion?" "How does the teacher introduce a new topic?"). Teaching variables generated include simple frequencies, sequence frequencies, and general teaching session descriptors. Simple frequency variables are tallies of the number of times a certain type of question or statement was used (e.g., higher-level question, rule, example), the total number of questions and statements used, the number of changes in topic, the amount of interaction with the student, the number of changes from verbal to algebraic representation, and the number of correct and incorrect student responses. Sequence frequencies are tallies of the number of times a certain type of question or statement was used to initiate a topic or to respond to a student's correct or incorrect response. Finally, teaching session descriptors are the total number of moves used to teach each student, the number of different statements used by the teacher in the teaching session, and the percentage of correct response by the student.

Teaching moves were first coded according to the specific rule or concept discussed, the content of the move (e.g., rule, relationships, example), the type of move (question or statement), and the student's response, if a question were asked. A computer program was then specifically developed to process the sequence of coded teaching moves and to provide frequency counts of the use of each type of move, the range of moves used, and the occurrence of particular sequences of moves. The primary dependent variables for analysis were 15 frequency variables and one ratio variable describing the teaching sequences. These variables are defined in Table 5 with the means and standard deviations given in Table 6.

Average Teaching Behavior

The means suggest that teachers used on the average fewer teaching moves than those available in the total repertoire to teach a "student" the gas laws (61 teaching moves made of 86 moves available). At the same time, they attempted to integrate the seven topics (three concepts and four rules) for they changed topics 15 times, touching each topic twice on the average. In addition, they tended to ask proportionally more questions (50% of all teaching moves in comparison to 43% available question moves in the repertoire) than to make statements. However, as would be predicted from classroom studies, teachers used relatively fewer questions calling for complex cognitive processing (52% higher-level questions asked of the question moves made in comparison to 62% higher-level questions available) than memory questions. A comparison of the average number of questions asked (33) and the average number of separate interactions with the student (13) suggests that teachers tended to ask several questions in a row. If the teacher followed a student response with another question, 53% of the time the question was higher-level. Teachers introduced

TABLE 5

Teaching Variables

Variable name	Aspect of teaching measured	Variable definition
Total moves	Quantity of teaching behavior	Total number of teaching moves used
Range of statements	Diversity of statements used	Number of different statement moves used
Higher-level questions	Teacher inquiry emphasizing student comprehension	Number of higher-level question moves used
Rules	Teacher emphasis on formal statement of gas laws	Number of rule moves used (questions and statements)
Relationships	Teacher emphasis on relationships underlying rules	Number of relationship moves used (questions and statements)
Examples	Teacher emphasis on applications	Number of example moves used (questions and statements)
Percent correct student response	Proportion of questions the student answered correctly	Ratio of correct student responses to total question moves
Topics initiated with questions	Teacher use of inquiry in introducing topics	Number of times a teacher initiated discussion on topics with question moves (string of two moves on the same topic necessary for inclusion)
Topics initiated with rules	Teacher use of statements of gas laws immediately in introducing topics	Number of times a teacher initiated discussion on topics with rule moves (questions or statements; string of two moves on the same topic necessary for inclusion)
Topics initiated with relationships	Teacher emphasis on relationships underlying rules in introducing topics	Number of times a teacher initiated discussion on topics with relationship moves (questions or statements; string of two moves on the same topic necessary for inclusion)
Teacher response with higher-level questions	Teacher tendency to continue interaction with the student with an empahsis on student understanding	Number of times a teacher followed student responses with higher-level questions
Teacher response with rules	Teacher tendency to follow interaction with the student with an emphasis on statement of gas laws	Number of times a teacher followed student responses with rule moves (questions and statements)
Teacher response with relationships	Teacher tendency to follow interaction with the student with relationships underlying rules	Number of times a teacher followed student responses with relationship moves (questions and statements)
Changes in topic	Integration of concepts and principles by the teacher	Number of times a teacher changed topic (e.g., volume to Boyle's Law to Charles' Law)
Interaction	Amount of teacher interaction with the student	Number of times a teacher changed from using statement moves to question moves and vice versa
Verbal symbol	Teacher emphasis on the relationship of algebraic representation to verbal statement of rules and relationships	Number of times a teacher changed from using moves involving verbal statement (questions and statements) to moves involving algebraic representation (questions and statements) and vice versa

TABLE 6
Teaching Style Group Means and Standard Deviations[a] for Summary Teaching Variables, Cognitive
Measures, and Gas Law Achievement Test

Variable	Group 1 (N = 6)	Group 2 (N = 6)	Group 3 (N = 6)	Group 4 (N = 4)	Total including unclassified teachers (N = 32)
Total moves	47.3	72.0	70.0	33.3	61.2
	(1.9)	(6.1)	(6.5)	(6.2)	(18.4)
Range of statements	21.1	23.8	32.5	17.8	25.8
	(3.7)	(2.4)	(2.9)	(3.6)	(6.9)
Higher-level questions	13.3	23.2	18.7	5.0	16.4
	(2.9)	(2.7)	(3.3)	(5.1)	(6.8)
Rules	3.8	3.5	3.8	3.5	3.7
	(0.8)	(0.8)	(1.3)	(1.7)	(1.4)
Relationships	5.7	10.2	13.0	4.0	8.8
	(2.1)	(1.0)	(2.5)	(3.7)	(3.7)
Examples	3.0	6.5	9.0	1.5	6.2
	(1.4)	(0.8)	(2.8)	(1.7)	(3.7)
Percent correct student response	0.85	0.75	0.87	0.86	0.85
	(0.06)	(0.08)	(0.05)	(0.08)	(0.09)
Topics initiated with questions	2.7	7.2	2.2	2.0	3.9
	(2.9)	(1.5)	(1.0)	(1.4)	(3.5)
Topics initiated with rules	2.0	1.2	0.2	2.0	1.7
	(1.4)	(0.8)	(0.4)	(1.4)	(2.7)
Topics initiated with relationships	0.8	2.8	3.5	0.3	2.1
	(0.8)	(0.8)	(1.5)	(0.5)	(1.6)
Teacher response with H−L questions	7.7	12.8	8.7	2.5	9.2
	(2.3)	(3.3)	(2.7)	(2.1)	(5.0)
Teacher response with rules	3.8	5.8	2.8	3.8	4.5
	(0.8)	(1.3)	(2.1)	(2.2)	(3.0)
Teacher response with relationships	4.0	9.3	8.0	1.8	6.2
	(2.1)	(2.3)	(1.3)	(1.5)	(3.3)
Changes in topic	12.7	15.8	14.2	11.5	15.1
	(2.3)	(1.5)	(5.5)	(2.5)	(6.6)
Interaction	21.8	34.5	31.2	16.0	26.1
	(6.2)	(5.1)	(5.9)	(4.2)	(8.8)
Verbal-symbol	19.0	27.8	27.7	18.3	25.8
	(2.5)	(*5.7)	(4.8)	(3.5)	(8.9)
Verbal ability[b]	40.8	40.3	38.7	38.3	38.6
	(1.9)	(5.2)	(5.0)	(4.6)	(4.8)
Reasoning ability	19.7	24.2	22.3	24.5	22.3
	(2.0)	(4.0)	(3.6)	(3.1)	(4.3)
Spatial ability	22.0	26.3	21.0	24.5	22.3
	(10.5)	(6.2)	(7.5)	(4.7)	(7.8)
Field dependence-independence	12.0	23.1	14.0	13.5	15.8
	(5.4)	(7.0)	(9.0)	(5.6)	(7.1)
Gas law achievement	8.0	8.8	9.2	8.0	8.3
	(2.1)	(1.2)	(0.8)	(1.8)	(1.6)

[a]The mean is given first, followed by the standard deviation in parentheses.

[b]A low score for a subject whose native language was Polish is not included in means and standard deviations for verbal ability.

topics — new or old — with questions only about a third of the time. "Students" answered questions correctly 85% of the time, probably because teachers tended to ask questions after a topic had been introduced. In content coverage, teachers gave or asked for a formal statement of each rule once on the average (3.7 moves for four laws), preferring to have rules expressed informally as relationships among gas conditions (8.8 moves for four laws). Application moves, however, were used infrequently in comparison to their availability (6.2 moves used in comparison to 35 moves available in question or statement form).

Finally, examination of the actual teaching sequences indicates that most teachers began by instructing the student on the basic concepts and then proceeded to cover the component gas laws (two variables) and then the full gas law (three variables). Eight of the teachers (25%) began with a gas law in teaching at least one of their students and then turned to the concepts to build "student" understanding. Since the learning algorithms required students to have an understanding of the basic concepts to learn the laws, teachers who did not adequately establish "student" comprehension of the concepts had to later return to teach the concepts. Few teachers, however, fully established "students' " initial knowledge of concepts or laws upon entering the session before beginning instruction. While the student learning ability dimension influenced teaching behavior more than the student knowledge dimension, the presence of previous knowledge sometimes made the slow learners appear to learn rapidly and the fast learners appear to learn exceptionally rapidly for the teacher who had not diagnosed initial "student" knowledge.

Effect of Student Characteristics on Teaching Behavior

Within the experimental situation, teaching behavior was found to be influenced by the characteristics of the simulated "student," as evidenced by repeated-measures analysis of variance. Here, data from each experimental "student" for each teacher were treated as independent observations. In addition, nine ratio variables were generated to control for differences in total quantity of teaching behavior and were included in these preliminary analyses. These variables were percent questions, percent higher-order questions, percent rules, percent relationships, percent examples, percent teacher response with higher-order questions, percent topics initiated with questions, percent topics initiated with rules, and percent topics initiated with relationships.

For fast versus slow learners, significant differences ($p < .05$) in teaching were found for 15 of the 16 primary teaching variables and for four of the nine ratio variables. When one considers the student learning characteristics, the observed differences in teaching behavior seem consistent with how teachers might be expected to behave with such students. Fast- and slow-learner algorithms differ along two dimensions: amount of information and sequencing of information needed for learning. The slow learners require more information and they need information sequenced in some rational order to a greater degree than do fast learners. With only two exceptions, subjects used more moves or a greater percentage of particular kinds of moves with the slow learners than with the fast learners. However, they initiated topics with rules a greater percentage of the time with fast learners. Since teachers did not differ in the number of topics initiated with rules, they apparently were most likely to introduce laws by a formal statement of the rule when the law was first introduced in the session. With fast learners, the greater proportion of topics initiated with rules indicates that fast students tended to learn the material the first time through a topic and did not need more extensive coverage later. Also indicative of their rate of learning, fast learners answered a greater percentage of teachers' question moves correctly.

Few significant differences in teaching behavior were found for high- versus low-knowledge students, probably because, as mentioned earlier, teachers did not adequately check for initial "student" knowledge of the concepts and laws. Therefore, even though "students" already knew some material, the teachers covered the material as if the "students" were not knowledgeable. The few differences in teaching behavior are, however, compatible with expectations. Teachers used more moves, a greater range of statements, and more example moves with low-knowledge than high-knowledge students.

Both the average teaching behavior across subjects and differences in teaching behavior due to student characteristics are compatible with general expectations of how teachers might reasonably act in such a highly structured teaching situation. Therefore, at least initially, the simulation procedure developed appears to be an adequate vehicle for studying cognitive aspects of verbal teaching behavior.

Teaching Patterns and Teacher Characteristics

One of the purposes of this study was to identify in the simulation situation patterns of teaching behavior and to attempt to describe possible teaching strategies represented by different patterns. Here, average scores across students for each of the 32 subjects on the teaching variables served as basic data. Two different approaches for grouping teachers with similar patterns were employed: (1) grouping on the basis of principal component score plots representing each teacher as a point in space (Guilford, 1965); and (2) grouping of teachers on the basis of teaching profile, where profiles were represented graphically by computer plotted diagrams (Chernoff, 1971). With the first method, groups of points representing individual teachers were readily identified when plotted. To facilitate interpretation of the first three principal components, a varimax factor rotation was applied, yielding factors appearing to represent (a) quantity and diversity, (b) structure, and (c) problem-solving aspects of teaching behavior. With the second method, Chernoff figures, groups were identified on the basis of agreement among three independent raters. Four groups were identified from the main body of teachers by grouping teachers with similar principal component scores or similar Chernoff figures, with two of these groups being defined by the overlap in membership of two principal component groups with comparable Chernoff figure groups. Means and standard deviations on teaching variables and teacher characteristics for the four groups are presented in Table 6.

The most distinct groups of teachers (i.e., groups identified by both grouping techniques) were:

Group 1: a deductive, lecture-oriented group (N = 6) who emphasized rules and presented material on a concept or principle before asking questions of the student, and

Group 2: an inductive, question-oriented group (N = 6) who used many questions, particularly higher-order questions, to introduce subject matter and to respond.

Definition of the proposed teaching strategies has been based on examination of the mean teaching profile of the group and the original teaching sequences of the group members. Teaching profiles of the above two groups are shown in Figs. 3 and 4 respectively.

Teachers in the deductive, lecture-oriented group (Group 1) received responses that averaged 85% correct when they asked questions; while the inductive, question-oriented group (Group 2) received responses that averaged 75% correct. This difference in student response reflects a greater use of higher-level questions by the second group and a different use of questions by each group. The first used questions more as a check on student knowledge during the discussion, whereas the second often used questions to initiate discussion on a topic not covered yet in the teaching session. Examples of teaching sequences of subjects in Groups 1 and 2 are given in Table 7.

Interviews supported the teaching profiles. Two-thirds of the teachers in Group 1 recognized they were using a deductive approach and some commented on the lecture format. For example:

T6: Well, usually I use a deductive approach more often than not, and I try to give an example as early as possible in the game so that people can be oriented with something they're familiar with, and I'll ask them questions about it.

T29: Somewhere in my own teaching I tend to present a lot of information rather than use a discovery method. I attempt to convey information . . . I tend to be fairly didactic in my teaching.

Three teachers particularly mentioned efficiency as a factor in determining their approach in the simulation setting, and all felt hindered by the lack of feedback from the student, particularly verbal feedback, and by lack of moves which particularly asked questions they wanted to ask or made comparisons they wanted.

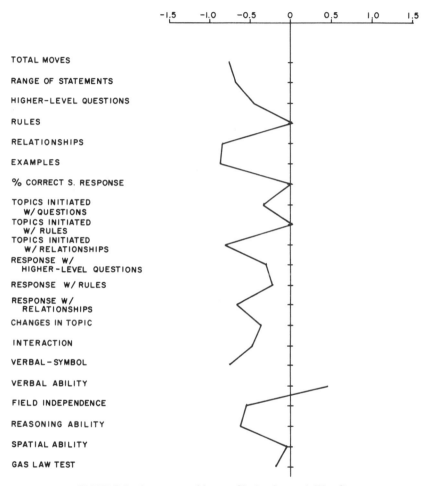

STANDARD SCORE

BASED ON SAMPLE MEAN AND STANDARD DEVIATION

FIGURE 3   Average teaching profile for Group 1 ($N = 6$).

In Group 2, four of the six teachers commented on using a questioning approach. For example:

T9: I tried to get a balance in terms of getting across generalizations or principles, questioning to try to get them to see relationships, also try to use examples to show relationships.

T14: I guess I always tended, tend a lot to ask questions before I state all of what's going on.

STANDARD SCORE

BASED ON SAMPLE MEAN AND STANDARD DEVIATION

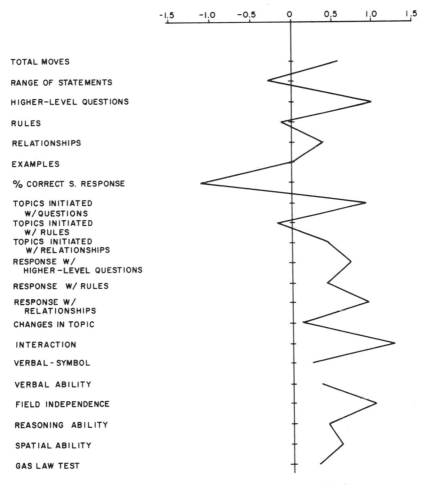

FIGURE 4 Average teaching profile for Group 2 ($N = 6$).

The two teachers who were particularly inductive in their approach expressed frustration with the students' slowness in picking up generalizations from examples or component laws. In addition, three teachers in this group commented on their uncertainty about how they wanted to teach the students and their search for different approaches, working out the sequence a little differently each time. T27: "I just wanted to try to get a different feel for the kids."

TABLE 7
Sample Teaching Sequences of Subjects in Groups 1 and 2

Group 1: T29 with the high knowledge, slow learner:

51. The pressure-temperature rule states that change in pressure of a given amount of gas is directly proportional to change in temperature at constant volume.

83. The pressure of a gas decreases when the temperature is decreased, if the volume remains constant.

76. Chemists have found that the pressure of a gas increases when the temperature is increased, if the volume remains constant.

56. How do changes in pressure relate to changes in temperature of a gas in a closed container? (Student answers "correctly.")

29. When you pump up a basketball, why does the pump become hot? (Student answers "incorrectly.")

31. What is the rule that describes the relationship between the pressure and temperature of a gas? (Student answers "correctly.")

63. The pressure-temperature rule may be represented by the equation: $P/T = c$, where "c" is a constant.

41. With V constant, if T increases, P increases proportionally.

86. Do you know the equation representing the pressure-temperature rule for a gas? (Student answers "correctly.")

19. Why shouldn't you put an aerosol can in an incinerator? (Student answers "correctly.")

24. Why is the pressure in your car tires greater after driving an hour than it was when you started? (Student answers "correctly.")

Group 2: T26 with the high knowledge, slow learner:

31. What is the rule that describes the relationship between the pressure and temperature of a gas? (Student answers "incorrectly.")

83. The pressure of a gas decreases when the temperature is decreased, if the volume remains constant.

51. The pressure-termperature rule states that change in pressure of a given amount of gas is directly proportional to change in temperature at constant volume.

56. How do changes in pressure relate to changes in temperature of a gas in a closed container? (Student answers "incorrectly.")

76. Chemists have found that the pressure of a gas increases when the temperature is increased, if the volume remains constant.

24. Why is the pressure in your car tires greater after driving an hour than it was when you started? (Student answers "incorrectly.")

59. When you are driving, the temperature of your car tires increases due to road friction, leading to an increase in air pressure in the tires.

31. What is the rule that describes the relationship between the pressure and temperature of a gas? (Student answers "correctly.")

86. Do you know the equation representing the pressure-temperature rule for a gas? (Student answers "incorrectly.")

63. The pressure-temperature rule may be represented by the equation: $P/T = c$, where "c" is a constant.

19. Why shouldn't you put an aerosol can in an incinerator? (Student answers "correctly.")

86. Do you know the equation representing the pressure-temperature rule for a gas? (Student answers "correctly.")

31. What is the rule that describes the relationship between the pressure and temperature of a gas? (Student answers "correctly.")

Two other teaching style groups were also identified, one by each of the grouping techniques. One identified by principal component scores was:

Group 3: an inductive, lecture-oriented group ($N = 6$) who emphasized relationships, presented subject matter to the student, but interacted with the student during the presentation by using questions to monitor learning (see Fig. 5).

A sample teaching sequence is given in Table 8. Interviews indicated that this group varied considerably in teaching background and that each teacher had to adapt his normal teaching in some way to fit the simulation situation. Two who were used to teaching college students found they had to gear their teaching down to the level of the simulated students by adding more explanation. One teacher had taught elementary school children and felt that she was going too fast and should make fewer logical leaps in the explanations. The remaining three teachers felt that they had to use a more directive, expository approach in the simulation situation than they would in the classroom, preferring to give an assignment, set up a laboratory experiment, or use a demonstration to introduce a new topic. Five out of the six commented that they would normally use more examples in their teaching than they could in the simulation situation.

The fourth group ($N = 4$) appeared from the interviews to have been alienated by the simulated teaching situation, particularly commenting on the lack of visual cues (for example, eye contact with the student, opportunities for instructional demonstrations). In teaching, they first presented subject matter with a strong emphasis on rules and then asked questions. Their teaching sessions were short and probably represented a minimum of effort on the part of the teachers in meeting the requirements of the situation (see Fig. 6). For example:

Group 4: T11 with the high knowledge, slow learner
76. Chemists have found that the pressure of a gas increases when the temperature is increased, if the volume remains constant.
56. How do changes in pressure relate to changes in temperature of a gas in a closed container?
(Student answers "correctly.")
63. The pressure-temperature rule may be represented by the equation: $P/T = c$, where "c" is a constant.
86. Do you know the equation representing the pressure-temperature rule for a gas?
(Student answers "correctly.")

The remaining teachers ($N = 10$) did not fall consistently into any group and shared few teaching characteristics, except that they generally tended to present subject matter before asking questions of the student (a lecture orientation).

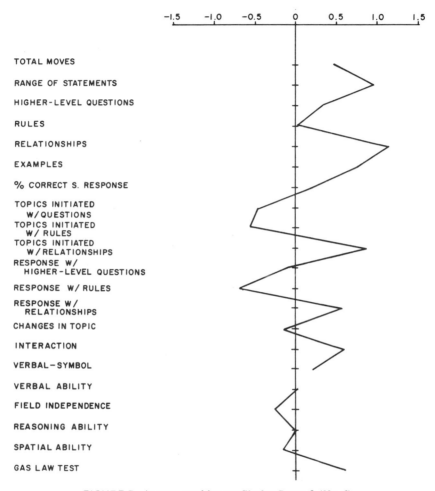

FIGURE 5   Average teaching profile for Group 3 ($N = 6$).

Teaching Patterns and Teacher Characteristics

The analysis of variance permitted by the research design showed few, but consistent differences in teaching behavior attributable to teaching experience and to the sex of the teacher. Experienced teachers placed less emphasis on the statement of rules, using fewer rule moves in general, in opening topics, and in following "student" answers, and initiated proportionally more topics with relationship moves. As for sex differences, women generally emphasized relationships underlying rules more than men did, using proportionally more relationship

TABLE 8
A Sample Teaching Sequence for Group 3:
T4 with the High Knowledge, Slow Learner

---

43. If an aerosol can is heated, the pressure inside the can becomes greater. Since the container cannot change in size, the can may explode under the increased pressure.
76. Chemists have found that the pressure of a gas increases when the temperature is increased, if the volume remains constant.
39. If a closed bottle of air were heated, the pressure inside the bottle would increase with increasing temperature. Under pressure, the cap may pop open.
56. How do changes in pressure relate to changes in temperature of a gas in a closed container? (Student answers "incorrectly.")
59. When you are driving, the temperature of your car tires increases due to road fraction, leading to an increase in air pressure in the tires.
76. Chemists have found that the pressure of a gas increases when the temperature is increased, if the volume remains constant.
83. The pressure of a gas decreases when the temperature is decreased, if the volume remains constant.
19. Why shouldn't you put an aerosol can in an incinerator? (Student answers "correctly.")
24. Why is the pressure in your car tires greater after driving an hour than it was when you started? (Student answers "correctly.")
31. What is the rule that describes the relationship between the pressure and temperature of a gas? (Student answers "correctly.")
41. With V constant, if T increases, P increases proportionally.
63. The pressure-temperature rule may be represented by the equation: $P/T = c$, where "c" is constant.
56. How do changes in pressure relate to changes in temperature of a gas in a closed container? (Student answers "correctly.")
86. Do you know the equation representing the pressure-temperature rule for a gas? (Student answers "correctly.")

---

moves particularly in opening topics. Women also used proportionally more example moves. Correlations between teaching behavior and the sex and teaching experience of the subjects were consistent with the analysis of variance results. Age was negatively correlated with initiation of topics with rules ($r = -.39$) and response with rules ($r = -.45$), reflecting the positive correlation between age and teaching experience.

All subjects in the inductive, lecture-oriented group (Group 3) and five of the subjects in the inductive, question-oriented group (Group 2) were experienced teachers, suggesting that a more inductive approach to teaching may be related to teaching experience. However, on the average, both inductive groups performed better than other groups on the achievement measure, indicating that they may have been more familiar with the subject matter than other teachers and therefore more able to take an inductive approach.

Of the cognitive variables, only cognitive style and verbal ability showed any correlation with teaching variables. Field independence was positively correlated

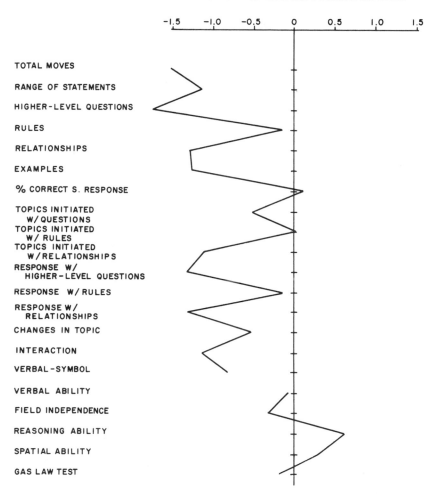

STANDARD SCORE

BASED ON SAMPLE MEAN AND STANDARD DEVIATION

FIGURE 6   Average teaching profile for Group 4 ($N = 4$).

with the number of higher-order questions used ($r = .50$), while verbal ability was negatively correlated with teacher response with rules ($r = -.35$). Allowing alpha = .10, field independence also was positively correlated with the total number of teaching moves used ($r = .33$), response with higher-order questions ($r = .30$), interaction with the student ($r = .32$), and changes from verbal statement to algebraic representation of rules ($r = .32$). Verbal ability was negatively correlated with the range of statements used ($r = -.34$), the number of examples used ($r = -.30$), changes in topic ($r = -.32$), and changes from verbal statement to algebraic representation of rules ($r = -.33$).

Profiles also indicated that the teacher groups differed on cognitive measures, suggesting that teacher cognitive characteristics may also affect teaching patterns. On the average, the deductive, lecture-oriented group (Group 1) scored higher on the verbal ability measure than on the other ability measures. This pattern of ability, along with their interview comments on feeling restricted by the lack of verbal feedback from the student and by the repertoire of teaching moves, may indicate that these teachers rely quite a bit on verbal communication in teaching. The inductive, question-oriented group (Group 2) scored above the sample mean on all ability measures and particularly on field independence. With their questioning approach, these teachers appeared willing to risk incorrect answers from the student and may have modified their teaching sequences more from student to student than other teacher groups. Although on the average the two groups scored the same on verbal ability, the group means on field dependence-independence contrasted sharply. The deductive, lecture-oriented group scored as more field dependent, while the inductive, question-oriented group scored as more field independent.

The group that was alienated by the simulation situation (Group 4) scored below the sample mean on field independence, but above the mean on spatial and reasoning ability measures. Along with these subjects' interview comments on the lack of visual feedback from the student, this pattern indicates that these teachers rely more on visual contact with the student than other teachers. Such a preference may have contributed to their alienation from the game situation, where no visual contact with the student was possible. The inductive, lecture-oriented group (Group 3) and the unclassified teachers scored at or slightly below the sample mean on all the cognitive measures. However, standard deviations were large, suggesting that there was little consistency on cognitive measures for these teachers.

Student Achievement

Student achievement as a measure of teaching success has not been emphasized in this study, since student learning in the game was defined by the learning algorithms. As would be expected on the basis of student characteritics, teachers were generally more successful in teaching the fast learners than the slow learners. However, since "students" in the simulation may not learn in the same ways that actual students learn, overall student achievement may not be used to evaluate teaching effectiveness for the different teacher groups. The effect of different teaching patterns on student learning should now be systematically investigated under teaching conditions involving real students.

CONCLUSION

The present research exploring the use of simulation techniques in the analysis of interactive speech has several implications for theory and practice in teaching. First, the technique of simulating dyadic interaction has proven effective for studying selected aspects of teachers' speech. By controlling conditions of interactive speech, the manner in which the teacher combines questions and statements in presenting subject matter and in interacting with the student can be rigorously studied. The capability of the experimental simulation to influence teacher behavior, to allow identification of teaching patterns, and to create an experience the subject could compare with everyday teaching suggests that the approach is a powerful tool for the study of teaching and of dialogue in general. While the experimental situation was not a natural teaching setting, the teaching component of the simulation was based on classroom teaching, specifically on research concerning teachers' use of speech to encourage student cognitive processing, teachers' psychological structuring and transmission of underlying content structure, and teachers' use of logical operations on content in presentation. Consequently, the simulation not only allowed description of patterns of teachers' questioning and explaining, but also implicitly provided a test of assumptions about the nature of information transmission in classroom teaching on which the simulation was based.

Second, the successful identification of teaching patterns in the simulation situation poses important questions for educational research and teacher training: What are the effects of different teaching patterns on student cognitive processing in class and subsequent learning? To what extent should attempts be made to develop or to modify teaching patterns? There are indications in the current study that teaching patterns may be related to other teacher characteristics, in particular, teaching experience, familiarity with the subject matter, verbal ability, cognitive style, and perhaps sex-linked characteristics. Although many characteristics of the training program and of the actual teaching situation may influence the teacher's techniques, the person's natural teaching patterns and personal characteristics may be important in acquiring and utilizing techniques. Identification of teachers who can most readily adapt their teaching to incorporate particular teaching skills and teaching strategies may be central for effective teacher training and reliable implementation of teaching models requiring specific techniques.

In addition, simulation techniques may augment teacher training programs by providing situations where teachers may learn specific skills under carefully chosen instructional conditions. A simulation situation of the type described in this paper could be employed for training in teaching techniques as well as for research purposes. Application of simulation techniques has already begun in medical education, where a number of simulation situations based on models of clinical decision-making have been developed for training medical students in the diagnosis of certain medical problems (Elstein, Kagan, Shulman, Jason, & Loupe, 1972; McGuire & Babbott, 1967; Taylor, 1972). In education, Flake (1974) has investigated the feasibility of computer-assisted simulation in teacher training. The program Flake has developed simulates an eight-student mathematics class and has been employed to aid student teachers in improving their questioning strategies in teaching mathematics. Evaluation of Flake's program as a training device indicated that teacher trainees showed an increased awareness of their teaching behavior and changed their teaching, such that they more frequently went beyond the first response of a "student" and modeled the prescribed problem-solving strategy. While Flake's research was concurrent, it was independent of the research described here, and the simulated teaching situations developed are quite different. However, together the studies illustrate the potential role simulation techniques can play in both basic research and in teacher training.

The power of simulation techniques, both as tools for analysis of interactive speech and as training devices, has yet to be firmly established. However, the promise that simulation offers for theoretical and practical developments in the study of dialogue warrants careful consideration of this avenue of research in the future.

ACKNOWLEDGMENTS

This research report is based on a dissertation submitted to the School of Education and Committee on Graduate Studies of Stanford University in partial fulfillment of the requirements for the degree of Doctor of Philosophy. Many grateful thanks are due to Dr. Richard E. Snow, Dr. N. L. Gage, and Dr. Janet D. Elashof for their direction and advice throughout the study. The research was conducted at the Stanford Center for Research and Development in Teaching, which is supported in part by the National Institute of Education, Department of Health, Education, and Welfare. Technical Report No. 39, 1973, published by SCRDT, also presents this study.

REFERENCES

Atkinson, R. C. Ingredients for a theory of instruction. *American Psychologist,* 1972, 27(10), 921–931.

Bellack, A. A., Kliebard, H. M., Hyman, R. T., & Smith, F. L. *The language of the classroom.* New York: Teachers College Press, 1966.

Berliner, D. C. *Microteaching and the technical skills approach to teacher training* (Tech. Rep. No. 8). Palo Alto: Stanford University, Stanford Center for Research and Development in Teaching, 1969.

Bloom, B. S., Engelhart, M. B., Furst, E. J., Hill, W. H., & Krathwohl, D. R. *Taxonomy of educational objectives. The classification of educational goals. Handbook I: Cognitive domain.* New York: Longmans, Green, 1956.

Bruner, J. S., Goodnow, J. J., & Austin, G. A. *A study of thinking.* New York: Wiley, 1956.

Chernoff, H. *The use of faces to represent points in n-dimensional space graphically* (Tech. Rep. No. 71). Palo Alto, California: Stanford University, Department of Statistics, 1971.

Dunkin, M. J., & Biddle, B. J. *The study of teaching.* New York: Holt, Rinehart & Winston, 1974.

Elstein, A. S., Kagan, N., Shulman, L. S., Jason, H., & Loupe, M. J. Methods and theory in the study of medical inquiry. *Journal of Medical Education,* 1972, **47,** 85–92.

Flake, J. L. The use of interactive computer simulations for sensitizing mathematics methods students to questioning behaviors (Doctoral dissertation, University of Illinois, 1973). *Dissertation Abstracts International,* 1974, **34,** 7623A. (University Microfilms No. 74-12,015)

Forsyth, I. J. Patterns in the discourse of teachers and pupils. In G. Perren (Ed.), *The space between . . . English and foreign languages at school.* London, England: Center for Information on Language Teaching, 1974.

French, J. W., Ekstrom, R. B., & Price, L. A. *Manual for kit of reference tests for cognitive factors.* Princeton, New Jersey: Educational Testing Service, 1963.

Gage, N. L., & Berliner, D. C. *Educational psychology.* Chicago, Illinois: Rand McNally, 1975.

Gagné, R. M. Some new views of learning and instruction. *Phi Delta Kappan,* 1970, **51,** 468–472.

Guilford, J. P. *Fundamental statistics in psychology and education.* New York: McGraw-Hill, 1965.

Heath, R. W., & Neilson, M. A. The research basis for performance-based teacher education. *Review of Educational Research,* 1974, 44(4), 463–484.

Johnson, P. E. Some psychological aspects of subject-matter structure. *Journal of Educational Psychology,* 1967, **58,** 75–83.

Johnson, P. E. On the communication of concepts in science. *Journal of Education Psychology,* 1969, **60,** 32–40.

Johnson, P. E., Cox, D. L., & Curran, T. E. Psychological reality of physical concepts. *Psychonomic Science,* 1970, **19,** 245–247.

Landa, L. Mathematical and cybernetic methods in education. In *Science in progress.* Novisti Press Agency Monthly No. 9, Moscow, 1968.

Landa, L. N. The construction of algorithmic and heuristic models of thinking activity and some problems in programmed learning. In W. R. Dunn & C. Holroyd (Eds.), *Aspects of educational technology.* London: Methuen, 1969.

McGuire, C. H., & Babbott, D. Simulation technique in the measurement of problem-solving. *Journal of Educational Measurement,* 1967, 4(1), 1–10.

Mehan, H., Fisher, S., & Maroules, N. *The academic and social aspects of classroom interaction.* (Classroom Interaction Study Research Group, Working Paper #2). Unpublished manuscript, University of California, San Diego, 1975.

Nuthall, G. An experimental comparison of alternative strategies for teaching concepts. *American Educational Research Journal,* 1968, 5(4), 561–584.

Rosenshine, B. Objectively measured behavioral predictors of effectiveness in explaining. In I. D. Westbury & A. A. Bellack (Eds.), *Research into classroom processes.* New York: Teachers College Press, 1971. Pp. 51–98. (a)

Rosenshine, B. *Teaching behaviours and student achievement.* Windsor, Berkshire, England: National Foundation for Educational Research in England and Wales, 1971. (b)

Rosenshine, B., & Furst, N. The use of direct observation to study teaching. In R. M. W. Travers (Ed.), *Second handbook of research on teaching.* Chicago: Rand McNally, 1973. Pp. 122–183.

Sanders, N. M. *Classroom questions: What kinds?* New York: Harper & Row, 1966.

Shavelson, R. J. *Basic teaching skills and student achievement: Some reasons for the absence of significant correlations and a proposal for future studies.* Unpublished manuscript, Stanford University, 1972.

Shavelson, R. J. What is the basic teaching skill? *Journal of Teacher Education,* 1973, **24**, 144–151.

Shavelson, R. J. Methods for examining representations of a subject-matter structure in a student's memory. *Journal of Research in Science Teaching,* 1974, **11**, 231–249.

Shavelson, R. J., & Geeslin, W. E. A method for examining subject matter structure in written material. *Journal of Structural Learning,* 1973, **4**, 101–111.

Simon, A., & Boyer, E. G. (Eds.) *Mirrors for behavior: An anthology of classroom observation instruments.* Philadelphia, Pennsylvania: Research for Better Schools, 1967.

Simon, A., & Boyer, E. G. (Ed.). *Mirrors for behavior: An anthology of classroom observation instruments continued.* Philadelphia, Pennsylvania: Research for Better Schools, Inc., 1970.

Smith, B. O., & Meux, M. O. *A study of the logic of teaching.* Urbana, Illinois: University of Illinois Press, 1962.

Smith, B. O., Meux, M. O., Coombs, J., Nuthall, G. A., & Precians, R. *A study of the strategies of teaching.* Urbana, Illinois: Bureau of Educational Research, University of Illinois, 1967.

Snow, R. E. *A second generation of microteaching skills research.* Paper presented at the annual meeting of the American Psychological Association, Washington, D.C., August, 1969.

Stasz, C. *Field independence and the structuring of knowledge in a social studies minicourse.* Unpublished Master's thesis, Rutgers University, 1974.

Taba, H. *Teaching strategies and cognitive functioning in elementary school children* (Cooperative Research Project No. 2404, U.S. Office of Education), San Francisco State College, February, 1966.

Taba, H., Levine, S., & Elzey, F. F. *Thinking in elementary school children* (Cooperative Research Project No. 1574, U.S. Office of Education). San Francisco State College, 1964.

Taylor, T. R. Computer-assisted instruction in medical education. *Programmed Learning and Educational Technology,* 1972, 9(5), 272–282.

14

What Is Remembered from Prose: A Function of Passage Structure[1]

Bonnie J. F. Meyer

Arizona State University

Most information a person acquires comes from reading or listening to prose. Thus, an important goal of education is to help people develop the ability to acquire information from their reading and listening. The primary handicap in developing programs to accomplish this goal is a lack of an adequate theory of learning from prose. There is very little data of the type needed for such a theory. Few studies have asked what people learn from their reading or listening and how this information is acquired; most studies have simply asked how much they learned.

The first step in developing a theory of learning from prose is to gather data about what kinds of information are, in fact, learned and remembered from prose. After reading or listening to a passage, people are unable to remember all the information it contained. When a number of people read or hear the same passage, some ideas from it are recalled by almost everyone, whereas other ideas are recalled by very few. Some studies have been conducted to investigate the effect of certain variables on which information is recalled from a passage.

In this chapter, experimental studies that have attempted to identify the kinds of information recalled from prose will be discussed. In addition, a presentation will be made of recent studies conducted by the author on the most powerful variable related to recall, the *content structure* or organization of information in a passage. These studies will be discussed in terms of the present knowledge dealing with learning from prose; some implications and theoretical speculations will be presented.

[1] Permission was generously given by North-Holland Publishing Co. to reproduce in this chapter tables and information from Meyer (1975a).

RESEARCH IN EDUCATION AND PSYCHOLOGY
DEALING WITH LEARNING FROM PROSE

Since much of what is learned in the schools is communicated through text or lecture, educators have been interested in studying learning from reading or listening to prose. Carroll (1971) has reviewed the research on learning from discourse by educators. In general, educators have tended not to examine the influence of aspects of the prose itself on which aspects of it are remembered. Instead, the effects of aids such as special instructions (Flanagan, 1939; Welborn & English, 1937), interspersed questions (Rothkopf & Bisbicos, 1967), training programs (Deverell, 1959), or other variables external to the text itself have been examined to ascertain their usefulness in increasing recall from a passage.

In contrast to educators' frequent use of prose in studies, in the past psychologists generally have tended to avoid research with natural prose. This avoidance was not due to a lack of interest, but resulted from a view that learning processes could better be studied with less complex and more easily controlled stimuli, such as lists of nonsense syllables or words, or pairs of these items. Thus, verbal learning research rarely involved the use of sentences or prose. Ironically, some of the learning principles consistently found with lists of words were not found with prose (Kircher, 1971). Not only is prose more complex and more complicated, but it contains an organizational structure designed to deliver a message; this primary attribute of prose materials is not found in lists of words or nonsense syllables.

Testing the Generalizability of Results
from Word Lists with Prose

Those psychologists studying verbal learning that did work with prose materials often contrived passages specifically to test the generalizability of some results found in word list studies. This prose has frequently sounded unnatural and has had unusual properties; for example, passages were often constructed to be reasonably sensible when the sentences in them were randomly assigned to different sentence orders (Deese & Kaufman, 1957; Frase, 1969; Kircher, 1971). Results found in word list studies which were tested for generalizability in prose materials included serial position effects, proactive and retroactive inhibition effects, stability of recall, and clustering effects.

Serial position effects have been consistently found in recall of word lists (Glanzer & Cunitz, 1966; Murdock, 1962). The serial position of a word in the sequence of words in a word list affects the frequency with which the word is recalled. People tend to recall the first few words presented in a series better than those in the middle of the series; this phenomenon is called the primacy effect. In addition, the last few words presented in a series are better recalled than those in the middle of the series; this phenomenon is called the recency effect. In contrast to these consistent findings with word lists, contradictory results have been found among studies examining serial position effects with prose. Primacy effects, the superiority in recall of the first few sentences of a passage, have been reported by Frase (1969), Jersild (1929), Kircher (1971) and Shaw (1896). Deese and Kaufman (1957) reported both primacy and recency effects. On the other hand, studies by Dell (1912), Richardson and Voss (1960), and Wilson (1931) reported that serial position had no influence on recall. Also, deVilliers (1974) and Kintsch, Kozimsky, Streby, McKoon, and Keenan (1974) reported no recency effects.

The research conducted by Meyer and McConkie (1973) presents a reasonable explanation for these contradictory results of research investigating serial position effects in prose. Their study investigated both serial position effects and effects of the structure among ideas in prose on recall. Two natural passages were used in the study; they were of approximately 500-words in length and were extracted from articles appearing in *Scientific American* magazine. The height of the ideas in the structure of a passage related to the frequency of recall of these ideas for both passages. In contrast, serial position was found to be related to recall in only one of the passages. In this passage ideas located in the first paragraph were recalled much better than ideal located in subsequent paragraphs. In addition, the top levels of the structure of the passage were also located in the first paragraph. A partial correlation between scores for the ideas of the passage based on recall frequency and scores based on serial position with scores based on height in the structure partialed out, showed that the height of ideas in the structure of the passage accounted for most of the variance attributed to serial position effects. In addition, the top level ideas, in the structure of the passage which produced no serial position effects, were dispersed throughout the passage and not concentrated solely in the first paragraph of the passage. Thus, the inconsistencies in previous studies on the effects of serial position in prose may be explained by examining the location of each passage of the ideas that are at the top of its structure of content.

In a recent study (Kintsch *et al.,* 1974) the higher-level information in 20–66 word paragraphs was found to occur more frequently in the beginning of the paragraphs, while subordinate-level information the paragraphs' structures more frequently occurred in the middle and end portions of the paragraphs. An analysis showed that the high-level information was recalled unusually well regardless of its serial position, and the recall of information was improved if it appeared at the beginning of the paragraph only if it occurred very high in the structure of the paragraph. Again, in this study there was no evidence for recency effects and most of the variance attributed to primacy effects could be accounted for by the height of ideas in the structure of the paragraphs.

Studies also have been conducted to see whether proactive and retroactive inhibition occurs in learning from prose; that is, whether old information interferes with the retention of new information, or whether new information causes a forgetting of previously learned information, phenomena which are commonly found in word list studies (Keppel, 1968). Again, as in the prose studies on serial position effects, contradictory results were reported from investigations of proactive and retroactive inhibition in prose. Some investigators have found statistically significant retroactive inhibition effects in prose (Crouse, 1970, 1971; Gillman, 1970; King & Cofer, 1960; Slamecka, 1960), but others have not (Ausubel, Robbins, & Blake, 1957; McGeoch & McKinney, 1933, 1934). These contradictory findings probably resulted from a failure to examine passages for structural similarities and differences as well as similarities and differences in topics and content. Recent research indicates that recall is facilitated when passages have the same structure but different content, while it is inhibited if passages have different structures but the same content.

Meyer (1971) looked at instability in just which ideas are produced on successive free-recall attempts from prose with no intervening presentations. Tulving (1967) using lists of words found considerable instability in successive recall attempts. With natural prose Meyer found that on successive recall attempts subjects recall somewhat different sets of items, although averaging about the same total number of items recalled. Stability in successive recalls from prose was not much greater than that obtained by Tulving with word lists. Thus, one free-recall attempt does not exhaust the actual number of ideas stored in memory from lists of words or passages.

Clustering in recall protocols from prose has also been studied. Research with word lists has demonstrated that the order in which word lists are recalled in a free-recall task is strongly influenced by the associative and conceptual relations among words (Bower, Clark, Lesgold, & Winzenz, 1969). Frase (1969) and Kircher (1971) both used simple passages contrived so that the sentences would make sense when randomly assigned to different sentence orders. For some passages they found increasing clustering of related ideas from the passages with more learning trials while in other passages they did not. Meyer (1971) did some preliminary work in studying the relationship between the occurrence of two ideas that were related together in the structure of a passage and the likelihood of the two ideas being recalled together in a recall protocol. Meyer found that although overall recall for a passage was only about 23% of the units of the passage, if a particular unit was recalled, then 70% of the time the unit directly above it in the structure was also recalled. The structures of passages should prove useful for studying clustering in prose.

This dimension of structure is an important attribute of prose. The organizational structure of a passage shows how the ideas in a passage were organized to convey its author's message. This dimension of prose is the prime factor differentiating prose from lists of words. Since studies investigating the generalizability of prose of findings in word lists dealing with serial position, proactive and retroactive inhibition, and, to a large extent, clustering have ignored the structure of the content of passages, these contradictory and confusing findings of studies with prose have resulted. Largely responsible for the investigators failure to consider the structure dimension was the lack of conceptual tools necessary to analyze the structure of a passage. Many of these necessary tools are now available through recent developments in linguistics (Fillmore, 1968; Grimes, 1972; Halliday, 1967a, 1967b, 1968; van Dijk, 1972) and artificial intelligence (Simmons, 1968, 1971; Simmons & Slocum, 1970; Schank, 1971). A few psychologists (Crothers, 1972, 1973; Frederiksen, 1972; Kintsch, 1974; Meyer, 1975a, 1975b) have utilized a number of these recent developments to develop prose analysis procedures to identify the structure of text. Application of prose analysis procedures of this type can be used in the future to clarify and explain the contradictory findings of these studies which have often ignored the structure differences between prose and word lists while investigating phenomena commonly found in word lists.

Although most investigations that have examined recall from prose have investigated the generalizability of the effects of variables studied with word lists, some have not. In these few studies, the only goal of the research was to examine which ideas were remembered from a passage under free-recall conditions, and then to relate those ideas to aspects of the information in the passage. These studies include the work of Bartlett (1932), Gomulicki (1956), Johnson (1970), Meyer and McConkie (1973), and Meyer (1975a) as well as the studies of Crothers (1972, 1973), Dawes (1966), Frederiksen (1972), Kintsch and Keenan (1972), and Meyer (1971, 1975a) which relate recall to aspects of structure in a passage.

Relating Recall to Nonorganizational Qualities in Text

In his book, *Remembering,* Bartlett (1932) described the types of information recalled by college students from passages over increasing time intervals from the initial presentation of a passage. He reported that accurate recall of prose is the exception and distortion is to be expected. Bartlett explained that recall was not a reproduction of a passage's ideas, but inferential reconstruction of the passage from a few assimilated details in the light of a person's "schema" at the time of recall. This "schema" is the organization of aspects of a person's past experiences that influence his current perception. New information is assimilated into existing schema and, except for a few outstanding facts, losses its particular identity. This view is somewhat similar to Ausubel's (1965) view that general ideas subsume details, whose individuality is soon forgotten.

Other investigators of recall from prose (Gomulicki, 1956; Kintsch *et al.,* 1974; Meyer, 1971, 1975a) have reported that distortion or intrusions of information external to a passage rarely occurred in their studies. The distortion reported by Bartlett is probably due to two factors. The first factor is the great lapses in time from presentation of a passage to its recall. The recall protocols in

Gomulicki, Meyer, and Kintsch *et al.*'s studies were written immediately or soon after presentation of the prose, while some of Bartlett's protocols were written as long as ten years after hearing a passage. The second factor is the differences in the passages used. Gomulicki used short and simple, unambiguous descriptive text or narratives, as did Kintsch *et al.*; Meyer's study employed factual, concrete, and unambiguous expository text. In contrast, Bartlett's text tended to be ambiguous. His selection, called *The War of Ghosts,* frequently used by later prose researchers, is a narrative. It is an Indian folktale, and aspects of it tend to be ambiguous and confusing. Perhaps a structural analysis of this passage could point out ambiguous aspects which may coincide with segments of the prose where Bartlett found distortions.

Gomulicki (1956) examined recall protocols from 37 prose passages, ranging from 13 to 95 words; two passages were descriptive text and the others were narratives. His goal was to identify and classify the kinds of information that dropped from recall of longer passages and that which remained in recall protocols. His results showed that descriptive, modifying segments of prose were poorly recalled in longer passages, while "agent-action-effect units" were recalled best. This observation and description of this well-recalled information is of particular interest in the light of recent developments in linguistics. Gomulicki's agent-action-effect units correspond to Fillmore's (1968) cases and Grimes' (1972) roles that are most actively involved in an action, the agent role and the patient and latter roles. Gomulicki claimed that an abstractive process occurred as subjects selected information from prose for memory. He pointed out that subject's recall protocols stated information that most closely corresponded to the total meaning of the passage and omitted secondary themes and descriptions.

Johnson (1970) also studied the relationship between aspects of prose and recall. He attempted to ascertain whether the ideas recalled from a passage were also those ideas which raters believed to be important to the passage. In order to get an index of the importance of an idea to a passage, which he called its structural importance, he had subjects divide narrative prose selections into pausal units, units where pauses seemed appropriate before and after a unit of text. Then other subjects were instructed to delete one-fourth, one-half, or three-fourths of these units according to their importance to the passage; the most important units were to be those not deleted. These units that were not deleted were given the highest structural importance scores, while the lowest scores went to the units that were first deleted, under the one-fourth deletion instructions. This structural importance score was found to be related to recall; that is, units with high-structural importance scores were better remembered.

Meyer and McConkie (1973) studied the relationship between the recall of ideas from a passage and the scores assigned to them by raters, according to their perceived importance of the passage. This perceived or rated importance measure was similar to Johnson's structural importance measure. Instead of assigning scores to units on the basis of a deletion task, in Meyer and McConkie's study ten independent raters rated each idea unit from a passage on a seven-point scale as to its importance to the message of the passage. The average rating of each unit was accepted as the rated importance score for that unit. Also, in this same study the investigators studied the relationship between the recall of ideas and their position in the content structure of the passage, or height in the organizational structure of the passage. In the two passages studied the recall of ideas from the passages was related to the ideas height in the content structure of the passage; ideas high in the structure were recalled better than ideas lower in the structure. Correlations between recall frequency scores and rated importance scores for ideas were approximately zero for one passage, while they were statistically significant for the other passage. In addition, in the passage where rated importance scores were not related to recall, they were not related to the scores based on the height of information in the content structure either. On the other hand, in the passage where rated importance scores were related to recall, they also were correlated significantly with scores based on the height of the ideas in the structure. A partial correlation between rated importance scores and recall frequency scores with scores based on height in the structure partialed out indicated that most of the relationship between rated importance and recall could be accounted for by the height of the idea units in the structure of the passage.

Meyer (1975a) conducted a study to see if the emphasis given certain information in a passage by its author, labeled *signaling,* could account for which ideas people tend to remember from a passage. Signaling is a noncontent aspect of prose which gives emphasis to certain aspects of the semantic content or points out aspects of the structure of the content. Words of signaling are not included in analysis of the structure and content of a passage since they do not add new content and relations, but simply accent information already contained in the content structure of the passage. Signaling in passages shows an author's perspective on the relative importance of the content related in his passage. A similar type of emphasis has been identified in sentences by Halliday (1968) as theme and by Grimes (1972) as staging. Signaling in Meyer's study included devices such as an author stating "There are *two* approaches. *One* is ____ and the *second* is ____," prematurely revealed information abstracted from content occurring later in a text, summary statements, and pointer words, like "an important point is ____."

In this study groups of college undergraduates read and recalled immediately after the reading and one week later passages with signaling and corresponding passages with the signaling removed. The presence of signaling tended to increase recall, but this effect was not statistically significant. The generally small signaling effect may have resulted from the fact that signaling was aimed primarily at information high in the content structure which was recalled well regardless of the presence of signaling. There was some evidence that signaling aimed at the middle levels of the content structure increased recall substantially.

In addition, certain types of signaling appeared to influence recall more than others. Anticipatory lists of topics to be discussed in a passage appeared to represent the most effective type of signaling investigated in the study. Also, in two of four pairs of passages with and without signaling there was some indication that substantial amounts of signaling robbed attention from non-signaled information low in the content structure, and subsequently reduced its recall. Thus, signaling, as identified, was not found to be powerful in determining what information is recalled from prose. Future research is needed to look at different types of signaling and signaling applied at different levels of a passage's structure.

Of all the variables studied, the structure variable appears to be the most promising in differentiating between ideas in a passage that will be well or poorly recalled. In addition, there is some evidence (Meyer & McConkie, 1973) that much of the effect of serial position and of rated importance can actually be explained in terms of the influence of the content structure on recall. Next will be discussed studies that have examined the relationship between structure in prose and recall.

Research Examining the Relation between Structure in Prose and Recall

Dawes (1966) was probable the first investigator to identify certain relationships between ideas in a passage and to examine recall protocols for the presence of these ideas and relationships. Dawes wrote meaningful declarative statements to assert set relationships, such as exclusion, disjunctive, inclusion, and identity relationships between two elements. He combined these statements of set relationships into passages. Then, Dawes examined recall protocols from these passages for any distortion of the set relationships and any differences in their recall frequency. Dawes' pioneering effort in relating structure in a passage to recall has prompted considerable interest in this undertaking. Other investigators, such as Frederiksen (1972), have used his passage of set relationships. Dawes' work was a starting point, but more comprehensive analysis techniques were necessary to analyze relationships in most passages since few if any passages not contrived by experimenters contain primarily set relationships. Even with Dawes' passages, many other relationships besides set relationships exist.

Frederiksen (1972), using one of Dawes' passages (Circle Island) comprised of set relations, diagrammed the passage as network of set relations. He made an additional diagram to indicate implications among propositions, information which could be inferred from a passage although not explicitly stated. In brief, Frederiksen examined the effects of various types of reading instructions on the recall of both explicitly stated concepts and relations and those requiring inference. Frederiksen's graph of the semantic structure of the Circle Island passage simply depicted the set relationships of the passage. A more comprehensive prose analysis system than the one described in his study is needed to diagram the relationships in natural prose. Frederiksen (1973) realized this need and has revised his prose analysis prcoedures, basing it on Simmons' work (1968, 1971; Simmons & Slocum, 1970).

Meyer (1971) analyzed the structure of ideas in natural prose. The two passages analyzed were approximately 500 words in length and were extracted from articles appearing in *Scientific American* magazine. The division of each passage into idea units was carried out subjectively. The investigator selected the most important idea in the first paragraph, then proceeded to select other ideas that described or gave further information about this main idea. Each resulting idea unit was felt to be a single, meaningful piece of information conveyed by the passage, whether it consisted of a word, a definition, or a phrase in the passage. A tree structure resulted from this division of each passage into units which described or modified other units; the tree structure spatially depicted the hierarchical structure among the ideas in the passage.

As a test of reliability, two independent judges were asked to arrange the idea units in an outline of the passage. A statement of each unit was printed on an individual slip of paper. The judges read each passage, then placed these slips in outline form on a sheet of paper marked off with a series of vertical lines. A main ideas was to be placed at the extreme left of the paper. An idea unit directly under it in a logical relationship was to be placed under it physically and displaced one column to the right. This procedure was continued until all idea units of a passage were placed in the outline form. Throughout the outlining task the judges had copies of the passage present and were free to refer to them at any time. The outline structures produced by each judge were compared to the original structure of each passage. For one passage, containing 78 idea units, the judges placed 72 and 74 of the units in positions identical to the original structure. For the other passage, containing 80 idea units, 71 and 72 of the units were in positions identical to the original structure. On those units in which a judge did not agree with the original placement of a unit, the judges did not agree between themselves. It was concluded that this method of identifying the structure of the passages was reliable, producing 91.5% agreement among judges and that the original structures could be accepted as describing the logical relationships among the idea units in the passages.

The height of an idea unit in this structure of a passage related to the likelihood of its being recalled. Ideas high in the structure were remembered more frequently than those low in the structure for both passages studied. This structure variable related to which ideas were recalled from a passage to a much greater extent than the other variables investigated in this study, the serial position of ideas in the passage and the perceived or rated importance of ideas to the passage. As has been previously discussed, the data indicated that much of the effect of serial position and of rated importance can actually be explained in terms of the influence of the structure on recall.

Kintsch and Keenan (1972) also have studied the relationship between structure in prose and recall. Their structural analyses were confined to sentences and short paragraphs. As in Meyer's study with passages, Kintsch and Keenan found that the height of an idea in the hierarchical structure influenced its recall. Ideas higher in the structure were more freuqently recalled than those lower in the structure. Their hierarchical structures are similar to those of Meyer (1971, 1975a).

In contrast, the structures of Crothers (1972, 1973) are not equivalent. Crothers has also studied the relationship between the structure of a passage and recall. Crothers (1972) predicted that ideas at superordinate nodes in his hierarchical structure of a passage would be better recalled than ideas at subordinate nodes. In addition, he expected secondary subtrees in his structure to be recalled less frequently than primary subtrees. These same predictions were made in Meyer's study (1971) and were supported by her recall data. In contrast, these hypotheses were not supported in Crothers' study. The differences are not due to any differences in the recall data collected, but to differences in the hierarchical structures resulting from the two discourse analysis methods. Ideas (nebula *outside* our galaxy, nebula *inside* our galaxy) that surprised Crothers by their low position in his structure and high recall are located at high positions in Meyer's structural analysis for the passage, and thus their high recall would be expected from Meyer's structure.

In summary, a number of recent investigations with prose have been conducted to examine the relation between structure and aspects of recall. Dawes investigated simple set relationships, and Fredericksen related graphs of explicit and inferred set relationships to recall. Meyer's research showed that a structure based on the relationships between ideas in a passage related to recall. Ideas higher in this structure tended to be better recalled from the passage than lower-level units. Kintsch and Keenan's study with sentences and paragraphs was in accordance with Meyer's findings. In contrast, Crothers' structure was not related to recall. His structures differ considerably from those of Meyer. This points out that although these researchers have all been interested in studying the structure of prose, their analyses of prose and resulting structures are not identical, but vary on different dimensions. Meyer (1975a) presents a discussion of these dimensions on which the prose analysis procedures of a number of investigators differ.

Although the investigators are not in complete agreement as to the form that the structure of prose is to take, they all appear to feel that this structure variable is important to study in order to increase knowledge in the area of learning from prose. When comparing the structure variable to any of the other variables that have been studied, the structure variable certainly appears to have the most potential for explaining which ideas in prose are well recalled and which are rarely recalled.

RESULTS OF STUDIES EXAMINING THE INFLUENCE
OF THE CONTENT STRUCTURE ON RECALL

Both Meyer (1971) and Kintsch and Keenan (1972) have found that the superordinate information, high in the content structure of a passage, is recalled better after reading a passage than subordinate information found lower in the structure. In these studies there was no control for the nature of the content of the passage high and low in the structure. Thus, the content high in the passage may have been more concrete, therefore having greater potential for imagery (Anderson, 1974; Yuille & Paivio, 1969), or the terms or concepts may have had a higher cultural frequency, or varied on some other dimension. The first study (Meyer, 1975a) to be reported employed better controlled stimulus materials to investigate the same question, whether information high in the content structure of a passage tends to be recalled better than information low in the structure. The second study (Meyer, 1975a) examines the influence of the content structure on the whole pattern of recall from a passage. In this study an investigation is made into the degree of correspondence between frequency of recall by a group of readers of units in the content structure of two different passages having different content, but the same structure and types of relationships among the content units.

For this research, Meyer (1975a) used a technique for analyzing a passage which yields a tree structure representing the structure of the relationships asserted in the text. The discourse analysis technique is based on Fillmore's (1968) case grammar and Grimes' (1972) semantic grammar of propositions. It views a passage as being a complex proposition which can be decomposed into subpropositions bearing certain relations to one another. Propositions are composed of a predicate and its arguments. There are assumed to be two types of predicates, with that term being used in the logician's sense: lexical predicates and rhetorical predicates. Lexical predicates are centered in a lexical item, typically verbs and their adjuncts, and take arguments which are ideas from the content of the text. The lexical predicates are related to the arguments by case or role relationships. Rhetorical predicates are not centered in lexical items, but still take arguments. These arguments can be single ideas from the content of the text, but are more often lexical propositions or other rhetorical propositions. The rhetorical predicates frequently appear at higher levels in the structure of a passage, representing intersentential relationships. The rhetorical predicates consist of a finite number of labels which classify and describe the relationships, particularly intersentential and interparagraph relations, found in prose. A complete description is available (Meyer, 1975a) of this technique for analyzing prose along with an explanation of how it compares to Meyer's (1971) previous procedure and procedures for other psychologists.

The passages used in the studies to be reported have from 8 to 15 levels in their hierarchically arranged content structures; the passages contain approximately 575 words. The ideas at the various levels in the content structure represent words and phrases from the text. In the passages used in the studies there were approximately 150 ideas or content words in each passage's content structure. In addition, in each structure there were approximately 150 labels comprised of case relations and rhetorical predicates, relationships units, which classified the relationships among these content words. Copies of the materials used in the studies reported in this chapter can be found in Meyer (1975a).

Experiment 1

In order to control for the nature of the content of the passage high and low in the content structure, six passages were carefully produced. Two were written on each of three topics: Nuclear Breeder Reactors, Schizophrenia, and Parakeets. On each of these topics a paragraph was written which was included in both passages of that topics. This is called the *target paragraph*. One of the passages on each topic, the high passage, was written in such a way that, when analyzed, the information in the target paragraph stood at the top of the content structure. The other passage, the low passage, was so written that in its content structure the information in the target paragraph stood at the lowest levels. Both passages on the same topic were the same length, and had the same number of words occurring prior to and following the target paragraph. Thus, physical position in the passage was constant.

The structural analysis of these passages appears to be reliable (Meyer, 1975a). Meyer and Grimes independently analyzed the passages and were in 95% agreement on the content structure. Disagreement centered on specifying the relationship labels; there was no disagreement on which content was high and low in the content structures.

Two groups of 21 Cornell University undergraduates each participated in the experiment. Subjects in each group read and recalled three passages. Group I read the Breeder Reactor High, Schizophrenia Low and Parakeet High passages. Group II read the Breeder Reactor Low, Schizophrenia High, and Parakeet Low passages. Order of presentation was counterbalanced within groups.

The experiment was conducted in two sessions. In the first, subjects read each passage and produced a written free recall of it immediately after reading. In the second session, one week later, subjects were again asked for a free recall of each passage. Then they were given lists of the content words found in the target paragraphs of each passage and asked to produce a third free recall of each passage, using these words to aid them. This is called the cued-recall task.

Subjects were tested in groups of five to fifteen. The entire task required about 3 hr, and subjects were paid $5.25 for their time. The experiment included other groups reading other types of passages to examine other variables.

The recall protocols were scored by assigning them 1 point for each content unit or relationship from the original content structure which was included in the recall. They were scored for substantive content, rather than for exact wording. Thirteen recall protocols were independently scored by two scorers, who agreed 99% of the time on where items from the content structure should be counted as present or absent in the recall. Complete information on scoring procedures can be found in Meyer (1975a).

Recall scores for the target paragraphs are presented in Table 1. Delayed recalls of the Parakeet passages have not been scored. As can be seen, in every case recall was significantly higher when the paragraph was high in the content structure, rather than low. This result was strong and consistent. This was not due to differences in passage difficulty, since total recall scores for the entire passages did not differ: 34% of the units were recalled from both Nuclear Breeder Reactor passages, and for the Schizophrenia passages 25% were recalled from the High version and 28% from the Low.

Table 2 reports the difference in target paragraph recall scores between immediate and delayed testing, and between delayed free and delayed cued testing. An analysis of variance of these data indicated significantly more loss over time for Target Paragraphs when low than when high in the structure ($F(1, 80\ df) = 5.814$, $p < .025$), with no significant effect for passage topic and no interaction. Difference between delayed free and cued recall did not vary with passage topic or content structure position. Thus, presence of the cues produced approximately equal increments of recall, over delayed free recall scores, in all conditions.

It appears, then that information high in the content structure of a passage is more likely to be recalled immediately after reading, and is subject to less forgetting over time.

One explanation for the recall superiority of high information might be that, since information high in the passage sets the theme of the passage, it is repeated

TABLE 1

Mean Recall for Target Paragraphs in High- and Low-Content Structure Positions for Immediate and Delayed Free Recall and Delayed Cued Recall Conditions

Target paragraph topic	Recall condition	Content structure high	Position low	df	t	Probability
Breeder Reactor (46 units in target)	Immediate free recall	18.05	13.43	40	1.981	.05
	Delayed free recall	14.81	4.48	40	5.186	.0005
	Delayed cued recall	25.57	19.67	40	1.945	.05
Schizophrenia (46 units in target)	Immediate free recall	19.71	13.90	40	2.319	.025
	Delayed free recall	14.14	7.09	40	2.823	.005
	Delayed cued recall	26.00	19.57	40	2.527	.01
Parakeets (88 units in target)	Immediate free recall	44.24	34.57	40	2.75	.005

TABLE 2

Mean Differences Between Immediate and Delayed Free Recall Scores, and Between Delayed Cued and Delayed Free Recall Scores for Target Paragraphs in High- and Low-Content Structure Positions

Passage	Content structure position	Mean recall condition differences	
		Immediate free–delayed free	Delayed cued–delayed free
Breeder Reactor	High	3.24	10.76
	Low	8.95	15.19
Schizophrenia	High	5.57	11.86
	Low	6.81	12.67

more frequently in the passage. To check this explanation, the High and Low versions of the Nuclear Breeder Reactor passage were searched for instances of four types of repetition of content units from the target paragraph: verbatim repetition, substantive repetition, detailed restatement and implicit reference. It was found that 12 of the 46 idea units in the target paragraph were repeated at least once in the text of the high version of the passage, while eight were repeated in the low version. Of these nine were repeated more frequently in the High version, and five were repeated more frequently in the Low version. Thus there was somewhat more repetition in the High version. However, amount of repetition did not seem to be related to likelihood of recall. Of the nine units repeated more frequently in the high version of the passage, eight were recalled better from that version. Of the five units repeated more frequently in the Low version, four were better recalled in the High version. These data were taken from immediate recalls, and the related recall showed an even greater tendency for better recall of units from the High version, regardless of repetition frequency. Thus, while there was slightly more repetition of target paragraph information in the High version of the passage, this could not account for the superior recall from that version.

The three findings of this study were:

1. Information is more likely to be recalled from a passage if it is high in the content structure than if it is low.

2. Information is more likely to be retained over time from a passage if it is high in the content structure than if it is low.

3. Providing cues for recall one week after the original reading increases the recall of information high and low in the content structure of the passage about equally.

First, these findings point out the importance of the content structure of a passage as a determiner of the learning and retention of information from the passage.

Second, these findings bear on various theoretical positions regarding learning from prose. The recall superiority of high information immediately after learning could be accounted for from either a selectivity in learning or a retrieval position. That is, it may be that the content structure guides the reader's attentional processes, causing him to be more likely to select for storage that information high in the passage structure. On the other hand, it may be that high and low information are equally stored, but that the laws of retrieval are such that high information is more likely to be recalled under free recall conditions. The present study does not allow the testing of these two alternatives.

In order to discriminate between these two alternative explanations some data are being collected. Collected so far are data from eighteen teachers attending a night class at Western Connecticut State College. Half of these subjects read the Breeder Reactor High and Parakeet High passages, while the other half read the Breeder Reactor Low and Parakeet Low passages. The subjects produced a written free recall immediately after reading which was immediately followed by a cued-recall task. The results show these subjects to recall a third to a half fewer ideas than subjects in the earlier experiment, but the same pattern of superior recall of the target paragraph high in the content structure is evident. The cues appear to assist recall for both high- and low-structural positions for both passages to about the same extent. Even with the assistance of cues, information high in the content structure is better recalled immediately after reading the passage. Thus, the data thus far collected support the first alternative that more information high in the structure is actually stored in memory.

The greater loss of recall of low information over time could be due either to a differential rate of loss from memory, or to structural changes which cause lower information to be less accessible to retrieval for free recall, though the information is still present in memory and is accessible in other ways. The subsumption theory of Ausubel (1965) takes the first position, suggesting that peripheral information (that which is lower in the content structure) is subsumed by the more central information (that higher in the structure) over time, thus losing its independent identity and becoming less available for recall. The cued recall data provide some help in discrimination among these theoretical positions. If the recall loss were due simply to structural changes which make the information less accessible to free recall, though still present in memory, it would appear reasonable that it would be recalled under cued conditions. A reasonable prediction might then be that information low in the structure, which has been most subject to loss of accessibility to free recall, would be aided most by the presence of cues. Although the data pattern was in this direction, the differences were not significant. Thus, low information appears to be more rapidly lost from memory or subsumed over time, and not to simply become inaccessible to free recall.

Third, the results from this study have certain practical implications. They suggest that those preparing curriculum materials should be careful to place important information high in the content structure of the instructional text, to insure its retention. Also, the type of text analysis developed, which reveals the structure of the content of a passage, may well have pedagogical value itself. If some students fail to detect the interrelations among ideas in the text, thus, acquiring a fragmented representation of the content, then giving them experience with this sort of text analysis in which they are able to see the total structural pattern of a passage may aid them in their reading.

There is potential for creating a valuable diagnostic tool for teachers, reading specialists, and school psychologists from research establishing norms for age levels on recall of high- and low-structure information from passages listened to and read. It may be that children with certain learning disabilities are not able to differentiate high structure information, which correspond to what educators have called main ideas, from low structure information, corresponding to details. They may not be processing for memory storage this higher level information to the degree of the more successful peers; instead, they may be distracted from the passage's message by paying undue attention to the lower level, detailed information.

Although the author has not examined recall protocols from children with learning disabilities in relation to the content structure of prose, a study (Meyer, 1976) was conducted with three different ability groups of sixth graders. The mean IQ scores of the three groups were 111, 100, and 86. Regardless of ability group the students remembered significantly more high structure information after listening to a passage than low structure information ($F_{2,75}$ = 496.05, $p <$ .001). The differences in the amount of information remembered among the three ability groups were statistically significant, but there was no statistically significant interaction between ability groups and recall of information high and low in the content structure. Thus, as with college students, information high in the content structure was better recalled than information low in the structure for the sixth-graders regardless of ability group. The brighter children simply recalled more information occurring both high and low in the content structure than children of lower ability. Developmental studies are necessary to look at when and how this differentiation in the recall of high- and low-level information occurs both in listening and reading.

Experiment 2

The second variety of study was designed to examine the degree of correspondence in recall frequency patterns for passages differing in the content units of their content structures, but having the same structural form and same specific relationship units. In order to examine the influences of the pattern of specific relationships in the content structure on recall, the Breeder Reactor High passage and the Schizophrenia High passage, mentioned in the first study, were designed to have the same pattern of specific relations in their content structures, but different content. The structural similarity of these passages was accomplished by following a series of steps. First, the Breeder Reactor High passage, a passage extracted from *Scientific American* magazine (Seaborg & Bloom, 1970), was analyzed and its content structure was identified. Then, an identical structure of relations was drawn with its content missing. The top levels of these structures related together problems with a solution to these problems. Thus, new content to be placed into this structure had to logically fit this organizational format, a typical plot structure; that is, the content topic had to possess problems and a solution. Once the topic of schizophrenia was found to meet these requirements, content related to the topic was placed in appropriate slots in the content barren structure of relationships. Then, the Schizophrenia High passage was written to express this set of relationships. Thus, both passages, when analyzed by Meyer's (1975a) analysis technique yield the identical content structure, except for the specific lexical units which enter into the structure. The relationship categories are all identical for the two passages.

Thus, the Breeder Reactor High passage and the Schizophrenia High passage have identical structures of specific relationships. In addition, the target paragraphs, discussed in the first experiment, dealing with breeder reactors and schizophrenia also are identical in structure. Therefore, the target paragraphs of all of the four versions of the Breeder Reactor and Schizophrenia passages have identical structures. In addition, four corresponding and additional versions to these passages with signaling (Meyer, 1975a) removed were written; thus, the passages and included target paragraphs for each pair of with-signaling and without-signaling passages have identical structures of relations, as well as identical content.

Four groups of 21 Cornell University undergraduates each participated in the experiment. The procedure and scoring was exactly the same as that described in the first experiment, except that two additional groups were added. These additional groups correspond to Group I and Group II, but instead of reading the passages in their original form with-signaling the words of signaling were removed from the passages of Group III and Group IV.

The recall frequency data from these passages were examined to see the degree to which the same structure results in the recall of the same items regardless of content. A Pearson Product-Moment Correlation Coefficient was computed between the recall frequency data for the Breeder Reactor High passage and that for the Schizophrenia High passage. The number of subjects ($N = 21$) recalling a unit in the content structure was tallied for each of the 193 units in the structure. The number of subjects who recalled each idea unit in the Breeder Reactor High passage was tallied. In addition, the number of subjects who recalled each idea unit in the Schizophrenia High passage was also tallied. Then, a correlation was run between these recall frequency scores for corresponding units in the two passages. The Pearson Product-Moment Correlation Coefficient for the Breeder Reactor High and Schizophrenia High with-signaling versions of the passages in the immediate free recall condition was .55 ($p < .001$). This degree of correspondence between the recall frequency patterns of these two passages was also found for the Breeder Reactor High and Schizophrenia High passages without-signaling and in the other recall conditions: the correlations were .52 ($p < .001$) for the without-signaling versions for immediate free recall, .56 ($p < .001$) for the with-signaling versions for delayed free recall, and .59 ($p < .001$) for the without-signaling versions for delayed free recall.

Table 3 compares these correlations for passages with the same structure of relations, but different content to correlations between passages with identical structures and content. The results are consistent for both the Breeder Reactor and Schizophrenia passages. The recall frequency patterns correspond to the greatest extent for with-signaling and without-signaling versions of the same passage in the same recall condition, next for the immediate and delayed free-recall conditions for the same passage, and least for the different passages with the same structure.

There are several conclusions which can be drawn from the data in Table 3. First, there is great stability in free-recall data in terms of the frequency with which different units are recalled by different groups of subjects. Recall frequency scores for with-signaling and without-signaling versions of the passages correlated about .88. Second, some of this correspondence can be accounted for in terms of passage structure alone. Two passages containing the same logical structure, but different content, correlate about .55 in the recall frequency scores of corresponding units. Third, from this it is seen that passage structure alone is not the only factor which determines the likelihood of units in the passage being recalled. The nature of the content occupying specific positions in the structure appears to have a substantial effect on whether these items will be well or poorly recalled. In a previous study (Meyer, 1971) it was observed that numbers tended to be recalled well, whether positioned high or low in the content structure of a passage. In the passages used in this study, there was no attempt to place this type of content at similar positions in the passages containing different content. Thus, if numbers tend to be recalled particularly well, this would reduce the correlation between recall frequency scores of the units of the two passages. To find out whether this was the case, the same correlations were computed on recall frequency scores of the passages having different content, but after having first deleted all data for units where numbers resided in either of the two passages. This reduced the number of pairs of scores in the correlation analysis from 193 to 172, and raised the correlation from .55 (accounting for 30% of the variance) to .63 (accounting for 40% of the variance). Thus, it was found that this particular type of content tends to be especially well remembered; numbers were, in general, better recalled than corresponding content units from the other passage.

In examining the .55 degrees of relation between the two passages with the same structure of relations, but different content, it is not apparent how much

TABLE 3

Pearson Product Moment Correlation Coefficients between Recall Frequency Patterns of the Content
Structure in Various Conditions

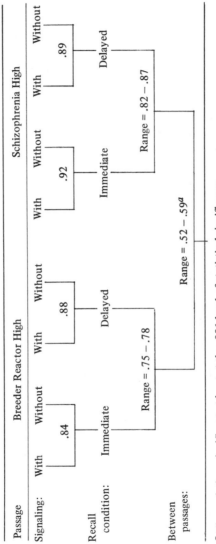

[a]All correlations significant at least at the .001 level of statistical significance.

of this relationship is due to the general effect of height in the content structure versus how much is due to the specific similarity of the function of the idea units as guaranteed by the same relationships in the content structures of both passages.

In order to examine this situation, any correspondence due solely to the same specific relationships in the two passages was eliminated. This was accomplished by identifying the height in the content structure of each unit in the Breeder Reactor High passage, and the number of people recalling that unit. Then, the recall freqeuncy of each unit in the content structure was replaced by the recall frequency of another unit with the same height in the structure through random selection. This procedure was followed for every idea unit in the content structure so that the height in the content structure of each unit was preserved while the specific functional relationships characterizing each unit was destroyed. A correlation was computed between these mixed recall frequency scores for the Breeder Reactor High passage and the original recall frequency scores of the Schizophrenia High passage. This provided a measure of the degree of relationship between the two passages due solely to height in the content structure.

The Pearson Product-Moment Correlation Coefficient for this relationship was .22 ($p < .001$) in comparison to the .55 ($p < .001$) correlation with the presence of both the factors of height in the structure and the same pattern of specific relations. Therefore, it appears that most of the relationship between the recall patterns from passages with identical structures is due to the similarity of their pattern of specific relationships in the structure and not just to height in the structure. Thus, both the factors of height in the structure and the pattern of specific types of relationships are needed to account for the correspondence in the patterns of recall from passages with identical structures of specific relations and different contents.

Through analyzing numerous passages and examining recall data the author came to believe that the pattern of specific relationships at the top levels of the content structure has a greater influence on what units are recalled than the pattern of relationships at the lower levels in the content structure. At the lower levels of the content structure the particular content of idea units determines whether or not they are recalled rather than the specific function the information takes in the passage in relation to other information. Data from this study were available to test this hypothesis.

The data used to investigate the validity of this hypothesis were the recall scores for each idea unit in the breeder reactor and schizophrenia target paragraphs read high and low in the content structure. The breeder reactor and schizophrenia target paragraphs have the same structure of specific relations and different content. The correlation between the recall frequency scores for the idea units in the breeder reactor and schizophrenia target paragraphs when the paragraphs were high in the structure would indicate the influence of the pattern of specific relationships at the top levels of the content structure on which units are recalled. On the other hand, correlations between the recall frequency scores of the idea units when these same paragraphs were low in the structure would indicate the influence of the pattern of specific relationships at the low levels of the content structure on which units are recalled. Thus, if the pattern of specific relations high in the structure greatly influences recall, while this pattern of relations only minimally influences recall low in the structure where peculiarities of content play the most important role in recall, then a correlation between recall frequency patterns from the paragraphs high in the structure should be high, while the correlations for the same paragraphs low in the structure should be low.

Table 4 presents the Pearson Product-Moment Correlation Coefficients between the breeder reactor and schizophrenia target paragraph high in the structure and between these paragraphs low in the structure. As can be seen in Table 4 the correlations between the breeder reactor and schizophrenia target paragraphs are high for the immediate free-recall condition, $r = .83$, and the delayed free-recall condition, $r = .67$. Thus, although the content of the ideas for the two paragraphs was different, the same pattern of specific types of relationships in the paragraphs appears to have produced similar recall patterns from the two paragraphs when they were high in the structure. In contrast, the correlations between these same paragraphs when they occur low in the content structures are approximately zero for the immediate and delayed free-recall conditions as seen in Table 4.

Thus, these data support the hypothesis concerning the differential influence of the pattern of specific relations in the content structure on recall depending on its height in the content structure. A further investigation of this hypothesis was made by examining the correspondence in the recall patterns from target paragraphs with identical patterns of relations as well as content. If content primarily determines the recall of information low in the structure, then the correlations between the recall frequency patterns for target paragraphs low in the structure with identical content structures should be much higher than those for the target paragraphs low in the structure with identical structures, but different content. In fact, the correlations between the recall frequency patterns

TABLE 4

Effect of Pattern of Specific Relationships on Target Paragraph Recall when High and Low in the Content Structure as Indicated by Pearson Product Moment Correlation Coefficients
($N = 46$)

Target paragraphs correlated	Free-recall condition	
(With signaling versions)	Immediate	Delayed
Breeder Reactor High with Schizophrenia High	.83	.67
Breeder Reactor Low with Schizophrenia Low	.09	−.11

from the target paragraphs with identical structures and content should be high when they are high and low in the structure. The recall patterns from the target paragraphs with the presence of signaling and without it were examined since these passages have identical content structures and only differ on signaling, a noncontent aspect of passages.

Table 5 presents the Pearson Product-Moment Correlation Coefficients between the with and without signaling pairs of target paragraphs high and low in the content structure for immediate and delayed free-recall conditions. All of these correlations are high (.74—.97) and show a great deal of similarity in which idea units were recalled from the with-signaling paragraphs and without-signaling paragraphs. When the target paragraphs have the same content and relations in their content structures, their recall patterns are very similar regardless of their height in the content structure.

Subtracting the values, converted by Fisher's z-transformations to z_r scores, in Table 4 from those in Table 5 gives a general indication of the amount of correspondence in recall pattern due to content alone. From the hypothesis under investigation subtracting the correlations from target paragraphs with different content and identical structures from those with identical content structures would be expected to yield large values, representing the effect of content on recall, for the paragraphs low in the structure and smaller values for the paragraph high in the structure. The subtraction for the low-target paragraphs yielded very large values for the immediate free recall condition, $r = .88$, and the delayed free-recall condition, $r = .85$. In contrast, these values were considerably smaller for the target paragraphs high in the structure for the immediate free-recall condition, $r = .44$, and the delayed free-recall condition, $r = .62$. It is evident from these data that the particular content of idea units has a great effect on what is recalled at low levels in the structure, while it has a considerably smaller effect on what is recalled high in the structure. These data support the proposed hypothesis that at the top of the content structure the

TABLE 5

Effect of Both Content and Pattern of Specific Relationships on Target Paragraph Recall when High and Low in the Content Structure as Indicated by Pearson Product Moment Correlation Coefficients ($N = 46$)

With signaling and without signaling pairs of target paragraphs correlated	Free-recall condition	
	Immediate	Delayed
Breeder Reactor High with and without signaling	.93	.93
Breeder Reactor Low with and without signaling	.90	.88
Schizophrenia High with and without signaling	.94	.86
Schizophrenia Low with and without signaling	.89	.74

pattern of relations has a very strong effect on what is recalled, while at the bottom of the structure what is recalled is determined almost entirely by aspects of the particular content of the specific units.

Table 6 displays more supporting evidence for this differential effect of the relations in the content structure on what units are remembered. The correspondence between the patterns of recall is extremely high (.83) from the top levels of the content structure of two passages with different content and the same structure of relations, but when the lower levels of the content structure are included in this correlation the correspondence of the recall patterns from the text drops (.55). This drop is due to the lesser influence of the pattern of specefic relationships in determining recall and the greater effect of particular content on recall. When both content and relations are constant in two passages as they are in the with-signaling and without-signaling versions of passages the correspondence between what is recalled from the passages is very high (.92) since the relations are the same at the top levels where they have the most influence on recall and the content is the same at the lower levels where specific content determines recall.

This study showed that passages with identical structures of specific relations, but different content produce similar patterns of recall. This structural dimension of prose appears to be a useful dimension on which to classify types of passages. Since the structure of relationships at the top levels of a passage's content structure is more powerful in predicting recall than the structure at the bottom levels of a passage's structure, it may be necessary only to classify passages into various types on the basis of their top-level structures. Classifying passages according to this structure variable along with content variables and traditional readability measures would help to ensure equivalency of passages often needed in experiments and for constructing equivalent forms of reading tests. Future research is necessary to determine whether it is the pattern of

TABLE 6
Pearson Product Moment Correlation Coefficients between Immediate Free Recall
Frequency Data

Commonalities of content structure	Segment of text	Text correlated	Correlation coefficient
Pattern of specific relations	Target paragraph	Schizophrenia High with Breeder Reactor High	.83
Pattern of specific relations	Total passage	Schizophrenia High with Breeder Reactor High	.55
Content and pattern of specific relations	Total passage	Schizophrenia High with signals with Schizophrenia High without signals	.92

information is recalled, or whether it is the particular types of role relations and rhetorical predicates that determine recall, or a combination of the two.

Due to these findings that point to the importance of the top levels of the content structure, Meyer and Freedle (1976) examined the effects of four different types of top-level structures. Four passages were written with 58 identical units in their content structures; the passages differed on 11 units in their content structures which corresponded to the different top-level structures, different rhetorical predicates, and a few content units necessary to vary the top-level rhetorical predicates. The results of a recall experiment with these materials clearly showed that certain top-level structures, such an antecedent—consequent relations, are superior in increasing the recall of the identical 58 units than other top-level structures, such as a list of attributes. These findings have practical implications for the design of comparable materials in reading tests and learning experiments, as well as important implication for a theory of learning and memory from discourse.

SUMMARY AND IMPLICATIONS

The content structure variable is important in determing which information is learned from a passage. Information that is located high in a passage's structure is recalled better immediately after reading or listening to it and with time. Less forgetting of this high-level information takes place over time. There are more ideas stored in memory immediately after reading a passage and a week later than a person can recall, but cues to aid retrieval profit low- and high-structure information about equally. Thus, differences in what is remembered from different levels in the content structure is not due solely to high-level information being more easily retrieved. Instead, it appears that more high-level information is actually stored in memory.

The pattern of specific functional relations at the top levels of the content structure appears to dictate which top-level information will be remembered by almost everyone in a group and which will be remembered by only a few. The pattern of specific relationships of the content structure has no influence over what is recalled at the lowest levels of the structure. Information at this level is not recalled by many people and what information is remembered by some people appears to be due to the particularities of the content, striking qualities such as familiar proper names and numbers.

The top-level information in the content structure is similar to what educators have identified as the main ideas of a passage and the interrelationships among these ideas. The top levels of the structure appear to carry the central message of a passage. In contrast, the low-level information in the content structure corresponds to ideas identified as detailed information. The low-level information in the content structure is not part of the central message of a passage although it often supports various aspects of the message; instead, the low levels of the structure appear to contain information peripheral to the central message of a passage.

One reasonable explanation for the data involves the identification by readers of the central organization of information in prose, as represented by the top levels of the content structure. Readers rehearse and subsequently store in long-term memory concepts and interrelationships most centrally related to the higher-level organization in a passage. Peripherally related information is rehearsed less in short-term memory and what information is processed for long-term storage tends to be particular clusters of content that in some way catch the reader's attention. In memory the information that is more centrally related to a passage's overall organization is retained longer, while the peripherally related clusters of information tend to be more quickly forgotten.

In the experiments discussed in this chapter, the recall protocols contained few intrusions or distortions, and aside from omissions the information recalled from a passage tended to be accurate in substance. Spiro (1975) contends this accuracy of recall and the superior recall of high structure information result from the artificial situation of the recall experiment. He explains that in the recall experiment the subject's goal is to remember as much as possible of the passage presented; the subject realizes that relating the information to his existing cognitive structures in memory is not a necessary or useful procedure in the experimental situation. Spiro states that when one interacts with discourse outside of the laboratory experiment he usually selects aspects of the discourse to remember that are of particular interest to him or that update and therefore modify his existing cognitive structures. Thus, in nonexperimental situations Spiro would predict that recall of groups of people would not relate to the content structure of a discourse, but instead by unique to the individuals as dictated by their varying interests and existing knowledge.

The author would concur with Spiro that the recall experiment encourages the subject to select a strategy to accurately remember the passage. However, much of school learning and learning throughout a person's life require him to ascertain a writer or speaker's message. In debate, conversation, and critical reading it is necessary to discover and remember the other person or writer's message, the top level of the content structure of the discourse. The listener must be able to store in memory the patterning of ideas or schema (Anderson, 1976) of the speaker before he can criticize the discourse or agree with it and integrate it into his own thinking. In addition, it is often necessary, particularly in school, to accurately recall the top-level structure or main ideas of another person's oral or written presentation. Thus, the strategy for processing and recalling the top level of the content structure of discourse, containing the main ideas, is a strategy frequently used by people throughout life.

It is true that there are a number of situations in which one does not need to remember the writer's message and can adapt a strategy to remember that structure alone at the top levels of the content structure that influences what information from a passage which updates his knowledge base. This information could come from any level of the content structure of the original passage and its selection for memory would depend on the interests and existing knowledge of the individual. This would seem to be the strategy when a reader skims a passage for particular details of interest.

Whether one is reading for the prupose of accurately remembering the message of a passage or to update his knowledge, it appears that the reader must have some strategy for organizing the information for storage in memory. In the recall experiment and most formal learning situations the most efficient learning strategy is to utilize the schema or top-level content structure of the writer to organize the information for storage in memory. Thus, with this strategy the reader's schema for processing the passage's information and that used by the writer to present the information coincide.

Evidence from the Meyer and Freedle (1976) study points out that when the top-level structure of the writer of a passage contains a message contrary to the reader's belief he will not use the writer's schema, but will provide his own different schema for organizing the ideas of the passage in order to process them for memory and subsequent recall. In this study public school teachers were presented with information about loss of body water with a problem and solution top-level structure, usually an effective discourse schema. The problem in the passage dealt with school coaches requiring atheletes to lose weight to make weight requirements for certain sports by losing harmful amounts of body water. The solution was the immediate dismissal by school boards of coaches requiring loss of body water. The recall of this passage was low compared to other passages used in the study with the same content and different, but comparable, top-level structures. This finding was puzzling. A rating of the passages used in the study by a different but similar group of public school teachers and their written reactions to the passages showed that they believed the solution, dismissal of the coaches, to be a harsh, unfair, and poor solution to the stated problem. The recall by the subjects in the experiment of the top-level structure was very low for the passage, indicating that the subjects did not use the writer's problem – solution schema – but provided their own individual organization to remember the detailed information of the passage. Thus, when a reader employs a strategy requiring the use of a schema different from that used by the writer of the text, his recall will not necessarily relate to the content structure of the passage.

The two main findings of the studies reported in this chapter were (1) that the information high in the content structure is better recalled and retained than low-level information, and (2) that the pattern of relations at the top levels of the content structure is powerful in predicting which top-level idea units will be recalled, while the pattern of relations low in the content structure has no influence on which low-level idea units will be recalled. These findings are in concordance with the explanation that in recall experiments and many learning situations the most efficient learning strategy is to use the writer or speaker's schema — the top level of the content structure of a passage — to organize the information presented for storage in memory. When the writer's schema is incongruent with one's belief or purpose in reading a passage, the reader may provide his own, different schema. In memory, information stored with the assistance of the writer's structure or one's own structure no doubt becomes stored in different structures or schemata as the ideas are integrated in time with existing and new knowledge.

Further research is needed to determine how people identify the major organizing information in prose, the top-level information in the content structure. Developmental research is required to show when people begin to process the main ideas and filter out peripheral information in normal reading and listening behavior. Research is also needed concerning what happens with time to information paralleling the top levels of the content structure in memory, and how, or whether, new schemata of relationships in memory are formed after reading a number of passages dealing with the same topic. There is much potential for the use of the content structure as a tool to understand the processing, storage, and alteration with time of information to be learned and remembered. The content structure variable in itself is valuable in clarifying many questions resulting from investigations of learning from prose, and for solving practical problems.

The content structure can be used to investigate practical problems in reading. The recall protocols written by students after reading a passage can be analyzed for their content structures. The content structures from the recall protocols of students with reading problems can be compared with the content structures from recall protocols of effective readers. The content structure can also be used to specify what types of information and types of organization are employed by students when they are instructed to read for different purposes, such as main ideas, details, and skimming. A theory of writing questions can be derived from the use of the content structure to define what kinds of information questions tap. In conclusion, there are potentially many uses for this variable of the content structure in reading and memory research.

REFERENCES

Anderson, R. C. Concretization and sentence learning. *Journal of Educational Psychology,* 1974, 66, 179–183.

Anderson, R. C. The notion of schemata and the educational enterprise. In R. C. Anderson, R. J. Spiro, & W. E. Montague (Eds.), *Schooling and the acquisition of knowledge.* Hillsdale, New Jersey: Lawrence Erlbaum Assoc., 1976.

Ausubel, D. P. Cognitive structure and the facilitation of meaningful verbal learning. In R. C. Anderson & D. P. Ausubel (Eds.), *Readings in the psychology of cognition.* New York: Holt, Rinehart & Winston, 1965. Pp. 103–115.

Ausubel, D. P., Robbins, L. C., & Blake, E., Jr. Retroactive inhibition and facilitation in learning of school materials. *Journal of Educationa! Psychology,* 1957, 48, 334–349.

Barlett, F. C. *Remembering: A study in experimental and social psychology.* Cambridge, England: Cambridge University Press, 1932.

Bower, G. H., Clark, M. C., Lesgold, A. M., & Winzenz, D. Hierarchical retrieval schemes in recall of categorized word lists. *Journal of Verbal Learning and Verbal Behavior,* 1969, **8**, 322–343.

Carroll, J. B. *Learning from verbal discourse in educational media: Review of the literature.* Final Report Project 7-1069. Princeton, New Jersey: Educational Testing Service, 1971.

Crothers, E. J. Memory structure and the recall of discourse. In R. O. Freedle & J. B. Carroll (Eds.), *Language comprehension and the acquisition of knowledge.* New York: Wiley, 1972. Pp. 247–284.

Crothers, E. J. The psycholinguistic structure of knowledge. In K. Romney & K. Wexler (Eds.), *Cognitive organization and psychological processes.* National Academy of Sciences, 1973.

Crouse, J. H. Transfer and retroaction in prose learning. *Journal of Educational Psychology,* 1970, **61**, 226–228.

Crouse, J. H. Retroactive interference in reading prose material. *Journal of Educational Psychology,* 1971, **62**, 39–44.

Dawes, R. M. Memory and distortion of meaningful written material. *British Journal of Psychology,* 1966, **57**, 77–86.

Deese, J., & Kaufman, R. A. Serial effects in recall of unorganized and sequentially organized verbal material. *Journal of Experimental Psychology,* 1957, **54**, 180–187.

Dell, J. A. Some observations on the learning of sensible material. *Journal of Educational Psychology,* 1912, **3**, 401–406.

Deverell, A. F. Are reading improvement courses at the university level justified? *Invitational Conferences on Education.* Canadian Educational Association, 1959. Pp. 19–27.

deVilliers, P. A. Imagery and theme in recall of connected discourse. *Journal of Experimental Psychology,* 1974, **103**, 263–268.

Fillmore, C. J. The case for case. In E. Bach & R. Harms (Eds.). *Universals in Linguistic Theory.* New York: Holt, Rhinehart, & Winston, 1968. Pp. 1–81.

Flanagan, J. C. A study of the effect of comprehension of varying speeds of reading. In *American Educational Research on the Foundations of American Education.* Official report, 1939. Pp. 47–50.

Frase, L. T. Paragraph organization or written materials. The influence of conceptual clustering upon level or organization. *Journal of Educational Psychology,* 1969, **60**, 394–401.

Frederiksen, C. H. Effects of task-induced cognitive operations on comprehension and memory processes. In R. O. Freedle & J. B. Carroll (Eds.), *Language comprehension and the acquisition of knowledge.* New York: Wiley, 1972. Pp. 211–246.

Frederiksen, C. H. Representing logico-semantic features of knowledge acquired for discourse. Unpublished article, 1973.

Gillman, S. I. Retroactive inhibition in meaningful verbal learning as a function of similarity and review of interpolated material. *Journal of General Psychology,* 1970, **82**, 51–56.

Glanzer, M., & Cunitz, A. R. Two storage mechanisms in free recall. *Journal of Verbal Learning and Verbal Behavior,* 1966, **5**, 351–360.

Gomulicki, B. R. Recall as an abstractive process. *Acta Psychologica,* 1956, **12**, 77–94.

Grimes, J. E. *The thread of discourse.* Ithaca: Cornell University, 1972.

Halliday, M. A. K. Notes on transitivity and theme in English. *Journal of Linguistics,* 1967a, **3**, 37–81.

Halliday, M. A. K. Notes on transitivity and theme in English, Part 2. *Journal of Linguistics,* 1967b, **3**, 199–244.

Halliday, M. A. K. Notes on transitivity and theme in English, Part 3. *Journal of Linguistics,* 1968, **4**, 179–215.

Jersild, A. Primacy, recency, frequency and vividness. *Journal of Experimental Psychology*, 1929, **12**, 58–70.

Johnson, R. E. Recall of prose as a function of the structure importance of the linguistic units. *Journal of Verbal Learning and Verbal Behavior*, 1970, **9**, 12–20.

Keppel, G. Retroactive and proactive inhibition. In T. R. Dixon & D. L. Horton (Eds.), *Verbal behavior and general behavior therapy*. Englewood Cliffs, New Jersey: Prentice Hall, 1968. Pp. 172–213.

King, D. J., & Cofer, C. N. Retroactive interference in meaningful material as a function of degree of contextual constraint in the original and interpolated learning. *Journal of General Psychology*, 1960, **63**, 145–158.

Kintsch, W. *The representation of meaning in memory*. Hillsdale, New Jersey: Lawrence Erlbaum Assoc., 1974.

Kintsch, W., & Keenan, J. Reading rate and retention as a function of propositions in the base structure of sentences. *Studies in mathematical learning theory and psycholinguistics*. Boulder, Colorado: Computer Laboratory for Instruction in Psychological Research, Publication No. 6, April, 1972.

Kintsch, W., Kozminsky, E., Streby, W. L., McKoon, G., & Keenan, J. M. Comprehension and recall of text as a function of content variables. Unpublished manuscript, University of Colorado, 1974.

Kircher, M. C. The effects of presentation order and repetition on the free recall of prose. Unpublished master's thesis, Cornell University, 1971.

McGeoch, J. A., & McKinney, F. Retroactive inhibition in the learning of poetry. *American Journal of Psychology*, 1933, 1934, **46**, 19–33.

Meyer, B. J. F. Idea units recalled from prose in relation to their position in the logical structure, importance, stability and order in the passage. Unpublished master's thesis, Cornell University, 1971.

Meyer, B. J. F. *The organization of prose and its effects in memory*. Amsterdam, The Netherlands: North-Holland, 1975a.

Meyer, B. J. F. Identification of the structure of prose and its implications for the study of reading and memory. *Journal of Reading Behavior*, 1975b, **7**, 7–47.

Meyer, B. J. F. The structure of prose: Effects on learning and memory and implications for educational practice. In R. C. Anderson, R. J. Spiro, & W. E. Montague (Eds.), *Schooling and the acquisition of knowledge*. Hillsdale, New Jersey: Lawrence Erlbaum Assoc., 1976.

Meyer, B. J. F., & Freedle, R. O. The effects of different discourse types on recall. Paper in process, Educational Testing Service, 1976.

Meyer, B. J. F., & McConkie, G. W. What is recalled after hearing a passage? *Journal of Educational Psychology*, 1973, **65**, 109–117.

Murdock, B. B., Jr. The serial position effect of free recall. *Journal of Experimental Psychology*, 1962, **64**, 482–488.

Richardson, P., & Voss, J. F. Verbal context and recall of meaningful material. *Journal of Experimental Psychology*, 1960, **60**, 417–418.

Rothkopf, E. Z., & Bisbicos, E. Selective facilitative effects of interspersed questions on learning from written material. *Journal of Educational Psychology*, 1967, **58**, 56–61.

Seaborg, G. T., & Bloom, J. L. Fast breeder reactors. *Scientific American*, 1970, **223**, 13.

Schank, R. Intention, memory and computer understanding. Stanford Artificial Intelligence Project Memo AIN-140, 1971.

Shaw, J. C. A test of memory in school children. *Pedagogical Seminary*, 1896, **4**, 61–78.

Simmons, R. F. A semantic analyzer for English sentences. *Mechanical Translation and Computational Linguistics*, 1968, **11**, 1–13.

Simmons, R. F. Some semantic structure for representing English meanings. Paper prepared for COBRE Research Workshop on Language Comprehension and the Acquisition of Knowledge, March 31–April 13, 1971.

Simmons, R. F., & Slocum, J. Generating English discourse from semantic networks. University of Texas at Austin, Computer Science Department, Preprint, November, 1970.

Slamecka, N. J. Retroactive inhibition of connected discourse as a function of practice level. *Journal of Experimental Psychology,* 1960, **59,** 104–108.

Spiro, R. J. Inferential reconstruction in memory for connected discourse. Technical Report No. 2, Laboratory for Cognitive Studies in Education, University of Illinois at Urbana-Champaign, 1975.

Tulving, E. The effects of presentation and recall of material in free-recall learning. *Journal of Verbal Learning and Verbal Behavior,* 1967, **6,** 175–184.

van Dijk, T. A. *Some aspects of text grammars.* The Hague, The Netherlands: Mouton, 1972.

Welborn, E. L., & English, H. B. Logical learning and retention: A general review of experiments with meaningful verbal materials. *Psychological Bulletin,* 1937, **34,** i–20.

Wilson, F. T. A comparison of difficulty and improvement in the learning of bright and dull children in reproducing a descriptive selection. *Genetic Psychological Monographs,* 1931, **9,** 395–435.

Yuille, J. C., & Paivio, A. Abstractness and the recall of connected discourse. *Journal of Educational Psychology,* 1969, **82,** 467–471.

Author Index

Numbers in *italics* refer to pages on which the complete references are listed.

337

Subject Index